The Mystery of Marriage

The Mystery of Marriage

How To Find True Love And Happiness In Married Life

Rabbi
Yitzchak Ginsburgh

Gal Einai
Jerusalem • New York • Los Angeles • Toronto • Zürich

THE TEACHINGS OF KABBALAH SERIES

THE MYSTERY OF MARRIAGE:
HOW TO FIND TRUE LOVE AND HAPPINESS IN MARRIED LIFE

RABBI YITZCHAK GINSBURGH
Editor: Rabbi Moshe Yaakov Wisfensky

Printed in the United States of America and Israel
First Edition

For information:

Israel: GAL EINAI
PO Box 1015
Kfar Chabad 72915
tel. (in Israel): 1-700-700-966
tel. (from abroad): 972-3-9608008
email: books@inner.org
Web: www.inner.org

GAL EINAI produces and publishes books, pamphlets, audiocassettes and videocassettes by Rabbi Yitzchak Ginsburgh. To receive a catalog of our products in English and/or Hebrew, please contact us at any of the above addresses, email orders@inner.org or call our orders department in Israel.

ISBN: 965-7146-00-3

THE PRINTING OF THIS BOOK WAS MADE POSSIBLE BY THE GENEROSITY OF

VARDA BAT ESTHER (ROSETTE)

DELUG

MAY THE SPREADING OF THE LIGHT OF THE TORAH BRING HER BLESSINGS ALWAYS

"נכון שיכתוב בצורת ספר השיעורים
שלומד. בברכה להצלחה..."

"...It would be proper to publish your classes in book form. With blessings for success..."

—from a letter from the Lubavitcher Rebbe to the author, Elul 5741

Table of Contents

Preface

In *The Mystery of Marriage*, Rabbi Yitzchak Ginsburgh presents an in-depth study of the loving union that the Torah envisions as the crown of married life.

Judaism's foremost aspiration is to establish and continuously enhance the conscious bond between man and G-d. The Torah conceives of this bond as a marriage; the image of G-d and Israel as groom and bride, the parable of the Song of Songs, is alluded to throughout the Torah.

This motif and imagery becomes sharply focused in Kabbalah and *Chassidut*—the inner dimension of the Torah, commonly known as "Jewish mysticism." In fact, the entire corpus of teachings that comprise this aspect of the Torah can be considered an exposition of the dynamics of the intimate relationship between G-d and Israel. Thus, its teachings, which reveal to the meditative soul the reality of the Divine, have always been seen in the eyes of its astute students as an allusion to the ways of marital harmony.[1]

Still, consistent with the subtlety and delicacy appropriate to the subject, this understanding was rarely articulated, and in fact, until recent times, there has been

---

1. See *Tanya*, ch. 49.

no major text explicitly devoted to it. Nonetheless, inasmuch as interest in the Torah's teachings on this subject has increased even as familiarity with the language of the Torah's "hidden" teachings has waned, the need for such a work has grown.

Rabbi Yitzchak Ginsburgh published his original distillation of the teachings of the Torah's inner dimension on this subject in Hebrew in 1986, as *Shechinah Beineihem* ("The Divine Presence between Them"). Over the following years, Rabbi Ginsburgh has given numerous classes and lectures on this topic in English and Hebrew, some of them based on *Shechinah Beineihem*, others containing new material. Several of these classes were transcribed[2] and published in English in 1990[3] as a 64-page booklet titled *The Covenant of Marriage: Chassidic Insights.* This booklet was then translated into Hebrew[4] and published in 1994 as *Brit HaNesuin*; a revised and expanded edition appeared in 1997. The present work is a greatly expanded edition of the previous English booklet, and includes much new material.[5]

In addition to the main flow of ideas in the text, *The Mystery of Marriage* contains a wealth of more advanced material intended for seasoned students of Torah in

---

2. by Drs. Mordechai Banayan and Tuvya Buchbinder.

3. edited and supplemented with additional material from the Hebrew *Shechinah Beineihem* by the present editor, and published by Targum Press.

4. by Aligal Kaploun, edited by Yonadav Kaploun.

5. Mr. Gershom Gale, Mr. Yechezkel Annis, Mrs. Orna Ferenz, and Rabbi and Mrs. Asher and Sara Esther Crispe contributed valuable editorial suggestions.

general and of Kabbalah and *Chassidut* in particular. We have placed these expositions chiefly in the footnotes and—in certain instances—in additional notes at the end of the relevant chapter. Despite its advanced nature, this material should be understandable with some effort even by the general reader; we are confident that the enrichment gained will justify the effort.[6]

At many points in the text and footnotes, ideas and concepts are summarized by means of charts. In general, these charts are meant to be read from the bottom up.

We have adhered to the convention of indicating both genders by the masculine, rather than replacing the generic "he," "him," and "his" with the feminine forms, or using alternate constructions such as "his/hers," "s/he," "his or hers," and so on. We hope it is understood that this decision was taken only to ease the flow of the text.

The use of Hebrew in the main text has been kept to a minimum for the sake of the general reader. Whenever a Hebrew term is used for the first time, it is transliterated, defined and given in Hebrew in parentheses; thereafter it is used in transliteration only. In the footnotes, however, Hebrew has been used much more liberally, and many

---

6. Nonetheless, the subject has by no means been exhausted; additional elaboration on the subject of this book may be found at the Gal Einai web-site, http://www.inner.org.

Many of the elaborations and explanations make use of Jewish Numerology (*gematria*). This much-maligned technique is actually a bona-fide, rigorous system of Torah interpretation. It is planned at some future date to publish a work detailing the "rules" of *gematria*, how to distinguish between legitimate and spurious examples, and so forth.

concepts are not defined even when first introduced. Their definitions may be found in the glossary.

Both the various Names of G-d and the word for "G-d" itself are considered sacred in Jewish law. Therefore, we have adhered to the following conventions:[7]

1. "G-d" is spelled with a hyphen instead of an "o."[8]
2. The spelling of the various Names of G-d is deliberately altered (usually substituting a *kuf* or "k" for the first vowel or *hei*/"h"). See Appendix 2.
3. The Tetragrammaton (G-d's holiest, four-letter Name), is referred to as it generally is in Jewish texts: "the Name *Havayah*." "*Havayah*" is both a rearrangement of the letters of the Name and the Hebrew word for "existence," serving to indicate the relation of this holy Name to the verb "to be."
4. When both Names *Havayah* and *Elokim* appear in the same verse, we have translated them both as "G-d." If it was necessary to distinguish between them, we have italicized the word "G-d" that corresponds to the Name *Havayah*.

We have chosen to transliterate Hebrew words according to their Sefardic pronunciation. Although both the Ashkenazic and Sefardic systems are holy, the Sefardic is more generally used at present.

We have used the half-cross (⊥) rather than a full cross to indicate addition, and a dot (·) rather than an "x" to indicate multiplication.

---

7. These conventions are standard in books written by followers of Jewish law, except for books intended for liturgical use or actual sacred texts, where the Names of G-d and the word "G-d" itself are spelled in full.

8. See *Shulchan Aruch, Yoreh Deah* 179, 276; *Shulchan Aruch HaRav, Orach Chaim* 85:3.

When mention is made of "our sages," this generally refers to the sages of the oral Torah, who flourished in Israel and Babylonia roughly during the first six centuries of the Common Era.

In most cases, only one source has been cited in the reference footnotes, since standard texts usually contain cross-references. The systems of reference followed are explained in the bibliography.

Although this book's explicit subject is the husband-wife relationship, its scope is actually much broader. This is because the man-woman relationship is simply the most intense and prototypical form of relationship, and thus the lessons that apply to it apply (albeit in somewhat abstracted form) to any social relationship, even the most casual. In every interchange, there is a "male" role-player and a "female" role-player (and indeed, in the course of any such interchange, these roles may alternate), and thus we generally find ourselves experiencing, throughout any given day, dozens of quasi-marital interactions.

So *The Mystery of Marriage* is actually about life in general, and about how one can be a true and effective partner with everyone with whom he comes in contact. But the rectification of one's character and fulfillment of one's life's purpose in general are ultimately dependent on the rectification of his marital life.

We mentioned that the inner dimension of the Torah may be considered a guide to the ways of marital harmony. The inverse is also true: the study of true marital harmony is instructive regarding the dynamics of the intimate relationship between G-d and Israel, the subject of Kabbalah and *Chassidut* in general. In this sense, *The Mystery of Marriage* may be considered an introduction to the study of Jewish Mysticism, and indeed, in the course of its pages most of the basic concepts of Kabbalah and *Chassidut* are introduced and elaborated upon.[9]

We are deeply grateful to the Almighty for being able to offer the public this work. We hope that the lessons and inspiration to be gleaned from our holy Torah's inner teachings with regard to marital harmony and intimacy will enhance the lives of all those who study them. May we soon merit to witness the restoration of the true Marital Harmony, that of creation with its Creator, with the advent of *Mashiach* and the true and complete Redemption.

Rabbi Moshe Yaakov Wisnefsky
19 Kislev 5760

---

9. For example: The *sefirot* are explained on pp. 33 ff., 57 ff., 142; the Names of G-d on pp. 109, 120 ff., 124-123, 229 ff.; the levels of the soul on pp. 15 ff., 378 ff. Chassidic and Kabbalistic insights to the Jewish calendar may be found on pp. 30, 181, 204, 315 ff. (Shabbat), 20 (*Rosh HaShanah*), 22, 221 ff. (*Yom Kippur*), 277 ff. (*Pesach*, *Sefirat HaOmer* and *Shavuot*), and 22 (the 15th of *Av*). Fundamental concepts of *Chassidut* are explained throughout the text, as well. The footnotes, as even a cursory perusal of the book will testify, contain extensive structuralization of concepts presented in the text into Kabbalistic patterns. Additional references may found, of course, in the index.

1

True Love

Finding One's Soul Mate

The Talmud[1] relates that it was customary in ancient Israel to ask a newly wed groom: "Have you *found* or do you *find*?"

The question refers to an apparent contradiction between two statements of King Solomon, the wisest of men. In the book of Proverbs[2] he declares:

מָצָא אִשָּׁה מָצָא טוֹב.

He who has found a woman has found good.

Yet in the book of Ecclesiastes[3] he states:

וּמוֹצֶא אֲנִי מַר מִמָּוֶת אֶת הָאִשָּׁה.

And I find woman bitterer than death.

---

1. *Yevamot* 63b.
2. 18:22.
3. 7:26.

Although these two verses seem to convey conflicting images of woman, if we examine them closely we can detect some subtle grammatical differences that will explain the apparent discrepancy.[4]

To begin with, the verb in the former verse is in the past tense—"he who *has found* a woman," whereas in the latter it is in the present tense—"and I *find* woman."

According to our tradition, the souls of the truly matched couple derive from a common soul-essence.[5] For this reason, the two are destined even before birth to unite in matrimony.[6] The use of the past tense in affirming the good to be found in marriage suggests that—both in the process of seeking a wife and in relating to the woman he has married—a man should strive to discover and focus on this deep-rooted, shared mutual identification.

---

4. As is evident from the context in which they are discussed in the Talmud, the simple, basic resolution of these verses is that the former refers to a good wife and the latter to a bad one. On a deeper level, however (see *Meor Einaim* [Pinto] to *Berachot* 8a), they describe different ways in which a man's wife reflects his level of self-refinement.

5. *Zohar* 3:43b, 1:85b; *Sefer HaGilgulim* 24; *Mishnat Chasidim, Seder Nashim, Masechet Zivug HaNashamot* 1; *Cf. Vayikra Rabbah* 29:8.

The full value of the phrase "he who has found a woman has found good" (מצא אשה מצא טוב) is 585. 585 = 45 · 13. 45 = "man" (אדם); 13 = "one" (אחד) and "love" (אהבה). From this we learn that man and woman were created to unite (in love) and become "one man," as it is said: "Male and female He created them, and He blessed them, and He called *them* 'man' [אדם] on the day He created them" (Genesis 5:2).

6. *Sotah* 2a.

Should he ignore this instruction and focus instead on the transient gratification of his immediate desires and predilections—as implied by the present tense employed in the second verse—the relationship will inevitably prove to be a bitter one.

This is further alluded to by the fact that in the first verse the verb ("he who has found") is followed directly by its object ("a woman"), implying that what the husband has sought and found is indeed his wife. His mind and heart focus on her, and his conscious concern is to meet her needs and the needs of his family, as opposed to his own.[7] This is the foundation of a happy married life.

In the second verse, however (which in the original literally reads: "and find I bitterer than death the woman"), the subject ("I") is interposed *between* the verb ("find") and its object ("woman"),[8] thereby implying that the man is really more concerned with finding himself—i.e., with his own self-gratification.

Thus, selflessness is the key to "finding" and relating to one's wife at the level of their common soul-root. The egocentric husband will be unable to achieve a genuine, mutual relationship with his wife that will sweeten with time rather than grow bitter.[9]

---

7. "One should eat and drink less than his means allow, dress in accordance with his means, and honor his wife and children beyond his means" (*Chulin* 84b).

8. As if the subject of the verb were also its primary object.

9. Our sages say that one should "come down a step to marry a wife" (*Yevamot* 63a). The simple meaning of this is that one should marry a woman of lower social status so that she not look down on

Although in such a case the husband is apt to feel that his wife has become "bitterer than death," it is in fact his own interposed "I" (which he projects on her) that has become so. This is indicated by the fact that the phrase "bitterer than death" directly follows the word "I," even before the mention of "the woman."

Let us look at these verses again. The first verse reads in full:

מָצָא אִשָּׁה מָצָא טוֹב,
וַיָּפֶק רָצוֹן מֵה'.

He who has found a woman has found good,
and will elicit [good] will[10] *from G-d.*

The second verse reads in full:

וּמוֹצֶא אֲנִי מַר מִמָּוֶת אֶת הָאִשָּׁה,
אֲשֶׁר הִיא מְצוֹדִים וַחֲרָמִים לִבָּהּ, אֲסוּרִים יָדֶיהָ.
טוֹב לִפְנֵי הָאֱלֹהִים יִמָּלֵט מִמֶּנָּה, וְחוֹטֵא יִלָּכֶד בָּהּ.

And I find woman bitterer than death,
for her heart is snares and nets,
and her hands are fetters.
He who is good before G-d will flee from her,
but he who sins shall be caught by her.

---

him. In the present context, however, we may interpret it to mean that lowering one's self-esteem is prerequisite to a successful marriage.

10. This "[good] will" refers to the revelation of the common soul-root of a couple; see below, footnote 18.

In other words, just as King Solomon calls the positive relationship between husband and wife "good," so does he call the flight from a negative relationship "good." The previously self-seeking husband begins his return to the "good" state by reorienting his consciousness such that he stands "before G-d" rather than being concerned solely with himself. By doing this, he "flees from her," i.e., from the image of his own ego that he has projected onto his wife. Only then can he proceed to find his true soul mate.[11]

Not surprisingly, the pivotal verb of these verses, "to find," figures prominently in the creation of Eve, the archetypal woman:

וַיֹּאמֶר ה' אֱלֹהִים:
לֹא טוֹב הֱיוֹת הָאָדָם לְבַדּוֹ, אֶעֱשֶׂה לּוֹ עֵזֶר כְּנֶגְדּוֹ.
וַיִּצֶר ה' אֱלֹהִים מִן הָאֲדָמָה
כָּל חַיַּת הַשָּׂדֶה וְאֵת כָּל עוֹף הַשָּׁמַיִם,
וַיָּבֵא אֶל הָאָדָם לִרְאוֹת מַה יִּקְרָא לוֹ,
וְכֹל אֲשֶׁר יִקְרָא לוֹ הָאָדָם נֶפֶשׁ חַיָּה הוּא שְׁמוֹ.
וַיִּקְרָא הָאָדָם שֵׁמוֹת
לְכָל הַבְּהֵמָה וּלְעוֹף הַשָּׁמַיִם וּלְכֹל חַיַּת הַשָּׂדֶה,
וּלְאָדָם לֹא מָצָא עֵזֶר כְּנֶגְדּוֹ.

And G-d said:
"It is not good for man to be alone,
I shall make him a helpmate."
So G-d formed from the earth

---

11. The numerical value of the phrase "He who is good before G-d will flee from her" (**טוב לפני האלהים ימלט ממנה**) equals that of "the Divine Presence [dwells] between them" (**שכינה ביניהם**, 502; see below, ch. 5). This indicates that when "He who is good before G-d will flee from her," he will find his true soul mate and merit that "the Divine Presence [dwells] between them."

all the beasts of the field and the birds of the sky,
and He brought them to the man to see what he would call them,
and whatever the man called any living being was its name.
So the man named all the animals and birds of the sky and the beasts of the field,
but for himself, Adam did not find *a helpmate.*[12]

It evidently was not enough for G-d to simply create Eve and present her to Adam; a true wife must be looked for and *found*.[13]

Upon her creation, Adam gave his wife the generic name "woman" (אִשָּׁה), which in Hebrew is simply the feminine form of the word "man" (אִישׁ):[14]

---

12. Genesis 2:18-20.

13. Furthermore, this is the first appearance of the root "to find" (מצא) in the Torah, and "everything goes after the beginning" (*Pirkei d'Rabbi Eliezer* 41). This is thus a clear indication of the essential relationship between the reality of woman and the concept of finding.

Here, as in the verse "He who has *found* a woman has *found* good," the root appears in the past tense. The first instance in the Torah of this root in the *present* tense is in reference to the punishment of Cain for killing his brother Abel (Genesis 4:14-15).

14. Genesis 2:23. "From this verse it follows that the world was created in the holy language [i.e., Hebrew]" (Rashi *ad loc.*; *Bereishit Rabbah* 18:4). Speaking and thinking in Hebrew is thus conducive to recognizing one's true soul mate. Language in general is associated with the woman, and Hebrew corresponds to the highest level of woman, the prophetess (*Likutei Moharan* 1:19).

זֹאת הַפַּעַם עֶצֶם מֵעֲצָמַי וּבָשָׂר מִבְּשָׂרִי,
לְזֹאת יִקָּרֵא אִשָּׁה,
כִּי מֵאִישׁ לֻקֳחָה זֹּאת.

This time, bone of my bones and flesh of my flesh,
This one shall be called 'woman,'
for she was taken from man.

Having found his true soul mate, Adam named her after himself, recognizing the common origin of their souls.

Looking at the original two verses yet again, we notice that in the verse "And I find the woman bitterer than death," "woman" appears with the definite article. This implies that one is relating to one's wife as a member of a generic group rather than as an individual who shares his soul-root. This fundamental lack of unity prevents one from finding good in his relationship with his wife.

In contrast, in the verse "He who has found *a* woman," "woman" appears without the definite article. This implies that one who finds his true soul mate names her after (i.e., recognizes) their common source, as happened in the story of creation. And therefore, "He who has found *a* woman—has found good."

To be sure, viewing one's spouse as part of oneself can be the sign of an exaggerated ego as well. In such a case, one sees his spouse as merely an appendage of himself and thus feels no need to relate to her as a distinct individual. This is alluded to in the verse "And I find the woman bitterer than death," in which the egocentric husband sees only himself in his wife.

The proper way to see one's wife as part of oneself is by sensing their shared soul-root, which, as we have said, is possible only by cultivating true selflessness. As we will explain, one's true individuality originates in one's soul-root. Paradoxically, it is only when spouses relate to each other with this awareness of their common source that they can see each other as truly unique individuals.[15]

Our sages teach us that "it is the way of man to search for woman,"[16] for he is in fact searching for his own

---

15. According to the sages (*Eiruvin* 18a; Rashi on Genesis 5:2), Adam and Eve were originally attached, back to back. In this state, Adam and Eve were "one," but Adam could not see her; he was conscious of her only as an appendage (an extra "rib"). In order to make her his wife, G-d "sawed" her off. Once Adam was able to see her for the first time as an independent being, they could join face to face, as husband and wife.

The two opposing types of oneness described here can be said to reflect the condition of Adam and Eve before they were sawed apart and afterwards. Before, husband and wife are one, but they cannot unite, since the husband sees his wife as nothing more than a part of himself. After they are separated, if he continues to see her in this light, nothing has been accomplished. To unite with her, he must focus on the oneness which preceded their physical creation, i.e., that of their common soul-root.

According to Kabbalah (*Etz Chaim* 29), in the sawing-off process (נסירה, *nesirah*) the male retains the states of *chesed* ("kindness," i.e., generosity) while the states of *din* ("judgment," or discrimination based on worthiness and gratitude in receiving) are passed to the female. Psychologically, this means that the husband loses awareness of himself as an object of attention; the sole object of his attention becomes his wife. He remains only as a giver of attention and concern.

Thus, the *nesirah* is the passage from egocentricity to recognizing the objective independence of the "other." In popular parlance, one's relationships change from "I-it" to "I-thou."

16. *Kidushin* 2b.

lost side or rib.[17] Spiritually, this lost side is the unconscious level of his own soul.

When one learns to relate to ("find") one's wife on the level of their common soul-root, he "finds" not only a good marriage, but the goodness inherent in the unconscious level of his own soul, as well.[18] A good wife is thus one who makes her husband conscious of the depths of his own will to be good. This is the deeper meaning of "He who has found a woman has found good."

In sum, by referring to the contrasting language of these two verses, those who posed the above question to the groom were hinting to him that the outcome of the union, for good or for bad, depends on his attitude. The blessings of marriage are contingent upon the abandonment of egocentricity and a positive reorientation toward inner truth and reality.[19]

---

17. *Bereishit Rabbah* 17:6; *cf. Berachot* 61a.

18. The statement of our sages: "Who is a proper wife? She who *performs* [עושה] the will of her husband" (*Tana d'vei Eliahu Rabbah* 9), is interpreted in *Chassidut* to mean "she who *rectifies* the will of her husband" (our sages often interpret the word עושה to mean "rectify"). As we will note, one's will is the primary expression of the deepest, super-conscious realm of one's soul. See additional note 1 at the end of this chapter (p. 39).

19. The numerical value of the Hebrew word for "found" (**מצא**, 131) is equal to that of the word for "humility" (**ענוה**), reinforcing the idea that humility and self-nullification are prerequisites to success in finding one's true soul mate.

The Two Trees of the Garden of Eden

The fact that a good marriage is dependent on abandoning egocentricity is alluded to in the passage immediately preceding the description of the creation of woman:

וַיַּצְמַח ה' אֱלֹהִים מִן הָאֲדָמָה
כָּל עֵץ נֶחְמָד לְמַרְאֶה וְטוֹב לְמַאֲכָל
וְעֵץ הַחַיִּים בְּתוֹךְ הַגָּן
וְעֵץ הַדַּעַת טוֹב וָרָע....
וַיְצַו ה' אֱלֹהִים עַל הָאָדָם לֵאמֹר:
מִכֹּל עֵץ הַגָּן אָכֹל תֹּאכֵל,
וּמֵעֵץ הַדַּעַת טוֹב וָרָע לֹא תֹאכַל מִמֶּנּוּ,
כִּי בְּיוֹם אֲכָלְךָ מִמֶּנּוּ מוֹת תָּמוּת.
וַיֹּאמֶר ה' אֱלֹהִים: לֹא טוֹב הֱיוֹת הָאָדָם לְבַדּוֹ,
אֶעֱשֶׂה לּוֹ עֵזֶר כְּנֶגְדּוֹ.

And G-d made grow out of the ground
every tree pleasant to sight and good to eat,
and the tree of life in the midst of the garden,
and the tree of knowledge of good and evil....
And G-d commanded Adam, saying:
You may eat from all the trees of the garden,
But do not eat from the tree of knowledge of good and evil,
for on the day on which you eat of it you shall surely die.
And G-d said: It is not good for man to be alone;
I shall make him a helpmate.[20]

20. Genesis 2:9,16-18.

Evil takes root in man when he focuses on himself and his own desires rather than on G-d and His desires (or, on a deeper level, when he considers himself independent or separate from G-d). When so oriented, he evaluates all experience only in terms of his own subjective sense of good.

In Kabbalah and *Chassidut*, it is explained that good tainted by selfishness is represented by the tree of knowledge of good and evil, while true, unadulterated good is represented by the tree of life.[21] By commanding Adam not to eat the fruit of the tree of knowledge of good and evil, G-d was warning him not to mix good and evil by choosing the path of self-centeredness and self-orientation.[22]

Eating the forbidden fruit caused man's psyche to become overtly self-conscious and egocentric. His sensation of good is no longer pure and Divine but a mixture of good and evil; he considers something good only if it is self-gratifying. If this attitude is left unrectified, the evil will eventually swallow up the good, as in Pharaoh's dreams;[23] one's appreciation for good—and even belief that anything can truly *be* good—will evaporate. This in turn will engender a feeling of

---

21. See additional note 2 at the end of this chapter (p. 41).

22. The two extremes of good and evil are referred to in *Sefer Yetzirah* (2:4) as "pleasure" and "plague": "There is no good higher than pleasure, and no evil lower than plague." The words in Hebrew for "pleasure" (**ענג**) and "plague" (**נגע**) are in fact permutations of the same three letters; the choice between good and evil (or unmitigated good and good mixed with evil) is essentially one of orientation.

23. Genesis 41:1-7.

bitterness toward life as one comes to blame others for life's disappointments and suffering. Having thus placed the cause of his suffering outside his sphere of influence, a person views himself as a helpless victim of circumstance and malevolence.

The two states of consciousness symbolized by the two trees are primarily expressed in the way man relates to woman. In forbidding Adam to eat the fruit of the tree of knowledge of good and evil, G-d was teaching him how to relate to his soon-to-be-created wife: "Do not mix egocentric lust and desire for self-gratification with the experience of true, unadulterated good."

In the entire narrative of creation, the creation of woman is the only creative act described as righting an inferior situation.[24] Furthermore, the previous situation is not described simply as "bad," but as "not good," implying that the preceding state *appeared* to be good, but really was not. In order to achieve the truly good state, G-d had to create woman.

In this context, "not good" is the incorporation into man's psyche of relative, apparent good.[25] This apparent

---

24. The earth's state at the outset of creation—"without form, and void, and darkness was on the face of the deep" (Genesis 1:2)—is not explicitly termed "not good," although after the creation of light "G-d saw the light that it was good, and G-d separated the light from the darkness" (*ibid.*, 1:4).

Indeed, the bachelor-state is often referred to as being "without form" (תהו, or "chaos"). It is a state of relative void and darkness. The creation of Eve, and marriage, is the contrasting state of light.

25. Cf. the opening discourses of *Sefer HaMa'amarim 5670*, in which it is noted that the variety of light whose sole purpose is to

good is man's existential state of being alone, i.e., egocentric and solely concerned with himself.[26]

A husband with this orientation is feeding on the tree of knowledge of good and evil. Unless he reorients himself to true life and goodness, "on the day that you eat of it you shall surely die," that is, he will eventually say: "I find woman bitterer than death."

Cultivating Selflessness

In order for selflessness to be complete, it must be cultivated in all three areas of human interaction: with respect to G-d, with respect to others (one's marital relationship being the most personal and intense form of this), and with respect to oneself.

With respect to G-d, selflessness means humble submission to His will; with respect to one's spouse, it means finding in her one's predestined soul mate (*bashert*) and relating to her on this level; with respect to oneself, it means refining one's character.

Our normative consciousness, according to Kabbalah and *Chassidut*, is only a small part of our soul's consciousness, which comprises additional levels and

---

shine into and thereby enliven darkness is itself considered darkness relative to true light.

26. "Alone" refers to existential loneliness, which is referred to as "concealment of the Divine countenance." To be alone is to be "back to back" to G-d, one's spouse, or one's spiritual mentor. To be together is to be "face to face" (cf. *HaYom Yom*, 22 Iyar).

modes of consciousness of which we are not generally aware. These additional levels are said to "surround" us, since it is not normally within our power to focus on them. In contrast, our regular consciousness is said to be "within" us, meaning that we are able to access and control it to a great degree. The surrounding levels are said to be "higher" or more "distant," since they are generally beyond our grasp, while the inner levels are said to be "lower" or "closer" to our ken.

In general, the three aspects of spiritual effort required to cultivate true selflessness engage the three major divisions of consciousness: the "distant surrounding consciousness," the "close surrounding consciousness," and the "inner consciousness."[27]

sphere of rectification	level of consciousness
devotion to G-d's will	distant surrounding
recognizing one's soul mate	close surrounding
refining one's character	inner

In particular, we are taught that the soul comprises five levels of consciousness,[28] two "surrounding" and three "within." These, in descending order, are:

27. In Hebrew: אור מקיף רחוק (*or makif rachok*), אור מקיף קרוב (*or makif karov*), and אור פנימי (*or pnimi*), respectively.

28. The Midrash (*Bereishit Rabbah* 14:11) notes that there are five terms for the soul used in the Bible. In Kabbalah (*Sha'ar HaGilgulim*,

level of consciousness	level of the soul		
	Hebrew name		translation
distant surrounding	*yechidah*	יְחִידָה	"single one"
close surrounding	*chayah*	חַיָּה	"living one"
inner	*neshamah*	נְשָׁמָה	"breath [of life]"
	ruach	רוּחַ	"spirit"
	nefesh	נֶפֶשׁ	"innate life force"

The source of the Jew's commitment to fulfill G-d's will is the absolute devotion to Him intrinsic to the highest of the soul's five levels, the *yechidah*. The *yechidah* is the irreducible essence of consciousness, aware of nothing other than G-d's absolute and all-encompassing reality.

In practice, one is only rarely conscious of this level of his soul; we usually function in the context of shorter-term desires and motives. But all one's desires ultimately reduce to the will to exist (or to enhance or expand one's existence). This will is in turn based on and permeated with the pleasure experienced (or assumed) in existing, which itself is based on the faith that existence is real. Inasmuch as the only true reality is G-d, the *yechidah* recognizes G-d as its sole source of pleasure and the objective of its will. This awareness underlies all conscious thought. Thus, the *yechidah* is said to always be present in the wings, "surrounding" and motivating one's conscious

---

introduction 1) it is explained that these refer to the soul's five levels of consciousness.

cognition and influencing one's decision-making process from afar.

The ability to recognize one's true soul mate derives from the *chayah*, the second-highest of the soul's five levels. The *chayah* is the level at which the soul's innate wisdom (חָכְמָה, *chochmah*) is manifest. It, too, is normally outside the realm of awareness and is only occasionally revealed as Divinely inspired flashes of insight. Still, inasmuch as it penetrates the conscious mind more frequently than does the *yechidah*, it is described as surrounding one's conscious thoughts more closely.[29]

Although any flash of insight is an experience of one's *chayah*, the quintessential insight is the awareness that one's soul derives from a source common to all other souls, as it is said: "Have we not all one Father?"[30] The most personal case of this is the awareness of the soul-root one shares with his spouse.[31]

The ongoing process of self-rectification and character refinement involves relating to others with genuine loving-kindness[32] and altruism while doing one's

---

29. "Close" implies the "in-and-out-of-mind" dynamic referred to as "touching and not touching"; see below, p. 243.

30. Malachi 2:10. In Kabbalah, *chochmah* and *chayah* are associated with the "father" image (the *partzuf* of *Abba*). Cf. *Tanya*, ch. 32.

31. *Chayah* (חיה), as a proper name, is the rectification of *Chavah* (חוה), Eve, the first woman, who was given this name (instead of *Chayah*) in consequence of the primordial sin. *Chayah* is thus a generic name for one's true soul mate in her most rectified state of being.

32. Loving-kindness is the primary emotion of the heart and is said to "accompany" all the others (*Etz Chaim* 25:2; *Pri Etz Chaim*, *Sha'ar Chag HaSukot* 1; see *Zohar* 3:103ab, 191b).

utmost to nullify all selfish or egocentric motives. This concentrated effort of the mind and heart engages the three inner, conscious levels of the soul, the *neshamah*, the *ruach*, and the *nefesh*.

In particular, the *neshamah* is the level of the mind (the active intelligence of the soul); the *ruach* is the level of the heart (the emotional attributes); and the *nefesh* is the level of action in general and of innate behavioral traits in particular.

Through concentrated spiritual effort, one may refine his ability to perceive reality in truth and in depth, sensitize his heart to react appropriately to the phenomena of life, and acquire a rectified "second nature" when it comes to action and behavior.

To summarize:

sphere of rectification	**level of consciousness**	**level of the soul**	
devotion to G-d's will	distant surrounding consciousness	*yechidah*	faith, pleasure, will, absolute devotion
recognizing one's soul mate	close surrounding consciousness	*chayah*	wisdom, insight
refining one's character	inner consciousness	*neshamah*	perception of reality
		ruach	emotional sensitivity
		nefesh	action, behavioral patterns

Now, it is a general principle that "the higher an entity, the lower it descends."[33] Thus, we are taught in

33. *Likutei Torah* 2:34c, *et al.*

Kabbalah and *Chassidut* that the highest level of the soul, the *yechidah*—the origin of one's conscious commitment to fulfill G-d's will—is most manifest at the lowest level, the *nefesh,* through an individual's ever-increasing[34] good deeds.

The second-highest level of the soul, the *chayah*—the insight that recognizes the essential unity of all Jewish souls—is manifest at the second-lowest level, the *ruach,* as one rectifies his emotions and learns to relate to others with loving-kindness.

This leaves the *neshamah* as the pivotal center of the soul. And, indeed, the primary focus of one's spiritual effort *vis-à-vis* his soul is his *neshamah,*[35] his mature intellect and power of perception with regard to apparently separate reality. Through concentrated meditation, one can train his mind to perceive reality

34. The rectification of this level of the soul depends upon *ever-increasing* good deeds. One of the meanings of *nefesh* (נפש) is "to increase" (לפוש). See below, p. 349, footnote 99.

35. The *neshamah* may be seen as both an inner and surrounding level of consciousness: inner inasmuch as it is conscious, and surrounding relative to action. The intellect is only the indirect motivator of action, relative to emotion, which is the direct motivator (*Tanya,* ch. 16 [22ab]). Physically as well, the head is considered both a part of the body and a separate entity; we speak of head and body.

Furthermore, in the evolution of the soul's consciousness as detailed in Kabbalah and *Chassidut,* the full, fivefold structure we are discussing here develops out of the initial triad of *nefesh-ruach-neshamah.* In this process, the *neshamah* metamorphoses into the *yechidah,* the *ruach* into the *chayah,* and the *nefesh* into the new *nefesh-ruach-neshamah* triad. The *neshamah* is related both to the previous *nefesh* and the future *yechidah,* and thus embraces all the soul's levels.

correctly, both with regard to seeing G-d's presence in the world (Divine providence) and in understanding other individuals and their interrelationships.

One's refined perception of reality (*neshamah*) will then give rise to rectified emotions in the heart (*ruach*, inspired by the *chayah*), which will, in turn, motivate one to continuously increase his good deeds (*nefesh*, reflecting the *yechidah*).[36]

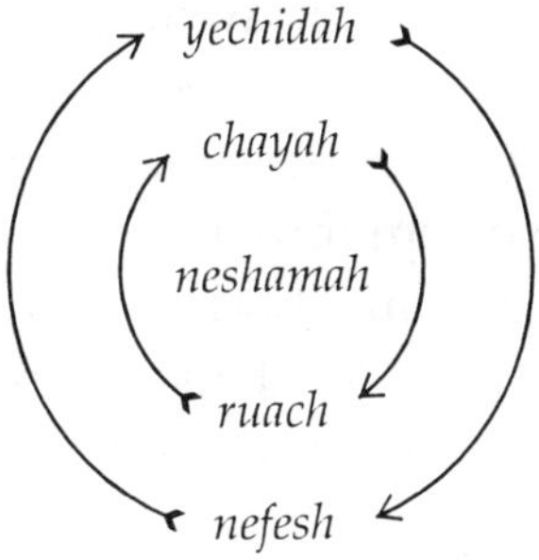

Remembering the Common Soul-root

Although, as emerges from the above discussion, finding one's soul mate and relating to her as such is no simple matter,[37] there are propitious times for identifying her (i.e., "remembering" her in their common soul-root).

---

36. This is the crux of the teachings of *Chassidut* in general and *Chabad Chassidut*—which maintains that Divine service begin with concentrated meditation, the level of *neshamah*—in particular.

37. The psychological process involved in choosing one's soul mate is the subject of a separate study, *The Unfolding of Consciousness*.

The first of these is *Rosh HaShanah*, the first day of the Jewish year. Adam and Eve were created on *Rosh HaShanah*; our sages teach us that they were created as 20-year-olds.[38] On the day they were created, G-d brought them to the garden of Eden, which He had prepared as an extended wedding canopy. *Rosh HaShanah* is thus both man's birthday and his wedding anniversary.[39]

We refer to *Rosh HaShanah* in our prayers as *Yom HaZikaron* (יוֹם הַזִּכָּרוֹן), which is commonly translated "the Day of Remembrance," but which more literally means "the Day of Memory." *Rosh HaShanah* is the day of judgment. G-d not only remembers us by judging us as we are in this world but also remembers us as we were before our souls descended into our bodies, when they were "an actual part of G-d above."[40] This arouses His mercy over us, since our souls have descended from such a height to such depths.

---

38. *Bereishit Rabbah* 14:7.

39. Thus, we may consider the inner reason why *Rosh HaShanah* is observed for two days to be that each day is one of mankind's anniversaries. The first day, which is pervaded by the harsher aspect of G-d's attribute of judgment (דינא קשיא, *Zohar* 3:231a), reflects mankind's collective birthday; the second day, which is pervaded by the softer aspect of G-d's attribute of judgment (דינא רפיא, *ibid.*), reflects mankind's collective wedding anniversary. In certain contexts of Jewish law, the two days of *Rosh HaShanah* are in fact considered to be one long day (*Beitzah* 4b; Rabbeinu Nissim, *Commentary on Sefer HaHalachot ad loc., s.v. VeIdach; Rashi ad loc., s.v. Asurah B'zeh*).

40. See *Tanya*, ch. 2. Cf. the parables of the Ba'al Shem Tov and Rabbi Levi Yitzchak of Berdichev (*Torat Shmuel, VeKachah 5637*, 70) regarding the blowing of the *shofar*.

Inasmuch as the world is continuously being created and sustained from G-d's consciousness, on *Rosh HaShanah* a Jew is also able to remember (i.e., sense) his origin in G-d's infinite light. This origin is the common soul-root he shares with his spouse.

Besides *Rosh HaShanah*, the collective birthday of mankind, one's individual soul-root (מַזָּל, *mazal*) is particularly accessible on his personal birthday.[41] One's birthday is thus another propitious time for identifying (i.e., "remembering") one's soul mate.

A third such time is one's wedding anniversary. Under the wedding canopy, a couple's soul-root shines in all its power, and draws down blessing and Divinely inspired consciousness (i.e., memory) of their essential oneness. One's wedding anniversary is thus an auspicious time for a couple to remember their common soul-root.[42]

Finally, "there were no more joyous days in Israel than the fifteenth of *Av* and *Yom Kippur*, for on these days the daughters of Jerusalem...went out and danced in the vineyards, saying 'Young man! Lift up your eyes and see what you will choose....'"[43] These two days are especially propitious for making matches.[44]

---

41. See *Y. Rosh HaShanah* 3:8; *Korban HaEidah ad loc.* Sources regarding celebrating birthdays have been collected in *Yom Malkeinu*.

42. Regarding celebrating one's wedding anniversary, see the Lubavitcher Rebbe's address of 14 *Kislev*, 5739.

43. *Ta'anit* 26b.

44. And for distinguishing between true love and profane misrepresentations thereof. Of the two days, the fifteenth of *Av* is the greater in this respect, despite the superior holiness of *Yom Kippur* (see *The Unfolding of Consciousness* and *Teshuvah MeiAhavah*).

These days, then, are the most conducive to remembering both the origin of one's individual soul and the soul-root one shares with one's spouse.

In order to "remember," one meditates on the fact that the source of one's soul is "an actual part of G-d above," thus realizing the great resources and potential it possesses, most of which are still untapped. One thereby achieves maximum awareness of his (or their common) task on earth and the spiritual strength to "choose life"[45] in the steadfast progression toward his (or their) goals.

In day-to-day life, this memory is reflected in a couple's shared hopes and plans for the future, as well as for their immediate and extended family (and indeed, for all those upon whom they have a positive influence).

This implies, as well, that the most important criterion for choosing one's soul mate (i.e., that which most identifies, albeit indirectly, the possession of a common soul-root), is: do we strive in the same way to realize the same ideals? The prospective partners should simply look for a general sense of mutual affinity and attraction, together with shared ideals and goals in life.[46] When they discuss the common future they envision building, or their common ideals and objectives in life, each should become excited about what the other says.

---

45. Deuteronomy 30:19.

46. In particular, a man will in most cases experience discreet instances of feeling that the match is "right," whereas a woman will experience a general feeling of dynamic potential, making her feel that the match is "well grounded." See below, p. 204.

"Oneness" in their past, present, and future is thus what defines a truly predestined (*bashert*) couple. They share a common soul-root (their past), common goals (their future), and always (in the present) remember their common origin as they proceed toward their common goal.[47]

Love at First Sight

It is clear from the above that one should not expect to be struck with an intense feeling of predestination when he first meets his predestined spouse. As a rule, the couple's love experience grows and develops as they nurture it together throughout their lives. Nonetheless, every rule has its exceptions, and we find examples in the Torah of the intense experience known as love at first sight.[48] Indeed, G-d Himself "fell in love" with His original vision of the Jewish people devotedly performing His will

47. In the terminology of Kabbalah, the present "memory" is the *reshimu* ("impression") of the past, i.e., G-d's infinite light, which filled all reality before the *tzimtzum* ("contraction"), and in which the origin of the soul is one with G-d. The *kav* ("ray" of light), which enters the vacuum created by the *tzimtzum* and proceeds to form the raw material of the *reshimu* into worlds, delineates the Divine path to the ultimate goal of the future.

48. The primary examples of this phenomenon in the Torah will be discussed presently.

on earth. According to our sages,[49] this love at first sight is what motivated G-d to create the world.[50]

It is important to remember, however, that this phenomenon is the exception that proves the rule.[51]

---

49. *Bereishit Rabbah* 8:7; *Zohar Chadash* 121c. See *Or Torah* 1, where the inspiration which the Jewish people provided G-d to contract His light in order to create the world is likened to a father's love for his child, which inspires him to pretend to be on his intellectual level (i.e., descend into his world) in order to relate to him. Inasmuch as the love between husband and wife is more ardent than that between parent and child, the *intensity* of G-d's inspiration to create the world is more aptly likened to love at first sight.

The intensity of love at first sight is the source of one's incentive to create a new reality, world, or family. The surge of strength afforded by love at first sight is illustrated in the account of Jacob's first meeting with Rachel (see below, 36).

The expression of G-d's *developing* love for the Jewish people (which does not provide immediate impetus to create), can be seen as the answer to the question posed at the beginning of *Etz Chaim*: why didn't G-d create the world before He actually did?

50. As noted above (p. 9, footnote 18), *Chassidut* interprets the statement of our sages (*Tana d'vei Eliahu Rabbah* 9), "Who is a proper wife? She who performs [עושה] the will of her husband," to mean that she "rectifies" it. The most literal reading of עושה is "to make," implying that the proper wife not only "rectifies" her husband's will but actually "produces" it. Before creation, the very *thought* of the "proper wife" sufficed to "produce" the will to create reality. See below, p. 118.

51. This is especially true in our days, since most of us have undergone numerous incarnations and the average person evinces the maturity of *tikun* ("multiplicity of vessels") more than the narrow individuality of *tohu* ("intensity of lights"). Our sense of inner identity is therefore more complex, making it harder to spontaneously identify our predestined soul mate. See below, p. 29, footnote 63.

There are thirteen general rules by which logical inferences may be drawn according to the Torah.[52] One of these is the following:

כָּל דָּבָר שֶׁהָיָה בִּכְלָל וְיָצָא מִן הַכְּלָל לְלַמֵּד, לֹא לְלַמֵּד עַל עַצְמוֹ יָצָא, אֶלָּא לְלַמֵּד עַל הַכְּלָל כֻּלּוֹ יָצָא.

When a particular case included in a general case is singled out to inform us about something novel [i.e., an exception], it is singled out not only to instruct us concerning itself, but is to be applied to the whole of the general case.

In other words, every exception tells us something about the rule that we would not otherwise have known.[53]

In our case, the exceptional experience of love at first sight is a graphic manifestation of the intensity and romance that developing love does eventually achieve as well. The converse is also true: if the experience of love at first sight is real, it will eventually achieve the stability and rootedness of developing love.

Instances of love at first sight are thus instructive even for the majority of couples, who do not experience such intensity at the start of their relationship. Rather than feeling that their love is somehow deficient or unromantic, they should view examples of love at first sight as

52. *Sifra*, introduction.

53. If an exception has no relevance to the rule, it cannot be considered valid; the temptation to consider it thus is a deception that the unrectified imagination (as will be explained) is attempting to foist upon us.

enlightening portents of the intensity into which their love should—and hopefully will—develop.

Those couples who *do* experience love at first sight should feel fortunate that their relationship has been blessed with such a great intensity from the outset. At the same time, however, they should be aware that the more impetuous a relationship's beginning, the more difficult it may be to stabilize it afterwards.[54] Still, with the necessary effort, the initial surge of genuine love at first sight will settle back into the "rule" and strike roots in the deeper essences of the couple. In this way the couple's love will develop and grow organically, just as in the more common case of developing love.[55]

---

54. In the terminology of Kabbalah, love at first sight involves the "unbounded lights of *Tohu*" (אורות מרובים דתהו). With devoted effort and Divine aid, these lights can be successfully drawn down into the mature, yet limiting "vessels of *Tikun*" (כלים רחבים דתקון). The effort begins with the acquisition of patience, which will be explained in chapter 9.

55. Since love at first sight is a foretaste of the intensity of mature love, its very experience can actually serve to humble a couple, making them realize that Divine providence "knew" that they lacked the patience to dedicate themselves to a lifetime of developing love. True, it is a *mitzvah* and blessing to taste the Shabbat dishes before Shabbat (see below, p. 181), but this in itself can be seen as a Divine concession, as it were, to those who otherwise would be unable to prepare for Shabbat in simple faith. Nonetheless, the complete "flavor" of Shabbat food can only be tasted on Shabbat itself (*Shabbat* 119a), just as the consummation of developing love exceeds the taste of it afforded by love at first sight. As will be discussed further (see below, footnote 69), any particular Shabbat is both the consummation of the preceding Shabbat and the beginning of a process that concludes with the following Shabbat. If the foretaste of Shabbat is considered a preview of the *second* Shabbat (which is related to the

Of course, not every case of what passes for love at first sight is genuine. If the exceptional experience carries within it nothing of the "rule"—if it contains no seed of settled, mature love—it is probably nothing more than an infatuation that will dissipate as quickly as it appeared.[56]

Experiencing Love at First Sight

As we said, recognizing one's soul mate depends on sensing their shared soul-root, and this is the most fundamental type of insight there is.

Normally, love[57] is born in the heart only after the initial, seminal flash of insight[58] has, through deliberate meditation,[59] ripened in the womb of the mind into a fully-developed idea and been assimilated into one's world view. Just as physical pregnancy requires time, so does this process, for the mentality that prevailed prior to

---

coming of *Mashiach*), it need not be understood as a Divine concession to human weakness but rather a manifestation of our ability to hasten the advent of *Mashiach*.

56. See below, p. 403.

57. Love is the emotion associated with the *sefirah* of *chesed*.

58. Sight (especially *first* sight and insight) is the sense associated with the *sefirah* of *chochmah*. *Chochmah*, the first *sefirah* of the mind, is the source of *chesed*, the first *sefirah* of the heart; this is why *chesed* appears directly beneath *chochmah* on the right axis of the sefirotic tree. *Abba* ("father") is the *partzuf* identified with the *sefirah* of *chochmah*.

59. Meditation (התבוננות) is the mental process associated with (and etymologically derived from) the *sefirah* of *binah* (בינה), which is identified with the *partzuf* of *Ima* ("mother").

the introduction of the new insight must come to grips with it. Since the mind and its thought-patterns are not fully refined and rectified, the introduction of a new element of truth requires that the previous mental structure be entirely re-evaluated and reconstructed in its light, and this takes time.

Exceptionally, however, one may experience love at "first sight"; love may appear simultaneously with the initial insight, without the time lapse typically required for it to develop and bear fruit. This can happen in one of two ways:

If the love is characterized by the non-self-awareness and non-self-orientation (בִּטּוּל, *bitul*) that accompanies the flash of insight, it is barely experienced as an "emotion" in the conventional sense of the word at all.[60] It can, in this way, shine with the brilliance of the original pristine insight. The essence of such a love-experience can be said to be contained within the mind's eye—as if the heart had "risen" into the eyes.

Alternatively, the seed of love can develop in the womb of the mind before being born in the heart, but without requiring the usual extended period of time, or in fact any time at all. Here, the emotion of love *is* experienced as an attribute of the heart, but one's mind is so refined that the emotion flows through it freely and

60. In the terminology of Kabbalah, this is the pure experience of *mochin d'Abba* when it does not couple with *mochin d'Ima*. This level is alluded to by the phrase "mighty in holiness" (נאדר בקדש, Exodus 15:11). At this level of consciousness, past, present and future exist simultaneously; the future ramifications of the seminal insight (the love) occur together with the insight itself (the first sight).

naturally. The self produces no "friction" to slow the birth of the emotions from the mind.[61]

We have likened the birth of love from the seminal insight deposited and nurtured in the womb of the mind to the conception and birth of a child, and further likened love at first sight to conceiving and giving birth without an intervening period of pregnancy. This absence of a gestation period will be the norm in the future.[62]

In the messianic era, both the relationship between husband and wife and that between G-d and the Jewish people will be one of constant falling in love at first sight.[63]

---

61. In contrast with the previous phenomenon, this experience is that of the refined union of *mochin d'Abba* and *mochin d'Ima*.

62. Our sages interpret the phrase "the pregnant woman together with the woman giving birth" (Jeremiah 31:7) to mean that "woman is destined in the future to give birth every day" (*Shabbat* 30b).

Gestation is a result of the sin of eating the fruit of the tree of knowledge of good and evil (Genesis 4:1, Rashi *ad loc.*; "in the eighth hour [of the sixth day, when they were created], two [i.e., Adam and Eve] entered the bed and four [i.e., they and their two sons, Cain and Abel] descended therefrom," *Sanhedrin* 38b). Therefore, when the sin is rectified, things will return to their former state. As we explained above, the primordial sin is synonymous with egocentricity. It is thus egocentricity that causes things to take time and undergo the process of development. In its absence, life becomes spontaneous, akin to a constant state of love at first sight (see *Muda'ut Tivit*, throughout).

Similarly, because of the sin of the spies, the Jews had to undergo a forty-year preparation process to enter the land of Israel instead of entering it directly after the exodus from Egypt (Numbers 14:34). This forty-year period is analogous to the forty days it takes for the fetus to form in the womb (*Nidah* 30a).

63. In general, the messianic era is seen as a restoration of the state of affairs before the destruction of the Temple or the primordial sin, as it is said, "renew our days as of old" (Lamentations 5:21). Thus,

Paradoxically, this continuous state of romantic passion will be fully integrated with the settled, stable love that characterizes seasoned relationships.

The foretaste of the world to come in this world is Shabbat (שַׁבָּת, "the Sabbath").[64] Shabbat is essentially above the normal time-consciousness of the six days of creation. During the six days of the week (which correspond to the six emotions of the heart), reality is aware of and focused on itself. On Shabbat, the consciousness of created reality returns to its source in the Divine plan, and the emotions ascend to the level of the mind's vision.[65] G-d re-experiences love at first sight, just as He did before creation. And since the world is continuously being created from G-d's consciousness, on Shabbat we too are able to experience love at first sight. We can both regain our inspiration with life in general, and fall in love anew with our spouses.

---

the fact that in the future love at first sight will become the rule rather than the exception suggests that this was the case originally, as well. We have seen that love at first sight characterized the relationships of most of the patriarchs and matriarchs, as well as those of King David, the progenitor of *Mashiach*. Finally, we noted above (p. 24, footnote 51) that love at first sight is the exception nowadays rather than the rule partly because of the complex psychological makeup we possess due to our history of previous incarnations. Obviously, then, before this was so, love at first sight was more the rule than the exception; concomitantly, it will again be so when this condition will be cured in the future.

64. *Berachot* 57b; *Yalkut Shimoni, Ki Tisa* 390; *Tamid* 7:4; *Midrash Eleh Ezkerah* (quoted in *Otzar HaMidrashim*, p. 442b).

65. I.e., *chochmah*.

The essence of the Shabbat experience is thus the first level of love at first sight.[66] The second level of love at first sight is the blessing that Shabbat bestows on the coming week.

From this it follows that when love at first sight is not experienced in the context of the holiness of Shabbat and its blessing for the coming week, it is a type of premature stillbirth.[67] This type of love at first sight is analogous to the appearance of a premature *Mashiach* (מָשִׁיחַ, "Messiah"). Our sages teach us that for the true *Mashiach* to come, we must keep two Sabbaths.[68] One interpretation of this is that we need to keep one Shabbat and project its light onto the days of the coming week, thereby preparing all reality for the following Shabbat. These two Sabbaths

---

66. In Kabbalah, Shabbat is identified with the power of spiritual sight, this being a manifestation of *mochin d'Abba*.

The word שבת itself is understood to allude to the eye (*cf. Zohar* 2:204a): the *shin* of Shabbat (שבת) possesses three heads which allude to the eye's three colors: the white, the red blood vessels in the white, and the hue of the iris (whether brown, blue, green, etc.). The remaining two letters of Shabbat (שבת) spell בת ("daughter"), the idiom in Hebrew for the black pupil (בת עין).

67. This is the manifestation of the love experience in the primordial world of *Tohu* (תהו, "chaos"), the unstable state of being whose immature vessels, unable to contain its lights, broke.

68. "Were Israel to observe two Sabbaths properly, they would be immediately redeemed" (*Shabbat* 118b). Elsewhere (*Y. Ta'anit* 1:1) this is stated with regard to *one* Sabbath; thus, the first statement is interpreted to mean that the Jewish people would be redeemed if they observed both aspects of even one Sabbath (*Zohar* 1:5b; *Likutei Torah* 2:41a).

correspond to the two manifestations of love at first sight we have described.[69]

Five Biblical Examples of Love at First Sight

We said above that the more impetuous a relationship's beginning, the more difficult it may be to stabilize it later. This is graphically illustrated by the five primary examples of love at first sight described in the Bible. The first of these, that of Adam for Eve, is implied in the account of their creation. The following four—that of

---

69. The first is associated with *Mashiach* ben Yosef, the second with *Mashiach* ben David. The three daily prayers (*Shacharit*, *Minchah*, and *Arvit*) correspond to the patriarchs (Abraham, Isaac, and Jacob, respectively). The unique Shabbat *Musaf* prayer corresponds to Joseph (both *Musaf* and *Yosef* derive from the root "to add"); the *Arvit* of *Motzaei Shabbat* and the *melaveh malkah* meal, which constitute the interface between the departing Shabbat and the coming week, correspond to King David. The influence of King David extends throughout the ensuing week, preparing the souls of Israel for the coming (second) Shabbat, which represents the epitome of the messianic era, when the natural order will be superseded.

Alternatively (in accordance with the interpretation cited in the previous footnote), the two types of love at first sight are reflected in the two spiritual levels of each Shabbat: Shabbat night is the celebration of the woman; in the terminology of Kabbalah, it is pervaded by the consciousness of the refined union of *mochin d'Abba* and *mochin d'Ima*. Shabbat day is a higher, "male" consciousness, that of pure *mochin d'Abba*. Shabbat night is the level of King David, who represents *malchut*, the woman; Shabbat day is the level of Joseph, who represents *yesod*, the man. In the future, when it will be manifest that "the woman of valor is the crown of her husband" (Proverbs 12:4), the level of King David will rise above that of Joseph.

Rebecca for Isaac,[70] of Jacob for Rachel,[71] of David for Abigail,[72] and of David for Bathsheba[73]—are described explicitly. These five, in their historical order, are descending examples of how the intensity of love at first sight can be focused into mature, rooted love. This ability to relate to another person with deep, concentrated attachment is known as *da'at* (דַּעַת, "knowledge").

When G-d created Eve and presented her to Adam, he exclaimed: "*This time*, bone of my bones and flesh of my flesh! This one shall be called 'woman,' for she was taken from man." Spontaneously saying "this time," he expressed his delight and emotional arousal—his love at first sight—for his newfound mate.[74]

---

70. Genesis 24:64-65.

71. *Ibid.* 29.

72. 1 Samuel 25; *Megilah* 14b.

73. 2 Samuel 11-12.

74. Our sages (*Bereishit Rabbah* 18:4) understand the words "this time" to imply that when G-d first created Eve for Adam by amputating her from him while he was awake, he saw her bleeding, and drove her away. G-d then created her a second time, while Adam was asleep. When he awoke and saw her in her consummate beauty (adorned by G-d Himself), he exclaimed, "*this time!*" The word used here for "time" (פעם) carries the sense of "arousal" of the heart and spirit (פעימה), as in the verse "And the spirit of G-d began to arouse him [לפעמו]..." (Judges 13:25).

In addition, let us note that the numerical value of פעם is 190, which equals $10 \cdot 19$, alluding to the full manifestation of the ten powers of the soul inter-included in the number 19. 19 is the numerical value of Eve (חוה). 190 is also the numerical value of the "rib" or "side" (צלע) of Adam from which G-d created Eve. $\Delta 19 = 190$. The number 19 is the only number whose triangle is equal to 10 times itself (for 10 is the "middle point" of 19).

Before Rebecca even saw Isaac, she had agreed, with devotion and self-sacrifice,[75] to be betrothed to him.[76] On

---

Notably, this prototypical instance of love at first sight occurs as a contrast to a previous disappointing experience. We may therefore infer that a rejected experience ("date" or *shiduch*) is often necessary for the subsequent experience of true love to be real. The very experience of disappointment serves to engender the sense of egolessness needed to relate to one's true mate as an individual soul sharing a common soul-root, rather than as just an extension of one's ego, as we have explained above. See however, below, footnote 76.

On a deeper level, however, the very rejection (whether immediate or after a period of time) of the disappointing experience(s) demonstrates that one does indeed possess an awareness (or "memory") of a common soul-root. This awareness enables one to recognize any encounter other than the true one as a mistake.

By rejecting improper candidates before affirming the proper one, man is unconsciously emulating G-d, in whose image he was created. We are taught that before creating this world, G-d "created and destroyed worlds, until He created this one, of which He said: 'this one pleases Me, while those displease Me'" (*Bereishit Rabbah* 9:2). This is understood to mean not that G-d failed at first to create His desired world, but rather that He desired to contrast, and thereby augment, the experience of light by that of darkness. G-d's acts are intended to be a lesson for man, to imbue in him an instinct for what is right ("pleasing") and what is wrong ("displeasing").

75. She had told her parents and brother that she would marry Isaac even against their will (*Bereishit Rabbah* 60:12; Rashi on Genesis 24:58).

76. The Torah praises Rebecca as being "a virgin, whom no man had known" (Genesis 24:16). By guarding her virginity, Rebecca avoided the necessity of undergoing a disappointing experience before meeting her true soul mate.

However, Isaac was at first not sure of Rebecca's virginity (see *Pirkei d'Rabbi Eliezer* 16, that he suspected Eliezer of having illicit relations with her) and therefore held himself back from experiencing

her way to meet him, she saw a man approaching in the field and knew intuitively that it must be him. She experienced such intense emotions of love at her first sight of him that she nearly fell off her camel. By virtue of having so completely bound herself to him beforehand, her soul was able to recognize (*know*) him as her true soul mate even before they had formally met.

In Kabbalah, the couple that more than any other personifies the love between G-d and the people of Israel—and exemplifies, as well, the ideal state of manifest love between husband and wife—is Jacob and Rachel,[77] whose relationship is also the Torah's prototypical example of romantic love.[78]

---

love at first sight. Only afterwards, "he took her into the tent of his mother Sarah...and he loved her" (*ibid.* 24:67). Once he was assured of Rebecca's personal integrity and saw that she was as righteous as his mother Sarah (Rashi *ad loc.*), he "allowed" himself to experience the full force of love.

77. Genesis 29. In the terminology of Kabbalah, they personify the union of the *partzufim Z'eir Anpin* and *Malchut.*

78. Significantly, the numerical value of the verse which expresses the climax of the love described in the Song of Songs (7:7):

מַה יָּפִית וּמַה נָּעַמְתְּ אַהֲבָה בַּתַּעֲנוּגִים.

How beautiful and pleasant you are, O love of delights!

is 1750, which is identical with that of the two names Jacob and Rachel, when each letter of their names is spelled in full:

יוד עין קוף בית ריש חית למד.

The average value of the 25 letters of the verse is 70 (1750 ÷ 25 = 70), the value of יין ("wine") and סוד ("secret"). The average value of the seven letters of יעקב רחל (when spelled in full) is 250

Like Isaac, Jacob knew that he was going to marry his relative's daughter.[79] When he arrived at the well near Haran, the shepherds told him that the approaching maiden was Rachel, his uncle Laban's daughter. His love at first sight enabled him to single-handedly roll back the boulder covering the well at which the shepherds watered their flocks, in order to let Rachel's flocks drink. And he cried, for he sensed that he would not merit to be buried with her[80] and that there would be difficulties and delays before they could marry.

However, his *da'at* was not complete enough to be immune to deception. He knew only that he was coming to marry one of Laban's daughters; since he did not know which, his psychological preparation was conditional. Therefore Laban was able to deceive him[81] by giving him

---

(1750 ÷ 7 = 250), the value of נר ("candle"). The *menorah* of the Holy Temple possesses seven candles, which represent the seven general levels of the souls of Israel (*Likutei Torah* 3:29c). Wine was poured on the altar of the Holy Temple. Of the equation of "wine" to "secret," our sages say: "when wine enters, the secret is revealed" (*Eiruvin* 65a). The ultimate secret revealed by the service in the Holy Temple is the "love of delights" of G-d and His people Israel (as personified by Jacob and Rachel). See *Sha'arei Ahavah V'Ratzon*, p. 112 ff.

79. Genesis 28:2. In addition, "everyone said, 'Rebecca has two sons and Laban has two daughters; the elder daughter will be for the elder son, and the younger for the younger'" (*Bereishit Rabbah* 70:17, 71:2; Rashi on Genesis 29:17). Laban had promised Rachel to Jacob; on the wedding night, he deceived Jacob by giving him Leah instead. He gave him Rachel only thereafter. Perhaps Jacob was susceptible to Laban's deception because since he had bought the birthright from Esau, he was in a certain sense both the elder and the younger son.

80. Rashi on Genesis 29:11.

81. In Hebrew, the idiom for deception is "stealing the other's *da'at*."

Leah first, in place of Rachel.[82] Despite the intensity of his love for Rachel, on his wedding night he did not *know* whom he was marrying.

In both of these cases, the parties were psychologically prepared to meet their soul mates, so events proceeded relatively smoothly. Psychological preparation for an event serves as a mental "guard" or protective shield, which controls and directs the intense emotions of the heart.

In contrast, King David was not psychologically prepared for either of his confrontations with love at first sight.

When he first met Abigail, he was on the way to avenge her husband Naval's extreme ingratitude and stinginess. Seeing her, he fell in love and wanted to marry her. Not having been prepared for their encounter, his love at first sight was initially devoid of mature *da'at* altogether.

But Abigail, the "woman of goodly intelligence,"[83] convinced him that they should not marry until the time

82. Although Jacob was a virgin when he married (see *Bereishit Rabbah* 98:4; Rashi on Genesis 49:3), he still had to marry Leah in order to be able to properly marry his soul mate, Rachel, toward whom he had experienced love at first sight. Rachel was Jacob's "revealed" soul mate, while Leah was his "concealed" soul mate. His disappointment with Leah did not lead him to reject her (as Adam did to the first creation of Eve, see above, footnote 74) but rather served to elevate him to a higher level of consciousness so that he could appreciate his concealed soul mate as well. His appreciation of Leah, the mother of six of his sons, also served to safeguard the intensity of his love for his revealed soul mate, Rachel, i.e., to draw down the unbounded lights of *Tohu* into the mature vessels of *Tikun*.

83. 1 Samuel 25:3.

was right.[84] Being a prophetess, she knew that David would fail with Bathsheba, and she succeeded in convincing him to wait in order not to fail in her case as well.[85] With her wisdom and charm, she succeeded in calming his emotions, allowing his approach to their relationship to be guided by his *da'at*.

In the case of Bathsheba, however, David's mind was not only unable to control his emotions but became subordinate to them. Although she was predestined to be his wife, he acted on impulse, and was unable to wait[86] to take her until the time was ripe.[87] Once she became pregnant, he arranged that her husband be killed in battle in order that he be able to marry her. This is clearly the lowest level of *da'at* that can accompany the experience of love at first sight.[88]

---

84. I.e., until Naval died and she would be unattached. *Y. Sanhedrin* 2:3; *Midrash Shmuel* 23:12.

85. *Megilah* 14b.

86. The power of the soul to wait is a function of its *da'at* (as it manifests its source in *keter*). As will be explained, in this incident, David demonstrated the lowest level of *da'at* (and thus was unable to wait).

87. *Sanhedrin* 107a; *Shabbat* 56a; *Zohar* 1:8b, 3:78b.

88. See additional note 3 at the end of this chapter (p. 42).

Additional Notes

1

to page 9.

In the terminology of Kabbalah, a wife reflects her husband's *keter*. This is the inner meaning of the verse quoted above: "...and he will elicit [good] *will* from G-d." Will is the Divine attribute associated with the *sefirah* of *keter*, the realm of the super-conscious relative to the *sefirot* below it, which in man are manifest as the conscious powers of the soul. *Keter* means "crown"; the super-conscious is depicted as being beyond the intellect just as a crown sits above the head. *Keter* is the origin of the common soul-root of the couple, as King Solomon states (Proverbs 12:4): "The woman of valor is the *crown* of her husband."

We are taught that "there are three crowns: the crown of Torah, the crown of priesthood, and the crown of kingdom, but the crown of a good name transcends them all" (*Avot* 4:13).

Inasmuch as *keter* is primarily manifest in the soul as the will, the "crown of Torah" is the will to know and become one with the Divine wisdom of the Torah; the "crown of priesthood" is the will to serve G-d in His Holy Temple; the "crown of kingdom" is the will to rectify society and the material world in accordance with the statutes of the Torah; the "crown of a good name" is the will to sanctify G-d's Name by exemplifying His good ways in one's day-to-day encounters with his fellows.

In Kabbalah and *Chassidut* it is explained that the light generated by the first three crowns descends into reality as "direct" or "male" light, whereas the light generated by "the crown of a good name" ascends from within the context of reality as "reflected" or "female" light. Thus, the female crown is primarily "the crown of a good name." It reflects back to its infinite source, which is higher than the origin of the first three crowns; it therefore "transcends [literally, 'rises above'] them all."

The "woman of valor"—her husband's "crown of a good name"—motivates him to exemplify goodness in his daily affairs, to love and be loved (just as her own fundamental consciousness and desire toward her husband is to love and be loved).

The word כְּשֵׁרָה, literally, "the *kosher* ['proper']" wife, can be read כְּשָׂרָה, "like Sarah," the first matriarch of the Jewish people. The whole quote will then read: "Who is a woman like Sarah? She who performs/rectifies the will of her husband." Our sages teach that Sarah was greater than her husband Abraham in prophecy (*Midrash Tanchuma, Shemot* 1; Rashi on Genesis 21:12). For this reason he was instructed to "listen to her voice" (Genesis 21:12), against his own initial will and innate inclination.

Sarah knew, better than Abraham, that Jewish continuity demanded that Ishmael be separated from Isaac. Since both were sons of Abraham, by promoting her son Isaac, she was advancing Abraham's own true self-development, whereas by banishing Ishmael, she was actually balancing Abraham's character, bringing him to a higher level of *bitul* ("selflessness") than he possessed before (as is clear from the fact that this—listening to Sarah and driving out Ishmael—is considered one of his ten trials, the last and greatest before that of the binding of Isaac).

The word "name" (**שם**, 340) in the idiom "a good name" (**שם טוב**, 357) is a multiple of the word "good" (**טוב**, 17): 340 = 20 · 17, and therefore 357 = 21 · 17. 21 is the value of G-d's Name **אהיה**, which is associated with the *sefirah* of *binah*; 17 is the value of G-d's hidden Name **אהוה**, which is associated with the *sefirah* of *da'at*, the power that unites *chochmah* and *binah*, so they can give birth to the emotions of the heart.

"If there is no *da'at*, there is no *binah*; if there is no *binah*, there is no *da'at*" (*Avot* 3:17). Thus, we see that *binah* and *da'at*, and their associated Divine Names (אהיה and אהוה) are interdependent.

Since the numerical value of the Name **אהוה** is the same as that of "good" (**טוב** = 17), it is referred to in Kabbalah as "the goodly Name." The literal meaning of the Name אהיה is "I shall be" or "I shall become." Thus, the product of these two Names—the secret of the crown of the "good name" (**שם טוב**, 357 = 21 · 17)—implies "I shall become good." This is the consciousness that the good woman projects onto her husband, the will to be good.

2

to page 11.

Life is the highest and truest good, as seen by the juxtaposition of these two terms in the verse: "See, I have set before you today *life* and *good*, death and evil" (Deuteronomy 30:15).

Furthermore, there are many pairs of verses in the Bible (especially in the book of Proverbs) that are stylistically or linguistically similar. The verse we have cited with regard to the goodness of marriage,

מָצָא אִשָּׁה מָצָא טוֹב, וַיָּפֶק רָצוֹן מֵה'

He who has found a woman has found good,
and shall elicit the [good] will of G-d.

is paired with the following verse (Proverbs 8:35), in which the Torah speaks in the first person:

כִּי מֹצְאִי מָצָא חַיִּים וַיָּפֶק רָצוֹן מֵה'.

For he who has found me has found life,
and shall elicit the [good] will of G-d.

As the Torah is likened to the good woman throughout the book of Proverbs, the phrase "he who has found me [the Torah]" corresponds to the phrase "he who has found [a] woman." These two verses thus demonstrate the equivalence of "good" and "life."

Moreover, the numerical value of the word "life" (**חיים**, 68) equals four times that of "good" (**טוב**, 17), and thus, the average value of the four letters of **חיים** equals **טוב**.

In particular, the love between husband and wife is referred to as "life," as it is written (Ecclesiastes 9:9):

רְאֵה חַיִּים עִם אִשָּׁה אֲשֶׁר אָהַבְתָּ.

See life with [a] woman you love.

Note that in this phrase, the word "woman" appears without the definite article, just as in the verse "He who has found [a] woman has found good."

Every other word in this phrase, **חיים אשה אהבת**, is a multiple of **טוב** (17). **חיים** = 68 = 4 · **טוב**; **אשה** = 306 = 18 · **טוב**; **אהבת** = 408 = 24 · **טוב**. Together they equal 782 = 46 · **טוב**, the value of the concluding phrase of the priestly blessing, **וישם לך שלום** ("And He shall place upon you peace"), which refers in particular to marital harmony (שלום בית).

The entire phrase "See life with [a] woman you love" (**ראה חיים עם אשה אשר אהבת**) equals 1599 = 13 · 123. 13 equals "love" (**אהבה**); 123 equals "pleasure" or "delight" (**ענג**). Thus, this verse alludes to the epitome of love between spouses, the love referred to in the Song of Songs (7:7) as "the love of delights" (אהבה בתענוגים).

The phrase possesses 19 letters. 19 = Eve (**חוה**), the first and archetypal woman, whose name derives from "life" (חיים), for she was "the mother of all life" (Genesis 3:20).

3

to page 38.

The five descending levels of *da'at* exhibited in the five levels of love at first sight which are described in these examples can be seen to correspond to the five levels of consciousness in the primordial, pre-rectified world of *Tohu*. These, in turn, may be associated with the four letters of G-d's Name *Havayah* and the transcendent upper "thorn" of the first of these letters, the *yud*. These levels of consciousness experienced differing levels of collapse or "breakage."

The first level, that of Adam and Eve, corresponds to the thorn of the *yud*, which in turn corresponds to the *sefirah* of *keter*.

In *keter*, there was a slight blemish in the "back" of its *netzach-hod-yesod*; its *da'at* remained complete. Adam's experience of delight with his newly created spouse, Eve, involved full recognition (*da'at*) of her being one with him, as he said: "bone of my bone, flesh of my flesh." The only blemish in their relationship followed from their inability to properly communicate with one another (see below, p. 165). This inability resulted from the damage done to the "back" of the *sefirot netzach, hod,* and *yesod.*

The next two levels are at the level of mind proper, the *yud* and the *hei* of the Name *Havayah,* which correspond to the *sefirot* of *chochmah* and *binah.*

At the level of *chochmah* (more precisely, the union of the two *partzufim* of the higher *Abba* and *Ima*), there was only a fall of its "back"; its *da'at* still remained intact.

The fact that Rebecca fell (she in fact leaned over, but did not actually fall to the ground) from the camel when she first saw Isaac reflects her intense state of *bitul* (the inner attribute of *chochmah*) at that moment. In the *Zohar* (2:236a) it is explained that by so doing, she actually subdued the evil force which inhered in the camel and rectified the slight fall experienced by *chochmah* in the world of *Tohu.* At that moment of love at first sight, accompanied by her complete state of *da'at,* she overcame the angel of death—personified by the camel—achieving the level of "they shall die, but not in [i.e., when possessing] *chochmah.*" Her fall, occasioned by her *bitul,* rectified the fall of *chochmah* of *Tohu,* caused by its lack of *bitul.*

This accords with the principle, especially applicable at the level of *chochmah,* that "the forest is felled with the ax [whose handle is] made of its own wood" (*Sanhedrin* 39b; *Tanya,* ch. 31). The Aramaic word used here for "forest" (אבא) is the same as the word for "father," the level of *chochmah.*

At the level of *binah* (more precisely, the union of the two *partzufim* of *Yisrael Saba* and *Tevunah*), *da'at* is mature in itself, yet experiences a slight "crack" which results in the shedding of tears. Thus, we see that Jacob cried when he first met Rachel.

The *vav* of the Name *Havayah* represents the emotions of the heart, which do not initially possess mature *da'at.* (In the world of *Tohu,* this level experiences total breakage. Were it not for Abigail's foresight, this would have occurred here, too.) They receive their *Da'at* from their "mother," the *partzuf Ima.* In the story of David and Abigail, Abigail acts as David's "mother," explaining the implications of his intended deed and convincing him to change his way. Changing one's way is an act of *teshuvah.* Throughout the *Zohar* and Kabbalah, *teshuvah* is identified with the *sefirah* of *binah,* the "mother."

David himself is the archetypal soul of the *sefirah* of *malchut*, which corresponds to the final *hei* of the Name *Havayah*. (In the world of *Tohu*, this level "faints," i.e., loses its consciousness, or *da'at*.) Bathsheba was David's soul mate at this most essential level of his soul; the entire lineage of the kingdom of David (until *Mashiach*) issues from this marriage. As the ultimate root of *malchut* is in the unknowable head of *keter* (see below, p. 377), it is clear why in this match in particular David possessed the least *da'at*.

In relation to these four levels, the love at first sight Adam experienced for Eve corresponds to the *sefirah* of *keter*, the "thorn" of the *yud* of the Name *Havayah*. In the world of *Tohu*, this level experienced the slight fall of the lower levels (*netzach-hod-yesod*) of its "back." For this reason, Adam had to experience the disappointment of the first creation of Eve. His experience of love at first sight for the second Eve in the pristine, shameless context of the garden of Eden reflected a level of consciousness unadulterated by sin, a purely natural and spontaneous attraction of first and only man for first and only woman, unsullied by the need to focus one's attention on him or her exclusively. This level of consciousness is thus above all the levels of *da'at* described above. (With regard to Adam and Eve, the term *da'at* refers to their physical union, as will be explained later [p. 138].)

In Kabbalah, we are taught that David and Bathsheba are the primary reincarnation of Adam and Eve in the Bible. Their sin is a reoccurrence of that of Adam and Eve (see below, p. 215). The present discussion thus presents us with an example of the principle that "the end is wedged in the beginning and the beginning in the end" (*Sefer Yetzirah* 1:7), or as expressed in the *Zohar* (*Tikunei Zohar*, introduction [17a]), "the supernal *keter* is itself the *keter* of *malchut*." The love at first sight of Adam and Eve before their sin was above *da'at*, whereas that of David and Bathsheba—which was responsible for their sin—was below *da'at*.

To summarize:

thorn of י	*keter*	Adam for Eve	love at first sight above *da'at*
י	*chochmah*	Rebecca for Isaac	love at first sight with complete *da'at*
ה	*binah*	Jacob for Rachel	love at first sight with mature *da'at*
ו	emotions	David for Abigail	love at first sight with immature *da'at*
ה	*malchut*	David for Bathsheba	love at first sight without conscious *da'at*

It is significant that the highest of the four explicit levels of love at first sight is that of the bride to her groom; the other three levels are described as the love of a groom for his bride. (Isaac only loved Rebecca after he had brought her into his mother's tent and saw that she was as righteous as his mother had been [Genesis 24:67, see above, p. 34, footnote 76].) From this it appears that it is the woman who is most fitted to experience love at first sight together with the complete *bitul* of *chochmah*. And so we find that *chochmah* is referred to as "my sister": "Say to *chochmah*, 'you are my sister'" (Proverbs 7:4). This is the same "sister" of whom it is said in the Song of Songs (5:2): "Open up to me, my sister...." In Kabbalah, "opening up to" is a function of *chochmah*.

2

The Power of Imagination

The Unrectified Imagination

Whether a couple's love develops naturally or they fall in love at first sight, the path to true love and romance can be as elusive as it is essential. This is because both love and romance are predicated on the rectification of one's power of imagination (כֹּחַ הַמְּדַמֶּה).

The principle meaning of "rectification" in Kabbalah is the taming and harnessing of otherwise unbounded, chaotic powers, talents and energies by limiting, defining and directing them.[1]

---

1. In the terminology of Kabbalah, "rectification" means "enclothing" an aspect of the unbounded "lights" of the world of *Tohu* (תהו, "chaos") in the limiting "vessels" of the world of *Tikun* (תקון, "rectification"). The fact that G-d's Name *Havayah* begins with a *yud* (י, the form of which, a point, signifies contraction or concentration [*tzimtzum*]) means that limitation is the *sine qua non* for beginning any rectified process. The challenge of spiritual life is to retain the unbounded energy and naïveté of *Tohu* even after having restrained them in the vessels of *Tikun* (see *Torah Or*, pp. 24-25).

No matter how rational we may like to think we are, imagination is the primary driving force in most people's psyche. When properly oriented ("rectified"), our rich and fertile power of imagination is a blessing, for it enables us to envision our ultimate life-goals and develop our G-d-given talents. A healthy imagination makes an individual an inspired, vibrant, and exciting person, and impels him to realize his dreams.[2]

But the imagination typically develops in an unrectified manner, assuming the values, forms, and frames of reference generously afforded by the as yet unrectified milieu into which we are born. Inasmuch as these are self-serving and conflicting, the imagination tends to become deceptive and weakened. The desires of this deformed and crippled imagination not only divert one's focus from his true purpose in life but trick him into fantasizing about unrealistic goals as well. The ensuing frustration weakens one's psyche in general. A warped or

---

In one instance (Deuteronomy 22:5), the Targum actually translates the Hebrew verb "to wear" (לבש) and the nouns used for "clothing" (כלי and שמלה) into Aramaic as three forms of the root תקן, the basic meaning of which in Hebrew is "to rectify." This is because clothing serves to define and direct the person who wears it (see below, p. 373).

Additionally, both the Hebrew and Aramaic words for "vessel" (כלי and מנא, respectively) also refer to "clothing" (as in the phrase כלי גבר in the above-cited verse). *Mitzvot* are referred to as the "clothing" of the Divine soul (see *Tanya*, ch. 4).

2. Moreover, the power of the imagination can itself *facilitate* the actualization of ones' dreams and goals, as in the saying of the Rebbes of Chabad: "Think good, and it will be good" (*Igrot Kodesh Admor Rayatz*, vol. 2, p. 537; vol. 7, p. 197).

weakened imagination thus inevitably leads one toward apathy, lethargy, or despair.

The untamed imagination is therefore the psychological base of one's evil inclination,[3] the ultimate goal of which is to lead man into the abyss of depression and apathy.[4] In one's imagination all the illusions of this world[5] find their expression.[6]

---

3. *Likutei Moharan* 1:54. It is first expressed as עין הרע ("the evil eye," an expression of jealousy or paranoia), which then degenerates into לשון הרע ("the evil tongue," as expressed by gossip and slander).

4. *Tanya*, ch. 26; *Ma'amarei Admor HaZaken 5562*, p. 52.

5. This world is known in Kabbalah as "the world of deceit" (עלמא דשיקרא, see *Zohar* 1:192b), meaning that things appear to be connected and dependent upon each other in ways that they really are not. The fact that the word for "deceit" (שקר) permutes to spell the word for "connection" (קשר) indicates that the rectification of this world is effected through proper use of the associative faculties of the imagination.

As explained in *Chassidut* (*Torah Or* 28c), all accurate dream-interpretation depends on the ability to "sew" together in correct order the disordered and wrongly connected associations of the imagination. The word for "dream interpreter" (פותר, see Genesis 40) permutes to spell the word for "seamster" (תופר). (This term is used with reference to Joseph, the archetypal dream interpreter; the word used to describe him as "attractive" [פורת, *ibid.* 49:22] is a further permutation of these two.)

Our sages teach us that Adam dreamt about Eve before she was actually created from him (*Bereishit Rabbah* 18:4). Since the first dream was about woman, it follows that the essence of dreaming reflects one's longing for his soul mate (see *Zohar* 1:149a). In the unrectified soul, this longing tends to appear in the form of degenerate sexual fantasies. It is not surprising, then,.that Joseph, who is known as "the righteous" (*tzadik*, צדיק) because he tenaciously guarded the purity of his sexuality, is also the archetypal interpreter of dreams. Sexual

A rectified imagination, on the other hand, enables one to sense if someone is truly compatible as a mate (or it can give a matchmaker the ability to sense compatibility between people).

Insight allows one to recognize his true soul mate, but this is nothing more than the bare awareness of their common soul-root. Insight alone is too ephemeral, too

---

purity purifies one's power of perception, one's ability to penetrate into the unconscious motivations expressed in dreams, "unravel" the unconscious "knots" of the psyche, and "sew" together, in a rectified manner, the threads of consciousness.

6. In the Torah, every spiritual or psychological state is typified as a human figure, a physical object, or a temporal event. The primary typification of the innate, unrectified power of imagination in general, and romance in particular, is the golden calf. In fact, the idiom for "the power of imagination" (כח המדמה) numerically equals "the golden calf" (עגל הזהב, 122).

The word for "calf" (עגל) is cognate to the word for "circle" (עגול). In Kabbalah, it is explained that the unrectified imagination derives from a consciousness of the "circular" revelation of Divinity (עגולים), in which all images and associations are equally legitimate, just as all points on the circumference of a circle are equidistant from its center. The rectification of the imagination is effected by the consciousness of the "straight" revelation of Divinity (יושר), which properly orders and orients concepts, thereby precluding false associations and establishing true ones (see *Torah Or, loc. cit.*).

The calf was worshipped by the Egyptians. The nation of Egypt itself is referred to as "the seat of lechery" (literally "the nakedness of the earth," see Genesis 42:9, 12; Isaiah 20:4; *Kohelet Rabbah* 1:4, end; see below, p. 95, footnote 46), and as a "beautiful calf" (Jeremiah 46:20). Lechery, of course, is the indulgence in false and illusory sexual associations. Of the ten dreams recorded in the Torah, four were explicit communications by G-d or His angel addressing the dreamer, and six had to be interpreted. Each of these six is in some way connected with Egypt.

nondescript to provide any sense of whether or not the other person is truly compatible.[7] The rectified imagination, however, can afford one a sense of whether or not the other person's psychological constitution agrees with one's own. An unrectified imagination, of course, will deceive a person in this regard.

It is of paramount importance, then, to rectify the imagination. There are two facets in this process: purging it of the effects of negative, unhealthy influences, and then reorienting it positively.[8]

---

7. It is theoretically possible for two people to be soul mates but not compatible. For example, it might be decreed on high that two incompatible people marry in order to rectify previous incarnations or bear children that could only be born by their union. There are, indeed, examples of Talmudic sages who had difficult wives (see *Yevamot* 63b), as well as righteous women who had problematic husbands (see below, p. 104). Such cases, however, are the exception.

8. This accords with the general principle of "turn from evil, and do good" (Psalms 34:15). Let us note, however, that the Ba'al Shem Tov, in accordance with the temperament of our generation, interprets this verse to mean that it is best to "turn from evil [simply] *by* doing [extra] good" (*Likutei Sichot*, vol. 1, p. 124; vol. 2, p. 474). This is in accordance with the principle that "even a little light dispels a great deal of darkness" (*Chovot HaLevavot* 5:5; *Tanya*, ch. 12 [17a], based on Ecclesiastes 2:13).

Actually, the Ba'al Shem Tov spoke of "turning from evil" by revealing the good kernel inherent in the evil itself, thereby *transforming* it into good (*Keter Shem Tov* 41, 69, 89). This is a most delicate undertaking, however, and is usually reserved for *tzadikim*. The Lubavitcher Rebbe, however (*Likutei Sichot, loc. cit.*), applies the principle of "turning from evil *by* doing good" to the common man by taking "turn from evil" to mean "ignore evil" and be solely concerned with (i.e., "*by*") "doing good." Even so, it is necessary to be aware of the successive stages, in accordance with the simple reading of the verse.

With regard to the negative influences, there are two obstacles that may need to be overcome.

In modern society, one's imagination is almost sure to become fixed on egocentric self-fulfillment unless intentionally trained otherwise. The constant onslaught of sensual stimulation—which is almost singularly antithetical to promoting Divine consciousness—insidiously invades the individual's imagination, habituating him to focus on self-fulfillment[9] and to seek it through mundane and temporal channels.

This selfishness underlies the secular ideal of romance, which is no more than a projection of the ego from the unconscious to the conscious level of the psyche, and the accompanying search for self-gratification. Clearly, someone with such an orientation cannot experience true love or romance, which are based on selflessness, concern for others, and giving.

Worse yet, one who has been betrayed often enough by the beguilements of his unrectified imagination may well develop, out of self-defense, a cynical suspicion of any promise of fulfillment.[10] Such a person has lost the

---

9. Even more insidious is when one is conditioned to serve someone else's purposes, even to his own detriment. In general, however, both the conscious and subliminal advertising promoted by the various media takes self-orientation as a given and simply aspires to convince or "program" one to feel that ascribing to its program (of lifestyle, buying preferences, etc.) will fulfill his selfhood.

10. True, one may remain outwardly eager for stimulation, as our sages state: "Man possesses a small limb; the more he feeds it, the hungrier it gets..." (*Sukah* 52b). But this outward hunger conceals an inward apathy and disbelief in spirituality and true romance. Hence the importance attached in the Torah to physical and emotional

innocence necessary to experience true romance. His whole emotional makeup, together with the potency of his imagination, has become dulled. He has become unconcerned with, and even unaware of, the true significance of love; the very concept of romance has lost its meaning.[11]

The cure for both these ills is twofold: one must first recognize that there is a problem.[12] It is of course possible to suffer from various types of malaise—mental (anxiety, depression, listlessness, etc.) and/or physical (tension, weakness, fatigue, etc.)—which may result from an uninspired or wrongly inspired life. On the other hand, one could be unaware of any such afflictions and appear to be living quite well. Some sort of spiritual arousal must therefore be sought which will raise one to a perspective from which he can view his state truthfully (or, if he already sees it truthfully, that will drive home the urgency of his situation). Any one of a number of so-called "religious experiences" can be inspiring in this regard; but the most effective is studying the Torah, inasmuch as it not

---

virginity (of both sexes) until marriage, fidelity in marriage, and all the social laws and practices of the Torah-lifestyle that are designed to limit gratuitous interaction between the sexes. The purpose of all of these is to preserve romantic innocence and avoid the dissipation and jading of the individual's romantic side. To be sure, "nothing can stand in the way of *teshuvah*" (*Y. Peah* 1:1; *Zohar Chadash* 19:4), and as stated above, determined rededication and reorientation to G-d and the Torah can grant one a second innocence. But one should try to avoid the need for this.

11. Eventually, such a person may even lose his desire to pursue any form of stimulation, including sexual relations.

12. *HaYom Yom,* 16 *Sivan; Igrot Kodesh Admor HaRayatz,* vol. 4, p. 354, vol. 9, pp. 194-5.

only gives one a glimpse of what kind of person he could be, but shows him as well how to reach this goal.[13]

Once one has been made aware of the problem, he can set about solving it. Realizing that the root of the matter is his own acquired self-centeredness, one can relinquish his present, egocentric world view and open himself to the next phase, which is the reconstruction of his way of thinking in accordance with his true, Divine soul. Abandoning the delusions of the unrectified imagination enables one to uncover a level of consciousness that is still pure and idealistic, which can then revitalize and purify the rest of his consciousness.

If one finds this difficult, or the inspiration he summons is not sufficient to prevent relapses, he should enlist G-d's assistance.[14] This is done through the tradi-

---

13. "The inner light within it will return him to the right path" (*Eichah Rabbah*, Introduction 2; *Y. Chagigah* 1:7).

14. Of course, we need to enlist G-d's assistance at all times. In the words of our sages: "Would that one pray the whole day" (*Berachot* 21a). The more open one's heart, the more spontaneous and flowing are his prayers. The Torah calls an "open" heart a "pure" heart (see *Tanya*, ch. 26). Purity of heart (טהרה, *taharah*) depends upon rectification of the imagination. Allusion to this may be found in the fact that the words for "imagination" (כח המדמה) and "blood" (דם) are etymologically related. Blood is a primary sign of impurity in Jewish law. Prayer is said to be offered "for one's blood" (see *Berachot* 10b).

The prayers of a pure heart are not intended to replace action but rather to motivate it (see *Tanya, loc. cit.*). They inspire one to first accomplish all that he can by direct action and only thereafter to rely on his prayers. In this context, the popular maxim "G-d helps he who helps himself" means that one who acts dynamically with G-d's continuous, implicit aid is assisted by Him to achieve above and beyond whatever he could accomplish otherwise.

tional means of heartfelt prayer[15] and other practices that the Jewish people have always used to open their hearts and minds to G-d.[16] Thus he is assured of the Divine grace

---

Ritual defilement (טומאה, *tumah*), on the other hand, is a spiritual condition resulting from some contact with death or a life-death nexus. Psychological "death" is the languidness that results from the melancholy or pessimism that results in turn from an unrectified imagination. (Even in the vernacular, we use the word "dead" or "deaden" to refer to insensitivity and callousness.) Just as the Torah prescribes various rituals of purification for the various levels of defilement, there are corresponding techniques to rid oneself of psychological defilement, or "deadness." Although, of course, all of these depend on Divine help, someone who is so uninspired that he feels totally incapable of motivating himself must rely entirely on G-d's mercy. Being spiritually "dead," he needs to be spiritually resurrected. Resurrection occurs through Divine mercy, as stated in the liturgy: "who in abundant mercy resurrects the dead." In the words of the prophet Amos (5:2): "The virgin of Israel has fallen, and can no longer arise." This can be understood to refer to a state of consciousness in which the innate innocence of the people of Israel has fallen to a level from which it can no longer arise by its own power. Only Divine mercy can lift it up, purify it, and restore it to its ideal level.

All that one can do in this state is to direct all his deeds and prayers to arouse G-d's mercy (on himself and all His people), and rely on Him with simple faith.

15. The chief objective of prayer is to arouse G-d's mercy (see *Likutei Torah* 3:78c), which is why our sages refer to prayer as "mercy" (רחמי).

16. These include: camaraderie and seeking the counsel of friends or wise elders; melody and dance; acts of kindness, charity and philanthropy; reciting psalms or passages from the *Zohar* and classic Chassidic texts (even if one does not fully understand their content); and immersion in a *mikveh*.

that alone[17] can engender true selflessness, and restore a sense of innocence and wonder to one who has become jaded and languid.[18]

Once these pitfalls have been overcome, one may proceed with the process of rectifying and reorienting his imagination in general and his conception of romance in particular.

---

17. The feeling of inspiration can only be as pure as its source. Since the Torah is the only pure source of Divine inspiration, only it can inspire in a totally potent and pure way.

18. Performing these practices for the explicit sake of reviving one's inspiration is an example of the teaching of our sages: "One should always occupy himself with Torah and good deeds, even if not for their own sake, for by [doing this] not for its own sake, he will come [to do this] for its own sake" (*Pesachim* 50b).

Occupying oneself with Torah and *mitzvot* "not for their own sake" (שלא לשמה) can refer to many different states and intentions. In Chassidic thought, the highest of these levels is when one intends that his study of Torah and performance of *mitzvot* be for the sake of spiritually rectifying himself. This borders on occupying oneself with Torah "for its own sake," which is purely for the sake of fulfilling G-d's will in creation.

Chassidut teaches that it is in reference to this highest level that our sages say (and promise): "One should always occupy himself with Torah and good deeds, even if not for their own sake, for by doing good not for its own sake, he will come to do good for its own sake."

(According to another interpretation, only when one *knows* that his present state of service of G-d is "not for its own sake" and is troubled by this will he merit to serve G-d "for His own sake." Abandoning self-deception is the first step toward the rectification of the imagination, as we have said.)

Association and Induction

Surprisingly, it is the rational, analytic part of the mind that is the key to rectifying the imagination. This is because rationality includes not only the power to *deduce* one fact from another, but also the power to *induce*—to abstract an archetype or distill the essence from an idea.

Let us examine the workings of the mind in general in order to understand this in greater depth.

The two primary poles of the intellect, seated in the right and left lobes of the brain respectively, are "wisdom" (*chochmah*) and "understanding" (בִּינָה, *binah*). Each possesses an independent source in the super-conscious (כֶּתֶר, *keter*), which supplies it with mental input.

The input of the super-conscious in *chochmah* takes the form of insight, the flash of new awareness that overtakes the mind and seems to appear out of nowhere.[19]

Binah, on the other hand, appears to process only the raw material supplied it by *chochmah*, developing the implications, applications, and ramifications of the new insight *vis-à-vis* one's existing thought structures. As it does this, however, *binah* is covertly drawing on its own source in the super-conscious. It is this input which enables it to successfully process the insights of *chochmah*.

Binah in fact receives two types of input from its super-conscious source.

---

19. "From where [מאין] shall *chochmah* be found?" (Job 28:12), is interpreted to mean: "*chochmah* appears out of nothingness [מאין]."

The first is the ability to perceive relationships, similarities and associations between disparate objects or concepts.[20] It is by virtue of this power that *binah* can integrate a new insight or idea into an already existing frame of reference. In the Talmud, this ability is referred to as "likening one thing to another,"[21] and the refinement of this ability is considered essential to the advanced study of Talmudic dialectics.

Association is a form of imagination; one uses his imagination to form an associative link between two apparently unconnected concepts.[22] Like the imagination,

---

20. The word *binah* (**בינה**) is derived from the root **בין**, which as a preposition means "between"; *binah* both sees the associations *between* entities and distinguishes *between* them.

21. *Berachot* 19a; *Mishneh Torah, Talmud Torah* 1:11; *Shulchan Aruch HaRav, Talmud Torah* 2:2. In Hebrew/Aramaic: מדמה דבר לדבר or מדמה מילתא למילתא.

22. The Hebrew term for "the power of the imagination" (**כח המדמה**) more literally means "the [native] associative power [of the mind]," for the word **מדמה** comes from the word for **דמות** ("likeness"), as in the words of G-d upon creating man (Genesis 1:26):

נַעֲשֶׂה אָדָם בְּצַלְמֵנוּ כִּדְמוּתֵנוּ.

Let us make man in our image, after our likeness.

The very word for "man" (**אדם**) is cognate to the word for "likeness" (**דמות**), for which reason "man" (**אדם**), though created from the "earth" (**אדמה**), is interpreted to imply "I shall be *like* the Most High" (**אדמה** לעליון, Isaiah 14:14), as though to say that the essence of *man* is the *earth imagining* itself in *heaven*.

In the account of creation, the word for "man" (אדם) means both man (Adam) and woman (Eve), as is explicitly stated: "...and He called *their* name 'Adam' on the day He created *them*" (Genesis 5:2; *Yevamot* 63a). The male component of the imagination is the nature to

the power of association is initially untrained, and unless properly directed (both in the logical and spiritual sense), it will, in its attempt to help the mind sort out the diverse stimuli that impinge on it, make all sorts of erroneous and inconsistent connections.[23] Based on faulty structures woven by the imagination, the mind will proceed to draw spurious inferences (an extreme example being the psychosis of paranoia). If allowed to be taken to its ultimate conclusion, the unrectified power of association will lead one to believe in superstitions and even idolatry, both of which, in the final analysis, are nothing more than incorrect associations between effects and their presumed causes.

It is for this reason that of all the exegetical devices employed in Talmudic methodology,[24] the one based on association[25] can only be invoked on the authority of a previous sage, who in turn must have received it from his teacher, and so on all the way back to Moses.[26] In Talmudic

---

ascend into heaven, whereas its female component is the nature to not lose touch with reality.

It is significant to note that the vernacular term "imagination" actually derives from "in our *image*." In order to establish *associations* (כדמותנו, "after our likeness"), one must first possess the power of *imagery* (בצלמנו, "in our image").

23. The primary example of this is the inconsistencies that are common in dreams. See above, p. 49, footnote 5.

24. These are listed in the introduction to the *Sifra*, and are recited as part of the daily morning prayer liturgy as well.

25. This is the "verbal analogy" (*gezerah shavah* [גזרה שוה]) between two verses that use the same terminology in different contexts. Based on the analogy, one applies laws pertinent in one context to the other.

26. It sometimes appears that a Talmudic sage is innovating a verbal analogy. Even in such a case, he is receiving it through the chain

study, one is only allowed to rely on one's own logic when reasoning by deduction,[27] since this does not require any exercise of the imagination.

Thus, the remedy for the tendency of unrectified association to lead the mind astray is the study of the Talmud,[28] which trains the rational mind to draw legitimate associations. Underlying and predicating the rational process, however, must be pure faith, both in G-d and in the Divine authority of the Torah and its methodology. The images of the imagination will then be real.[29]

The second type of input which *binah* receives from its super-conscious source is the power of induction,

---

of tradition (איש מפי איש) from Moses, only here it is being transmitted across the generations via the super-conscious levels of the sages' souls. This is the meaning of "inspiration." For this to be genuine, of course, the innovating sage must be truly self-effacing with regard to all the great souls that preceded him, as well as to the consistency of the chain of Jewish tradition, from Moses' time until his own. This true *bitul* then causes the Torah to be given anew in the present moment, as manifest in the "new" verbal analogy. The analogy, like a marriage, then gives birth to new dimensions of understanding.

The rectified imagination thus receives its inspiration from previous great souls and sages.

27. The primary example of this type of reasoning is the first of the thirteen Talmudic exegetical methods, inference *a fortiori* (called *kal vechomer* [קל וחומר, "(deducing) the heavy from the light"] or *din* [דין, "judgment"]).

28. Or the study of other parts of the Torah which employ Talmudic methodology.

29. As Rabbi Yitzchak Isaac of Homil points out (*Chanah Ariel* 2:47b), the logic of the Talmud, as distinguished from pure rational logic, is a unique method of reasoning germane to the Jewish psyche.

which is referred to by the sages as "understanding one thing out of another."[30]

In its simplest sense, induction is the mechanism through which the mind draws associations, for any association between two ideas is based on a perceived common denominator, or shared essence or archetype. In this sense, induction is merely the facilitator of the imagination, the tool it uses to draw inferences.

But beyond this, once it has successfully worked out all the associations between the old and new ideas, induction enables the mind to penetrate into depths of understanding it was not previously able to imagine. By distilling and abstracting the underlying essence of a particular idea or set of ideas, one uncovers new realms of insight. Here, induction actually expands the conceptual repertoire and the capacities of association.

The difference between associative imagination and inductive imagination is that associative imagination expands and broadens the surface of the mind's boundaries, enabling it to encompass more and more true associations which enrich one's general consciousness of reality. The literal reading of the term for induction, on the other hand, is "understanding one thing from *within* another," implying that one must penetrate into the depth

30. In Hebrew: להבין דבר מתוך דבר (*Shabbat* 31a; Rashi on Exodus 31:2; *Mishneh Torah* and *Shulchan Aruch HaRav, loc. cit.*; see *Teshuvat HaShanah*, ch. 21).

of the original concept in order to induce a new, greater understanding.[31]

---

31. Association is thus analogous to an "expanding universe"; induction, on the other hand, is like passing through the singularity point ("black hole") of an existing universe in order to enter a new one.

For this reason, the phrase "one thing from within another" (דבר מתוך דבר) equals 878, which in turn equals:

—"*Mashiach*" (משיח) when spelled in full (מם שין יוד חית),

—"darkness" (חשך) when spelled in full (חית שין כף),

—the three levels of darkness present at the giving of the Torah: "darkness, cloud, mist" (חשך ענן ערפל, Deuteronomy 4:11),

These three—"darkness," "cloud," "mist"—correspond to past, present, and future:

- Of the past it is said: "and the land *was* unformed and void, and darkness [חשך]..." (Genesis 1:2).
- Of the present, it is said: "The matter [עניין] which *occurs* on the earth" (Ecclesiastes 8:16). עניין is cognate to ענן; this word occurs exclusively in Ecclesiastes, and always in the context of the "bad" and dark state of present reality. The sorcerer who chooses propitious times (according to certain commentaries, by observing the clouds) is called an עונן or מעונן, cognate to ענן. In the liturgy of the High Holidays, our present state of being is compared to ענן כלה ("a vanishing cloud").
- Of the future, it is said: "In *conclusion* [literally, 'the end']: all has been heard..." (סוף דבר הכל נשמע, Ecclesiastes 12:13, the *end* of the book of Ecclesiastes, whose *final* letters spell ערפל).

—"the advantage of light [which issues from darkness]" (יתרון האור, Ecclesiastes 2:13),

—"I saw an inverted world" (עולם הפוך ראיתי, *Pesachim* 50a; *Bava Batra* 10b). This is said of the "world of truth," the "new heavens and new earth" (Isaiah 66:22), which appears inverted in relation to our present reality—"the world of deceit."

This string of equivalences teaches us that *Mashiach* will reveal a totally new universe from the deepest darkness of the existing one.

It is through the inductive process that the imagination exercises its primary creativity, for discovering or inventing new concepts is more daring than weaving new associations between existing ones.[32]

Although it is a rational function, induction is guided by the intuition,[33] one's super-rational sense of what is a legitimate induction and what is not. Here too, however, the accuracy of one's intuition can be obscured or warped by the unrectified imagination on its way to the conscious mind. By rectifying the imagination, one enables his intuition to accurately guide his inductive powers.

---

32. *Binah* is a "surrounding" power relative to both the seminal insight of *chochmah* (which it envelops and around which it constructs its mental structures) and to the emotions which it generates. The two faculties of *binah*, association and induction, express the two core-meanings of the word מקיף, "to touch" and "to surround." Association corresponds to the meaning "to touch" since it is the juxtaposition of ideas. Induction corresponds to the meaning "to surround" since any cause is said to surround its effect. In induction, the effect is the presently understood concept, which reaches up (or delves down) to find the distilled archetype which is its cause.

In the terminology of Kabbalah and *Chassidut*, the imagination is the most external, superficial manifestation of the *partzuf* of *Ima*. This dimension of the mind comes to the forefront of one's consciousness when the more inner dimensions recede (as when sleeping; dreams are the primary expression of the imagination [see above, p. 49 footnote 5, and *I am Asleep yet My Heart is Awake*, footnotes 1-3]). The imagination is rooted in the *gulgalta* (the מקיף of *Arich Anpin*), whereas intuition is rooted in the *mocha stima'ah* (the פנימי of *Arich Anpin*).

33. The Talmudic term for intuition is נכרים דברי אמת ("truth is recognizable," *Sotah* 9b, etc.). Intuition provides the sense of how far one can legitimately go in the process of induction.

Developing the ability to correctly induce one thing from another rectifies the inductive side of the imagination. This is accomplished by studying those parts of the Torah that employ and hone this type of reasoning.[34]

The ultimate rectification of the imagination is the gift of prophecy.[35] As we explained above, egocentricity was introduced into man's psyche when he ate the fruit of the tree of knowledge of good and evil.[36] When, in the messianic future, this sin will have been fully rectified, and with it man's power of imagination, "I will pour out My spirit on all flesh: your sons and daughters will prophesy, your old men shall dream [clear] dreams, and your young men shall see [true] visions."[37]

---

34. This includes the study of the Talmud, but as will be explained presently, it is the study of Kabbalah and *Chassidut* that best refine this aspect of the imagination.

35. The prohibition against misusing one's imagination to predict the future based on spurious extrapolations from the present is "you shall not divine" (Leviticus 19:26). Joseph, who uses his rectified imagination to correctly interpret dreams, says: "one such as I can surely divine" (Genesis 44:15). The verb "divine" (נחש) is also the word for "snake." However, it is also the numerical equivalent of the rectifier of the primordial snake and the fallen, corrupt imagination, *Mashiach* (משיח, 358).

36. p. 11. Man was created originally with a pure, rectified imagination, as it is said: "G-d made man upright, but they have sought out many fabrications" (Ecclesiastes 7:29).

37. Joel 3:1.

Meditation: Abstraction and Projection

Now, of all the experiences that contribute to the molding of the imagination (and the basic parameters of one's imagination are formed primarily in one's youth), those relating to love have the strongest influence.[38] In order to rectify the imagination, therefore, the common forms of romantic imagery must be abstracted to and reconstituted at their source, the love and romance between G-d and Israel.[39]

This is done through rationally directed meditation as prescribed in Kabbalah and *Chassidut*. The primary objective and focus of these parts of the Torah is the all-inclusive rectification of consciousness (behind which the imagination is the primary driving force). Since it is concerned with the dynamics of the relationship between G-d (the cosmic groom) and the collective or individual soul of Israel (the cosmic bride), the Torah's inner dimension is in effect one great exposition of love and romance.

By studying this dimension of the Torah, one comes to understand and feel love at its source. The ebb and flow of one's actual or anticipated marital affections becomes a springboard from which to perceive and experience the dynamics of the Divine love relationship, and in turn, project the rectified image of the romantic experience into

---

38. This is because love is the primary emotion, from which all others are derived. See above, p. 16, footnote 32.

39. Thus, rectifying one's concept of love and romance is the key to rectifying the imagination, which in turn enables one to experience true love and romance in his own life.

one's own life. One can then experience true love and romance in all avenues of life,[40] particularly in marriage, which becomes a reflection of the true and ultimate ideal of romance.

In summary, the rectification of the imagination in general, and of one's image of love and romance in particular, involves three stages: the abandonment of false conceptions of love and romance, the abstraction of worldly love and romance to Divine romance, and the resultant manifestation of Divine union in worldly love.[41]

---

40. In the words of Rabbi Shneur Zalman of Liadi, Rabbi: "True love of G-d is fully expressed only in one's love of his fellow Jew, for by loving one's fellow Jew, he loves what his Beloved loves" (*HaYom Yom*, 28 Nissan).

41. These three stages parallel the threefold dynamic of "submission, separation, and sweetening" (see below, p. 262). The latter two stages parallel the twofold dynamic of "run and return" (see below, p. 238).

abandonment of false conceptions of love and romance	הכנעה submission		
abstraction of worldly love and romance to Divine romance	הבדלה separation	רצוא run	הפשטה abstraction
manifestation of Divine union in worldly love	המתקה sweetening	שוב return	הלבשה enclothing

3

The Three Stages of Love

To Cling and Become One

As we have seen, the goodness inherent in relating to one's spouse at the level of their common soul-root is considered the very purpose of the creation of man:

וַיֹּאמֶר ה' אֱלֹהִים:
לֹא טוֹב הֱיוֹת הָאָדָם לְבַדּוֹ,
אֶעֱשֶׂה לּוֹ עֵזֶר כְּנֶגְדּוֹ.

And G-d said:
It is not good for man to be alone;
I shall make him a helpmate.[1]

This goodness is synonymous with the couple clinging together and becoming one:

---

1. Genesis 2:18.

עַל כֵּן יַעֲזָב אִישׁ אֶת אָבִיו וְאֶת אִמּוֹ וְדָבַק בְּאִשְׁתּוֹ,
וְהָיוּ לְבָשָׂר אֶחָד.

Therefore shall man leave his father and mother
and cling[2] *to his wife,*
and they shall become one flesh.[3]

The sequential relationship between the concepts of good, clinging, and oneness is as follows:

As we have said, the goodness in a good marriage is an echo of the Divine pleasure the couple experienced in their common soul-root, before their souls separated from one another in order to descend and enter individual bodies.

Once born, each individual feels an instinctive need to seek his "lost side,"[4] based on the subconscious recollection of the deep pleasure he experienced together with her in their primordial existence. When he does find her, he must then *cling* to her, which he does by leaving his parents' home,[5] becoming independent, and building a home for himself together with her. As our sages teach: "one's wife is his home."[6]

Becoming "one flesh" encompasses both the physical consummation of marital relations[7] (which begins with the

2. This is the first appearance of the root "to cling" (דבק) in the Torah (see above, p. 6, footnote 13).

3. *ibid.* 24.

4. See above, p. 9.

5. See Ramban on Genesis 2:24.

6. *Yoma* 2a. See below, ch. 10.

7. Ibn Ezra on Genesis 2:23.

couple's clinging together) and the birth of children, in whom their flesh becomes physically one.[8]

When they become one, husband and wife once again experience the goodness and Divine pleasure they knew in their common soul-root.[9]

---

8. Rashi on *ibid.*, 2:24.

9. As a noun, the Hebrew root דבק ("to cling") means "glue." The two words "good" and "glue" are juxtaposed in the verse: "...he says of *glue*, it is *good* [דבק טוב]..." (Isaiah 41:7).

The numerical value of this idiom (**דבק טוב**, 123) equals that of the word for "pleasure" (**ענג**). This is alluded to in *Sefer Yetzirah* (2:4): "there is no *good* higher than *pleasure*." The initial letters of the two words **דבק טוב** equal **אחד** ("one," 13).

When the three letters of **דבק** are coupled to the three letters of **טוב** in one-to-one correspondence and their products taken, we have: $4 \cdot 9 = 36$; $2 \cdot 6 = 12$; $100 \cdot 2 = 200$. The sum of these products ($36 + 12 + 200$) is 248, the number of "limbs" in the human body, and the number of positive commandments in the Torah (*Makot* 23b; *Ohalot* 1:8).

We may interpret this to mean that all 248 positive commandments serve as the "good glue" which connects man to G-d (just as the word *mitzvah* itself means "joining together").

Man was created "in the image of G-d" (**בצלם אלהים**; Genesis 1:27); the numerical value of this phrase is also 248, as is the value of the name of the first Jew, Abraham (**אברהם**). The Jew, in his performance of the 248 positive commandments, *clings* to G-d and becomes *one* with Him (of Abraham it is said: "Abraham was *one*" [Ezekiel 33:24]). This union of G-d and man on earth is the ultimate reason for which He created him.

Thus, goodness is both the beginning of a couple's relationship and its end, in accordance with the principle that "the end is wedged in the beginning and the beginning in the end" (*Sefer Yetzirah* 1:7).

In the terminology of Kabbalah, these three states are identified with the soul's three mental faculties. "One" (אחד) is identified with the *sefirah* of *chochmah* (see *Tanya*, ch. 35 in note, citing the Maggid of

Relationship, Togetherness, and Oneness

The goal of marriage, then, is that the couple manifest in their earthly consciousness the existential oneness they found in their celestial soul-root. This is the essence of true love.

Attaining this ideal is a three-stage process. This is because, according to Kabbalah, all of creation exists within three frames of reference: space, time, and soul.[10] Any rectification of reality must therefore address each of these three "dimensions." With respect to husband and wife, this means that the unity that exists at the level of their common soul-root must be made manifest in each of these three frames of reference.[11]

Mezerich), "good" (טוב) with the *sefirah* of *binah* ("the revelation of *Atik* is in *binah*" [see *Zohar* 3:178b]; *Atik* is synonymous with pleasure) and "clinging" (דבק) with the *sefirah* of *da'at*.

10. Based on the terminology of *Sefer Yetzirah* 3:3 ff. The word used there for "space" is "world" (עולם); the word used for "time" is "year" (שנה). The word for "soul" (נפש) is used there in the sense of the *living* human body (created "in the image of G-d"), which is a physical reflection of man's spiritual soul.

"Space" includes the three conventional dimensions of length, breadth, and depth. If we consider time the fourth dimension, soul (or morality, ethics) becomes the fifth dimension.

11. The word for "one" (אחד) appears three times in the account of creation, with regard to each of these frames of reference: "one day" (Genesis 1:5, time), "one place" (*ibid.* 1:9, space), "one flesh" (*ibid.* 2:24, soul).

Remarkably, each of these verses has 13 (= **אחד**, "one") words. The first verse contains 49 (= 7^2) letters. All three together contain 144 (= 12^2) letters. The most important verse of the Torah which contains the word "one" is the *Shema* (Deuteronomy 6:4), which itself contains

The first stage in this process is for a couple to learn how to relate to and interact properly with one another. In the early stages of their relationship, they think of themselves primarily as separate individuals, since their aspirations, desires, and interests have not consciously aligned or coalesced. Love, at this stage, is the soul's ability to project itself outside itself and to thereby touch another soul. As explained above, unrectified love is focused on oneself; one may think he's loving someone else, but he's really only loving himself.[12] Rectified love involves learning how to focus one's love and concern on someone else.

Since they consider themselves separate entities, the husband and wife may be said to be occupying at this stage separate realms of mental "space." Establishing and maintaining a proper loving relationship can therefore be seen as the rectification of the "spatial" manifestation of their intrinsic unity.[13] Over the course of time, a couple learns to express their love as a deepening sense of partnership in building a Jewish home and achieving their common goals, genuinely caring for one another, and becoming more and more sensitive to and respectful of each other's feelings.

---

25 (= 5^2) letters. The total number of letters in these four verses is thus $12^2 + 5^2 = 169 = 13^2$, i.e., the word **אחד** squared!

12. Such love may be described as "impotent," since it produces nothing lasting.

13. In Kabbalah, the six emotive attributes (from *chesed* to *yesod*) are the origin of the three dimensions of space, each attribute corresponding to one of the six extremities of the three spatial coordinates.

The second stage of a couple's consciousness is existential, continuous togetherness. Having aligned themselves to each other "spatially," they have closed the mental distance between them and become a husband-wife unit. Their consciousness and emotional boundaries have expanded to encompass each other; each spouse considers the other a part of himself.[14]

As a result, physical proximity or the lack of it does not affect their togetherness. They have transcended space and exist together in time.[15] As they experience time's cycles together, they focus on how life's varying moods impinge on their common consciousness and react productively to them together. As their love matures to this level of true togetherness, neither of them can picture his or her life apart from the other.

At the final stage of consciousness,[16] husband and wife come to experience themselves as a single entity. Their common soul-root is now fully manifest in both of them; as they were in heaven, so they are on earth. This is the fulfillment of G-d's intention that they "cling...and become one." In time, love and true romance deepen in

---

14. See above, p. 7, and below, p. 210, footnote 3.

15. In the dimension of time, two points that exist simultaneously are considered coincident although their spatial coordinates may be physically distant.

16. The transition from the second to the third stage of consciousness is provided by the *mitzvah* of procreation. Procreation is the culmination of their togetherness and the consummation of their most fundamental mutual time-experience, the wife's menstrual cycle, as will be explained in ch. 11.

both the conscious levels of their souls and in their mutual "collective unconscious."[17]

To the extent that the couple becomes absorbed in their true reality as a part of G-d, their sense of independent selfhood disappears. They no longer possess feelings and emotions directed toward one another, but have rather "become" one another. At this level, one can not only rectify or expand one's emotional makeup but actually change it. Once a person surrenders his selfhood to the infinity of G-d's reality, he can transform himself into a purer, higher version of himself.[18]

To summarize:[19]

---

17. The three Hebrew terms for these stages, יחס ("relation"), יחד ("together"), and אחד ("one"), are clearly phonetically related. The common consonantal letters of these words are חסד, "loving-kindness"; these are three levels of love.

More specifically, the ס of יחס transforms to the ד of יחד through the substitutional method of *albam;* and the י of יחד transforms into the א of אחד by virtue of their being vowel-letters (אהו"י) and through the substitutional method of *ayik becher*.

Using the metaphor of music, the first stage corresponds to the couple "singing" in counterpoint, the second in harmony, and the third in unison.

18. By doing this, one is in effect "procreating" oneself anew. This self-rebirth is just a more refined expression of the consummation of a couple's oneness, the procreation of children (see above, p. 68, and below, p. 334, footnote 57).

From this it is evident that true transformation is possible only if one is married.

19. In the terminology of Kabbalah, the spatial relationship is associated with the *partzuf* of *Z'eir Anpin*. In the temporal relationship, consciousness ascends to the *partzuf* of *Ima*, i.e., the couple conceive of

soul	oneness	nullification of individual emotions, transformation into one entity
time	togetherness	broadening the emotions so that they encompass the other individual
space	relationship	rectifying the emotions, reorienting their initial egocentricity

These three stages parallel the sequence of good, clinging, and becoming one described above.

The "good" in first stage, relationship, is simply the negation of the "not good" of living alone.

At the second stage, togetherness, the couple actually "cling" to each other; they are still two entities but consider themselves as parts of the same whole. This stage is thus an intermediate step between the consciousness of being two entities and being one.

At the third stage, they become truly one. They can then experience the higher "good" of their common soul-root.[20]

To summarize:

themselves as existing within a common womb. At the soul level, consciousness ascends further to the *partzuf* of *Abba*, i.e., the couple conceive of themselves as existing within a common seed.

20. This is alluded to by the fact that the words for "one" (אחד) and "good" (טוב) inter-permute in *atbach*.

soul	oneness	oneness; goodness at the level of the soul-root
time	togetherness	clinging
space	relationship	goodness as the negation of "it is not good for man to be alone"

At the beginning, as we said, a couple must learn how to relate to one another properly. This topic will be treated in the next seven chapters. In chapters eleven through thirteen, we will focus on the rectification of the couples' consciousness in the context of time. In the final two chapters[21] we will discuss the couple's unity on the level of soul.

---

21. Chapter fourteen, "Marital Union—the Mystery of the Sabbath," focuses on the dimension of time reaching up to and uniting with that of soul; it thus serves as an interface between these two dimensions.

4

Relationship

Mirror Psychology

The surest way to gauge one's success in the process of self-refinement is to observe his spouse's behavior toward him.[1] Both consciously and unconsciously, she senses the purity of his motives and responds accordingly, both intentionally and instinctively.

In a larger sense, this is true of all inter-personal relationships. "As [when looking in] water, face reflects face, so does one's heart find reflection in another's."[2] Thus, in accordance with the nature and extent of one's involvement with other people, one may gauge one's self-refinement by the way one is treated.

---

1. Our sages teach (*Avot* 3:10): "Whoever is pleasing to man is pleasing to G-d, and whoever is not pleasing to man is not pleasing to G-d." The Ba'al Shem Tov went to great lengths to implant this consciousness in his disciples. One's relation with mankind in general begins with his most intense, focused interpersonal relationship (which is also the first relationship ever to exist), that which he shares with his spouse.

2. Proverbs 27:19.

Since marriage is the most intense form of inter-personal relationship, this principle applies first and foremost to married life. It is here that one will confront most strikingly his successes and failures in self-refinement, mirrored in his spouse's behavior toward him.[3]

In general, this reciprocal attitude between spouses is on one of three levels, in accord with the stages of rectification of the imagination.

If the husband is still laboring under false, self-centered notions of love and romance, his behavior will certainly reflect this, and his wife will naturally resent his egocentricity and pit herself against him. Their relationship—that of two unrelating individuals occupying separate, colliding "spaces"—will be characterized by frequent and painful friction. Alienated from a husband whom she senses does not have her best interests at heart, she will disconnect from him as well and shirk her wifely obligations.

Once the husband extricates himself from his unrectified imagination, he can begin to work on himself. He gradually begins to redirect his intentions toward fulfilling G-d's will in all avenues of life (and in particular

3. This is all the more so the case when the couple lives in the land of Israel, where Divine Providence is most revealed, as it is said: "it is the land upon which the eyes of G-d always look" (Deuteronomy 11:12). Thus, the question cited at the beginning of this book, "have you *found* or do you *find*?" was reported as being asked specifically in ancient *Israel* (and not in the other center of Jewish life at the time, Babylonia).

in his marriage[4]), sense his and his wife's common soul-root, and refine his character. Even though he has not yet completed this process, his wife will sense his genuine effort and respond by striving to help and support him.[5]

Nonetheless, until the process is complete, she will maintain a separate sense of self. The two will view their marriage as a mutually beneficial relationship wherein each is happy and ready to give yet expects to receive in return.

If the husband succeeds in all the above-mentioned areas—purifying his intentions so that his sole motivation is to do G-d's will, attuning himself to his and his wife's common soul-root, and refining his character, always placing the needs of others before his own—the couple's consciousnesses will merge. His absolute devotion to her will inspire her to devote herself commensurately to him:[6]

---

4. Where husband and wife become "partners" with G-d in the act of creation.

5. The Targum translates the Hebrew עזר ("helpmate") as סמך ("support"; see below, footnote 9). To be of help and to be of support are complimentary concepts: "help" implies active involvement while "support" implies a more passive state. A wife supports her husband by enhancing his self-confidence, "projecting" her own faith and trust in the worthiness of his ambitions and his ability to achieve them.

This exemplifies the principle that the Hebrew text of the Torah and its Aramaic translation demonstrate a male-female, active-passive relationship (here, both in reference to the female, i.e., her own male and female sides).

6. The deepest meaning of "the Divine Presence dwelling between them" is that both husband and wife establish such a complete identification with the Divine Presence that each perceives the other as the only individual in need of attention.

This is alluded to in the verse (Leviticus 19:18), "And you shall love your fellow as yourself, *I am G-d*." In order to truly love one's

"as [when looking in] water, face reflects face, so does one's heart find reflection in another's."[7] She will feel an indivisible part of him, and all her deeds will reflect *total* devotion to him.

These three levels of relationship between a couple are alluded to in G-d's statement before He created Eve:

אֶעֱשֶׂה לּוֹ עֵזֶר כְּנֶגְדּוֹ.

I will make for him [i.e., for Adam] a helpmate.[8]

In Hebrew, the two-word idiom translated as "helpmate" (עֵזֶר כְּנֶגְדּוֹ) literally reads "a helper opposite him."[9] Our sages discerningly point out that two kinds of relationship are implied: "If he is worthy,[10] she shall be a

---

fellow as oneself, one must first nullify his own sense of selfhood to the extent that it becomes completely superseded by G-d's, which then functions through his consciousness (see *Klal Gadol BaTorah*).

7. Proverbs 27:19.

8. Genesis 2:18.

9. The Targum translates the idiom עזר כנגדו as סמך לקבליה, literally, "a support paralleling him." Thus, we can understand "opposite him" here to mean "complementing him." Indeed, as will be discussed, if the husband interprets his wife's contrariness properly, it will serve to improve both themselves and their relationship.

10. The Hebrew word for "worthy" (זכה) also means "refined" or "pure." Thus, the extent to which one's wife accords with him depends on the extent to which he has purified and refined himself.

Just as the *pure* olive oil (שמן זית זך) used in the Temple had to be "pressed to become a source of light" (Exodus 27:20), so must the husband, in order to "purify" and "refine" himself (and thus become "a source of light"), first "press" or "crush" his ego. The Lubavitcher Rebbe explains that for our generation, this is accomplished by feeling

help to him; if he is unworthy, she shall be *opposed* to him, and fight him."[11]

The third and highest level of relationship is implied by the word "for him" (לוֹ),[12] which precedes the two-word idiom for "helpmate." This level is also alluded to two verses later, when "helpmate" appears a second time:

---

the anxiety over the realization that *Mashiach* has not yet been revealed (*Sefer Ma'amarim Melukat*, vol. 6, p. 134 ff.). The pure olive oil will then bring about—as "a source of light"—the revelation of *Mashiach*. (The perfectly rectified state of marital harmony is truly a messianic revelation.)

11. Rashi *ad loc.*; *cf. Yevamot* 63b.

12. Our sages interpret the word לו ("to him") in another verse to refer to a wife, basing this interpretation on the use of the word לו in our verse (*Ketubot* 67b; Rashi on Deuteronomy 15:8).

The fact that this interpretation is derived through "verbal analogy" (גזרה שוה) alludes to the intrinsic relationship between the level of לו itself and the inner meaning of גזרה שוה. Literally, גזרה שוה means "an *equal* '*cut*.'" Adam and Eve were initially created "back to back." Eve was then *cut* apart from Adam and brought to him "face to face," to cling to him and become one ("*equal*") with him.

The fact that Adam and Eve were created "back to back" is interpreted in *Chassidut* to mean that initially, each one had only his own interests at heart. The rectified state of being "face to face" is that of true, selfless devotion to one another.

This rectified state of being "face to face" is also one of true modesty, for (as will be explained later) modesty is the expression of one's transcendence of self-orientation.

For this reason, the very fact that the word לו refers to a (level of) "wife" is "unknown" (i.e., "modest") in its own verse; it is only by comparison to another verse that this becomes revealed.

...וּלְאָדָם לֹא מָצָא עֵזֶר כְּנֶגְדּוֹ.

...but for himself Adam did not find a helpmate.

The words "for himself" are the translation of the two letters prefixed to the noun "Adam." These two letters (ול) spell the word "to him" (לו). In this allusion, the woman is totally connected to and even precedes her husband.[13]

Furthermore, as we have observed,[14] the word "found" alludes to the verse: "He who has *found* a woman has found good," where the use of the past tense means that he has found his soul mate in their mutual source. Thus, we can interpret the phrase "and Adam did not find for himself..." to read: "and man was still unable to find woman at the level of their common soul-root, the level of 'for him[self].'"[15]

---

13. As his "crown" (see above, p. 9, footnote 18).

14. p. 6, footnote 13.

15. Numerically, this is alluded to by the fact that the average value of the two words **לא מצא** (162) equals **ולאדם** (81), indicating that it is the level of **ולאדם** which Adam didn't find (לא מצא).

Furthermore, **לא מצא** = **בצלם** ("in the image"), alluding to the phrase "in the image of G-d He created him, male and female He created them." This indicates once more that Adam was unable to find his soul mate at the level on which both were created in the common image of G-d.

The numerical value of **ולאדם** is $81 = 9^2$. **אדם** = $45 = \Delta 9$ (the sum of all numbers from 1 to 9), and **לו** = $\Delta 8$. This accords with the general rule in mathematics that the sum of the triangles of two successive numbers equals the square of the larger number ($\Delta n \perp \Delta[n \perp 1] = [n \perp 1]^2$). Thus, the totally devoted wife precedes and complements her husband to become, together, a perfect being.

"for him"	לוֹ	unity of wife and husband
"a helper"	עֵזֶר	wife assisting husband
"opposite him"	כְּנֶגְדּוֹ	wife at odds with husband

The *Tzadik*: Absolute Devotion

These three levels of relationship between husband and wife reflect the three general levels of relationship between G-d and man.[16]

A *tzadik* (צַדִּיק, a consummately righteous person) is someone who is so completely devoted to G-d[17] that he never regards himself as a separate entity or individual.

---

16. On the classification of souls as *tzadik, beinoni,* and *rasha,* see *Tanya* (whose original title is "The Book of the *Beinonim*"), ch. 1-12. It is taught there that most of us, by our own efforts, can at most achieve the level of the *beinoni;* the metamorphosis of a *beinoni* into a *tzadik* is the prerogative of G-d (see, in a similar vein, *Mishneh Torah, Yesodei HaTorah* 6:5, regarding a prophet).

Nonetheless, "all Jews are responsible [עֲרֵבִין] for each other" (*Shavuot* 39a), which in *Chassidut* is interpreted to mean that "all Jews are present within [מְעֹרָבִים] one another" (and also "all Jews are pleasant [עֲרֵבִים] to each other").

In a similar vein, the word **צבור** ("congregation" or "public") is interpreted in *Chassidut* as an acronym for **צדיקים בינונים ורשעים**, "*tzadikim, beinonim,* and *resha'im.*" Every Jew is said to possess his own **צבור**, an inner identity containing each of the three levels. Thus, what is said with regard to any of these levels applies in a relative way to all people at all times.

17. As the *tzadik* perceives all Jewish souls as "actual parts of G-d" (*Tanya,* ch. 2), his devotion to G-d is reflected in his devotion to G-d's people.

True, his observance of Torah and the commandments is suffused with his intention to cling to and become one with G-d by fulfilling His will, and he experiences Divinity with love and fear. Yet he attributes it all to G-d's infinite grace and providence. As our sages say:[18] "Give [*i.e.*, attribute] to Him [לו] that which is His, for you and all that is yours are His."[19]

G-d responds by proudly attributing all the good in reality to the merit of the *tzadik*.[20] In fact, as mentioned above,[21] His motive in creating the world was the pleasure He would derive from the good deeds of the righteous.[22]

---

18. *Avot* 3:7.

19. For this reason, a *tzadik* is referred to by the word לו, literally "to Him," inasmuch as his very being is devoted to G-d, and because he ascribes the positive emotions he experiences and the good deeds he performs "to Him."

20. The Ba'al Shem Tov (*Keter Shem Tov* 193) interprets the verse (Psalms 62:13), "And kindness is Yours, G-d, for You recompense man according to his deeds": In Your kindness, You recompense man *as if* the deed was his. In the case of the *beinoni*, G-d accounts everything he does as if he himself did it, even though in truth it is G-d who does everything. In the case of the *tzadik*, G-d goes further and considers even what He himself does as if the *tzadik* had done it. Cf. *Berachot* 17b: "The whole world is sustained in the merit of My son Chaninah...."

21. p. 27.

22. Therefore, this level can be seen as a return of the soul to the consciousness it possessed before the *tzimtzum*, when it was one with G-d.

Inasmuch as "Your people are all righteous" (Isaiah 60:21), this applies in essence to every Jew.

The word "for him" (לו) itself alludes to the level of the *tzadik*, for its numerical value—36—is the number of *tzadikim* that live in every

The *Beinoni*: Mutual Interests

The second level of relationship corresponds to the consciousness of the *beinoni* (בֵּינוֹנִי, the "intermediate" servant of G-d).

In all modes of behavior—thought, speech, and action—the *beinoni* has renounced the lifestyle bred by the unrectified imagination and thus is free of sin, but his motives are not yet totally pure; he has not surrendered his selfhood. He is committed to helping G-d bring the world to perfection by fulfilling His will with joy, yet remains aware that he is working for his own good as well.

Our sages interpret the phrase which concludes the verse: "You shall therefore keep the commandments, the rules, and the laws which I command you *today to do*

---

generation (*Sukah* 45b). In Kabbalah, it is taught that in every generation there are 36 *revealed tzadikim* as well as 36 *concealed tzadikim*, two (complimentary) levels of לו (see above, footnotes 12 and 19). The common appellation for one of these *tzadikim* is "a *lamed-vavnik*," emphasizing the two letters that compose the word לו. The importance of the number 36 lies in its being the square of 6, indicating the inter-inclusion (and thus perfection) of all six emotional and behavioral attributes (*midot*). It is for this reason that the *tzadik* is associated with the sixth, summary *midah* of *yesod*, and that this very *sefirah* is alluded to (in 1 Chronicles 29:11) by the word "all."

The following two words, עזר כנגדו, equal 360, or 10 · 36. This implies that the essence (the tenth part) of these two contrary modes of relationship exists at the level of לו. As will be discussed, the *beinoni* and the *rasha* (potential *ba'al teshuvah*) each reflect their essential source, the *tzadik*, as is said: "And your people are all righteous [*tzadikim*]" (Isaiah 60:21).

them,"[23] as implying: "today [in this world] to do them and tomorrow [in the world to come] to receive their reward."[24]

The *beinoni* takes this to mean that though the challenge of this world ("today") is to perform G-d's commandments faithfully, in return, he will surely inherit ("tomorrow") the reward of the world to come.

A *tzadik,* on the other hand, understands this teaching to mean that one should "today" be concerned only with "today" and its tasks and have no concern for "tomorrow" and its rewards. For in truth, "one hour of *teshuvah* [תְּשׁוּבָה, "return" to G-d through self-rectification] and good deeds in this world is greater than all the life of

---

23. Deuteronomy 7:11. This is the concluding verse of *parashat VeEtchanan,* following the account of the giving of the Torah and the portion of the *Shema.*

Parashat VeEtchanan is always read on the Shabbat following *Tishah b'Av,* Shabbat *Nachamu,* so named after its *haftarah,* which begins נחמו נחמו ("Console, console...," Isaiah 40:1). Thus, the two (identical) words at the beginning of the *haftarah* directly follow the last words of the Torah reading, "today to do them."

As will be explained, the phrase "today to do them" has two interpretations, one for the *beinoni* and one for the *tzadik.* Each of these levels can be seen to correspond to one of the levels of consolation of the Jewish people, נחמו נחמו:

The consolation of the *beinoni* is the clear revelation to his soul that by clinging to G-d (by means of Torah study and the fulfillment of *mitzvot*) throughout the trials and tribulations of this world, he will surely merit the bliss of the world to come. The consolation of the *tzadik,* on the other hand, is that by clinging to G-d throughout the trials and tribulations of this world, he will merit the revelation of G-d's essence in *this* world.

24. *Eiruvin* 22a; *Avodah Zarah* 3a.

the world to come,"[25] for in this world one can unite totally with G-d by performing His will. The *tzadik*'s service of G-d is strictly for its own sake. His unconditional desire to serve and become one with Him precludes any concern with receiving a reward, even that of the world to come.

Rabbi Shneur Zalman of Liadi illustrates this idea as follows:[26]

> The story is told in the Midrash[27] of a Jewish woman who was married for many years, but had not had children. Her husband decided therefore to divorce her, so he went to Rabbi Shimon bar Yochai, of blessed memory, who told him that just as they celebrated their marriage with joy, so should they celebrate its severance with joy.
>
> The husband prepared a great feast, at the height of which he asked wife to choose whatever of his possessions she desired, assuring her that he would not refuse her anything.
>
> And what did she do? She served him so much wine that he got drunk and went to sleep, and then told her servants to take him on his bed into her bedroom.
>
> The following morning, when he awoke and found himself in her home, he asked her why he had been brought there—wasn't it clear that he intended to divorce her? She replied: "Didn't you tell me that I could take whatever I wanted? Well, I desire neither gold, nor silver, nor precious gems,

25. *Avot* 4:17.
26. *Ma'amarei Admor HaZaken HaKetzarim*, p. 461.
27. *Shir HaShirim Rabbah* 1:31.

nor pearls; all I want is *you*. You yourself are the sole object of my desire."

When the husband heard this, he again became enamored of his wife, and took her back. And in this merit, the Holy One, blessed be He, granted them children.

So it is with regard to the service of G-d. As it is stated: "I will serve you aromatic wine, the fragrance of my pomegranates"[28]—this refers to the fact that the least worthy of Israel is as full of [merits accrued by fulfilling G-d's] commandments as a pomegranate is of seeds. [The bride, Israel, serving the groom, G-d, means arousing Him] to descend [and dwell] among us, for [by doing so, we are in effect saying to Him:] "Who have I in heaven, and I desire nothing beside You on earth."[29] Meaning: I have no desire for any good thing or delight, neither in the higher garden of Eden nor in the lower garden of Eden; I desire nothing but *You*.[30]

In this merit, one will "bear" spiritual progeny—a son and a daughter, i.e., love and fear of G-d. [Love and fear of G-d are considered spiritual progeny inasmuch as they are the "offspring" of intellectual meditation].

And also on the physical plane, "he will have offspring and [merit] long life."[31]

---

28. Song of Songs 8:2.

29. Psalms 73:25.

30. see also *HaYom Yom*, 18 *Kislev*.

31. Isaiah 53:10. This verse is stated with regard to *Mashiach*, from which it becomes clear that this level of Divine service—"Who have I in heaven? And I desire nothing other than You on earth"—is a level of messianic consciousness and gives birth to the spark of *Mashiach* in the soul of every Jew who merits to serve G-d on this level.

The *Rasha*: Indignant Estrangement

The third and lowest degree of relationship—when the wife is pitted against her husband—corresponds to that between the *rasha* (רָשָׁע, wicked person[32]) and G-d.

---

32. There are many levels of *resha'im* (see *Tanya*, ch. 11). We are here referring to the most extreme case, the *rasha* who "knows his Master and intentionally rebels against Him" (*Midrash Tanchuma* [ed. Buber], *Bechukotai* 26:14), synonymous with the *rasha* who suffers—conscious or unconsciously—all forms of evil (רשע ורע לו). Someone who does not fulfill G-d's will out of non-belief (not "knowing his Master") or ignorance (not knowing his Master's will) is analogous to someone who does not know he is married or what being married entails. Though it is surely one's responsibility to "know" his Divine groom in order to "serve" Him, if nonetheless he is currently unaware, he cannot be held *fully* responsible for not fulfilling his marital obligations. It is incumbent on the spouse or community to enlighten him.

Just as the very highest level of *tzadik* is reflected in the souls of all *tzadikim* and all Jews (for "Your people are all *tzadikim*"), so is the very lowest level of *rasha* reflected in the souls of all *resha'im* and by association, in the souls of all Jews (each being a complete צבור, as explained above, footnote 16).

One of the greatest of the disciples of the Ba'al Shem Tov, Rabbi Pinchas of Koretz, once said: "Who is a consummate *tzadik*? He who loves a consummate *rasha*. Who is an incomplete *tzadik*? He who loves an incomplete *rasha*."

In the inner צבור of one's soul, it is the very highest level of *tzadik* that reaches down in love to raise up the very lowest level of *rasha*. The inherent goodness of the consummate *tzadik* sweetens the existential suffering of the consummate *rasha*.

And so, the lowest level of relationship between husband and wife, that of כנגדו, has the potential to rise to the very highest level, that of לו.

It is the level of the *beinoni*, referred to in *Tanya* (ch. 14) as "the level of all men," which serves as the spiritual mirror reflecting both

Intentional rebellion against G-d is usually the result of the *rasha*'s existential frustration over his inability to cope with life's trials and tribulations and/or the multitude of obligations expected of him by the Torah. Whether fully conscious of it or not, the *rasha*'s soul, imprisoned by the forces of evil (and not knowing how to distinguish between them and Divine providence[33]), rails against G-d in anguish: "Why have you made my life so miserable?"

The *rasha*'s complaints may appear legitimate:[34] at times, it may seem that G-d has unjustly abandoned His

---

the level of the *tzadik* which reaches down to the *rasha* and the level of the *rasha* which rises up to the *tzadik*.

33. Of course, everything that befalls one in life is ultimately by Divine providence. The very existence of "forces of evil" is a result of the free will of man, which itself is "overseen" by Divine providence.

34. And can be expressed, therefore, even by the *beinoni* or *tzadik*, albeit in a more refined form: they do not presume G-d to actually be malevolent but simply do not understand His "bad" behavior toward them (and the world), since they know Him to be benevolent and to be acting in their best interests.

On a deeper level, every Jew has to assume—in his relationship with G-d—the consciousness of all three levels. For example, the *tzadik* has to play the part of the *rasha* when he contends with G-d over His seemingly unbecoming conduct toward His people. The *Zohar* (3:153b) even states that "the *Mashiach* is destined to bring the righteous to repentance." This can be interpreted to mean that the *Mashiach* will bring the righteous, happy in their own portion, to feel the anguish of the entire world so intensely that they cannot but contend against G-d over His conduct. This will eventually compel G-d, as it were, to acquiesce and redeem us, to open our eyes to see His infinite goodness, which until then was exclusively the province of the faith of the *tzadik* and *beinoni*.

creation.[35] The *rasha* is thus reacting as any wife would when faced with a cruel or disinterested husband—by rebelling.

The rapprochement of the *rasha* with G-d (his *teshuvah*) can begin in either of two ways:

The *rasha* can choose to recognize[36] that he has only himself to blame for G-d's apparent distance.[37] G-d always desires to reveal Himself by showering His creatures with good but is "prevented" from doing so by the collective

---

Further allusion to these three approaches to G-d can be found in the way Rashi (to Genesis 18:23) describes Abraham's argument with G-d over the fate of Sodom and Gomorrah. He interprets the opening phrase of the verse, ויגש אברהם, "And Abraham approached [G-d]":

> We have found "approaching" [הגשה] to refer to "war"...or to refer to "reconciliation"...or to refer to "prayer".... Abraham approached G-d in all these ways, to speak harshly, to reconcile, and to pray.

"To speak harshly" refers to the level of the *rasha* in the *tzadik*. "To reconcile" (as two marriage partners) refers to the level of the *beinoni* in the *tzadik*, and "to pray" (in pure devotion and union) refers to the level of the *tzadik* in the *tzadik*—the inner essence of the *tzadik*.

35. As it is said: "Verily, you are a hidden G-d" (Isaiah 45:15).

36. One must first truly understand the consequence of sin before he can sincerely confess and return to G-d, as it is said, "His heart will understand and [then] he will return and be healed" (Isaiah 6:10).

37. From which he comes to recognize the hidden good inherent in G-d's apparently "bad" behavior. This hidden good becomes manifest at three levels: (1) G-d *wants* to be good to me, but I don't allow Him; (2) in the apparent "bad" which befalls me, there is indeed a "good" intention—to arouse me to introspection and *teshuvah*; (3) in the apparent "bad" which befalls me, there is a core of essential good, a "tasty fruit" concealed within a "coarse shell." See additional note at the end of this chapter (p. 106).

sins of the generation and those of particular individuals,[38] including, of course, the *rasha* himself.[39] Once he realizes this, the penitent *rasha* can forgive G-d for the trauma and disappointment he has experienced and resolve to stop hindering the revelation of G-dliness in the world by his rebellious attitude and deeds.

Or G-d may take the initiative, expressing His own "repentance" of "wrongdoings" toward the *rasha* (and the world in general),[40] and making, as it were, a serious effort

---

38. In the words of the prophet: "G-d's hand is not too short to save, nor is His ear too heavy to hear; rather, it is your iniquities that have separated you and your G-d, and your sins that have caused His face to hide from you" (Isaiah 59:1-2).

39. Cf. the statement of our sages: "One should always consider himself and the world equally balanced between merits and faults. Thus, if he performs one sin, he tips his and the world's scale, condemning himself and the world to punishment; if he performs one meritorious act, he tips both his and the world's scale to the side of merit, bringing himself and the whole world to salvation" (*Mishneh Torah, Teshuvah* 3:4, from *Kidushin* 40b).

40. G-d even admits His blame, as the Talmud (*Sukah* 52b) says, "There are four things that the Holy One, blessed be He, is sorry that He created: exile…." And again: "The Holy One, blessed be He, said, `Bring an atonement offering for Me on the New Moon, for my having diminished the moon'" (cf. Rashi on Genesis 1:16 and Numbers 28:15; *Shevuot* 9a; *Chulin* 60b). The diminution of the moon symbolizes the exile of G-d's presence in the world. When sanctifying the moon, we pray: "May it be Your will to fill the moon's lacking, that it should no longer be diminished, and may the light of the moon be like that of the sun, like the light of the seven days of Creation as it was before it was diminished."

Since the moon also represents woman, the diminution of its light—as well as the related phenomenon of exile—corresponds to a wife who falls in spirit when sensing her husband's waning interest. Our desire to see the moon's light restored to its original intensity

to court His spouse anew. He restores His spiritual or material beneficence.[41] This demonstration of Divine grace brings the *rasha* to realize that G-d's behavior toward him—past, present and future—has always been for his best interest. Here, too, he can forgive G-d and resolve to serve Him again.[42]

In either case, the *rasha* becomes totally transformed. No longer angry, bitter, or self-absorbed, his sole aspiration is now that G-d bestow His blessings openly on all people, and so he commits himself to work unceasingly toward that end. The ultimate focus of his life becomes the final Redemption, for only then will G-d's abundant kindness be revealed for all to see.

G-d—as a loving husband in response to the gestures of his once-estranged wife—will then reciprocate by forgiving the *rasha* his past sins. The *rasha*'s memory of his former attitude and behavior inspire him to remedy his

---

alongside that of the sun—the "two kings sharing one crown"—reflects the wish for the reinstatement of marital harmony, with the wife returned to her essential dignity and splendor alongside her husband. This lends added significance to the custom of Jewish women to observe extra practices in the celebration of *Rosh Chodesh* (*Shulchan Aruch, Orach Chaim* 417:1), the day on which the light of the moon, after having disappeared, is renewed.

41. G-d and the Jewish people are depicted as arguing over who should take the initiative in restoring good relations: "The congregation of Israel said to the Holy One, blessed be He: 'It is up to You, as it is said [Lamentations 5:21], "Return us to You, O G-d, and [then] we shall return."' But G-d said back to them: 'It is up to you, as it is said [Zechariah 1:3], "Return to Me, and [then] I shall return to you"'" (*Eichah Rabbah* 5:21).

42. See below, p. 315, footnote 2.

(and the world's) situation with a forcefulness of spirit and love for G-d greater than that of one who had never sinned.[43] On this account, G-d not only erases the negative effects of the former *rasha*'s past sins but even counts them as merits,[44] by virtue of their having propelled the *rasha* to take the action necessary to remedy his, and the world's, situation.

Thus, despite a problematic disposition or dark personal history, a *rasha* can aspire toward a sublimer and more rewarding "second nature."[45]

From the above description of how the relationship between a *rasha* and G-d becomes rectified, we may infer the following *vis-à-vis* husband and wife:

When a man sees his wife opposing him, he should suspect that he is to blame. Perhaps he has projected an image of disinterest and non-involvement. Recognizing this, he should forgive her lack of cooperation and devotedness, seeing these faults instead as useful indicators for gauging his own effectiveness in relating to her and to others.

---

43. "Even the wholly righteous cannot stand in the place where the penitent stand" (*Berachot* 34b; *Sanhedrin* 99a), for "they strive with a more intense longing of the heart, and with greater forcefulness, to approach the King" (*Zohar* 1:129b). See *Tanya*, ch. 7; *Igeret HaTeshuvah*, ch. 8.

44. *Yoma* 86b; *Bava Metzia* 33b.

45. Which is, after all, nothing more than a return to his true nature, which was temporarily eclipsed by his so-called "first nature," the product of his evil inclination and unrectified imagination. This is affirmed by the fact that the phrase "second nature" (טבע שני) numerically equals the word for "truth" (אמת, 441).

Domestic strife should thus serve—whether or not this is the wife's conscious intention—to deflate and neutralize the husband's ego.[46] By responding to his wife's expressions of dissatisfaction with understanding and consideration—rather than with defensiveness and hostility—the husband begins the process of his own self-correction. Subduing his own inclination to anger and relating to his wife with love instead will certainly inspire her to love him in return, and his simply ceasing to think of her negatively will help ameliorate the situation.[47]

---

46. This is an additional meaning of woman's being described as "a helpmate opposite him": by being adversarial ("opposite him"), a woman can unwittingly help ("helpmate") her husband temper his ego.

A woman is uniquely able to help her husband rectify his imagination. "In the merit of righteous women was Israel redeemed from Egypt" (*Sotah* 11b). Inasmuch as Egypt symbolizes obscenity and licentiousness (Leviticus 18:3; *Sifra, Acharei* 18; *Vayikra Rabbah* 23:7; *Tana d'vei Eliahu Rabbah* 7; *Sha'ar HaYichud VehaEmunah,* introduction; see above, p. 50, footnote 6), this means that a man's wife can help extricate him from his unrectified imagination. The first plague visited upon Egypt was the transformation of its water into blood (דם), which alludes to the imagination (כח המדמה). It is the woman's repeated passage through the interfaces between the images of life, potential life, and death associated with her menstrual blood (דם) that affords her this unique ability (see ch. 12).

Additionally, the rectification of the imagination is largely dependent on its "return" to and absorption into its ultimate source in the soul—faith—and a woman's faith is more deeply rooted in her soul than is a man's. See below, p. 112.

47. See below, p. 150. This is an example of the Chassidic teaching, "Think good and it will be good," referred to above (p. 48, footnote 2). Optimistic confidence (*bitachon*) is said to be especially pertinent once one is married, as opposed to mere faith (*emunah*), which is more relevant before marriage.

Of course, it also behooves the wife to consider a troubled marriage the result of her own failings. Perhaps her thoughts, words, or deeds are preventing her husband from acting on his natural desire to relate to her more positively. Recognizing this, she can come to forgive him[48] and reformulate her perspective on the relationship in a new and positive light.

The husband, seeing his wife take this initiative, will realize that her past negative behavior was in fact caused

---

48. The recurring motif of forgiveness that appears at this level of the *ba'al teshuvah* lies at the very heart of the covenant of marriage. The essence of the marriage covenant is the commitment to always forgive; this commitment transcends the natural bounds of common relationships between individuals and thereby lifts a couple to a Divine plane of existence.

By forgiving—especially by forgiving one's spouse—one emulates one's Creator most closely. G-d continuously forgives the misdeeds of His beloved spouse, His people Israel. In our prayers, we ask three times a day for G-d's forgiveness, and we are sure that He forgives us (see *Igeret HaTeshuvah*, ch. 11). This blessing in the *Amidah*—"Forgive us, our Father, for we have sinned..."—corresponds, in Kabbalah, to the *sefirah* of *chesed*, "loving-kindness," for [continual] forgiveness of the other is the greatest expression of absolute love for him.

In accordance with the general principle that arousal from above depends on prior arousal from below, the more we express our forgiveness for one another (and especially between married partners), the more we merit to experience G-d's forgiveness of us.

Forgiveness is most necessary with regard to "the blemish of the covenant" (פגם הברית; see at length *Igeret HaTeshuvah*). Thus, its most essential manifestation is the resolution of marital strife (פיוס, a permutation of יוסף, Joseph, the archetypal soul of תקון הברית, "the rectification of the covenant"), for the sake of continually reinforcing the covenant of marriage.

by her impression of unresponsiveness on his part. He can then set about improving himself, refining his character, and in particular begin learning how to relate to his wife with love.

In the meantime, the hurt spouse should remind himself that nothing occurs by accident, and it is certainly Divine providence that has placed him in his hopefully temporary predicament. Insofar as possible, he should try to cultivate an attitude of patience and trust in G-d, who certainly is subjecting him to this ordeal for a purpose.[49]

If the stress refuses to resolve itself in spite of such accommodations, the couple must face the possibility that perhaps theirs is a relationship that can be rectified only by being ended. Divorce, when required by the Torah, is compared in *Chassidut* to the exodus from Egypt: a husband who is not his wife's devoted partner is like a Pharaoh to her.[50] Divorce thus becomes a form of liberation, redeeming her from an enslaving environment and an unhealthy attachment. Though it is not easy, the woman must have faith that she will find her true match (*bashert*) elsewhere—just as the Jews loyally followed Moses into the desert and there discovered their true Beloved waiting for them at Mt. Sinai.

---

49. In general, one is encouraged to try as far as possible to preserve one's marriage, even if this means enduring an acrimonious spouse while working on one's own attitude (see *Pele Yoetz, s.v. Ahavat Ish veIshah*, based on *Yevamot* 63ab).

50. See the Chassidic commentary *Ramataim Tzofim* on the beginning of *Tana d'vei Eliahu Rabbah*. Clearly, the reverse situation is also possible: a husband may be enslaved to his wife, in which case, divorce (when mandated by the Torah) is his liberation from slavery.

Even if it is decided that divorce is necessary, there is still no reason the couple should bear any ill will toward each other—or G-d. In line with the attitudes outlined above, they should consider the time they spent together a decree of Divine providence, either as a necessary way of bringing about a certain stage of the rectification of their souls or as a way of achieving some other part of G-d's plan for the world. If they have been blessed with children, they may certainly consider the purpose of their marriage to have been in order to bring these souls into the world.

Yet again, despite these consolations, divorce should always be considered the final resort, only contemplated when all other approaches have failed, for, as our sages say: "the altar itself sheds tears when one divorces his first wife."[51]

First Nature and Second Nature

Our sages teach us that one's first wife is his predestined soul mate, while—should he need to marry a second time—his second wife is given to him in the merit of his deeds.[52] This does not mean, however, that one's merits do not at all determine what kind of wife one first marries, or that one's second wife is in no way predestined. In every marriage, "first wife" and "second wife" may be understood to signify the initial, unrectified

51. *Gitin* 90b.

52. *Sotah* 2a.

way and subsequent, rectified manner in which one relates to his spouse.

If one gets married before he has begun or progressed very far in the process of self-rectification, what he searches for in a spouse will be accordingly colored by his unrectified perceptions. He is apt to confuse a transitory thrill for a sense of predestined affinity and embroil himself in a relationship that has no real basis.

Still, we are taught that ever since the exile from the garden of Eden, "there is no good in which there is not an element of evil, and no evil in which there is not an element of good."[53] Thus, there is perforce a kernel of reality in the initial feelings this couple feel for each other. Even though it is channeled through less than ideal motives, it nonetheless expresses a deep, unconscious connection that will always occupy a special place in these individuals' psyches.[54]

If this core of true affinity can be isolated and developed, the couple can indeed transform their relationship into a "second marriage," as they progressively refine themselves and rectify their perspectives.[55]

---

53. *Likutei Diburim* 87a (see *Sefer Yetzirah* 6:2 [6:4 in Ari version] and commentaries).

54. Allusion to the uniqueness of "first love" may be found in the Torah's injunction that the priestly class, who embody and express G-d's attribute of love, be married only to wives who have not undergone the trauma of divorce. The high priest is forbidden to marry a widow as well, and is only allowed to marry a virgin (Leviticus 21:7,13).

55. Therefore, even in the most extreme cases, when divorce *is* called for, "the altar itself sheds tears when one divorces his first

Conversely, if the parties are seeking their mates based on rectified and proper perspectives, even their initial attraction will be based on their rectified natures. To the extent that they refine themselves, they will be able to identify their predestined soul mates in the context of those qualities that provide a solid basis for a lasting relationship.[56]

In this case, their "second marriage" will be coincident with their first; they will be able to synthesize the intensity of raw attraction with their "second," rectified natures.[57]

The Biblical archetypes of the "first marriage" and "second marriage" are those of Adam and Noah, respectively. The complimentary verse to "And Adam did not find for himself a helpmate"[58] is:

---

wife." Attempting to rectify a marriage on the verge of collapse by refining oneself, etc., is fulfilling—in an allegorical sense—our sages' preference (*Vayikra Rabbah* 34:14) that one *remarry* one's divorced wife (provided she has not been married to someone else in the interim).

Of course, one could have to marry a second time because he became widowed rather than divorced. This would cast no aspersions on the quality of his first marriage; rather, it would mean that the couple concluded whatever they were meant to accomplish on earth as a couple, and the departed spouse, whatever he or she was meant to accomplish as an individual.

56. Thus, our sages counsel one to *endeavor* to marry the daughter of a Torah scholar (*Pesachim* 49a). This implies that one should make efforts to be worthy of the finest match possible.

57. This is thus an instance of clothing the "lights of *Tohu*" in the "vessels of *Tikun*," explained above (p. 26, footnote 54).

58. Discussed above, p. 6 ff.

וְנֹחַ מָצָא חֵן בְּעֵינֵי ה׳.

And Noah found favor in the eyes of G-d.[59]

---

59. Genesis 6:8. These complimentary phrases are the only two in the first Torah-portion, *Bereishit,* in which the verb "to find" appears in the past tense.

The combined numerical value of these phrases is 1024, which is 32^2. 32 is the numerical value of the word for "heart" (לב). Thus, these two phrases together reflect the full inter-inclusion of the emotions of the heart.

Thirty-two is also the number of "pathways of wisdom" which shine into the heart (*Sefer Yetzirah* 1:1), as it is said: "my heart has seen much wisdom" (Ecclesiastes 1:16). This number is derived as follows: In the *Zohar* (*Tikunei Zohar* 21 [51b]), the intellect is identified as the "double song" (שיר כפול), the union of the two primary powers of the intellect, *chochmah* and *binah.* Thus, each "linear measure" of intellect is 2. In particular, however, there are four (2^2) "brains" or seats of intelligence (*chochmah, binah,* and the two facets of *da'at*), which enliven the emotions of the heart. Each of these four exists in three dimensions (and is thus envisioned as a "cube"), giving $4 \cdot 2^3 = 32$.

Besides being 32^2, 1024—the combined numerical value of these phrases—is 2^{10}. This indicates that these two phrases together allude to the married couple (2) as they together fully develop the ten powers (each of which manifests as a unique dimension) of their souls.

1024 is also the number of letters in the full Hebrew text of the *Shema.* (The three Biblical paragraphs themselves contain 1000 letters, and the phrase "Blessed be the Name of the glory of His kingdom forever and ever" contains 24 letters. This phrase, recited between the first and second verses, was added by our sages in accordance with the tradition that it was recited by our forefather Jacob in response to his sons' declaration of the first verse.) Thus, the two phrases that refer to the archetypal "first" and "second" marriages together allude to the couple becoming an expression of G-d's unity in the world, as well as to their commitment to His Torah and its commandments, these being the subject of the *Shema.*

In the first verse, the verb "found" is negated ("and Adam did *not* find"); in the second, it is positive ("and Noah found"). This is as if to say that what Adam did not merit to find by virtue of his deeds[60]—a mate—Noah did.

We may therefore apply to Adam the statement of our sages: "If one says 'I have toiled, but have not found,' do not believe him [i.e., that he has indeed toiled sufficiently]," and to Noah, its continuation: "If one says 'I have toiled, and have found,' believe him."[61]

"First nature" thus corresponds to Adam and Eve, who sinned, whereas "second nature" corresponds to Noah and his wife Na'amah,[62] who "found favor in the eyes of G-d."[63]

---

60. By naming all the creatures, Adam was able to realize that he did not have a mate, but this did not help him find one. Nonetheless, this realization itself was enough to "induce" G-d to give him Eve. Noah, on the other hand, was able to find his soul mate on his own, and through her, his own soul-root. This is why it is stated that he "found favor in the eyes of G-d," which is not said of Adam.

Every revelation comprises a preliminary "dark" version, which is followed by the full, open revelation itself. This is alluded to in the phrase: "And there was *evening*, and there was *morning*, one *day* [i.e., 'revelation']" (Genesis 1:5; see *Shabbat* 77b). In the present context, Adam was the "dark" version of mating that preceded and paved the way for the "full" version embodied by Noah and his wife.

61. *Megilah* 6b.

62. Rashi on Genesis 4:22. The word "Na'amah" (נעמה) means "pleasant": "Why was she called Na'amah? Because her deeds were pleasing" (*Bereishit Rabbah* 23:3; cf. *Zohar Chadash* 19b).

63. The verse "And Noah found favor in the eyes of G-d" is the first appearance in the Torah of the idiom "to find favor in the eyes of...." The word Noah itself (נח) is the word for "favor" or "grace" (חן) spelled backwards. Thus, "finding grace in someone's eyes" is in

The Wife's Influence

Whereas the husband is to approach marital harmony as a reflection of his own inner spiritual development, the following story from the Midrash[64]

---

effect gazing at one's own reflection in his eyes, which can be done only if one is facing the other directly, i.e., relating to him in complete spiritual congruence.

In the Song of Songs, finding favor or grace in the eyes of one's spouse is referred to by the imagery of a dove—"My dove in the clefts of the rocks" (2:14); "My sister, my beloved, my dove, my unblemished one" (5:2); "One is my dove, my unblemished one" (6:9); "Your eyes are like doves" (1:15, 4:1, 5:12)—since doves love to gaze into each other's eyes (see *Likutei Torah* 5:39a; *I am Asleep yet My Heart is Awake*, p. 27).

Noah sent a dove from the ark to see if he had indeed found favor in the eyes of G-d, i.e., if the earth was dry. The dove represents the eyes of Noah searching for grace (his own reflection) in G-d's eyes.

In general, "grace" is personified throughout the Torah by the female. In Kabbalah, it is identified with the *sefirah* of *malchut*, the feminine realm. It is said (Proverbs 11:16): "A woman of grace supports honor." To "support honor" is understood to mean "to support one's husband's and children's' learning of Torah," for "there is no 'honor' other than Torah" (*Avot* 6:3). The numerical value of the phrase "the honor [or 'glory'] of G-d" (כבוד יהו-ה, 58) is equal to that of the word for "grace" (חן).

In addition, throughout the writings of Kabbalah, the word חן appears as an acronym for חכמה נסתרה, "the concealed wisdom" (i.e., the inner wisdom of the Torah, or Kabbalah itself). חכמה נסתרה = 788 = שלום בית ("marital harmony"). Thus, we may infer that the "woman of grace" encourages her husband to learn the inner dimension of the Torah in particular, and that this in turn brings true marital harmony.

64. *Bereishit Rabbah* 17:7.

implies that the wife has the power to *directly* improve the behavior of her husband:

> Once, a certain pious man was married to a pious woman, but they did not have children. They said, 'we are not doing G-d any good,' and divorced one another. The pious man subsequently married a wicked woman, and she made him wicked. The pious woman married a wicked man, and she made him pious. Thus, we see that all is dependent upon the woman.[65]

---

65. Throughout this chapter we have illustrated how the wife's behavior is a reflection of the husband's level of refinement, and it is therefore within his power to determine *her* attitude and behavior. However, we prefaced this by saying that this is the case only with regard to inter-spousal (and by extension, all interpersonal) relationships. In other words, it is his wife's behavior *toward him* that the husband may view as a gauge of his own refinement and that he may reasonably expect to be able to influence. If she is antagonistic or wicked *in general*, he should be wary of the lesson implied in this midrash! Indeed, the Torah prescribes divorce "if he finds in her some *immoral* thing [ערות דבר]" (Deuteronomy 24:1).

Still, even in such a case the husband should try to reform his wife before contemplating divorce. "G-d's attribute of goodness is greater than His attribute of punishment" (*Sanhedrin* 100b), meaning that goodness is more powerful than evil, and with sufficient effort, he may well succeed. In the case recorded in this midrash, we must surmise that the husband was either not righteous enough to influence his wife or that he did not succeed in attuning himself to their common soul-root and thus did not share his righteousness with her.

In Yiddish, the term for such a privately righteous person is *tzadik in peltz*, "a righteous man in furs." The image is that of a person who, in a cold room full of people, puts on a fur coat, instead of making a fire, which would warm everyone (*Likutei Sichot*, vol. 3, p. 880).

A wife improves her husband's behavior through her innate faith in him, projecting her vision of his true, noble nature onto him and seeing him, as it were, through the eyes of G-d.

A man therefore works on his marriage by correcting himself in relation to his wife, gauging his progress by noting her attitude (and feedback) toward him. A woman, on the other hand, works on her marriage by focusing on her husband, helping him (whether or not he is aware of it) correct himself and fulfill his potential. She does this by deepening her faith in G-d and His providence, and her awareness of His purpose in creation (which entails the rectified image of her husband and their marriage). For this reason she is called his "helpmate."

We will now proceed to examine the ways in which husband and wife can and should individually and mutually perfect themselves as they ascend toward the re-merging of their souls into one.

This recalls a Chassidic teaching based on the verse: "And the unimpassioned [of the flock] were Laban's, while the impassioned ones were Jacob's" (Genesis 30:42). The word used here for "unimpassioned" means, as Rashi interprets it, that "they were well-covered with skin and wool, and did not desire to be warmed by the males." In contrast, the word used for "impassioned" means literally "bound" or "connected," i.e., always seeking the companionship of a mate (see Ramban *ad loc.*). Based on this, Rabbi Shneur Zalman of Liadi said that if one fails to connect concernedly to one's fellows (this being the characteristic of Jacob, personifying good and holiness), he will eventually become "unimpassioned" and the "property" of Laban (personifying evil).

Additional Note

to page 91.

Together with the initial recognition that it is the person himself who is to blame, we may here identify four levels of consciousness *vis-à-vis* the *rasha*'s perception of who is responsible for his suffering. These correspond to the four letters of G-d's Name *Havayah*, as follows:

י	*yud*	wisdom	essential core of good in apparent bad
ה	*hei*	understanding	potent, good intention in apparent bad
ו	*vav*	emotions	G-d's desire to express good, thwarted by the individual or the generation
ה	*hei*	kingdom	acceptance of one's own existential guilt

In Kabbalah, the "taste" of hidden good is identified with the power of clarification of *chochmah* (of which is said: "All are clarified by wisdom" [*Zohar* 2:254b; *Nitzotzei Orot ad loc.* §3; *Sefer HaMa'amarim 5708*, p. 206, note 11]), the *yud* (inner, essential point) of G-d's Name.

The first *hei* of G-d's Name, associated with the *sefirah* of *binah*, is identified throughout the *Zohar* with *teshuvah*. Understanding entails the inner intention of the mind and soul. Here it represents G-d's intention in all that He does—to arouse the soul of man to return to Him.

The essence of G-d's desire to express His goodness to man is represented by the *vav* of His Name, which corresponds to His Divine attributes (especially to loving-kindness and mercy). While the two higher letters of G-d's Name, the *yud* and the *hei* are referred to as "the concealed levels," the two latter letters, the *vav* and the *hei*, are referred to as "the revealed levels." The *vav* represents G-d's "innate" desire to reveal good.

The final *hei* corresponds to the "kingdom of G-d" on earth (i.e., in the consciousness of man), the Divine "mirror" which reflects the state of rectification of the "ego" of man, who is created to be the servant of the King. The first stage toward the rectification of the ego is the recognition and acceptance of guilt, as we find with regard to King David, the archetypal soul of *malchut* ("kingdom"), who spontaneously responded to the accusation expressed by Nathan the prophet with the words "I have sinned to G-d" (2 Samuel 12:13. See *Tanya*, ch. 29 and *Igeret HaTeshuvah*, ch. 12, in reference to King David's statement: "And my sin is always before me" [Psalms 51:5]).

The highest level of consciousness depicted here, the recognition of the essential good concealed within the apparent bad, is in fact a bridge between this first way of *teshuvah* (based upon taking the blame for all the bad that befalls one) and the second way (G-d's taking the initiative to "shower" one with goodness).

5

Dwelling with the Divine Presence

Divine Presence and Holy Fire

The Hebrew words for "man" (אִישׁ) and "woman" (אִשָּׁה) are each composed of three letters, two of which—the *alef* (א) and *shin* (ש)—are common to both, and one of which—the *yud* (י) in the word for "man" and the *hei* (ה) in the word for "woman"—is unique in each. This phenomenon is the key to understanding the respective uniqueness of man and woman, how they complement each other, and how they may utilize their differences to merge and become one.

The two common letters of the words for "man" (אִישׁ) and "woman" (אִשָּׁה) spell the word for "fire" (אֵשׁ) and the two unique letters (יה) spell *Kah,* one of the Names of G-d. We can thus think of man and woman as two fires that together can serve as an abode for the Divine Presence.

Thus, our sages teach, "if they merit, the Divine Presence dwells between them. But if they do not merit"—

and the letters signifying the Divine Presence are withdrawn—"fire devours them."[1]

"To merit" here is understood to mean "to be sufficiently refined."[2] The "fire" that devours a couple in the absence of the Divine Presence is the untamable lust, envy, or anger that inevitably appears in its wake.

However, when they do merit, the fire shared by husband and wife is the holy flame of Divinely inspired love for one another which serves to weld the two into one.[3] The holy fire both consumes whatever profane,

---

1. *Sotah* 17a. Significantly, this was said by Rabbi Akiva, who also said that the *mitzvah* to love one's fellow as oneself (Leviticus 19:18) is "the fundamental principle of the Torah" (*Y. Nedarim* 9:4; cf. *Shabbat* 31a). Loving one's fellow begins with loving one's spouse.

As will be explained, according to Kabbalah, the *yud* signifies the *sefirah* of *chochmah*, while the *hei* signifies the *sefirah* of *binah*. In contrast to the lower *sefirot*, whose union is intermittent, these two are in a constant state of union (*Zohar* 3:4a, 120a, 290b). Their presence in the couple (as the *yud* and *hei* of איש and אשה) thus indicates that the couple's union reflects something of the supernal union of these two *sefirot*.

2. The root זכה means both "merit" and "refining." See above, p. 80, footnote 10.

3. The intense love between husband and wife is "strong as death; jealousy is harsh as the grave. Its coals are coals of fire, the flame of G-d. Many waters cannot quench love...." (Song of Songs 8:6). In *Kidushin* 56b (quoting Deuteronomy 22:9), the word "holy" (קדש) is seen as a contraction of the words "burning fire" (יקוד אש). G-d's first revelation to Moses, in which He articulated His love and concern for the Jewish people, was in a "bush that burned, but was not consumed" (Exodus 3:2). The fire of Divine love burns but cannot be quenched.

In *Chassidut* we are taught that marital love manifests the spiritual element of fire, in contrast to fraternal love, which manifests

destructive fires might have been present between the couple and converts them into holy fire itself.[4]

Truth and Faith

The holy fire is manifest differently in each of the marriage partners:

The husband's holy fire is his "intellectual light" (אוֹר שִׂכְלִי, the initials of which spell אֵשׁ, "fire"), which he introduces into the home as the wisdom of the Torah.[5]

---

the spiritual element of water (see *I am Asleep yet My Heart is Awake*, p. 19). Marital love, as fire, possesses the power to weld two into one. This is the secret of the numerical equivalence of אהבה ("love") and אחד ("one," 13), as is said in the story of creation, "and he shall cling to his wife, and they shall become *one* flesh" (Genesis 2:24).

4. Our sages teach us (*Yoma* 21b) that there are six levels of fire, the lowest being physical fire and the highest being the fire of the *Shechinah*. This highest fire is referred to as אש אוכלת אש, "the fire that consumes all other fires." When husband and wife merit this holy fire (when "the Divine Presence dwells between them"), all other fires are consumed therein.

As explained elsewhere (see *Sod HaShem Lireiav*, ch. 11), this highest fire corresponds to the ray (or "line," *kav* [קו]) of G-d's infinite light that permeates the vacuum created by the initial contraction (*tzimtzum* [צמצום]) and brings all worlds and souls into being, sustains them, and ultimately bestows Divine consciousness on them.

Just as the *kav* enters the vacuum, so does the *Shechinah* enter the home and heart of a husband and wife who, by denying their own egocentricity, create "room" for the *Shechinah* to enter and "create" new life within them.

Both men and women are obligated to learn Torah. But whereas both are obligated to learn all those parts necessary for (or that will enhance) their observance of the *mitzvot* (מִצְוֹת, "commandments") incumbent upon them,[6] men are additionally commanded to study Torah ceaselessly and to learn even those parts that do not directly impinge on their observance of the *mitzvot*.[7] It is this abstract, intrinsic level of Divine intellect that the husband contributes to the household, thus bringing a unique level of truth and enlightenment to his family.[8]

The wife's holy fire is her "complete faith" in G-d (אֱמוּנָה שְׁלֵמָה, the initials of which also spell אֵשׁ, "fire"),[9]

---

5. The Torah is referred to as fire, as in "Are not my words like fire?" (Jeremiah 23:29), and "From His right hand He [gave Israel] a law of fire" (Deuteronomy 33:2). For a deeper understanding of the term אור שכלי, see Rabbi Avraham Abulafia, *Or HaSechel*.

6. This includes those *mitzvot* classified as "duties of the heart," such as love and fear of G-d, which apply to both men and women. These *mitzvot* are elucidated fully only in the inner dimension of the Torah; thus both men and women are equally obligated to study those topics in Kabbalah and *Chassidut* (see the source cited in the following footnote).

7. See *Sefer HaSichot 5750*, pp. 456ff, published also in *Sha'arei Halachah Uminhag, Yoreh Deah* 63.

8. This is represented by the *yud* in the word איש, which signifies the *sefirah* of *chochmah* ("wisdom" and penetrative insight). The insight of *chochmah* is often described as a "flash of lightning" across the dark screen of the mind.

9. Our perfect faith in G-d's inscrutable essence is reflected in the Torah's prohibition against worshipping any form of idolatry. In this context, the Torah refers to G-d as אש אכלה, "a consuming fire" (Deuteronomy 4:24). The positive implication of this Divine appellation is that one's own (feminine) fire of faith in G-d consumes one's entire being, elevating him to a totally higher, Divine level of existence.

expressed chiefly through her heartfelt prayers and blessings,[10] as well as through her general attitude toward

---

The Biblical origin of the phrase אמונה שלמה is in the words of the wise woman to Yoav (2 Samuel 20:19): אנכי שלמי אמוני ישראל, "I am of the completely faithful of Israel." From here we see that complete faith is the essential attribute of woman, and that her ability to properly express her complete faith depends on the "wisdom" (Torah) she receives (directly or indirectly; consciously or unconsciously) from the soul of her husband.

In the terminology of Kabbalah, based on the verse: "G-d founded the world with wisdom" (Proverbs 3:19): "*Abba* founded the daughter," or *malchut*, via *Z'eir Anpin* (*Zohar* 3:248a, 256b, etc.).

10. This is expressed by the *hei* in the word אשה, signifying the *sefirah* of *malchut*, which is associated with the faculty of speech.

Both men and women are obligated to pray and perpetually reinforce and express their faith in G-d. The woman, however, contributes the sense of being constantly dependent on G-d's benevolence, as is indicated by the fact that the word for "faith" (אמונה) is related to the Aramaic word for "[an empty] vessel" (מנא). Thus, through her influence, the Jewish household is permeated with the feeling that life is a continuous state of prayer. This accords with the fact that she manifests the *seifrah* of *malchut*, the seat of the ego, which when rectified is expressed as "I am prayer." See our essay, *Living in Divine Space*.

The numerical value of the word for "woman" (אשה, 306) is three times that of the word for "faith" (אמונה, 102). In other words, "faith" is the average value of the three letters of "woman," as if to say that woman in her entirety is the embodiment of faith.

Thus, while a wife draws her inspiration to learn Torah in general from the source of her husband's soul, the husband draws his inspiration to pray from the source of his wife's soul. This is alluded to in Genesis 25:21: "And Isaac prayed to G-d in the presence of [i.e., inspired by] his wife." In Kabbalah we are taught that the origin of Isaac's soul was in "the feminine world," and that the union of Isaac (יצחק = 208) and Rebecca (רבקה = 307) equals "prayer" (תפלה = 515). See below, p. 198 footnote 10, and p. 197, footnote 8.

life. Her firm, enduring faith strengthens her husband and family, providing them with a warm hearth and protective refuge from the storms and vagaries of life. Her flame of faith penetrates and ignites the faith of her husband and family.[11]

Husband and wife ideally inspire each other to contribute their respective qualities, each fanning the flames of the other's holy fire. When the holy fires of Torah and faith unite, the *yud* and *hei* of G-d's Name descend upon the home, gracing it with the Divine Presence.[12]

Mutual Completion

The numerical value of the letter *yud* (י, the unique letter in the word for "man," אִישׁ) is ten, while that of the letter *hei* (ה, the unique letter in the word for "woman," אִשָּׁה) is five.

As we mentioned above,[13] *da'at* ("knowledge") is the power of the soul through which one "knows" reality, which is to say, how one relates to it.[14] One can view his

11. See, for example, the story related in the introduction to *Pokeiach Ivrim* (§18 ff.).

12. Note that the final letter of the phrase אור שכלי is the *yud* of איש, whereas the final letter of the phrase אמונה שלמה is the *hei* of אשה. Thus the *notrikun* of אור שכלי is אש י, while that of אמונה שלמה is אש ה.

13. p. 33.

14. See *Tanya*, ch. 3; *Igeret HaKodesh* 15.

environment in an optimistic light, considering things and people to be generally friendly, or view it critically and apprehensively. In the terminology of Kabbalah, these propensities are called, respectively, the five degrees of *chesed* (חֶסֶד, "loving-kindness") and the five degrees of *gevurah* (גְּבוּרָה, "severity") of *da'at*—its "right side" and "left side," respectively.[15] These are the mental origins of the heart's two primary emotions, love and fear, which become manifest after an intellectual process is completed.

A man naturally possesses all ten (*yud*) degrees of *da'at* and is thus more-or-less balanced in his perception of his environment. A woman, though given an extra measure of understanding (*binah*),[16] is initially lacking in her faculty of *da'at*; before marriage she possesses only the five (*hei*) degrees of *gevurah*.[17] It remains for her husband to introduce her to the positivity (the "right side") of the

---

15. See *The Hebrew Letters*, pp. 238-9. Normally, we speak of seven emotions (*midot*). We would expect, then, that there would be seven "proto"-emotions in *da'at*, which would serve as the sources for the seven actual emotions that result from the intellect. The reason there are only five is because all the emotional content of any given process is actually contained within the first five emotions. The final two, *yesod* and *malchut*, are, in contrast, functions of effective coalescence, transmittal and manifestation of the first five (see *Siddur im Dach*, p. 303 ff.).

"*Chesed* is the right arm; *gevurah* is the left arm" (*Tikunei Zohar*, introduction [17a]). The fact that there are only five fingers at the end of each arm—and not seven—also serves to indicate that there are only five states each of *chesed* and *gevurah*.

16. *Nidah* 45b; *Bereishit Rabbah* 18a.

17. See additional note 1 at the end of this chapter (p. 131).

chesed-aspect of *da'at*[18] and thereby to complete her *da'at*. It is his responsibility to complete his "better half."[19] This is done by using his "light of the intellect" to help his wife see matters objectively and positively.

What the *hei* lacks numerically it compensates for in form. The form of the *yud* (י) is virtually that of a dimensionless point, whereas the *hei* (ה) is composed of three lines representing the three dimensions of space.[20] The *yud*'s form signifies undeveloped potential, the seminal yet ephemeral lightning-flash of insight (*chochmah*); the *hei*'s shape signifies the expansion and

---

18. Her "complete faith," mentioned above, gives her a positive attitude that all will turn out for the best, as King Solomon says in praise of the ideal wife: "She looks cheerfully ahead *to the latter day*" (Proverbs 31:25). It is primarily with regard to the events of the present and the immediate future that she needs her husband's help in developing a positive attitude.

19. The material aspects of this responsibility are stipulated in the text of the *ketubah*, the Jewish marriage contract. See additional note 2 at the end of this chapter (p. 132).

20. The left, disconnected line of the *hei* is seen to represent the dimension of depth, the coordinate perpendicular to the page on which it is written.

Note that in explaining the function of the man, we refer to the letter's numerical value, while in explaining that of the woman, we refer to its shape. This accords with a basic difference between man and woman, whereby the male relates to things of an abstract nature (number) while the female identifies with concrete reality (form).

The association between the male and mathematical abstraction is alluded to in the following verse (Numbers 23:10): "Who can count... the *number* of the *seed* of Israel...." The male contributes the abstract, formless seed while the female concretizes it and gives it form.

substantiation of this potential and its assimilation into the real world (*binah*).[21]

The assistance the wife can offer her husband is therefore to help him manifest his potential. Her implicit faith (אֱמוּנָה שְׁלֵמָה) in his potential encourages him to actualize it. Through the influence of her *hei* on his *yud,* he becomes aware of his latent sensitivities and talents and can thus work to develop them.[22] In the same way that the wife physically cultivates her husband's seed to fruition,[23]

---

21. As is explained in *Chassidut, binah* not only expands and develops the initial insight of *chochmah* but also purifies it, ridding it of the element of illusion inevitably accompanying any new revelation.

22. The *yud* of the husband represents the full array of his ten soul-powers, which are grouped into four divisions of super-rational pleasure (*keter*), the two powers of the mind (*chochmah* and *binah*), the three primary emotions (*chesed, gevurah,* and *tiferet*), and the four secondary emotions (*netzach, hod, yesod,* and *malchut*). The wife's *hei* (5) follows this matrix of 1 ⊥ 2 ⊥ 3 ⊥ 4, extending them into reality and full revelation.

23. This power of woman to give birth not only physically to her children but figuratively to her husband, is implied by our sages' statement that "an extra measure of understanding was given to woman beyond that accorded to man." To "understand" something—either a concept or an other—means to embrace and surround it, to support and nurture it to full development. The woman "understands" both her children and her husband: She is an "understanding mother" by virtue of both the womb from which her children are born as well as her power to nurture and raise them. But in addition, she possesses a higher "womb," her being the "understanding wife" from whom her husband's latent potential is born. G-d gave this extra measure of understanding to Eve directly upon her creation while her husband Adam was in deep sleep (for this level of understanding was unable to pass through his consciousness).

she helps develop and give birth to his latent potential by spurring it into concrete expression.

But together with spurring him on, she must also take care to gauge the level of pride and self-satisfaction he takes in his achievements.[24] It is her task to permeate her household with a sense of humble thanksgiving[25] to G-d for all accomplishments and blessings. As explained above, one's wife is his pillar of faith. She constantly reinforces his faith—whether directly or indirectly—that it is G-d "who gives you strength to achieve,"[26] and not, as his ego may cause him to think, that "*my* strength and the power of *my* hand has accomplished this."[27]

It is in this sense that *Chassidut* interprets the statement of our sages that "a good woman is one who performs the will of her husband"[28] to imply that she

---

24. *Malchut*, the feminine *sefirah*, represents self-consciousness and ego-sensitivity. It is therefore the function of the woman to identify conditions of ego and know how to handle them. She is G-d's instrument in selectively shaping man's sense of self. This ability to gauge and know how to rectify ego is the unique quality of a king (*malchut* means "kingship"), as the verse in Psalms (75:8) states: "This one [whom He senses to be haughty] He puts down and that one [whom He senses to be lowly] He raises up."

25. In the terminology of Kabbalah: "*Binah* extends until *hod*" (see *Tikunei Zohar*, introduction [7a]). *Hod* is the sincere gratitude born of the extra measure of understanding (*binah*) granted the woman.

26. Deuteronomy 8:18.

27. *Ibid*. 8:17.

28. *Tana d'vei Eliahu Rabbah* 9.

actually (re-)constructs and rectifies his will.[29] This rectification comes about by her facilitating and encouraging both his self-development and his self-effacement.[30]

Through the couple's love of G-d, whom they recognize to be the ultimate, single source of their own souls, they arouse His love for them, which He showers on them when they unite with one another in love.[31]

The Third Partner in Procreation

The ultimate fruit of the union of husband and wife, to which they each contribute their holy fire and thus enable the Divine Presence to dwell between them, is their children. G-d is thus called the third partner in procreation.[32]

---

29. In line with the connotation of "rectification," which the verb "performs" (עשה) also carries (see Rashi on *Bereishit Rabbah* 11:7). See above, p. 9, footnote 18, and p. 24, footnote 50.

30. In the *Zohar* (176b, beginning of *Sifra d'Tzeniuta*), *tikun* is defined as a state of equilibrium. The hips serve as the "fulcrum" of equilibrium, supporting the entire body. Our sages note that the breadth of the female body at her hips provides her with a heightened stability, enabling her to carry a fetus (Rashi on Genesis 2:22). Similarly, on the spiritual plane, with her greater sense of balance, she helps her husband balance his ongoing drive for self-development with his continual need for self-effacement.

31. Just as the husband and wife each possess their respective "fires" of love for one another, so does G-d—who is also referred to as "fire" (see notes 4 and 9, above)—manifest His fire of love for them.

32. *Kidushin* 30b.

A child born of holy fire may be called "a child of fire" (יֶלֶד אֵשׁ). This phrase in Hebrew is a permutation of another of G-d's Names, *Kel Shakai* (אל שדי, "G-d Almighty"). The initials of this Name, as well, spell the word for "fire" (אֵשׁ); the remaining letters spell the word for "child" (יֶלֶד).

And indeed, the Name *Kel Shakai* is associated with the Divine power of procreation[33] and figures prominently

---

33. In Kabbalah, this Name refers to the *sefirah* of *yesod* ("foundation"), which is associated with the male and female reproductive organs, the "foundation" of human continuity.

In particular, the Name שדי ("Almighty," denoting G-d's power to direct and channel the creative process) is associated with the *sefirah* of *yesod*, and the Name אל (which also means "power") is associated with the *sefirah* of *chesed* ("loving-kindness"; the connotation of this Name is thus "the power of love"). When they are joined and used as one Name, it implies that the procreative power is motivated by and a function of the strength of love.

The Ramban (on Genesis 17:1, *s.v. Kel*) explains that by His Name "G-d Almighty," G-d works miracles in the guise of nature, whereas by His Name *Havayah* He works miracles that transcend nature.

So it is with husband and wife, the "patriarch" and "matriarch" of their home: the miracles involved in building a home together, bearing and raising children, seeing grandchildren, etc., all garbed in nature, reflect the holy fire of the *Shechinah*, אל שדי, present in the home.

The Name יה, the essential level of "the Divine Presence dwells between them," corresponds to the "white flame" (שלהבת) above the "dark-bluish fire" (אש, see R. Eliahu of Vilna, *Commentary on Sefer Yetzirah*, 1:7).

Both levels of fire are expressed in the Song of Songs (8:6) with regard to the love between groom and bride: "Its [i.e., the love's] coals are the coals of fire [אש], the flame [שלהבת] of G-d [יה]."

By the power of the Name יה (the first two letters of the Name *Havayah*, corresponding to its "higher unity"), the manifest miracle of in the appearances of G-d to the patriarchs and matriarchs,[34] especially when He promised to make them the progenitors of our people.[35]

We can identify two unique permutations of this Name—one which embodies the power of the male in procreation and the other which embodies the power of the female.

The "male" permutation of *Kel Shakai* is "he shall give birth to fire" (יֹלד אֵשׁ). This alludes to the "birth" of the husband's seed in his wife's womb.[36]

The "female" permutation is "a pitcher of fire" (דְלִי אֵשׁ),[37] i.e., a container which draws fire into it.[38] This

---

"exodus," transcending even the confines of refined nature, transpires in the Jewish home. The home becomes a sanctuary wherein G-d openly reveals His presence to husband, wife and children (and guests, see ch. 6). The great *tzadik*, Rabbi Menachem Mendel of Vitebsk, when told that *Mashiach* had arrived, had to look (and "smell") outside, for within his own home the light (and "fragrance") of *Mashiach* was already present.

34. As G-d told Moses before the Exodus: "I appeared to Abraham, to Isaac, and to Jacob as *Kel Shakai*, but My Name *Havayah* I did not make known to them" (Exodus 6:3).

35. Genesis 35:11.

36. See Rashi on Genesis 4:18.

37. Note that the "female" permutation is the inverse of the "male" one, implying that the former is the "reflected light" (אור חוזר) of the latter.

38. According to Rabbi Avraham Ibn Ezra (on Exodus 31:18, Esther 3:7), although "Israel is above the influence and forecasts of the signs of the zodiac" (*Shabbat* 156a), the sign which nonetheless most reflects the innate character-traits of the Jewish people is Aquarius (דלי, "the pitcher" or "water-carrier"). The water-carrier is also a favorite symbol of the Ba'al Shem Tov (*HaYom Yom*, 21 *Tevet*),

alludes to the wife's womb, which receives her husband's seed along with her own.[39]

When the word for "fire" (אֵשׁ) in each of these phrases is expanded to spell out its particular connotation for the husband (אוֹר שִׂכְלִי, "intellectual light") and for the wife (אֱמוּנָה שְׁלֵמָה, "complete faith"), the following two phrases are produced:

יֵלֵד אֵשׁ ← יֵלֵד אוֹר שִׂכְלִי

He shall give birth to the light of the intellect

---

symbolizing blessing, and it appears in *Chassidut* as a description of the form of the letter *alef* (which alludes to the manifest presence of the Creator in His creation).

Inasmuch as Jewish identity is determined by the mother, we can understand why innate Jewish attributes derive from the דלי אש, the female "pitcher of fire."

39. Both the male form ילד and the female form דלי equal 44, which equals the sum of "father" (אב, 3) and "mother" (אם, 41), who together give birth to a "child" (ילד, 44)!

44 is also the numerical value of דם ("blood"), the two final letters of אדם ("man"). The first letter of אדם, the א, represents the "breath of life" given to man by the third partner in marriage, G-d A-lmighty.

The average value of the two parents (אב and אם) is 22, corresponding to the 22 letters of the Hebrew alphabet, which find their physical manifestation as the 22 chromosomes contributed by each parent to the genetic identity of the child. G-d unites the additional, 23rd pair of chromosomes to determine the sex of the child. (This pair corresponds to the א of אדם, whose very form is interpreted in Kabbalah to depict the unity of the male and female seed.)

The word ילד or דלי (= 44), when written in full (יוד למד דלת) equals $528 = 44 \cdot 12 = 22 \cdot 24 =$ ילד $(22 \cdot 2) \perp 22^2$!

דְלִי אֵשׁ ← דְלִי אֱמוּנָה שְׁלֵמָה

[She is] the pitcher of complete faith.

These two phrases are numerically equal to the two words for "Torah [study] and prayer," the fires of the husband and wife,[40] respectively:

יֶלֶד אוֹר שִׂכְלִי = תּוֹרָה

דְלִי אֱמוּנָה שְׁלֵמָה = וּתְפִלָּה

Thus we see that the holy fires that the husband and wife each contribute to their common household are also their respective procreative powers.

G-d is One

As we have mentioned, the two main facets of the intellect, *chochmah* and *binah,* are the figurative "father" and "mother" of the emotions born of any particular idea. These emotions are then expressed through thought, speech, or action, which also originate in the intellect. Thus, emotion and expression are the figurative "son" and "daughter" of *chochmah* and *binah.* The creative process therefore proceeds through four stages: the flash of insight, its development

40. The connective *vav* of "*and* prayer" alludes to the law mentioned above that women, in order to pray with love and fear, must (like men) study those parts of the Torah that arouse love and fear of G-d in the heart.

into a conceptual structure, the emotions it engenders, and the form in which it is expressed.

Now, any creative process is a manifestation of G-d's power to create, which is the Divine attribute associated with G-d's Name *Havayah*. Indeed, the literal meaning of this Name is "He [continuously] creates."[41] Moreover, the fourfold creative process of insight-development-emotion-expression is alluded to by the four letters of this Name:[42]

י	*yud*	*chochmah*, wisdom	father
ה	*hei*	*binah*, understanding	mother
ו	*vav*	emotions	son
ה	*hei*	expression	daughter

The *yud* (י), the smallest letter of the Hebrew alphabet, represents the seminal point of insight. The *hei* (ה), which is composed of three lines, represents the expansion of the seminal insight into the three dimensions of length, breadth, and depth. The *vav* (ו), a straight line or vector, represents the descent of the idea from the mind to the heart, the level of emotion. The latter *hei* (ה) again represents expansion, but here it is that of the emotion into the three forms of expression: thought, speech, and action.[43]

41. *Sha'ar HaYichud VeHaEmunah*, ch. 4 (79a).

42. The four letters of the Name *Havayah* correspond to the four essential levels of every complete being, whether world, *partzuf*, angel or man.

43. *Torah Or 95b; Siddur Im Dach 282a; Or HaTorah, Shemot*, p. 1514; *Sefer HaMa'amarim 5710* p. 122 ff.; *Likutei Sichot*, vol. 8, p. 108 ff.; *Sod HaShem Lireiav*, p. 57.

Although everyone of course possesses the full array of powers of intellect, emotion, and expression, the predominant power in each individual is determined by the role he is playing in the above scheme. We have already described how husband and wife contribute their "holy fires" of *chochmah* and *binah* to their common household; full emotional experience and effective expression are contributed by the sons and daughters, respectively. This is the mystical reason why Jewish law requires that one give birth to at least one son and one daughter in order to fulfill the commandment to "be fruitful and multiply."[44] Only then does a household possess the full matrix of creative powers, thus becoming a comprehensive vessel for the expression of Divine unity in the world.

As we said above, a married couple becomes "one flesh" by having children. This idea is one of the mystical meanings of the *Shema*: "Hear, O Israel, *Havayah* is our G-d, *Havayah* is *one*."[45]

Thus, before a couple has children, they are on the level of the *vav-hei* of the Name *Havayah*. In this context, the *yud-hei* hovering over them represents, besides their own parents, the Divine Presence that dwells between them. As we said, this Divine Presence is represented by the Name *Kah;* it is here manifest as the couple's Divine potential to *become* parents.

To summarize:

---

44. Genesis 1:28. See below, p. 349.

45. Deuteronomy 6:4.

י	*yud*	"father" to be
ה	*hei*	"mother" to be
ו	*vav*	groom
ה	*hei*	bride

When they have children, a husband and wife ascend by means of their new roles as parents to the level of *yud-hei* themselves, and their children become the *vav-hei* of a new manifestation of G-d's Name *Havayah*.

Thus, from generation to generation, *vav-hei* becomes *yud-hei*, and a new *vav-hei* is born. The entire process begins with and depends on the initial *Kah* (יה), the Divine Presence, dwelling upon and between the holy fires of husband and wife. And so we see that it is the power of G-d's essential Name *Havayah* that generates all generations from the outset of creation forever and ever.

Intention and Experience

A husband and wife experience the Divine Presence that dwells between them in subtly different ways.

Of all the sacred Names of G-d,[46] three are termed "essential"[47]: *Havayah* (יהו־ה), *Ekyeh* (אהיה), and *Kah* (יה).

---

46. See *Mishneh Torah, Yesodei HaTorah* 6:2, with regard to the seven Names of G-d which it is forbidden to erase.

47. In Hebrew: שמות עצם, as opposed to "descriptive" names (שמות תואר).

The *most* essential is the ineffable Name *Havayah*.[48] These three Names are associated with the intellect, in contrast to G-d's other Names, which are associated solely with the emotional attributes.[49] Intellect without emotional involvement is directed inward (one thinks to himself). Emotion and behavior, on the other hand, are directed outward (one loves, fears, and so forth, things external to oneself).

In particular, the Name *Havayah* relates to *chochmah*, the Name *Ekyeh* to *binah*, and the Name *Kah* to the level of *chochmah* that unites with *binah*.

To summarize:

---

48. All three Names are composed solely of the four letters of the Hebrew alphabet that serve both as consonants and vowels (אהו״י). These four letters are symmetrically situated at the beginning, end, and two middle-points of the initial ten letters of the alphabet: 1 (**א**), 5 (**ה**), 6 (**ו**), 10 (**י**). Together they total 22, indicating that these four letters are indeed the inner soul and essence of the entire 22-letter alphabet.

As consonants without vowels are inaudible (i.e., inanimate), it is explained in Kabbalah that the vowels, relative to the consonants, are as soul to body. Thus, we understand that G-d's essential Names (constructed solely of the four letters of the alphabet that serve as vowels) are the inner soul of all the words.

49. Actually, the Name *Havayah* is generally associated with mercy (רחמים), one of G-d's emotional attributes. But mercy differs from the other emotional attributes in that it derives from the inner dimension of *keter* (while the others derive from *keter*'s external dimension) and its arousal is dependent on one's *da'at* (one's ability to truly empathize with the other).

יהו־ה	*Havayah*	*chochmah* ("wisdom")	father, husband
אהיה	*Ekyeh*	*binah* ("understanding")	mother, wife
יה	*Kah*	the level of *chochmah* that unites with *binah*	third partner in procreation

Looking at these Names in Hebrew, we see that the letters that make up the Name *Kah* (יה) are the first two letters of the Name *Havayah* (יהו־ה) as well as the last two of the Name *Ekyeh* (אהיה).

If we understand the Names *Havayah* and *Ekyeh* to reflect the consciousness of the husband and wife in marital relations, it follows that the husband experiences the Divine Presence—the "third partner" in the couple's union—at the beginning of marital relations, while the wife experiences it at the end.[50]

"Beginning" and "end" here refer to the temporal beginning and end of marital relations, i.e., the preparatory stages and the climax. But as well—and primarily—they refer to the "beginning" and "end" of *consciousness*: the spiritual/mental and physical/emotional planes. That is to say, the husband experiences the Divine Presence more spiritually, in his abstract mind, while the wife experiences it more in the innate psyche of her body.[51]

---

50. The same is true of the way men and women experience the Divine Presence in life in general. Men tend to experience it chiefly in their abstract, initial vision of reality, which serves to inspire them in their everyday life, while women tend to experience it more in the concretization of its revelation in the real world (see below, p. 236 ff.).

51. In Kabbalah, the woman herself (in mind and body) reflects and symbolizes the *Shechinah*, G-d's presence and immanence in reality.

Looking again at these two Names in Hebrew, we see that their remaining four letters spell the Name *Akvah* (אהוה).[52] This Name is associated with *da'at*, the Divine power that unifies *chochmah* and *binah*[53] and signifies the experience of the couple becoming "one flesh." The first two letters of this Name are the first two of *Ekyeh* (אהיה), and its last two letters are the last two of *Havayah* (יהו־ה).

This teaches us that the wife experiences the merging with her husband into "one flesh" at the beginning of marital relations, while the husband experiences it at the end. Again, in addition to referring to the temporal beginning and end of marital relations, this refers also (and principally) to the spiritual/mental beginning and physical/emotional end. The wife experiences the relatively spiritual dimension of becoming one with her husband; he is conscious of their becoming one more on the physical plane.

This is an example of the principle "the end is wedged in the beginning and the beginning is wedged in

---

52. In Kabbalah, this Name is termed the "secret" Name of G-d. This is because, first of all, it does not appear explicitly in the Torah. Secondly, it corresponds to the *sefirah* of *da'at*, which is not initially manifest as one of the *sefirot* (which number "ten, and not nine; ten, and not eleven" [*Sefer Yetzirah* 1:4]). Finally, its numerical value is 17, that of the word for "good" (טוב). Of the light that was created during the first week of creation, it is said that "G-d saw the light, that it was good" (Genesis 1:4). Our sages interpret this to mean that G-d saw that "it was proper to hide it" until the future (*Chagigah* 12a).

53. See above, p. 127, where we explained that husband and wife are unified by the Name *Kah*, i.e., the aspect of *chochmah* that unites with *binah*. The Name *Akvah* is the power that effects this union.

the end."[54] The end of the wife's experience of the Divine Presence is wedged in the beginning of the husband's: the experience of her body links to the experience of his mind. Reciprocally, the beginning of the wife's experience of "becoming one flesh" is wedged in the end of her husband's: the experience of her mind links to the experience of his body.[55]

To put it another way: the primary (or ideal) *intention* of the husband in marital relations should be to manifest the presence of the third partner, while that of the wife should be to become "one flesh." The essential *experience* of the husband, however, is becoming "one flesh," while that of the wife is the presence of the third partner.

To summarize:

	beginning experience	end experience
husband	Divine Presence	becoming one
wife	becoming one	Divine Presence

54. *Sefer Yetzirah* 1:7.

55. See additional note 3 at the end of this chapter (p. 133).

Additional Notes

1

to page 115.

The woman personifies the *sefirah* of *malchut*, which is initially constructed entirely out of the five states of the *gevurah* of *da'at* (*Etz Chaim* 34; *Likutei Torah* 4:31a, etc.). Before marriage, she is referred to as "the beautiful maiden without eyes" (*Zohar* 2:95a). Rabbi Yitzchak Luria interprets "without eyes" (in the plural) to mean that she innately possesses only one eye, the left, which embodies the five *gevurot* of *da'at*, which see reality critically and with trepidation.

In the words of our sages (*Sifrei, Shelach* 15:21): "Man's eye looks favorably [upon guests], whereas woman's eye looks critically [on them]."

The word עין ("eye") = 130 = 5 · 26. Each eye possesses five powers of *Havayah* (הוי'. = 26). At the level of *da'at*, each of the five *chasadim* as well as each of the five *gevurot* is represented by G-d's Name *Havayah*. This is so because the essence of *da'at* is the force that motivates the synthesis of *chesed* and *gevurah*, the attribute of mercy (*rachamim*), which is the essential attribute of G-d's Name *Havayah*.

At the level of the emotions of the heart, the attribute of *chesed* is represented by G-d's Name *Kel* (אל), whereas the attribute of *gevurah* is represented by His Name *Elokim* (אלהים). The six emotions of the heart correspond to the six days of creation described in the first account of creation and thus to man's "first nature." *Da'at* is essentially above nature, and so the origin of mercy, the Name *Havayah*, appears only in the second account of creation, as a rectified "second nature." (As our sages teach [*Bereishit Rabbah* 12:15], G-d saw that the world could not exist solely on the principle of strict judgment, signified by the Name *Elokim*, which alone appears in the first account of creation. In the second account, therefore, He also used the Name *Havayah*, which signifies mercy.)

The woman, who personifies the *sefirah* of *malchut*, or created reality in general, initially possesses only a left eye, the five *gevurot* of *da'at*, which even in "second nature" itself (the second account of creation, which includes the Name *Havayah*) are still vulnerable to the seduction of the primordial snake. She innately feels intimidated by her environment, which she tends to view critically (*gevurah*), though optimally with a sense of pity (*rachamim*). This is so because her *gevurot* themselves are Names of *Havayah*, the Name of mercy (*rachamim*). She is thus motivated to turn to G-d in heartfelt prayer and arouse His mercy on herself and on the world around her.

Her husband, on the other hand, possesses two eyes, all ten Names of *Havayah* belonging to his *da'at*. He envisions the world in a positive light, as being (already) full of G-d's mercy. His orientation is thus to increase the Divine blessing already inherent in nature (for blessing requires a pre-existent substance on which to rest). This he does primarily through studying and teaching Torah.

In response to the wife's heartfelt prayer, G-d draws down to her, via the holy union with her husband, the five *chasadim* of *da'at*, which she integrates into her consciousness as her second, right eye.

2

to page 116.

According to Kabbalah (especially as explained in the writings of Rabbi Avraham Abulafia), true perfection (as manifest in marriage) is the state of a *whole* entity being joined by an additional *half* (שלם וחצי), rather than the isolated completeness of a whole entity by itself.

In our statement of perfect faith in G-d's absolute unity—"G-d is one" (הוי' אחד)—this numerical phenomenon appears three times, at the beginning (the ratio of the first two letters), at the end (the ratio of the last two letters), and in general (the ratio of the two words themselves):

The first two letters of "G-d [is one]" (יהו־ה אחד) are יה (the י of איש and the ה of אשה). They possess the ratio of 2:1 (10:5 = 2:1).

The last two letters of "[G-d is] one" (יהו־ה אחד) are the letters ח and ד (which, according to the sages, signify the seven heavens and earth

[8], the vertical axis of physical space, and the four lateral directions of physical space). They also possess the ratio of 2:1 (8:4 = 2:1).

The two words "G-d is one" (יהו־ה אחד) possess this same ratio, for *Havayah* equals 26, and **אחד** ("one") equals 13 (26:13 = 2:1).

If the *half* is taken to represent the feminine component inherent in true perfection, we may thereby infer that the *revelation* (in the future, see Rashi on Deuteronomy 6:4) of G-d's oneness (the word **אחד** = 13, the *half* of **יהו־ה** = 26) corresponds to the feminine principle of Divinity, the Divine Presence.

In addition, let us note that when the *whole* (the **י** of **איש** = 10) and the *half* (the **ה** of **אשה** = 5) are joined (in marriage) at "right angles," the hypotenuse of the right triangle equals (approximately) **וה** (11; more exactly: 11.180...; 1,118 = 26 · 43 = 86 · 13 = **שמע ישראל יהו־ה אלהינו יהו־ה אחד**, "Hear O Israel, *G-d* is our G-d, *G-d* is one").

As we have explained, the four letters of 'הוי represent "father," "mother," "son," and "daughter," respectively. Thus we see that the progeny (the son [ו] and daughter [ה]) of the parents (the father [י] and mother [ה]) are present, *in potentia*, from the moment of marriage as the "hypotenuse" of their parents' "right triangle."

3

to page 130.

This will become clearer by picturing the Name *Ekyeh above* the Name *Havayah* and grouping the four letters of each into two halves:

אה יה

יה וה

Thus arranged, the two Names can be read either horizontally or vertically. No matter how they are read, the end of the first is wedged in the beginning of the second.

Though, in general, especially in the writings of Rabbi Yitzchak Luria, the Name *Ekyeh* is identified with the *sefirah* of *binah*, its origin is in *keter* (*above* the Name *Havayah* that appears in *chochmah*). The Name *Ekyeh* appears in the phrase אהיה אשר אהיה ("I shall be that which I shall be," Exodus 3:13), where it is mentioned twice. In Kabbalah it is explained that the first אהיה is in *keter*, whereas the second is in *binah* (the word אשר corresponds to *chochmah*, between *keter* and *binah*). This is one of the main indications in the Torah that the origin of woman is higher than that of man.

Note that only by arranging the two names in this fashion, with *Ekyeh* above *Havayah*, reflecting its higher origin, does the Name *Akvah* appear in its proper order. This indicates that in order for husband and wife to truly unite, they must possess some consciousness of the wife's higher origin.

There are two other primary instances in the Torah of the phenomenon of an intrinsic pair of words that can be read both horizontally and vertically:

The inner emotions associated with the two *sefirot* of *chesed* and *gevurah* (the two "hands" or "wings" of the soul) are love (אהבה) and fear (יראה), respectively. Fear is related to the feminine soul: "A woman who fears G-d shall be praised" (Proverbs 31:30); the feminine soul is "formed" by the power of *gevurah*. Love is related to the male soul: "He has remembered [זכר, the word for 'male'] his loving-kindness" (Psalms 98:3); the male soul is "formed" by the power of *chesed*. By picturing the word יראה above the word אהבה, we observe that "the end [of fear] is wedged in the beginning [of love]:

יר **אה**
אה בה

In Kabbalah we are taught that the souls of the evil Balaam (בלעם) and Amalek (עמלק) are intimately related. "The end [of Balaam] is wedged in the beginning [of Amalek]." The blessings of Balaam (whose name is interpreted to mean בלא עם, "without a nationality") *end* with the prophecy: "Amalek is the *first* of the nations, but his end will be utter destruction" (Numbers 24:20). The first two letters of Amalek (**עמ**לק)—his *beginning*—mean "nation"; the final two letters (עמ**לק**)—his *end*—mean "destruction."

בל **עם**
עם לק

The relationship of these two phenomena is that through our fear and love of G-d, we ultimately transform the souls of Balaam and Amalek into good: **יראה** (216) rectifies **בלעם** (142), which together equal **משיח** (*Mashiach*, 358); **אהבה** (13) rectifies **עמלק** (240), which together equal **אבנר** (Abner, 253), the "commander-in-chief" of the army of *Mashiach*, as taught in Kabbalah. (In number theory, the "triangle" of 253 [32,131] is the "middle point" of the "triangle" of 358 [64,261].)

The four related words: **יראה** (216), **אהבה** (13), **בלעם** (142), and **עמלק** (240) together equal 611 (**תורה**, "Torah") = 13 · 47. 13 = **אהבה**; 47 = 21 (**אהיה**) ⊥ 26 (**יהו־ה**), our original pair!

6

Words of Love and Kindness

Man the Speaker

The Torah describes the creation of man as follows:[1]

וַיִּיצֶר ה' אֱלֹהִים אֶת הָאָדָם עָפָר מִן הָאֲדָמָה,
וַיִּפַּח בְּאַפָּיו נִשְׁמַת חַיִּים,
וַיְהִי הָאָדָם לְנֶפֶשׁ חַיָּה.

And G-d formed man from the dust of the earth,
and He blew into his nostrils the breath of life,
and man became a living soul.

Rashi explains that the seemingly redundant third phrase refers to the additional level of soul with which

---

1. Genesis 2:7. The fact that the Torah precedes the description of the ascendancy of man by pointing out that he was created "from the dust of the earth" indicates that man's *first* rectification of consciousness is to see himself as "dust of the earth," to achieve the state of genuine lowliness which will be explained in the following chapter.

mankind has been endowed above the lower forms of life. Surprisingly, however, he identifies this uniqueness not as man's pure intelligence but as "knowledge and speech."[2] The Targum also translates the term "living soul" in this verse as "a speaking spirit."[3] The sages as well differentiate man from the lower forms of life by referring to him as "the speaker" rather than "the thinker."

The power of speech is thus seen as the hallmark of humanity, the quality that sets man apart from the rest of creation. As important as intellect and the higher faculties are, man's singularity lies not in that he can think for himself but in his ability to communicate his innermost thoughts and feelings to others.

"Speech," the ability to convey a part of oneself to another, is thus used by the sages as a euphemism for marital relations,[4] since marital relations are, of course, the most intense and intimate form of communication. Likewise, "knowledge" in the Bible is often used to refer to marital relations, beginning with those of Adam and

---

2. In Hebrew: דעה ודבור. Inasmuch as we understand "knowledge" (*da'at* or *deah*) as the ability to relate to an other, "knowledge and speech" are simply the mental and physical correlates of each other.

3. In Aramaic: רוח ממללא. In contrast, when the phrase נפש חיה ("living soul") is used with regard to lower forms of life (Genesis 1:20, 21, 24, 30; 2:19), the Targum translates it literally (נפשא חיתא). We may thus surmise that the Targum is the source on which Rashi bases his explanation of this phrase. (He apparently understands the word רוח to mean דעה, as in Isaiah 11:2 [רוח דעת], just as on Exodus 31:3 he explains דעת to be רוח הקדש.)

4. *Ketubot* 13a.

Eve: "And Adam *knew* his wife, Eve."[5] We have thus gone full circle: speech alludes to marital relations, marital relations are equivalent to knowledge, and knowledge and speech are the unique endowments of mankind.

Verbal communication and marital relations are thus closely intertwined.[6] Misusing one's faculty of speech is tantamount to a misuse of one's sexual energy, since both result in the dissipation of the ability to relate potently to an other. Likewise, consciously working to rectify one's faculty of speech will directly and positively affect his marital relations.

It is not surprising, then, that the Torah attaches great importance to the proper use and rectification of speech and discusses at length both its constructive and destructive powers.[7] For if it is speech that makes us human, it is *how* we speak that determines what kind of human being we are.

Rectified Speech

The key to genuine communication through speech is sincerity, or in the words of our sages: when "mouth

5. Genesis 4:1. See *Tanya*, ch. 3.

6. See *Sefer Yetzirah* 1:3.

7. There are many *mitzvot* that revolve around the sanctification of speech. See the chapter titled *Shemirat Brit HaLashon* in *Malchut Yisrael*.

and heart are the same."[8] When the mouth expresses what is truly in the heart, the "words which issue from the heart [of the speaker] enter the heart [of the hearer]."[9] Since the most essential emotion of the heart is love,[10] the words

---

8. *Terumot* 3:8. The antithesis of this—unrectified speech—is speaking with "one thing in the mouth and [a different] one in the heart" (*Pesachim* 113b).

The ideal state of speech is alluded to in the name of the first letter of the Hebrew alphabet, the origin of all speech: *alef* (אלף), which as a number equals one, and as a word is an acronym for אמת למד פיך, "teach your mouth [to speak] truth" (*Otiot d'Rabbi Akiva*, beginning) and אחד לב פה, "one [and the same] in heart and mouth." The phrase אחד לב פה (= 130) equals 10 times אחד (= 13), "one," itself, indicating that when one's verbal expression reflects the depths of his heart, he has unified all ten powers of his soul.

9. Cf. *Berachot* 6b. *Shirat Yisrael*, p. 156. In proportion to the intensity of the "*heart* of the fire" (לבת אש) of the speaker, its *flame* (להבה) of love and desire ascends and *enflames* the *heart* of the hearer.

The prophet Obadiah (1:18) identifies the two levels of "fire" (אש) and "flame" (להבה) with "the house of Jacob" and "the house of Joseph": "The house of Jacob will be fire and the house of Joseph a flame...." When the flame of Joseph encounters a negative, unreceptive object, it consumes it, as the verse continues: "and the house of Esau will be straw, and they will set them on fire and devour them...." But when it encounters a positive, receptive object, it "enflames" and inspires it.

The relation between the two words לב ("heart") and להבה ("flame") is obvious. When the first letter of אש ("fire") is added to the final three letters of להבה, the word אהבה ("love") is formed. Thus, אהבה can be seen as a *notrikun* for אש להבה (in addition, א and ל interchange in the system of *albam*). אש = 301 = 7 · 43; להבה = 42 = 7 · 6. The full phrase אש להבה = 343 = 7 · 49 = 7^3.

10. Love is the primary emotion of the heart (the inner experience of the *sefirah* of *chesed*); it "accompanies" and "leads" all the others, as explained above. Its archetypal soul is Abraham, who is referred to as "the greatest of [*gadol*] the giants" (i.e., the greatest of

which most truly "issue from the heart" are words of love and concern for the welfare of an other.[11]

King Solomon states:[12]

---

the archetypal souls of Israel, Joshua 14:15). In Kabbalah, *chesed* ("loving-kindness") and *gedulah* ("greatness") are synonyms for the same power of the soul.

That love is the most essential emotion of the heart is implied by the fact that the vernacular word "love" (and its cognates in related languages) etymologically derives from the Hebrew word for "heart," *lev* (לב).

Our sages teach that the greatest, most intense of all loves between mates in the animal kingdom is that between the lion and the lioness (*Sanhedrin* 106a). In Ezekiel's vision of the Divine chariot, the lion is "to the right" (Ezekiel 1:10), corresponding to the *sefirah* of *chesed*. One of the seven synonyms for "lion" in Hebrew (*Midrash Mishlei* 20:2), לביא, derives from the Hebrew word for "heart," *lev* (לב). In addition, "lion" (*leib*) in the vernacular derives from *lev*, and appears in the idiom (both Hebrew and other languages) "lion-hearted." The very phrase לב אריה ("heart of a lion") equals 248, which equals אברהם ("Abraham").

11. That the purpose of the mouth is to express the words of love and kindness which issue from the heart is indicated by the numerical equivalence between the word for "mouth" (פה, 85) and the combined value of the words for "love" and "kindness" (אהבה + חסד = 13 + 72 = 85).

85 itself (פה) is the middle-point of 169 = 13^2 (13 = אהבה, "love").

In addition, 85 = 5 · 17; 17 = טוב, "goodness." In Kabbalah, we are taught that *da'at* projects five powers of goodness into the heart which thereafter become expressed as rectified speech (the five initial categories of rectified speech, presently to be discussed).

The sum of the two prime factors of 85 (5 and 17) is 22, the number of letters in the Hebrew alphabet, and the value of the word טובה, the feminine form of "good" (the letter ה = 5 being added to the word טוב = 17).

12. Proverbs 27:19.

כַּמַּיִם הַפָּנִים לַפָּנִים כֵּן לֵב הָאָדָם לָאָדָם

As [when looking in] water, face reflects face,
so does one's heart find reflection in another's.

Speaking and relating "face to face" is thus synonymous with doing so "heart to heart."[13] In the *Zohar*[14] we are taught that the ability to relate "face to face" is the very essence of all rectification. Man is virtually the only creature that engages in marital relations face to face.[15] This is because for him, marital relations are meant to be an expression of his uniquely human capacity to convey his love, the innermost attribute of his heart, to his spouse.

As we mentioned,[16] there are five positive propensities (degrees of *chesed*) within *da'at* ("knowledge," or the power to connect and relate). Inasmuch as speech is the paradigm of connection and relation, it is through speech that these five degrees of *chesed* become manifest. As the *Zohar* states: "*Da'at* is hidden in the mouth."[17] Each of the five, projected on the faculty of speech, defines a different

---

13. In Hebrew, "face" (פנים) also means "inner consciousness" (פנימיות), for the face expresses the wisdom of the soul (as in Ecclesiastes 8:1: "the wisdom of a man radiates in his face") and the innermost emotions of the heart.

14. *Zohar* 2:176b, in the *Sifra d'Tzeniuta*. Kabbalah describes the lower levels of communication, when one party or both does not expose his inner self, as "[male] face to [female] back," "[male] back to [female] face" or "back to back."

15. *Bechorot* 8a. The other two are the snake and the fish, "since the *Shechinah* spoke with them"—the snake in the creation story, and the fish in the book of Jonah.

16. p. 114 ff.

17. *Zohar* 2:123a. See *The Hebrew Letters*, p. 252.

category of rectified speech. One should therefore try to rectify[18] his manner of speech, especially with his spouse, in accordance with these five categories:

1 *Words of Love*

The importance of sincere avowals of love and unqualified affection cannot be overstated. Challenging though it may be to continually seek new ways to convey one's love to one's spouse without sounding trite, one must never assume that it "goes without saying" or that it can be taken for granted.[19]

---

18. Ideally, by simply purifying one's thoughts, one's faculty of speech will follow suit, and one will not have to concentrate explicitly on controlling his speech. However, for most people, it is necessary to tackle the problem on both fronts. See *Ma'amarei Admor HaEmtza'i*, p. 455 (*Pokeiach Ivrim*, p. 9 in 1973 edition).

From an even deeper perspective, the letters and words of speech reflect and express the super-conscious levels of the soul, which is not manifest in one's thoughts. In *Chassidut* we are taught that the "letters of thought" and the "letters of speech" have two independent sources in the very essence of the soul (see Rabbi Hillel of Paritch, *Commentary on Sha'ar HaYichud*, end of ch. 3).

By paying close attention to one's speech, one learns to channel the super-conscious powers of one's soul into the conscious levels of mind, heart and deed.

19. In general, it is the husband who must express his love for his wife explicitly and directly. The wife's expression of love for her husband is in general more indirect (and implied in the tone of her voice).

It is interesting to note that the expression **אני אוהב אותך** ("I love you," the husband speaking to the wife) equals 502, which in turn equals **שכינה ביניהם** ("the Divine Presence [dwells] between them").

This degree of *chesed* is termed in Kabbalah "loving-kindness within[20] loving-kindness" (חֶסֶד שֶׁבְּחֶסֶד).

The attribute of *chesed* is associated in Kabbalah with the first day of creation.[21] The first words G-d spoke on this day—His first words recorded in the Torah—were "Let there be light."[22]

From the fact that the first instance of speech recorded in the Torah is the creation of light, we learn that the beginning and essence of all speech is light;[23] the verbal expression of light is words of love.[24] As mentioned

---

20. In all these terms, the word "within" is equivalent to "expressed as."

21. Of all six days of creation, it is said: "The world shall be built by *chesed*" (Psalms 89:3). Our sages teach that all the working of creation took place during the 12 daytime hours of each of the six days. $6 \cdot 12 = 72 =$ חסד. The *chesed*-hours of creation are what is alluded to in the verse: "The world shall be built by *chesed*." Thus, each of the attributes that correspond to one of the days of creation is to be understood as the inner degree of *chesed* shining into and appearing through that attribute.

22. Genesis 1:3.

23. "Everything goes after the beginning" (*Pirkei d'Rabbi Eliezer* 41). This is evident also from the verse: "The beginning of your words shall shine light" (Psalms 119:130), and the expression: "Open your mouth, that your words may shine" (*Berachot* 22a). According to Kabbalah, the word for "speech" used in the account of creation (אמר) is an acronym for the three stages of creation, "light" (אור), "water" (מים), and "firmament" (רקיע). See above, p. 29, footnote 62.

24. The word for "love" (אהבה) can be seen as an acronym for אור הקדוש ברוך הוא ("the light of the Holy One, blessed be He"; see the chapter of this name in *Sha'arei Ahavah v'Ratzon*). Furthermore, the word for "light" (אור) is a *notrikun* for אהבה ורצון ("love and good will").

previously, emotions are outwardly directed, as opposed to the intellect, which is directed inward. Thus, one's emotions may be thought of as "radiating" or "shining" outward to the world. Love is the first and primary emotion; it makes one care enough to extend oneself into and relate to reality.

2 *Words of Rebuke: Constructive Criticism*

Words of rebuke are constructive only after the previous category of speech (words of love) has been adequately employed, so there can be no doubt that one's criticism is predicated by love and concern. In fact, sincere rebuke should not only be predicated by love but be a direct result of it. One's love and concern for one's spouse should be the sole motivation for criticizing him.[25]

Like all the *mitzvot*, there are laws surrounding the *mitzvah* of rebuking one's fellow.[26] These must be studied and observed in order for one's rebuke to be administered properly and effectively.

---

25. The word for "rebuke" in Hebrew (תוכחה) may be seen to be constructed of two syllables: תוך, which means "from the midst of" or "from a state of" and חה, which equals the word אהבה ("love"). Thus, the word תוכחה reads as תוך אהבה, "from a state of love."

This is further supported by the fact that the first appearance of the word תוכחה in the Torah is when Abraham rebuked Abimelech after the latter's slaves seized his well (Genesis 21:25). As Abraham personifies loving-kindness, this teaches us that all rebuke should issue from love. See *The Dynamic Corporation*, p. 27, footnote 17.

26. These may be found in *Shulchan Aruch, Orach Chaim* 156 (in *Shulchan Aruch HaRav*, 156:6-8).

In addition, one must always bear in mind the Ba'al Shem Tov's teaching[27] that when a person is confronted with a shortcoming in another, it is first and foremost because G-d is showing him, through the mirror of the other person, a fault that in some way exists in himself. The first response, then, should be to seek out and correct the corresponding fault in oneself. Only then, with the benefit of perspective and when there is no trace of anger or indignation, may one proceed to criticize and correct.[28]

This degree of *chesed* is termed "loving-kindness within severity" (חֶסֶד שֶׁבִּגְבוּרָה).

The attribute of *gevurah* ("severity") is associated in Kabbalah with the second day of creation, on which G-d created the firmament to separate the higher waters from the lower waters: "Let there be a firmament in the midst of the waters."[29]

---

27. Cited in *Meor Einaim*, beginning of *Chukat*, *et al.*

28. See at length, *Likutei Sichot*, vol. 10, pp. 24-29. The mental attitude that enables one to do this is discussed below, p. 211.

29. Genesis 1:6. On the meaning of the higher and lower waters, see *The Hebrew Letters*, p. 27.

Additionally, water allegorically signifies the intellect (*Zohar* 2:19b, etc.); the firmament in the water thus signifies the ability of the intellect to discriminate, i.e., recognize the differences between even very similar situations and contexts. This ability is crucial in administering rebuke, since it is very easy to misconstrue the circumstances surrounding an act and the motives behind it, as well as to fail to find the proper words and tone with which to rebuke. (See *Igrot Kodesh Admor HaRayatz*, vol. 4, pp. 14-15; *HaYom Yom*, 22 Elul.)

This is alluded to by the phenomenon that when the commandment "you shall surely rebuke your fellow" (הוכח תוכיח את עמיתך, Leviticus 19:7) is written as a perfect square, the corner letters

In Kabbalah, water represents *chesed* and love. Rashi[30] explains that the essence of the firmament is G-d's rebuke, in response to which the upper waters remain suspended in space. The fact that the firmament of rebuke is spoken of as being "in the midst of the waters"[31] teaches us that criticism must be constructive, that is, issuing from and phrased in terms of love.

3 *Words of Praise and Admiration*

Every Jew possesses infinite positive qualities. Unfortunately, these may, either in a particular situation or in the person's life in general, lay dormant, sometimes to such an extent that the person is himself unaware of them. By praising someone for a particular property or attribute, however, one can draw it forth.[32] Persistent reinforcement

---

spell the word for "wisdom" (חכמה), as if to say that rebuke must be framed in wisdom.

ח	כ	ו	ה
י	כ	ו	ת
ע	ת	א	ח
ך	ת	י	מ

This lends additional meaning to the verse: "The words of the wise, when spoken gently, are heeded" (Ecclesiastes 9:17; see further, p. 219).

30. *ad loc.*

31. In Hebrew, "the midst of the waters" is תוך המים; since water represents love, this becomes **תוך אהבה**, which in turn numerically equals **תוכחה**, as pointed out in footnote 25, above.

32. See, *inter alia*, *Derech Mitzvotecha*, *Shoresh Mitzvat HaTefilah* 9 (p. 118-19).

of the attribute in the mind of the person builds his character, and he will gradually begin to live up to the image of himself he is being praised for.

In light of what we have explained regarding how husband and wife complete each other,[33] it follows that each will use the ability to praise his spouse somewhat differently. The husband, personifying the *yud* (the point), will focus directly on his wife's good qualities and praise them as his insight flashes on them.

The Ba'al Shem Tov taught that it is often efficacious to do someone a physical favor before doing him a spiritual one. Benefiting someone in a physical way demonstrates the sincerity of one's intentions, since spiritual advice can easily sound patronizing or be seen as a cheap substitute for real help. Once one has thus won the other's confidence, he can help him spiritually, as well.

So it is with regard to praise. A wife may appreciate being praised for her physical (and relatively mundane) virtues,[34] and her husband must be sensitive enough to

---

33. See above, p. 114 ff.

34. The husband is responsible to provide his wife with "her food, her clothing, and her conjugal rights" (Exodus 21:10). However, if he simply provides these physically and does not compliment her in their regard, it is questionable if he has truly satisfied her need for them. Part of his duty, then, is to praise her (in a sensitive and appreciated manner) for her prowess as a housekeeper (chiefly represented by her cooking), her taste in dress, and her physical attractiveness.

The Torah praises Rachel as being יפת תאר ויפת מראה, "of beautiful form and beautiful appearance" (Genesis 29:17; see below, p. 392, footnote 46). Although these both refer to physical beauty, "beautiful form" refers specifically to the shape and proportion of the

know when this is so. In such cases, he should praise her for these qualities before praising for her spiritual, more sublime qualities in order to make this latter praise more credible and profound.[35]

---

limbs, while "beautiful appearance" refers specifically to the complexion or shining of the face (see Rashi, Ibn Ezra *ad loc.*). The beauty of one's facial radiance, we are told, is dependent on his spiritual condition: "The wisdom of a man radiates in his face" (Ecclesiastes 8:1). Relative to each other then, "beautiful form" describes physical beauty, and "beautiful appearance" the more spiritual. Here we see, then, that the Torah first praises Rachel's physical qualities and only then her spiritual ones.

Furthermore, the *sefirah* of *tiferet* in Kabbalah is called "the body" (*Tikunei Zohar*, introduction [17a]), indicating that praise is associated with the body. Below (p. 313), we associate the wife's self-adornment with the *sefirah* of *tiferet*; her jewelry, etc. reveal her inner beauty.

The fact that how well one is dressed is a subject for praise may be inferred from the verse that introduces the commandments regarding the priestly garments: "And you shall make garments of holiness for your brother, Aaron, for honor and for *praise*" (Exodus 28:2).

See additional note at the end of this chapter (p. 183).

35. Corresponding to the three physical qualities the husband must praise in his wife are the spiritual virtues he must also praise her for: her generosity to others, her intelligence and good character traits (*midot*, see below, p. 183), and the way she raises their children. These are the main qualities for which he should praise her.

responsibility of the husband	**physical praise**	**spiritual praise**
conjugal rights	attractiveness; beauty	raising and educating children
clothing	taste in clothing	intellect and character traits
food	cooking; housekeeping	acts of generosity

The wife, too, must praise her husband for both his physical and spiritual qualities.[36] However, inasmuch as she personifies the *hei* (space in general), she will tend to focus on her husband's potential, embracing an overall vision of him rather than focusing on specific qualities. By praising him in these general terms, she cultivates him, thus helping him realize her higher vision of him.

Of course, the praiser must sincerely see the quality he is praising or believe that it is indeed there, and must couch his praise in a convincing manner. After one's care and concern has been expressed through constructive criticism, praise will sound more genuine. Implicit in loving rebuke is the assumption that the other person contains hidden potentials that have not yet been actualized.

To be sure, simply thinking well about a person and emphasizing his positive traits in one's mind is important and efficacious.[37] In many cases, treating a person *as if* he is already exhibiting a desired trait will itself enable and

---

In his poem of praise to the woman (which closes the book of Proverbs and is recited as part of the Sabbath-night home liturgy), King Solomon writes: "Grace is false, and beauty is vain, but a woman who fears G-d shall be praised" (Proverbs 31:30). This means that if the woman is not righteous, her grace and beauty are of no value, but if she is, they are praiseworthy (*Kesef Tzaruf ad loc.*).

The simple reason that the woman's beauty is not openly praised in this poem is that King Solomon wrote it in honor of his mother, Bathsheba (see *Zohar* 3:74b; Rashi and Ibn Ezra on Proverbs 31:1), and it is not proper for the son to praise his mother's physical beauty.

36. Men may also be praised for their physical appearance, just as the Torah describes Joseph as being—like his mother Rachel—"of beautiful form and beautiful appearance" (Genesis 39:6).

37. See *Likutei Moharan* 1:282.

encourage him to rise to the expectations held of him. Nonetheless, this is not always enough, since it usually fails to build the other person's character sufficiently and actively enough in his own mind. Ideally, one's positive vision of the other person should be articulated.

This degree of *chesed* is termed "loving-kindness within beauty"[38] (חֶסֶד שֶׁבְּתִפְאֶרֶת).

The attribute of *tiferet* (תִּפְאֶרֶת, "beauty") is associated in Kabbalah with the third day of creation, on which G-d said: "Let the water under heaven be gathered to one place, so that the dry land may appear."[39] The dry land already existed, but it was covered by the sea. In effect, G-d was "praising" the dry land (by saying that it should be revealed), and this "inspired" it to reveal its latent self. Then, "G-d said: Let the earth bring forth grass, herb yielding seed, and fruit trees...."[40] This "praise" served to activate the earth's inherent but latent potential to produce plant life (כֹּחַ הַצּוֹמֵחַ).[41]

---

38. The root פאר means both "beauty" and "praise." In the reflexive, it means "to consider oneself praiseworthy," i.e., "to take pride."

The *sefirah* of *tiferet* comprises both "revealed states of *chesed*" and "concealed states of *chesed*." Praising physical qualities corresponds to the former; praising spiritual qualities to the latter.

39. Genesis 1:9.

40. *ibid.* 1:11.

41. This series of "praises" reflect the same three aspects of physical praise we described above: G-d's praise of the land, causing it to be revealed, is like the spouse praising his partner's physical beauty. G-d "praising" the earth's ability to cover itself with verdure is like the spouse praising his partner's beautiful clothing. G-d "praising" the earth's ability to bring forth fruit trees is like the spouse praising his partner's ability to provide for their needs. And

The people of Israel is likened to the earth: "For you shall be a land of desire, said G-d of Hosts."[42] The Ba'al Shem Tov interpreted this verse to mean that like the physical earth, each and every Jew possesses infinite latent potential and hidden treasures. "It is these treasures and bountiful harvest," he said, "which I wish to reveal in every Jew,"[43] and he did this by continuously praising even simple Jews. Activating a person's latent potential in

---

indeed, G-d originally permitted man to eat only the produce of the third day of creation, i.e., vegetation (Genesis 1:29).

In Kabbalah, the dry land, or earth, is a referent to the *sefirah* of *malchut*, which corresponds to the woman. The above pattern of praises applies particularly, then, to how the husband must praise his wife.

We are taught that each of the four kingdoms (mineral, vegetable, animal, human) are inter-included of the others. The "vegetative" aspect of man is his hair, which is constantly growing. (The imagery of one's hair as a garment covering the body may be seen from the phrase "a raiment of hair" [Genesis 25:25].) The above praise of the earth's vegetation would thus correspond in the couple, besides to the beauty of the spouse's clothing, to the beauty of her hair, as well.

42. Malachi 3:12.

43. *HaYom Yom*, 17 *Iyar*. One's latent potential is those powers of one's soul which are presently dormant. The Ba'al Shem Tov said his soul was sent down from heaven to awaken the Jewish people from its deep spiritual dormancy. Just as a person in a state of deep "faint" (or coma) can be revived by whispering his Hebrew name to him, so did the Ba'al Shem Tov say that his own name, Israel, the collective name of the Jewish people, is in fact such a whisper in their ears. As explained throughout Kabbalah and *Chassidut*, there is no greater praise of the Jewish people than to call them by the name "Israel." The name "Israel" is identified with the *sefirah* of *tiferet*, as in the phrase "the beauty of Israel" (תפארת ישראל, Lamentations 2:1). The numerical value of ישראל (541) is the middle point of the numerical value of תפארת (1081).

a sense turns him into a new person; in fact, we are taught in *Chassidut* that G-d's continuous re-creation of the world is most evident in the power of producing vegetation latent in the earth.[44]

Thus, despite the fact that *chesed* is the foremost, leading attribute of the heart, and words of love are the basis of one's relationship and communication with one's spouse, one's deepest effort should be spent in praising her. *Tiferet* refers to the harmonious blending of different colors[45]; one's praise of one's spouse should encompass as wide a spectrum of compliments as possible.

Furthermore, praising one's spouse can help fan the fire of love.[46] Recognizing and actualizing more and more of her potential provides all the more reason to love her.[47]

---

44. *Igeret HaKodesh* 20 (p. 132ab).

45. In Kabbalah, *tiferet* is the central fulcrum of the emotions (manifesting itself in the widest spectrum of emotive shades), and is identified with the torso, out of which grow all the body's limbs.

46. See *Tanya*, end of ch. 32 and end of ch. 44, based on the verse "Jacob, who redeemed Abraham" (Isaiah 29:22). Jacob personified the *sefirah* of *tiferet*; Abraham personified the *sefirah* of *chesed*.

47. As mentioned above (p. 140, footnote 10), an alternative name for the *sefirah* of *chesed* is *gedulah* (גדולה, "greatness"). This indicates the thematic connection between love and praiseworthiness, specifically with regard to one's infinitely great potential to express loving-kindness.

Moses praised G-d as being "great, mighty, and awesome" (Deuteronomy 10:17); this phrase is the opening expression of G-d's praises in the *Amidah* prayer. Thus, the first and foremost praise is of G-d's greatness (loving-kindness). In the course of Jewish history, there were times when the appropriateness of mentioning His might or awesomeness in the liturgy was questioned, but never the appropriateness of mentioning His greatness (*Yoma* 69b).

4 *Words of Control and Direction*

Since everyone finds himself at some point in a position of authority over someone else, it is important to learn how to direct without condescension. Giving orders in a domineering or patronizing fashion may glean quick results in the short run, but in the long run it will only foment discontent and resentment.

Rather, one should learn how to direct in a spirit of love and deference. If one phrases instructions as requests rather than demands—both acknowledging the other person's autonomy (even though he is functioning as a subordinate) and minimizing one's own authority (even though he is functioning as a superior)—one will generally elicit a positive response. When approached in the proper manner, most people will gladly extend themselves.

In addition, the sensitivity and tact with which one conveys his instructions will subliminally communicate his inner conviction of their correctness. Autocratic exhibitions of force are an attempt to compensate for a lack of conviction by invoking the authority of power and position. If the subordinates sense the inner certitude of the orders, rather than just the authority being wielded, they will be certain to comply wholeheartedly. As King Solomon said: "The words of the wise, when spoken gently, are heeded,"[48] i.e., when one's words are spoken gently, it is clear that one is wise, and thus one will be heeded.[49]

---

48. Ecclesiastes 9:17. See below, p. 219.

49. In the sefirotic tree, *netzach* is below, and thus is seen to derive from, *chochmah*. Moreover, in the chain of development of the

But here, too, sincerity is paramount; the one giving the instructions must truly recognize and value the other person's intrinsic worth and integrity. If the one to whom directions are given senses that the attitude of the instructor is feigned, his compliance will be forced, at best.[50] It is for this reason that this category of speech follows the previous one, praise.

This degree of *chesed* is termed "loving-kindness within victory" (חֶסֶד שֶׁבְּנֶצַח). The word for "victory" (*netzach*, נֶצַח) also means "conducting" or "supervising" (נִצּוּחַ).

The attribute of *netzach* is associated in Kabbalah with the fourth day of creation, on which G-d created the sun, the moon, and the stars. "And G-d put them in the firmament of the heavens to shine on the earth, to rule over the day and the night, and to separate between the light and the darkness."[51]

We are taught that the celestial bodies possess souls and are aware of both G-d and the affairs of our world.[52] In the natural order ordained by G-d, they control and direct the seasons and affairs of earth, acting as commanders, giving orders and making order.

Nonetheless, they give full autonomy to the earth and its mortal beings. They certainly do not feel they are owed anything, for they are aware that they are no more

---

partzufim, the *netzach* of the higher *partzuf* is vested within the *chochmah* of the lower one.

50. In the context of business management, this idea is elaborated on in ch. 2 of our essay *The Dynamic Corporation*.

51. Genesis 1:17-18.

52. *Mishneh Torah, Yesodei HaTorah* 3:9.

than "a hatchet in the hand of the woodcutter."[53] They are the humble servants of G-d, just as was Moses, the humble leader and commander of the Jewish people.[54]

5 *Words of Gratitude*

After one's request has been fulfilled, care must be taken to express proper gratitude. If this is neglected, the entire deferential tone of the request is undermined and adversarial responses are sure to follow.

Compliance with one's requests should be treated as an unexpected and undeserved gift.[55] Just as one should express gratitude for any other gift—especially if it is *truly* unexpected—so should one articulate appreciation for the fulfillment of one's wishes.

This degree of *chesed* is termed "loving-kindness within thanksgiving" (חֶסֶד שֶׁבְּהוֹד).[56]

---

53. *Zohar* 36a.

54. In Kabbalah, Moses is associated with the *sefirah* of *netzach*.

55. The Hebrew word for "thanksgiving" (הוד) also means "acknowledgment." As implied by its English etymology, acknowledgment depends on knowledge, i.e., recognition that what one has received is a gift. Only after one has truly acknowledged the giver and the gift in his mind and heart can he express his thanks in words.

56. In Kabbalah, the Divine Name which corresponds to the *sefirot* of *netzach* and *hod* is "Hosts" (צבאות), from the root of the word for "army" (צבא). *Netzach* represents the victorious army; *hod* represents the surrendering army, or the power of the victor to bring the other side to surrender. From this we learn that a crucial part of our power to rectify creation (i.e., "subdue" or "conquer" its *a priori* materialism) depends on the rectification of our speech at the levels of

Although sincerity is crucial in all aspects of speech (and character), it is the very essence of expressing thanks,[57] since by giving sincere thanks one authenticates the love that has hopefully underscored the entire communication process. The truest way to ensure sincerity in gratitude is to cultivate one's awareness that none of us is in fact deserving of anything, and that everything we possess or benefit from is a result of G-d's unmitigated kindness.[58]

The attribute of *hod* (הוֹד, "thanksgiving") is associated in Kabbalah with the fifth day of creation, on which G-d created the fish and birds.[59] Here, for the first

---

netzach and *hod*. The Exodus from Egypt, as explained in *Chassidut*, is an ongoing spiritual process and is the archetype for the final exodus from all exiles. When the Jewish people left Egypt, we were referred to as "the hosts of G-d."

57. Of the five categories of speech, the greatest degree of sincerity (תמימות, the inner property of *hod*, see *Sod Hashem Lireiav*, p. 49-50) is reflected here. As explained above, through praise one reveals qualities that are dormant in the soul of the one being praised. These qualities are the soul's "inner lights" (such as wisdom, loving-kindness or mercy). To the extent that one's thanksgiving is sincere, he also reveals an aura of splendor (*hod* also means "splendor"), an encompassing (majestic) light above the acknowledged one. The act of thanksgiving is thus similar to coronation, entailing the total commitment (another implication of *hod*) of the one acknowledging to the one acknowledged.

58. See *Lev LaDa'at* pp. 1-49, and below, ch. 7.

59. Genesis 1:20. Both fish and birds were created from the lower waters, which are referred to in Kabbalah as "the depth below," an appellation of the *sefirah* of *hod* (*Sefer Yetzirah* 1:5, commentary of R. Eliahu of Vilna *ad loc.*; *Kehilat Yaakov* 2:22a; *Tikunei Zohar* 70 [125a]). In the soul, "the depth below" is the state of submission from which one offers sincere thanks to his benefactor.

time, G-d blesses His creation: "And G-d blessed them, saying: 'Be fruitful and multiply and fill the water in the seas, and let the birds multiply on earth.'"[60]

Aside from possessing mobility, the animal kingdom is distinguished from the mineral and vegetable kingdoms by its active consciousness.[61] Our sages teach us that fish and birds possess enough consciousness to experience Divine providence and continuously acknowledge their destiny at His hands.[62] Because the fish and the birds were

---

(In the second account of creation, it is stated [Genesis 2:19] that the birds were created from the earth. Our sages resolve this apparent contradiction by explaining that the birds were created from the swamps, an intermediate state between water and earth [*Chulin* 27b; Rashi on Genesis 2:19].)

60. Genesis 1:22. G-d continued to bless creation on the sixth and seventh days (*ibid.* 1:28, 2:3). In this sense, these two final days can be considered extensions of the fifth. This reflects the principle that the manifestation of the degrees of *chesed* culminates in the fifth emotional attribute, *hod*, and then extends to and includes the final two attributes of *yesod* and *malchut*. See further, p. 162.

61. This is the significance of the term "living being" (נפש חיה), which is first applied to the animal kingdom (Genesis 1:20). Rashi (*ad loc.*) explains this term to mean that animals possess "vitality," which is synonymous in Kabbalah with consciousness.

62. The Talmud (*Chulin* 63a) applies the verse (Psalms 36:7) "Your judgments are in the great deep" to when a bird catches a fish; that is, even a fish is not eaten without being judged. The fact that the fish is judged means that, on some level of consciousness or proto-consciousness, it knows it is being judged. (This judgment does not imply that animals are responsible for their actions, for animals do not possess free will. Nonetheless, G-d judges whether each animal is destined to fulfill its role in creation by living or dying, by consuming—elevating another—or being consumed—being elevated into another.)

capable of recognizing and acknowledging G-d's blessing, He blessed them.

The ability and willingness to receive gratefully is what elicits the gift. The desire to give (or to fulfill requests) is deeply rooted in every individual, since giving and contributing validate one's sense of worth.[63] Someone who feels he has nothing to give may succumb to a sense of worthlessness and lose interest in life. But equally deep-rooted is the revulsion at squandering one's energy. Someone who feels his time and effort are going to waste, or that he is accomplishing nothing with his gifts, may succumb to feelings of frustration and emptiness.[64]

By articulating one's appreciation, therefore, the recipient becomes the giver and the giver the recipient—of validation.[65] Thus validated, the giver is encouraged to give further or comply with additional requests.[66] And so begins an infinite cycle of mutual giving and receiving.[67]

---

63. "More than the calf wants to suck, the cow wants to suckle" (*Pesachim* 112a).

64. Note how this contrasts with the popular notion that there is nothing wrong with "wasting seed." The admonition of not wasting one's G-d-given energies may be considered an extension of the prohibition against wasting in general (בל תשחית, *bal tashchit*).

65. *Hod* (הוד) comes from the word for "echo" (הד). The emotion in giving thanks must echo the inner desire of the giver to receive thanks.

66. This is indicated by the fact that *hod* is the reflection of *chesed*; one gives thanks for acts of kindness. We are also taught that "*binah* extends as far as *hod*" (בינה עד הוד אתפשטת, *Etz Chaim* 29:8), i.e., the final stage of understanding is giving thanks.

This is the mystical meaning of the statement: "One who gives a morsel of bread to a child should inform its mother" (*Shabbat* 10b). Its "mother" (*Ima*) is its consciousness; making one conscious of the fact

In any coupling process, Kabbalah teaches that "the male position is that of *netzach* [command], while the female position is that of *hod* [gratitude]."[68] Thus, in the cycle of continuous giving and receiving, the husband and wife constantly exchange roles.

This is why giving, as it were, looks for appropriate recipients; once an appreciative receiver is found, the gift can be given.[69]

---

that he has received a gift allows him to give thanks and thereby receive more. This is similarly expressed by our sages' statement that "Beloved is man, for he was created in G-d's image; it is an even greater love that it was made known to him that he was created in G-d's image" (*Avot* 3:14).

67. Although vegetation can also reproduce itself *ad infinitum*, this is due to the ongoing presence of the original power of creation *ex nihilo* invested in the earth. Because this original power is less manifest in the animal and human kingdoms, animals and man require G-d's blessing in order to procreate infinitely.

This is similar to the fact that as time progresses, deeper dimensions of the Torah are revealed in order to counter the effect of the waning of the spiritual capacities of the generations (ירידת הדורות).

Whereas the *chesed* of *tiferet* brings forth a latent or dormant quality in another person, the *chesed* of *hod* links it to its source in the infinite, since by thanking the person one is thanking G-d, the true source of the gift.

68. *Sha'ar HaKavanot*, first discourse on *Chanukah*; *Mavo Shearim* 3:1:2, 5:1:1. More than any two other powers of the soul, *netzach* and *hod* act as "marriage" partners. They are compared to the feet, which only enable a person to walk when they function together.

69. "The Holy One, blessed be He, found no vessel that could contain blessing for Israel other than peace, as it is written, 'G-d will give strength to His people; G-d will bless His people with peace' [Psalms 29:11]" (*Uktzin* 3:12).

In order to be successful and fruitful, however, this cycle of giving and receiving requires G-d's blessing.[70] The original and archetypal blessing that G-d bestowed upon creation was the ability to procreate, which in turn implies the drive or instinct to procreate, i.e., the search for and attraction to a mate.[71] Procreation is a mutual relationship of giving and receiving.

According to the Talmud (*Berachot* 60b), a Jew should begin his day by reciting a series of blessings. But since blessing requires a "vessel" of acknowledgment in which to rest, Jewish custom is to recite first the statement "I *thank* You, living and eternal King, for You have kindly restored my soul to me; Your faith is abundant" (*Seder HaYom*, beginning).

70. All human endeavor requires G-d's blessing to be successful. The human effort is no more than the "vessel" which man prepares to receive G-d's blessing.

71. This may be seen from the Talmudic report that when the sexual urge was removed from the world, not only people ceased procreating, but so did the animals (*Yoma* 69b).

In contrast, vegetation is self-propagating and has no consciousness of mating. Thus, G-d did not bless (or need to bless) vegetation by telling it to be fruitful and multiply, since its regeneration is either asexual or occurs through forces outside itself (pollination, etc.). In the Talmudic report just cited, it is not recorded that vegetation ceased to reproduce when the sexual urge was removed.

This difference between animals and plants is also evident in the account of Noah and the flood. When Noah took the animals into the ark in order to recommence life after the flood, he took a male and female of each. (The exception was the ritually pure animals, of which he took seven pairs each in order to sacrifice the extra ones when he emerged from the ark. [Genesis 7:2, 8:20; Rashi *ad loc.*]) This would seem to indicate that in the original creation, too, G-d created each animal as a single male-female couple (although this is said explicitly only with regard to the leviathan [*Bava Batra* 74b; Rashi on Genesis 1:21]), and Noah was following this example. Upon emerging from

Just as G-d is the ultimate source of blessing, so is He the ultimate object of all thanksgiving. Whenever one thanks someone for a gift received or for a favor done, his gratitude should carry the awareness that he owes G-d thanks as well. Sincerely thanking others is in fact a good way to develop a sense of indebtedness to G-d.[72] And as we said, by cultivating awareness of one's indebtedness to G-d, one elicits His blessing. Thus, couples who have not yet been blessed with children should pay particular attention to cultivating this aspect of speech, i.e., acknowledging each other's kindness.

Pure Communication

As we have said, one should be sure to invest adequate time and effort in articulating the above five states of *chesed* in communicating with his spouse. The ultimate goal of communication, however, is not just to forge a courteous or even loving relationship between husband and wife, but to afford them the opportunity to bond and unite with each other. Thus, the aim of rectifying one's speech in accordance with the five categories detailed above is to apply it to the couple's common life together.[73]

---

the ark, G-d commanded the animal-couples to reproduce (Genesis 8:17). Vegetation, in contrast, was initially created *en masse* (see Rashi on Genesis 1:11), and Noah did not take any plants with him into the ark, except for use as food.

72. *Chovot HaLevavot* 3, introduction.

73. Speech is an expression of closeness, while silence is in most cases considered a sign of distance.

It is therefore important for a couple to discuss their separate lives with each other. By taking the time to share at least part of their respective days' experiences, the fact that they lead individual lives can serve to bring them closer together rather than make them feel as though they live in different worlds.[74]

And certainly a couple should discuss the *common* aspects of their lives, such as their shared goals and dreams, the running of their home, the education of their children, and family affairs. For in these areas it is imperative that they not only feel united but act as one as well.

By discussing and sharing these aspects of their lives, a couple progresses from "talking to" and "talking about" to "talking with" each other. The actual act of conversation becomes a binding agent in itself, in addition to a way to initiate or conduct some other activity.[75] Sharing thoughts and feelings is in some ways an even more profound expression of love than saying "I love you."

The previously detailed five aspects of rectified speech serve as the skeletal frame of a couple's communication. As such, speech at this level is an expression of the attribute of *yesod* (יְסוֹד, "foundation"), into which the

---

74. Thus, we are taught that even the narratives in the Torah bind the soul of the one who studies them with G-d's supernal wisdom (see *Tanya*, ch. 4; *Kuntres Acharon* 1). We find that the patriarchs (Genesis 31:4-17) and the sages (*Berachot* 27b) consulted with their wives.

75. See below, ch. 8. Jewish law requires a husband to eat with his wife (*Shulchan Aruch, Even HaEzer* 70:2, gloss of R. Moshe Isserles).

preceding five emotions (from *chesed* to *hod*) flow and coalesce.[76]

Of course, a couple should not let conversation become an end in itself; this is counterproductive. By continuing to talk past the natural conclusion of a discussion, they run the risk of letting their conversation degenerate into overfamiliarity and invasion of each other's privacy, not to mention transgressions of the prohibitions of gossip, slander, tale-bearing, etc., which usually result from overextended conversation. Talking with one's spouse on this level is in fact insulting to her.[77]

---

76. *Yesod* means "foundation." The foundation of a building is the part that connects it to the earth. This *sefirah* is thus where connection, communication and interchange between two parties takes place. Intimate communication is the "secret" of the two parties, hence the connection between the word *yesod* (יסוד) and the word for "secret," *sod* (סוד). Another term for close communication is "secret talk" *sod siach* (סוד שיח).

77. Thus, our sages teach (*Avot* 1:5): "Do not converse excessively with women. This refers [even] to one's wife; how much the more so with another's wife. Hence the sages have declared that whoever converses excessively with women brings evil upon himself, neglects the study of Torah, and will in the end inherit Purgatory." Idle talk is the source of the foreign thoughts that invade one's mind when he is trying to pray or learn Torah (*Torah Or* 102c; see the chapter titled *Shemirat Brit HaLashon* in *Malchut Yisrael*). The classic case of foreign thoughts is thoughts about other women; thus, idle talk with one's wife can bring him to "how much the more so with another's wife."

Rashi (on this passage from *Avot*; see also *Beit HaBechirah ad loc.*) points out that although discussing one's experiences with one's spouse is generally salutary, discussing matters in which they do not share common concern or expertise can be counterproductive. Both these extremes are illustrated in the case of the wife of Korach and the

The archetypal example of this occurred on the sixth day of creation, the day associated in Kabbalah with *yesod*. On the one hand, it was on this day that Adam and Eve first joined in marital relations,[78] which expressed their deep communion and bonding. On the other hand, the events of this day indicated that they had not quite learned how to communicate deeply.

G-d commanded man not to eat the fruit of the tree of knowledge of good and evil.[79] In conveying this to Eve, Adam did not make it clear that G-d had only forbidden them to *eat* the fruit.[80] When the snake asked her what fruits were forbidden to eat, she said it was forbidden even to *touch* the tree of knowledge. Adam had not taken the trouble to communicate with her properly, as would befit a loving spouse. Instead, he conveyed G-d's command vaguely, assuming that this would suffice and spare him the need to discuss the issue at length. This, we

---

wife of On (Numbers 16; *Sanhedrin* 109b). One must therefore carefully assess the readiness and/or capability of his spouse to understand him before engaging in conversation.

According to Kabbalah, as the messianic era approaches, the spiritual stature of women rises. (During the first period of the messianic era, the spiritual status of men and women will be equal; during the second, eternal period, that of women will exceed that of men.) Thus, as we draw closer to the Redemption, husbands can more naturally confide in their wives than was the case in earlier generations.

78. According to Kabbalah as well, *yesod* is closer to *da'at* in essence than are any of the other emotions. *Da'at* is the inner dimension of communication, whereas *yesod* is the act of communication itself.

79. Genesis 2:17.

80. *Or HaChaim* on this passage.

are taught, is why the snake was able to enter into a protracted conversation with Eve and finally seduce her into eating the forbidden fruit. In the end, she seduced Adam to eat as well.[81]

The most profound type of conversation a couple can share, of course, is the Torah they learn, either by discussing what they have learned while apart or by learning together.[82] As is explained in *Chassidut*, when one studies Torah, one is "totally and truly united with the blessed, infinite light [of G-d]"[83] in a "wondrous union, like which there is no other, and which has no parallel anywhere in the material world, whereby complete oneness and unity from every side and aspect can be attained."[84] When husband and wife learn or share Torah knowledge with each other, they participate together in this consummate union with G-d.

By discussing and learning Torah together, a couple becomes part of the ongoing process of revealing G-d's will in this world, which is the purpose in particular of the oral Torah.[85]

---

81. Thus, by improperly "conversing excessively" with his wife, she caused him "to inherit Purgatory."

82. As will be explained below (p. 171), Torah study is in fact a sublime form of kissing.

83. *Tanya*, ch. 23 (29a).

84. *Ibid.*, ch. 5 (9b).

85. The oral Torah is traditionally studied in pairs, each individual challenging the other's understanding until they reach a common ground. This "sparring partnership" is called "the battle of Torah" (*Sanhedrin* 111b), in which each partner plays the role of the other's "helpmate, opposite him." The word for this study-partnership is

The oral study of Torah, and the oral Torah in particular, are identified in Kabbalah with the final attribute, *malchut* (מַלְכוּת, "kingdom"),[86] since, as we said, the chief objective of learning the oral Torah is to understand and adhere to G-d's will. Inasmuch as our study of the oral Torah is an expression of our belief in the integrity of the transmission of G-d's will through our sages, it is here that the twin fires of the "light of the intellect" (the "male fire") and "complete faith" (the "female fire") truly fuse into one.

---

chavruta (חברותא), from the word for "friend" (חבר). As will be explained in ch. 8, husband and wife are intended to be each other's best friends.

The study of the written Torah, in contrast, is a more private endeavor, whereby the individual binds himself to the transcendent aspect of Divinity (see *Torah Or* 57d-58a).

86. *Tikunei Zohar*, introduction (17a). These two arenas of speech, the mundane and the holy, are the two consummations of the preceding five rectifications of speech. Similarly, in Kabbalah, *yesod* and *malchut* are considered the two "seals" of the preceding five *sefirot*. We are thus taught that there are two aspects of rectification (*tikun*). The first is that of the physical and mundane realm, which consists of separating (*birur*) the non-holy from the holy; this is the focus of our attention during the week. The second is that of the spiritual and holy realm, which consists of unifying (*yichud*) things with their source; this is our focus on Shabbat (see below, p. 320, footnote 16). The two, archetypal agents of these two types of *tikun* are *Mashiach* ben Yosef and *Mashiach* ben David, respectively. Joseph personified the faithful provider of the needs of his people; David personified the yearning "to continuously dwell in the House of G-d" (Psalms 27:4). The first type of *tikun* is prerequisite to the second, as our sages say, "He who toils before Shabbat will eat on Shabbat" (*Avodah Zarah* 50a).

Malchut is associated in Kabbalah with the seventh day of creation, Shabbat. Inasmuch as G-d rested on the seventh day from the mundane speech used in creating the world, Shabbat is seen as a day of rest from mundane speech, to be devoted rather to contemplative prayer and the study of the Torah.[87] Shabbat is the ideal time, then, for husband and wife to learn Torah together.[88]

On a yet higher level, the essential holiness of Shabbat cannot be expressed by *any* type of speech.[89] This reminds us that there are levels of communication which speech is unable to express. It is to these levels of communication that we now turn our attention.

Kissing

Rectified speech is essential for a couple to effectively communicate their mutual love and forge a common bond. However, inasmuch as speech presumes a dichotomy of speaker and listener, it can never be more than a means of communication and exchange between two individuals; it cannot express a couple's essential unity. To return to the words of the *Zohar*, "*Da'at* is *hidden*

---

87. See *Kuntres Acharon* 9 (163a).

88. The Torah they learn on weekdays is the projection of Shabbat of that day. See below, p. 319, footnote 13, with reference to how the daily prayers are the projection of Shabbat into the week.

89. See *Y. Shabbat* 15:3. Although we pointed out above (p. 162, footnote 73) that not speaking typically betrays hostility, here we are referring to speech being transcended by deeper, more sublime forms of communication.

within the mouth": speech can convey the five degrees of *chesed* within *da'at,* but *da'at* itself—the sense of true union—is too profound for even rectified speech to convey; it remains forever hidden in the mouth. The sages state further: "the heart cannot reveal [its essence] to the mouth."[90] Even though, as we said above, for speech to be effective it must issue from the heart, it is incapable of expressing the heart's innermost secret.

The most hidden and secret connection between the couple can be expressed only through the kiss.[91] In kissing, both parties simultaneously give and receive;[92] there is no subject-object dichotomy. Whereas speech reflects the revealed connection between husband and wife, kissing manifests their hidden connection, their shared secret.

Above,[93] we noted that when conversing with one's wife, one should preserve a sense of inner connection to her and not allow their conversation to degenerate into extraneous, vapid, and eventually forbidden talk. To this we may now add that one should not converse with one's spouse beyond the point at which soul-to-soul communication flows naturally into kissing; doing so disrupts the

---

90. *Midrash Tehilim* 9:2; *Kohelet Rabbah* 12:10.

91. See *Or HaTorah, Bereishit*, p. 217.

92. See *Etz Chaim* 39. Kissing is intrinsically a double-phenomenon, since it is a simultaneous meeting of two breaths (as opposed to speech, in which the two parties take turns talking). As will be explained later (p. 175), there are two dimensions of kissing. Shabbat, which is also a double-phenomenon (see below, p. 318, footnote 9), is associated with kissing, in contrast to the weekdays, which are associated with speech (p. 317, footnote 9).

93. p. 164.

spontaneous intensification of closeness they have reached.[94] If a couple continue to talk at this point, the energy and intensity their conversation has developed is apt to spill over into undesirable channels.[95]

Still, the inner kiss of the heart can only be manifest to the extent that speech has been rectified and the mouth has been transformed into a channel for the expression of the five degrees of *chesed*. This is why kissing is in general meaningful only after all that should be said has been said, and in an appropriate way. Defective or frustrated communication between spouses can make either or both of them lose their desire to kiss.[96]

---

94. This idea lends an additional level of understanding to our sages' directive not to "converse excessively" with one's wife (see above, p. 164, footnote 77).

95. The more deeply the couple has communicated during the conversation-phase, the more profound will be their experience of union and the less they will need to continue to converse if they progress to kissing and eventually to marital relations. Thus, our sages say that the verse "He declares to man what is his talk" (Amos 4:13) refers to "even the unnecessary conversation between a man and his wife" during marital relations, i.e., beyond what is necessary to establish the proper atmosphere (*Chagigah* 5b; cf. Rabbi Ovadiah of Bartenura, *Commentary on the Mishnah*, *Avot* 1:5).

96. As we saw above (p. 141, footnote 11), the "mouth" (**פה** = 85) equals the combined value of "love" (**אהבה** = 13) and "kindness" (**חסד** = 72).

When the two words for "love" (**אהבה**) and "kindness" (**חסד**) are combined with the word *da'at* (**דעת** = 474), their initials spell **אחד** ("one") and their total numerical value is 559. This number, multiplied by two (reflecting the presence of the love, kindness, and knowledge in the mouths of both husband and wife), equals 1118, the exact numerical value of the *Shema*:

Union with G-d

We see, then, that the mouth possesses two dimensions: its outer dimension conveys and experiences the reality of the spoken word, while its inner dimension conveys and experiences the sublimity of the kiss.

In our relationship with G-d, kissing is the level of union we achieve through the study of the Torah and is contrasted with performing the commandments, through which we are said to embrace G-d.[97]

שְׁמַע יִשְׂרָאֵל יהו־ה אֱלֹהֵינוּ יהו־ה אֶחָד.

Hear O Israel, G-d *is our G-d,* G-d *is One.*

In Kabbalah and *Chassidut,* it is explained that the *Shema* is the affirmation of the "higher unity," the awareness that all creation exists within G-d (יחודא עילאה). This "higher unity" is expressed as the sublime kiss of husband and wife. In contrast, the "lower unity" (יחודא תתאה), G-d's omnipresence within His creation (expressed by the second verse of the *Shema*) corresponds to marital relations.

97. *Tanya,* ch. 45. The Zoharic term for this union is "the clinging of spirit to spirit" (אתדבקות רוחא ברוחא). It is clear from the final sentences of this chapter in the *Tanya* that learning Torah is not termed "kissing" unless it entails concentrated thought. For Torah study to be considered a kiss, there must be a silent level within the speech.

Once one has achieved this union with G-d through Torah-study, however, it may then manifest itself in all the other facets of one's life as well (see *Igeret HaTeshuvah,* ch. 9).

The same three people through whom the Torah was given—Moses, Aaron, and Miriam (*Chidushei Agadot, Meor Einaim,* and *Etz Yosef* to *Shabbat* 88a; cf. *Chulin* 92a)—were those who died by the kiss of G-d (Deuteronomy 34:5; Numbers 33:38 and Rashi *ad loc.; Moed Katan* 28a). Both love and Torah study are likened to death, since they both entail the dissolution of the ego (Song of Songs 8:6; Numbers 19:14, *Berachot* 63b).

By observing the *mitzvot*, the body is transformed into a vehicle by which G-d can express Himself in the world, so to speak, and we can come to emulate G-d through our actions. But through Torah study, the mind is bound, as it were, with the mind of G-d, since the Torah is G-d's will and wisdom. Torah study is therefore a much more profound level of union with G-d than *mitzvah*-observance.[98]

Of course, Torah-study is itself a *mitzvah*. Thus, in Torah study we may observe both aspects of union with G-d: by using the faculty of speech to articulate the Torah's words, the physical body is sanctified, and by using the mind to understand G-d's will and wisdom, the Divine soul clings to and unites with its source.[99]

Torah study	inner union with G-d	kiss
mitzvah observance	external union with G-d	embrace

Rabbi Shimon bar Yochai once asked[100] why G-d didn't create man with two mouths, just as He created him

---

Similarly, when the Jewish people received the Torah at Mt. Sinai, they expired from the ecstatic experience and had to be revived (*Shemot Rabbah* 29:4; *Shir HaShirim Rabbah* 6:3).

98. The advantage and necessity of *mitzvah*-observance lie in the fact that only through it can one sanctify his own body and portion of the physical world, and thus contribute toward fulfilling the purpose of creation (*Tanya*, ch. 38).

99. See *Tanya*, ch. 5.

100. *Y. Berachot* 1:2. Rabbi Shimon bar Yochai was one of "those whose Torah-study is their profession," i.e., who study Torah without interruption. Such people are exempt from interrupting their studies in

with two eyes, two ears, and two nostrils. One mouth could then be used for mundane speech and the other purely for Torah study.

The answer is that G-d intended us to use our faculty of speech solely for Torah study, as it is said: "'And you shall speak of them'[101]—*them,* and not other things."[102] Even when we engage in mundane conversation, it is meant to be infused with holiness,[103] just as the worldly conversation of true Torah scholars is itself considered Torah and to be worthy of study.[104]

True, a Torah scholar's apparently mundane talk issues from the outer dimension of his mouth, while his words of Torah issue from its inner dimension. But since everything he says is infused with Divine inspiration, and he consciously intends to unite the two dimensions of his mouth, the dichotomy between the inner and outer dimensions disappears.

The two dimensions of the mouth are alluded to in G-d's description of His relationship with Moses, the greatest of all prophets: "I speak to him mouth to mouth."[105] The literal meaning of this phrase, of course, is

---

order to pray (*Shabbat* 11a), since Torah study is considered of eternal value, whereas prayer is for the needs of the moment (*ibid.* 10a).

101. Deuteronomy 6:7.

102. *Sifrei ad loc.*

103. See above, p. 139, footnote 7.

104. *Avodah Zarah* 19b. The word "Torah" (תורה) is cognate to the word for "guidance" (הוראה) (*Gur Aryeh,* beginning, quoting Rabbi David Kimchi; *Zohar* 3:53b).

105. Numbers 12:8.

that G-d addressed Moses directly, face to face.[106] Its inner meaning, however, refers to the two dimensions within Moses' mouth: the inner dimension experienced, in total selflessness, the kiss of the Divine Presence, while the outer dimension conveyed G-d's teachings to the people of Israel.[107] By speaking to Moses "mouth to mouth," G-d unified the two dimensions within his mouth. This is the ultimate end for which man was created with one mouth.

Inasmuch as every Jew may and should aspire to the example of Moses,[108] each of us should endeavor to use the power of speech to convey, as far as possible, his ineffable experience of the sublimity of G-d's Presence. And to his

---

106. The epitome of this phenomenon was when "the Divine Presence spoke from the mouth of Moses" (*Zohar* 3:232a). This applies to the book of Deuteronomy, which was received during the last 37 days of Moses' life (*Megilah* 31b; *Likutei Torah* 5:20c; *Likutei Sichot*, vol. 4, p. 1087).

This number (37) is the numerical value of the word for "breath" (הבל), alluding to the G-d's breath which He blew into Adam, giving his lifeless body its soul. Inasmuch as this word is also the Hebrew name of Abel, the soul-root of Moses (*Sha'ar HaGilgulim* 20, etc.), it follows that the "breath" which G-d blew into Adam was in fact the soul of Moses.

107. The average value of the three words of the phrase "mouth to mouth" (פה אל פה = 201) is 67, which equals the word בינה ("understanding"). Our sage state: "Fifty gates of understanding were created in this world; all were given to Moses save one" (*Rosh HaShanah* 21b). This, then, alludes to our interpretation that both mouths of the phrase "mouth to mouth" relate to Moses himself.

108. Hence, the sages of the Talmud occasionally address each other as "Moses" (*Shabbat* 101b; *Sukah* 39a; *Beitzah* 38b; *Chulin* 93a, etc.). According to *Chassidut* (*Tanya*, ch. 42), there is a reflection of Moses' soul in the soul of every Jew by virtue of which every Jew may know G-d through meditation.

spouse, his rectified speech should convey as much as possible of the shared secret of their kiss.

The Kiss of the Future

The Song of Songs, the most sacred of the Hagiographa[109] and the Divine parable for the love between G-d and Israel, begins its imagery with the delight of the kiss:

שִׁיר הַשִּׁירִים אֲשֶׁר לִשְׁלֹמֹה:
יִשָּׁקֵנִי מִנְּשִׁיקוֹת פִּיהוּ,
כִּי טוֹבִים דֹּדֶיךָ מִיָּיִן.

The song of songs, of Solomon:
May He kiss me with the kisses of His mouth,
for Your affection is better than wine.[110]

According to Rashi,[111] the affection referred to in this verse is the Jewish people's experience of receiving the Torah, and the longed-for kiss is the experience of the future revelation of its inner dimension:

> [The Jewish people say of G-d:] "Would that He kiss me with the kisses of His mouth, as He did once!"... For He gave them His Torah and spoke with them face to face, and [the

---

109. *Yadaim* 3:5.
110. Song of Songs 1:2.
111. *ad loc.*

> memory of] this display of affection is still more pleasing to them than any worldly delight [symbolized by wine]. They have been promised that He will appear to them again to reveal its secret meanings and hidden mysteries, and they entreat Him to fulfill His word. This is the meaning of "*may* [in the future tense] He kiss me with the kisses of His mouth."

The simple meaning of this passage, then, is that the memory of receiving the Torah is dearer to the Jewish people than any worldly pleasure, and this makes us yearn for the revelation of its inner dimensions.[112]

---

112. Although the inner dimension of the Torah was given at Mt. Sinai together with the rest of the Torah, it was communicated cryptically, and the study of what little of it that was revealed was confined to the spiritual elite of each generation. As history progresses toward its messianic fulfillment, more and more of this dimension of the Torah has been revealed and publicized, but the fullness of its revelation awaits the advent of *Mashiach*.

Thus, Rabbi Shneur Zalman of Liadi said that although there will be another exodus and redemption from exile, "there will not be another giving of the Torah." The Torah that *Mashiach* will reveal is contained, though hidden, within the Torah of the present.

Nonetheless, since the Torah that *Mashiach* will reveal transcends whatever will have been revealed until then, "the Torah of this world is considered vanity relative to the new dimension of the Torah that *Mashiach* will reveal" (*Kohelet Rabbah* 11:8).

The original and future revelations of the Torah are alluded to in the word for "affections" (דדיך, in the plural). The full spelling of the word for "affection" (דוד) is the same as that of "David" (דוד), and thus the word "affections" alludes to the two Davids: the original

affection	future kiss	future revelation of inner dimension of the Torah
	past kiss	experience of receiving the Torah at Mt. Sinai
wine		worldly delights

Although we have identified Torah study in general with kissing, this passage indicates that a more sublime kiss associated with the future revelation of Torah will occur in the messianic era.

Relative to this future kiss, today's Torah study is not considered a kiss at all. Indeed, according to the deeper understanding of this verse, "wine" refers not to the mundane pleasures of this world but to the Divine pleasure of studying the Torah[113] and meditating on its secrets, idiomatically referred to as "drinking the wine of the Torah."[114] Understood in this light, this verse describes how we yearn for G-d's future kiss—the revelation of the

---

King David and his consummate descendent, *Mashiach*. Inasmuch as the five books of the Psalms are said to parallel and express the emotional dimension of the five books of Moses, King David here represents the original revelation of the Torah, and *Mashiach* its future revelation. Since the coming revelation will be infinitely more sublime than its present revelation, King David is referred to in this context as a viceroy and *Mashiach* as a full king (*Sanhedrin* 98b).

113. "'Wine' refers to the Torah" (*Midrash Tanchuma, Vayechi* 10; *Tana d'vei Eliahu Zuta* 14; see *Sifrei, Eikev* 48; *Shir HaShirim Rabbah* 1, *s.v. Ki Tovim Dodecha* 3).

114. *Avodah Zarah* 35a; *Vayikra Rabbah* 30:1, etc. The term "the wine of Torah" is applied by Rabbi Shneur Zalman of Liadi to the commentary of Rashi on the Torah, which is a digest of the teachings of the sages (*Sefer HaSichot 5696-5700*, p. 197; *HaYom Yom*, 29 *Shevat*). The numerical value of the word for "wine" (יין) is 70, alluding to the seventy facets of Torah interpretation (*Bamidbar Rabbah* 13:15-16).

inner dimension of the Torah—because we know it will be infinitely more sublime than even the "wine" of its present manifestation.

		basic understanding	deeper understanding
affection	future kiss	future revelation of inner dimension of the Torah	future revelation of inner dimension of the Torah
	past kiss	experience of receiving the Torah at Mt. Sinai	experience of receiving the Torah at Mt. Sinai
wine		worldly delights	study of the Torah

True, it is said that "when wine enters, the secret is revealed."[115] Thus, there is a secret that is revealed through drinking wine—by learning the Torah of this world: the essential connection between G-d and the Jewish people. When learning Torah, one subliminally senses or "hears" G-d "whispering" the secrets of His love. There is a level of love, however, that remains too sublime to be expressed even in this way but which will be communicated through the future kiss.[116] Relative to the secret revealed by the wine of Torah, the secret revealed by this future kiss is called the "secret of secrets."[117]

---

115. *Eiruvin* 65a; *Midrash Tanchuma, Shemini* 5; *Zohar* 3:39a.

116. The expressible secret is likened to wine, whereas the inexpressible secret of secrets is compared to oil. Pure olive oil symbolizes the revelation of *Mashiach*, the kiss of the future (see above, p. 80, footnote 10).

117. The "secret" of G-d's love for the Jewish people which is communicated through learning Torah is "a love which is dependent on something" (*Avot* 5:16), i.e., dependent on the observance of Torah and *mitzvot*. When the Jew learns Torah and fulfills G-d's command-

The phrase "the heart cannot reveal [its essence] to the mouth" is said with reference to the appointed time of the coming of *Mashiach*. G-d Himself, as it were, cannot yet articulate the innermost desire of His heart, the consummation of reality as His "dwelling place," which will come to pass when *Mashiach* comes.[118] The Torah revealed to us in this world is G-d's instructions regarding how the world should be run, His secret dream of the perfect world that he shares with us. The future revelation of the Torah—its "secret meanings and hidden mysteries"—is the reasons *behind* these instructions, G-d's innermost desires that motivated Him to create the world.

Understood in this light, the verse now can be read: "May He send us *Mashiach*, who will reveal the inner dimension of the Torah, for we value this revelation more than the pleasure of learning the Torah of this world, even though this does allow us to sense something of His love."

---

ments, he senses the aspect of G-d's love for him that is based on this obedience.

The "secret of secrets," however, is G-d's love for the Jewish people "that is not dependent on anything" (*ibid.*), i.e., He and we are inextricably, existentially bound to each other, and He, so to speak, cannot live without us. This is His motivation in desiring "a dwelling place in the lower worlds." This "secret of secrets" cannot be communicated in this world because it would undermine man's free choice and its resultant reward and punishment. The exceptions to this are the forefathers, "who were given a taste of the future world in their lifetimes" (*Bava Batra* 16b-17a), and, as will be explained presently, one who studies the inner dimension of the Torah.

118. Of which Rabbi Shneur Zalman of Liadi said: "One cannot question a desire" (*Or HaTorah, Bamidbar*, p. 997; *Sefer HaMa'amarim 5666*, p. 7).

With the advent of *Mashiach*, the kiss of the present will become the spoken word of the future; G-d will "articulate" His kiss. When the "secret meanings and hidden mysteries" of the Torah are revealed, the kisses of this world, which convey a depth of connection inexpressible in words, will become the words of that world.

In a similar vein, we are taught that Moses is "both the first and the final redeemer."[119] Although in his first incarnation, as G-d's chosen agent to reveal the Torah, his outer mouth expressed his inner mouth (as we described above), what was revealed to the Jewish people was primarily the explicit words of the Torah, his outer mouth. In his final incarnation as the redeemer of Israel, he shall reveal the "new Torah." He will "speak" exclusively from his inner mouth and reveal to Israel the infinite delights of the kisses of G-d.

Our sages teach us that the Torah of this world is considered vanity relative to the dimension of the Torah

---

119. See *Shemot Rabbah* 4:2; *Zohar* 1:253a; *Sha'ar HaPesukim, Vayechi*. This is alluded to in the verse (Ecclesiastes 1:9): "That which was shall be" (מה שהיה הוא שיהיה), where the name "Moses" (משה) appears as the initial letters of the first three words. The word "that" (מה, which also means "what" and implies an inner state of selflessness) refers in particular to Moses, who said about himself and his brother Aaron, "What [מה] are we?" (Exodus 16:7, 8). When Moses was born (and not yet named) he was called "he" (הוא): "And she [i.e., his mother Jochebed] saw him that *he* was good" (*ibid.* 2:2). Thus, we may infer from the phrase "*that* which was, it [*he*] shall be," that in his first incarnation, Moses primarily revealed the level of מה (מה שהיה), whereas in his final incarnation, as *Mashiach*, he will reveal the absolute source of his soul, the concealed "third person" הוא (הוא שיהיה), which shined at the moment of his birth. See *Teshuvat HaShanah*, ch. 22.

that *Mashiach* will reveal.[120] Just as the worldly conversation of a Torah scholar is considered mundane relative to his words of Torah study, so will his study of the Torah in this world be considered mundane relative to the Torah insights he will receive and reveal with the coming of *Mashiach*. As we hear the new dimension of the Torah being spoken by *Mashiach*, each and every one of us will be touched by the kiss of G-d.

As part of the Shabbat preparations, it is customary to taste the Shabbat food on Friday afternoon.[121] Similarly, *Chassidut* is the foretaste of the dimension of the Torah that will be revealed in the messianic future, which is likened to Shabbat.[122] By studying *Chassidut*, one becomes privy to "the secret of secrets," a foretaste of G-d's future kiss. Inasmuch as this kiss is the secret of G-d's ineffable vision

---

120. *Kohelet Rabbah* 11:8. This follows the general principle in Kabbalah that all levels of revealed reality are essentially relative in nature (see *Rechovot HaNahar*, the introduction to *Nahar Shalom*). If even apparently antithetical entities (such as *tohu* and *tikun*, as explained there) are relative, non-antithetical entities (such as the Torah of this world and the Torah of the world to come) are surely relative.

What this implies is that once a relativity is established between two concepts—even non-antithetical ones—they may be considered antithetical. Each concept thus serves to bring the other into bold conceptual relief, as it serves as its theoretical, abstract negation.

121. *Magen Avraham* to *Shulchan Aruch, Orach Chaim* 250:1:1; *Sha'ar HaKavanot* 62b (vol. 2, p. 26 in Brandwein ed.).

122. *Sanhedrin* 97a.

for the world, learning *Chassidut* increases one's sensitivity to and awareness of the imminent coming of *Mashiach.*[123]

We have thus identified five progressive levels of the revelation of the Torah, all of which are part word, part kiss. As the revelation of the Torah proceeds, the "word," originally in the foreground, recedes as the "kiss" comes to the fore; the nature of the revelation progresses from speech to kiss. In the beginning, when the Torah was first given, the word was heard while the kiss was hidden; in the future, the kiss will be fully revealed and overshadow the word.[124]

level of Torah study	speech/kiss continuum
the future revelation of the Torah	the future kiss
Chassidut, the taste of the future revelation of the Torah	foretaste of the future kiss
the wine of the Torah in this world	the kiss of this world, awareness of G-d's love for the Jewish people within the words of the Torah
the Torah we study in this world	speech
the experience of the giving of the Torah on Mt. Sinai	the "former kiss" the Jewish people remembers; Moses spoke with both dimensions but we heard primarily the outer dimension, speech

123. The teachings of *Chassidut* were originally conceived as the most potent way of hastening the messianic redemption (letter of the Ba'al Shem Tov, printed in *Ben Porat Yosef* 127b; *Keter Shem Tov* 1).

124. This accords with our understanding (above, p. 169) of our sages' direction not to "engage in excessive conversation with one's wife"—the "wife" being here the Jewish people.

Additional Note

to page 149.

Taking physical beauty to comprise "beautiful form" and "beautiful appearance" (as in footnote 34, above), we have thus four types of physical praise. These may be corresponded to the four letters of the Name *Havayah*, as follows:

"Beautiful appearance," the more spiritual aspect of the physical body, which is dependent on *chochmah*, corresponds to the *yud* of the Name *Havayah*.

"Beautiful form," referring to the shape and proportion of the limbs, corresponds to the first *hei* of the Name *Havayah*, since it signifies *binah*, which gives form to the seminal point of *chochmah*.

Beautiful clothing corresponds to the *vav* of the Name *Havayah*, since it corresponds to the emotional attributes. These are known in Hebrew as the *midot* (מדות), which literally means "measures," since (1) one's emotions are a direct result of and proportionate to his intellect, and (2) they "clothe" and express it precisely (i.e., they are "tailored" to fit it perfectly). The word מדה itself is used (in the masculine form מד) to mean "clothing" (e.g. Leviticus 6:3, etc.).

Prowess in housekeeping corresponds to the latter *hei* of the Name *Havayah*, since this letter corresponds to *malchut*, the domain of the king and queen. Housekeeping includes cooking, interior decorating, and providing for one's family in general.

י	*yud*	*chochmah*	"beautiful appearance"
ה	*hei*	*binah*	"beautiful form"
ו	*vav*	*midot*	clothing
ה	*hei*	*malchut*	housekeeping, providing

7

Humility

The Basis of Humility

The key to improving one's character, and in particular to reducing one's tendency to get angry,[1] is to recognize one's own existential lowliness.[2]

This does not mean to imply that one should not recognize his own self-worth. Every Jew possesses a unique Divine soul, complete with a full array of the most sublime and noble capacities of intellect and emotion, and this fact itself endows him with inestimable potential and worth.[3]

---

1. See the end of *Igeret HaTeshuvah.*

2. This is a fundamental teaching of the Ba'al Shem Tov and his disciples.

3. See *Hayom Yom,* 17 *Iyar* in the name of the Ba'al Shem Tov, and above, p. 151, footnote 43.

In the opening chapters of the *Tanya,* before Rabbi Shneur Zalman of Liadi outlines the essentials of a Jew's service of G-d, he describes the resources with which a Jew is to undertake this service: the nature of his Divine soul and its powers of intellect and emotion.

Yet, the very awareness of our own great worth paradoxically makes us painfully aware of how dismally we betray it. In fact, the more one appreciates the exalted nature of his Divine soul, the more his own self-estimation plummets when measured against the record of his faithfulness to it.

The archetypal figure of humility is Moses: "And Moses was the humblest man on the face of the earth."[4] But surely Moses knew that he was chosen by G-d to receive the most intimate communications with Him that any mortal would ever have and to teach the Torah to all Israel for all time. How could he be so humble in spite of this obvious superiority?

The answer given in *Chassidut*[5] is that yes, Moses was quite aware of all this. But he reasoned that his great accomplishments and the favors shown him by G-d were due to the exceptional qualities with which G-d had endowed him; had someone else been granted these same qualities, he would have surely accomplished much more. Reckoning thus, Moses truly considered himself the lowliest of men, despite—and in fact, because of—his greatness.[6]

---

4. Numbers 12:3.

5. *Likutei Sichot*, vol. 1, pp. 278-9.

6. It is important to note that Moses followed this train of thought precisely because he was humble by nature. He did not have to logically and rationally *induce* humility.

With regard to the four general levels of humility: selflessness, humility (the two primary attributes of Moses), submission, and lowliness (the two primary attributes of David), see below, p. 374, footnote 9.

King David also exemplifies the epitome of lowliness. When chastised by his wife Michal for seeming to demean the throne by dancing before the ark of the covenant in view of the maidservants, he said: "I am [and shall remain] lowly in my own eyes."[7]

One's essential shame before G-d is due to the fact that the vast majority of one's thoughts and sensations are void of Divine consciousness. Jewish faith affirms that "there is no space void of Him,"[8] "space" meaning not only physical space but psychological and temporal space as well.[9] Every thought and sensation occupies "space" in one's consciousness. It is our purpose on earth to fill all such space with the awareness of G-d's omnipresence. When we fail to do this, we stand before G-d full of shame,[10] for just as nature abhors a vacuum, the mind cannot remain empty. If it is not filled with holy thoughts, it will be filled with unholy ones.[11]

Just as David personifies the existential lowliness of the Jewish soul, so does Joseph, the archetypal *tzadik*, personify the Jew's ideal state of Divine consciousness, his essential worth. His very presence in the "pit" (the empty

---

7. 2 Samuel 6:22.

8. *Tikunei Zohar* 57 (91b), 70 (122b).

9. See *Sod Hashem Lireiav*, ch. 3.

10. Cf. The liturgy of *Yom Kippur*, "I am before You like a vessel full of shame and embarrassment."

11. The Biblical symbol for the mind not occupied by holy thoughts is the pit into which Joseph's brothers cast him. This pit is described as being "empty, void of water" (Genesis 37:24); our sages comment: "since it was void of water, it was filled with snakes and scorpions" (*Shabbat* 22a).

mind) expels the foreign, unholy thoughts (the snakes and scorpions) that otherwise fill it.

Thus, Joseph and David[12] unite the recognition of essential worth and the awareness of existential lowliness.

The Source of Happiness

When one is aware of his own lowliness, one no longer makes demands on others or expects anything from them; he knows that he deserves nothing.[13] And so with one's relationship to G-d: to the extent that one cultivates true humility, he will demand nothing from G-d and consider the infinite goodness He showers upon him to be undeserved.[14]

---

12. Joseph and David are the two messianic figures in the Torah, and the progenitors of *Mashiach ben Yosef* and *Mashiach ben David*, respectively. Revealing one's own messianic spark, which means identifying and pursuing his unique purpose in life, thus involves a combined consciousness of one's essential worth on the one hand and existential lowliness on the other.

13. This state of consciousness is reflected in the fourth and fifth categories of speech discussed above (p. 143 ff.).

14. As stated in Psalms 16:2: "You do not owe me the goodness that I receive." G-d's bestowing of undeserved goodness is called *chesed chinam* (חסד חנם, "undeserved [literally, 'free'] loving-kindness").

Although one should accustom himself to ask G-d for all his needs, thus acknowledging that He is the source of all material and spiritual beneficence (*Mishneh Torah, Tefilah* 1:2), this should be done as a request rather than a demand.

This humility was exemplified by our patriarch Jacob. When he was about to confront his brother Esau after having fled from him thirty four years previously, he prayed to G-d for protection, saying: "I have been humbled by all the loving-kindness and truth which You have done with your servant."[15] He felt that whatever merits he might have possessed had been more than exhausted by the infinite kindness G-d had already bestowed upon him.[16]

The Torah states that this attitude is intrinsic to the Jewish people: the more goodness we receive, the humbler we become.[17] In contrast, one characteristic of an evil person

---

While one should strive to recognize that all he receives in life is due to G-d's *chesed chinam*, G-d, on His part, wishes to give man a sense of achievement in order that he not experience the reward for his good deeds as "the bread of shame" (the shame of one who receives an undeserved gift). See above, p. 84, footnote 20, and *Lev LaDa'at*, pp. 1-49.

15. Genesis 32:11.

16. Rashi *ad loc.* In the course of one's Divine service, one first becomes aware that G-d's benevolence toward him infinitely exceeds his merits. Higher than this is the awareness that his achievements and merits themselves can in fact only be ascribed to the benevolence of G-d (see above, footnote 14), and that all he receives is thus a gift from G-d's *chesed chinam*.

17. "You are the least of all peoples" (Deuteronomy 7:7)—"for you [by your very nature] are continually diminishing yourselves, as Abraham did when he said 'For I am dust and ashes' [Genesis 28:27], and as Moses and Aaron did when they asked: 'What are we?' [Exodus 16:7]..." (Rashi *ad loc.*).

The initial letters of the phrase **טובתי בל עליך** ("You do not owe me the goodness that I receive," quoted above in footnote 14) spell **טבע**, "nature." It is the Jew's true nature to feel that he is continually receiving undeserved kindness from G-d. If one's materialistic ego appears to have become his true nature, he must work on himself until he regains his original orientation.

is that success and prosperity inflate his ego, since his self-reinforcing conceit convinces him that all his accomplishments and fortune are due to his own efforts or merits.[18]

Conversely, when seemingly bad things happen, a lowly person will immediately assume full responsibility, and recognize that G-d is causing him to suffer in order to effect atonement for his sins.[19]

Releasing all one's demands on G-d and man on the one hand, and accepting full blame for misfortune on the other, spare one the pain of being hurt or offended in life. Anger and depression result from the belief that one really deserves better in this world and that his assumed right to gratification is being infringed.[20] The proper attitudes, in

---

Furthermore, the final letters of this phrase, טובתי בל עליך, spell (backwards) **כלי**, "vessel." This essential Jewish lowliness and unworthiness is the ultimate vessel for receiving blessing.

The *Mishnah* concludes with the statement that the vessel for G-d's blessing is peace: "The Holy One, blessed be He, found no vessel capable of holding [His] blessing for Israel other than peace, as it is said: 'G-d will give His people might; G-d will bless His people with ["*in*"] peace' [Psalms 29:11]."

In *Chassidut*, we are taught that true peace between people depends on their existential lowliness. See *Sod HaShem Lireiav*, ch. 33.

18. See *Igeret HaKodesh* 2.

19. See *Igeret HaTeshuvah*, ch. 11. This attitude supplements our basic belief in Divine providence and goodness, which imply that nothing "bad" ever really happens anyway; everything is ultimately for the good. (See *Igeret HaKodesh* 11.)

20. In Hebrew, the word for indignant "insistence" on rights is **הקפדה**. Its numerical value (194) equals that of the word for "righteousness" (**צדק**), here taken in the sense of "self-righteousness" or "self-justification."

contrast, enable one to be sincerely and continuously happy and optimistic.[21]

True and Illusory Humility

The humility we have just described should not be confused with the unfortunately common psychological pitfalls of self-deprecation and poor self-image. These result from desensitization to spirituality, in which one

---

Self-justification originates in the very root of man's unrefined character. In fact, it derives from one's innate egocentricity, one's love of and concern with oneself alone, and it is referred to in *Chassidut* as "the enemy disguised as the ally" (see *K'lalei HaChinuch veHaHadrachah*, ch. 3).

The root of the word הקפדה is קפד. In Biblical Hebrew, a קפוד (from this root) is a bird of prey (see Isaiah 34:11); in later Hebrew, a "porcupine." Just as a porcupine's quills repel anything that happens to trespass on his domain, so does an indignant individual "prick" all those around him (see *Sefer HaMa'amarim 5659*, p. 56 ff. [*Kuntres Hechaltzu*, ch. 4]).

The rectification and transformation ("sweetening") of הקפדה is the reorientation from being sensitive and demanding of one's own rights to being sensitive to and feeling responsible for the rights of others—particularly the rights of one's spouse. The root **קפד** thus permutes to spell **פקד** ("to remember," usually in the sense of remembering one for the sake of redeeming him, and specifically "remembering" one's wife's conjugal rights) and **דפק** ("pulse" or "knock"). "The voice of my beloved knocks" (Song of Songs 5:2), exciting me with anticipation of his coming to "redeem" me in love.

21. This optimism does not, of course, imply denial of the gravity of evil or suffering. On the contrary, it is an effective means of either attacking it indirectly, or preserving one's confidence while dealing with it directly.

loses one's connection to his Divine soul or allows it to become weakened. The less one identifies with his Divine soul, the more one focuses on his animal nature, which he correctly perceives to be a complex labyrinth of base urges and drives. When this happens, a deep depression grips his consciousness and lends a subtle sense of desperation to everyday life. This desperation can manifest itself in various ways.

The obvious cure for poor self-esteem, then, is to simply redouble one's efforts to and realign one's consciousness with his Divine soul.

The cultivation of proper self-esteem balanced by proper humility is one of the main challenges parents face in raising their children. To a lesser but nonetheless significant extent, friends, business associates, and of course, spouses, can also either undermine or reinforce both one's proper self-image and one's sense of humility.

In view of the importance of humility in one's relationships to his fellow man and to G-d, it is essential to cultivate it continuously.

With regard to marriage: when there is conflict between husband and wife, each should consider himself the primary cause of the difficulty, as explained above.[22] If this does not suffice to resolve the problem, one's next thought should be: "What makes me think that I deserve to be treated any better?" One should remember that everything one has is an undeserved gift from G-d, and

---

22. See above, pp. 94-96.

that this includes one's spouse and children, along with all one's material and spiritual possessions.[23]

23. Even while in a fit of temper (having been taken over by his evil inclination), one should nonetheless try to remember his innate love for G-d. This is the meaning of our sages' statement (*Berachot* 54a) that the commandment to love G-d "with all your heart" (Deuteronomy 6:5) means "with both your inclinations." Thereby he will calm his anger and begin to rectify his emotions in general (Maimonides, *Commentary on the Mishnah, Berachot* 9).

8

Trusted Friends

Sharing

Of course, spouses must learn not only how to avoid conflict but how to be each other's truest friends. They must be able to approach one another with their most intimate thoughts, hopes, and fears, and be assured they will find an open ear and heart.[1]

This includes sharing their weaknesses and faults with each other. Although most people are loath to bare the less appealing aspects of themselves to anyone, least of all their spouse, it is here that the depth of a couple's relationship and their ability to understand each other is truly shown.

Anxiety about sharing private and personal concerns generally stems from insecurity. One fears that an honest revelation of facts and feelings will be met by rejection or loss of respect, or perhaps be used against him later. Ironically, such fear and insecurity actually results from an

1. Cf. *Mishlei Yisrael* 588: "A good wife is one's good friend."

exaggerated ego; one is so concerned about one's self-image[2] that he is reluctant to endanger it by exposing weaknesses or shortcomings. His inferiority complex is a result of a deeper superiority complex. If he were not so protective of his ego, he could afford the openness that allows true intimacy to develop between spouses.

This is particularly true with concerns about marital relations: sharing insecurities with one's spouse reflects the depth of the relationship. When sensual gratification is the sole basis of the couple's bond, any exposure of weakness regarding one spouse's ability to satisfy the other potentially undermines the whole relationship. The other partner could justifiably withdraw rather than support and encourage his troubled spouse.

But when a husband and wife are good and trusted friends, there is nothing to fear from self-disclosure. Either can confide knowing that the other will be accepting and offer loving counsel. In such a context, one can view one's weaknesses as challenges dealt him by Divine providence rather than as threats to his self-image and integrity.[3]

---

2. His extended "body." As explained in *Tanya*, ch. 32, in order to properly fulfill the commandment to love one's fellow, one must learn to emphasize his soul over his body; this allows him to transcend the limitations of the body, which separate people from each other. The Lubavitcher Rebbe (address of *Shabbat VaYakhel Pikudei* 5724, cited in *Tanya b'Tzeiruf Ma'arei Mekomot*, vol. 2, p. 612) explains that, in addition to one's physical body, "body" here also means one's self-image.

3. Nonetheless, a husband should recognize that his wife, by virtue of her innate modesty, is naturally more reticent in disclosing her innermost feelings. See below, p. 337.

In truth, sexual dysfunction should never be viewed as a personal shortcoming but rather as a reflection of Divine providence—and related to accordingly. Man's greatest test is not to fall into the trap of thinking that "my own strength and the power of my own hand has accomplished this."[4] This is true for all one's gifts, including one's sexual prowess.[5] One must always remember that "He is the one who grants you strength to succeed."[6]

In fact, the first and only declaration of manifest Divine providence in the Torah is when Rebecca's family exclaimed about her match with Isaac: "The matter has issued from G-d!"[7] Based on this, we are taught that the greatest revelation of Divine providence involves meeting one's spouse-to-be, as well as all subsequent aspects of marriage and its fruition, childbearing.[8]

It is thus no coincidence that the founders of Judaism, the patriarchs and matriarchs, were almost all barren for many years.[9] At this inceptive phase of the Jewish psyche, G-d needed to instill in our forefathers the awareness that sexual prowess is a Divine gift, in order that it be inherited by their progeny. He desired their

---

4. Deuteronomy 8:17.

5. Sexual prowess is rooted in the *sefirah* of *yesod* ("foundation"), and is the fundamental source of all one's strength and power.

6. *Ibid.*, 8:18. The idiom "*strength* to succeed" (as well as the phrase "my *strength*...has accrued all this success for me" in the previous verse) implies sexual prowess.

7. Genesis 24:50.

8. See additional note at the end of this chapter (p. 206).

9. Abraham, until the age of eighty-six; Sarah, until the age of ninety; Isaac and Rebecca, for twenty years; Rachel, for six years.

heartfelt prayers for children,[10] for with each and every prayer they reached new depths of faith in their Creator and His providence.

In light of the above, we see that a couple need not be afraid to discuss the physical aspects of their married life with each other.

This does not mean that the natural inhibitions of modesty and embarrassment should be at all abrogated. To be sure, if one's embarrassment stems from his self-consciousness, it is just a manifestation of the ego and can be the source of many varieties of sexual complexes. This type of embarrassment or shame is detrimental and should be shunned.

But embarrassment that stems from the fear of profaning the sacredness of life in general or one's marital relationship with his spouse in particular is both healthy and wholesome.[11] By articulating an idea, one is implying

---

10. *Yevamot* 64a. The word for "prayer" itself, **תפלה**, equals 515, the combined value of **יצחק** and **רבקה**. See above, p. 113, footnote 10, and below, footnote 8.

11. Adam and Eve originally engaged in marital relations "and were not ashamed" (Genesis 2:25). Once they ate of the tree of knowledge of good and evil, however, they became ashamed of their nakedness and clothed themselves. However, by having partaken of the fruit of the tree of knowledge of good and evil, their consciousness in general and sense of shame in particular became primarily based on feelings of self-consciousness and ego. The rectification of the primordial sin may thus be conceived as the rectification of shame, extricating proper shame and embarrassment from its egocentric adulteration.

Before the giving of the Torah, the Jewish people possessed the attributes of mercy (רחמנים) and generosity (גומלי חסדים) but not shame (ביישנים). In fact, they were known as "the most impudent of

that it can in fact be fully articulated; talking about the more sublime aspects of life therefore entails the risk of implying that they embrace no higher, ineffable dimension. A couple must therefore strive to weigh the advantages of self-disclosure and candidness against the risk of loss of mystery and modesty they entail.[12]

In addition, one should avoid focusing on weaknesses, especially out of bitterness,[13] lest one become ob-

---

the peoples" (עזים שבאומות). Only when the Torah was given did they acquire an innate sense of shame, which mellowed their impudence. This is alluded to by the verse in which Moses describes the purpose of the Divine revelation of the giving of the Torah (Exodus 20:17): "so that the fear of G-d be upon your faces." Our sages teach: "This [fear of G-d] refers to shame" (*Nedarim* 20a). According to *Chassidut*, shame is the most inward form of fear, as alluded to in the expression "upon your faces" (על פניכם), which may be read, "in your innermost being" (פנימיותכם). The term "shameful fear" (**ירא בשת**) is a permutation of the first word of the Torah (**בראשית**), indicating that acquiring this fear is the inner purpose for which the Torah was given.

We will later contrast modesty (צניעות, *tzeniut*), the more instinctive, natural state of selflessness, with humility (ענוה, *anavah*), the actively imposed state of selflessness. Shame (בושה, *bushah*) is an intermediate state between these two, in which one oscillates between the self-awareness which necessitates humility and the true selflessness which characterizes modesty. When one falls out of selflessness back into self-awareness, the impression of the awareness of G-d he experienced in his state of true selflessness transforms his sense of self-awareness into an experience of existential embarrassment, the state of "shameful fear" (ירא בשת) described above.

12. Hence the importance of the use of euphemism and metaphor in discussing marital relations. Avoiding explicitness (as far as possible) serves to preserve the sense of transcendence and holiness of the subject, and avoids debasing it.

13. One's ability to so refrain depends upon his state of lowliness, as explained in the previous chapter.

sessed with them. Exaggerated concern about shortcomings betrays a lack of faith in G-d's constant goodness. One must never forget that "all that the All-merciful does, He does for the best,"[14] even if we are presently unable to see the good within the apparent bad. If he is able, one should endeavor to look so deeply into the apparent bad that he actually sees its hidden core of good, so that he can say: "*everything* is indeed for the best."[15]

The Mind and the Heart

The fact that a couple's relationship is intended to be based mainly on their spiritual bond of true friendship and only secondarily on their physical bond is alluded to in the famous statement of the *Zohar*:[16] "the mind rules the heart."

In the imagery of Torah, the terms "mind" and "heart" often allude to heaven and earth, i.e., the spiritual and physical realms, respectively. Thus, in the above statement, "the mind" signifies the power to relate to another person on the spiritual plane, as a sensitive, loving friend, while "the heart" signifies one's innate emotional makeup motivated by physical attraction or repulsion.

Thus, a happy marriage is one in which "the mind rules the heart." The couple's friendship and spiritual bond takes precedent over their physical relationship. This

14. *Berachot* 60b.

15. *Ta'anit* 21a.

16. 3:224a, in *Ra'aya Mehemna*.

does not mean that the mind negates the heart's feelings, but rather that it matures and refines them so they reflect the sensitivity of the mind.[17]

Nonetheless, we are taught in *Chassidut* that this is just the beginning. After having reached the level at which "the mind rules the heart," a couple may strive to realize even higher orders in their union and service of G-d. The first of these is the level where "the inner dimension of the heart rules the mind."[18]

The reason the mind must generally rule the heart is that the unrectified heart embodies all the egocentric perversions of the unrectified imagination. The physical extremes of lust and repulsion spouses may feel for each other may thus in many cases be the result of less than holy factors. The inner dimension of the heart, however, is that part of the heart that has not been sullied by the descent of consciousness into the unrectified imagination; it is the emotions as they exist in one's soul-root, where the couple are one, united essence. At this level, the physical attraction of the spouses has been divested of all the negative appurtenances of the unrectified imagination and simply expresses their natural affinity for each other. This level of consciousness, when it is reached, may be allowed to "rule the mind": the rectified physical attraction between the spouses can and should enhance and intensify their spiritual relationship, making them even closer, truer friends.

---

17. See further, p. 332 ff. regarding the elevation of profane thoughts.

18. See *Likutei Torah* 54d.

Still, although this level of consciousness derives from the couple's intrinsic unity in their common soul-root, it is expressed in their mutual attraction as separate individuals. Higher than this level, therefore, is that at which "the inner dimension of the mind rules the inner dimension of the heart."[19] The inner dimension of the mind is the consciousness of the essential unity of the couple as one, undifferentiated entity. This level, once reached, "rules" the inner dimension of the heart: it informs the couple's physical attraction for each other with a sense of underlying unity, which in turn imparts to it the permanence and eternity characteristic of an essential bond.

In the creation story, Adam and Eve are said to personify the mind and the heart.[20] After they ate the forbidden fruit, Eve was told that "[Adam] shall rule over you."[21] Thus, man's dominance over woman is not an intrinsic condition of creation but rather a circumstance of the exile, the present state of our world, which resulted from the primordial sin and the expulsion from Eden. Only during the present order must the mind descend to the heart in order to rule and rectify it. The couple's

---

19. See *Besha'ah Shehikdimu*, pp. 90, 328.

20. *Moreh Nevuchim* 2:30. This may be understood as well from the fact that *chochmah* is associated with man (Ecclesiastes 8:1: "the *chochmah* of a *man* radiates in his face") and *binah* with woman (*Nidah* 45b: "an extra measure of *binah* was given to woman beyond that accorded to man"), and that *binah* is called "the heart" (*Tikunei Zohar*, introduction [17a]).

21. Genesis 3:16.

spiritual friendship must oversee and steer their unrectified physical passion towards refinement.[22]

In the messianic future, however, it will be once again revealed that "a woman of valor is the *crown* of her husband." The inner dimension of the heart will rule the mind, and the unmitigated joy of pure, unsullied attraction will overtake and steer the mental dimension of the couple's relationship.

But this itself will be penultimate to the highest level, in which the inner dimension of the mind will rule the inner dimension of the heart. The essential blessing of the curse of the garden of Eden will be revealed,[23] and the intrinsic unity and absolute friendship of the couple will overtake and continuously elevate the joy of marital relations.

The initial state, in which "the mind rules the heart," is the nature of the Jew's service of G-d during the workweek, when he experiences his exile from the garden of Eden. Though all Divine service should be performed with joy,[24] the joy of the weekday service of G-d is by its very nature relatively constrained due to the necessity of

---

22. This is another way of understanding the statement of our sages: "come down a step and marry a wife" (*Yevamot* 63a; see above, p. 3, footnote 9). The mind ruling the heart is the level of the *beinoni* (see above, p. 85 ff.).

23. It is axiomatic in Chassidic thought that every curse is simply a blessing of such a high order that the goodness it contains cannot be absorbed in the context of the limited spiritual level of our fallen world. Only in the future—or in moments of exceptional spirituality in the present—can a curse's true goodness be revealed (*Keter Shem Tov* 87; *Likutei Torah* 2:48a, etc.).

24. As is said: "Serve G-d with joy" (Psalms 100:2).

constantly contending with the negative forces of unrectified reality.

In contrast, the festivals are marked by the experience of true, Divinely inspired joy (שִׂמְחָה).[25] This joy is the experience of the inner dimension of the heart,[26] the experience of Eve.[27] On the holidays, "the inner dimension of the heart rules the mind."

Shabbat, in contrast, is the day of pleasure and delight (עֹנֶג), which are higher than joy. Whereas the exuberance of joy manifests itself on the physical plane, the sublimeness of pleasure manifests itself on the spiritual plane.

As will be explained later,[28] the most ideal time for marital relations is the Sabbath night, for then, the physical element of the union attains the joy of the holidays[29] as "ruled" by the pleasure of the Sabbath. "The inner dimension of the mind rules the inner dimension of the heart."

Thus, if the workweek can be likened to the exile from the garden of Eden, the holidays may be likened to

---

25. As it is said (Deuteronomy 16:14): "You shall rejoice on your festival." The term "festival" here refers specifically to the annual pilgrim festival of *Sukot* (which therefore is termed "the time of our joy") and, by extension, to those of *Pesach, Shavuot,* and *Shemini Atzeret* as well. See *Sod HaShem Lireiav*, p. 261.

26. As it is said (Psalms 4:8): "You have given *joy in* my *heart*."

27. Eve is "the mother of all life" (Genesis 3:20) and "the mother of the children is happy" (Psalms 113:9).

28. p. 318 ff.

29. On Shabbat, in addition to the primary *mitzvah* to experience pleasure (ענג), there is a *mitzvah* to experience joy (שמחה) as well (*Sifrei, Bamidbar* 87, *s.v. Uv'yom*).

Adam and Eve re-entering the garden, and Shabbat to their reaching the tree of life, partaking of its fruit, and achieving eternal, Divine life.[30]

inner dimension of mind rules inner dimension of heart	Shabbat	delight (and subdued joy)	eating the fruit of the tree of life
inner dimension of heart rules mind	festivals	true joy	return to the garden of Eden
mind rules heart	workweek	limited joy	outside the garden of Eden

30. The Tree of Life is "the source of life" (Psalms 36:10), which is interpreted to be "the source of all pleasure" (*Likutei Torah* 1:1a), the pleasure of Shabbat.

Additional Note

to page 197.

A common euphemism for marital relations used by our sages is "the way of the land" (דרך ארץ). In the book of Psalms (37:23), it is stated that "Man's steps are established by G-d, and He desires his *way* [דרך]." We may thus understand these Divinely ordained "steps" and "way" to refer not only to his ability to function in the world in general but particularly with regard to his virility.

Our sages further state (*Vayikra Rabbah* 9:3; *Tana d'vei Eliahu* 1) that "the way of the land [דרך ארץ] precedes the Torah." Although "the way of the land" here is generally understood to mean "good behavior" in general, we may apply its meaning of "marital relations" here as well. In this light, the statement implies that learning how to relate and deal with one's Divinely-ordained strengths and weaknesses in marriage is prerequisite to achievement in the way of the Torah (see *Kidushin* 29b). In addition, a married person's Torah study is more potent and fruitful than an unmarried person's, inasmuch as the word "Torah" itself (תורה) is cognate to the words for "insemination" (יורה [כחץ]) and "pregnancy" (הריון). As taught in Kabbalah, "rectification" begins with being happily married. Only then can one merit the "crown of Torah."

As we have seen (in footnote 10, above), the combined value of the names **יצחק** and **רבקה** is 515, the numerical value of **תפלה** ("prayer"). This number is also the value of **דרך ארץ** ("the way of the land"), which further indicates the close dependence of sexual prowess on prayer and Divine providence.

We are also taught that Moses prayed 515 prayers (the value of the word **ואתחנן**, "And I supplicated" [Deuteronomy 3:23]) to enter the land of Israel. 515 (**תפלה** and **דרך ארץ**) is the number that connects G-d (whose essential Name *Havayah* = 26) to Israel (**ישראל** = 541): 26 ⊥ 515 = 541. Moses prayed 515 prayers to unite the Divine consciousness of the Name *Havayah* to the souls of Israel in the land of Israel. The land of Israel is the land where "heaven" (spirituality) and "earth" (physicality) unite, where Divine consciousness becomes manifest in the context of the seemingly mundane. In the desert (before entering the land of Israel), the Jews were only able to live a spiritual life, unable to link it to the physical plane.

The marital union, more than any other act of man, possesses the potential to unite the spiritual and physical realms. For this reason, the prophets employ it as a metaphor for the Jewish people entering into and settling the land of Israel: the people of Israel are the groom and the land of Israel their bride (see Isaiah 62:5). Their union arouses G-d, the celestial groom, to unite with His bride, the people of Israel. Thus, relative to the land, we are male, whereas relative to G-d, we are female (see below, p. 317).

From the time the Torah was given, Moses did not engage in marital relations (*Sifrei, Baha'alotecha* 99; Rashi on Numbers 12:1). In Kabbalah, we are taught that had he merited to enter the land of Israel, he would have become *Mashiach,* who will be physically married (see Isaiah 53:10).

We will explain later that the land of Israel is conducive to cultivating patience and that patience is a crucial factor in marital relations. Since Moses was distinguished in his humility and patience (Rashi on Numbers 12:3), it was in this regard that he was tested, and because he on one occasion exhibited impatience (Numbers 20:7-12), he was denied entry into the land of Israel, the land of patience.

9

Infinite Patience

Rectifying Oneself, Rectifying Others

It is indeed a great achievement to become genuine enough to discuss one's shortcomings with one's partner. But one must take care to apply this objectivity only to one's own imperfections and problems, enlisting his partner's aid and support as he works to rectify them through prayer and self-refinement.

With regard to judging (or condemning) the apparent shortcomings and misdeeds of another, our sages have said: "Do not judge your fellow until you have reached his place."[1] *Chassidut* explains that since one can never really reach another's "place"—that is, never fully understand another's conscious or unconscious motivations—one can *never* judge him.[2]

---

1. *Avot* 2:4.

2. *Sefat Emet ad loc.* Only G-d, of whom it is said, "no *place* is devoid of Him" (*Tikunei Zohar* 57 [91b], 70 [122b]) "reaches" man's true place and is thereby able to judge him.

Nonetheless, by saying "*until* you have reached his place," the sages imply that one should try to understand his fellow as best he can, and to draw as close to his "place" as possible. Drawing close to another means relating to him, both intellectually and emotionally, with empathy and love.[3]

---

3. As we have noted (above, p. 187), "place" often refers to the state of one's psyche (see *Sod Hashem Lireiav*, ch. 3). In particular, it refers to *binah*, as is said: "Where is the *place* of *understanding*?" (Job 28:12, 20). Thus, to "reach the place" of another is to understand him. Understanding creates "space" around the understanding soul which expands (by the power of love) to encompass the other. One never reaches the other's place *per se*, but rather expands his own place to include him. In the terminology of Kabbalah, *binah* is the "mother" principle and the common "womb" of all souls. This common womb is the place that encompasses us all.

Just as one loathes being critically judged by others, so will he be loathe to judge a fellow soul together with him in the common womb; one's innate "love of self" has expanded to include his fellow, who is now on an equal par with himself. Just as he ignores his own shortcomings, so will he ignore those of one whom he loves, as it is said: "Love covers all sins" (Proverbs 10:12). (This is the "mother" state of consciousness with regard to the *mitzvah* to love one's fellow Jew as oneself. See *Derech Mitzvotecha*, p. 29a.)

Above (see p. 72, footnote 15), we explained that the attainment of this level of consciousness indicates that one's love has ascended from the dimension of space to that of time. Even though we are here still discussing the rectification of interpersonal relationships, the "spatial" dimension of love, this "temporal" consciousness is what enables one to exhibit infinite patience in "space." When one is together with the other person in time, the discrepancies in their "spatial" relationship lose their urgency; this affords him patience.

Here, in the common "womb," whether one is conscious of it or not, the way one envisions his fellow reflects his own state of being. As taught by the Ba'al Shem Tov (*Likutei Moharan* 1:113; *Binah LaItim*

As one comes closer to another person, one's perspective changes. He begins to see him more appreciatively and is now able to fulfill the complementary dictum of our sages:[4] "Judge all men favorably." One begins to recognize that the apparent blemishes one had observed are actually reflections of identical, though less apparent, blemishes in oneself.[5] One can then fulfill the *mitzvah* of rebuking his fellow[6] according to the teaching of the Ba'al Shem Tov:[7] first one must rebuke oneself with regard to the same fault, and only then is one able to rebuke his fellow constructively. This teaching of the Ba'al Shem Tov lends additional insight to the advice of our sages:[8] "First rectify yourself, and then rectify others."

63; *Likutei Sichot,* vol. 4, p. 1207, in interpretation of *Avot* 3:16), by judging one's fellow one is in fact judging oneself—even if he is unaware of being together with him in the common womb. Thus we are taught that "judgments are aroused from *binah*" (*Zohar* 2:175b).

4. *Avot* 1:6.

5. *Meor Einaim, Chukat,* beginning; *Toldot Yaakov Yosef, Terumah,* end.

6. "You shall surely rebuke your fellow" (Leviticus 19:7). See above, p. 146.

7. The verse quoted in the previous footnote literally reads: "Rebuke you shall rebuke your fellow," implying a double rebuke: "rebuke [yourself and then] you shall rebuke your fellow."

8. *Bava Batra* 60b. The word here used for "rectify" (קשוט) literally means "adorn." Since "adorning" alludes to the relationship of husband and wife (*Ketubot* 59b; *Ta'anit* 31a), we may infer that the general teaching "First rectify yourself and then rectify others" applies especially to husband and wife.

This is further supported by the fact that the first historical incident in connection with which this principle is articulated centers

The Antidote to Anger

When one realizes that the rectification of others depends upon one's own self-rectification, one learns to be patient with them. Patience is the antidote to anger.

The only legitimate object of anger is one's own evil inclination, as our sages teach: "One should always stir up the anger of his good inclination against his evil inclination."[9] With regard to others in general, and to one's

---

on marital relations. In the Midrash (*Bereishit Rabbah* 23:4; cf. Rashi on Genesis 4:25) it is told that:

> Lamech [the descendent of Cain] went to Adam and complained about his wives [who refused to cohabit with him for fear that their children would be wiped out by the impending flood]. Adam said to them, "Is it for you to fashion your behavior in accordance with G-d's decrees? Do what you are commanded to, and He will do as He pleases." They retorted, "*Rectify yourself first!* Have you not separated from your own wife for one hundred and thirty years—ever since death was decreed for mankind because of your sin!?" As a result of this, "Adam knew again his wife." Why does it state "*again*"? To teach us that his passion for her was greater than ever before.

This same word for "rectify" and "adorn" also means "truth," as in the verse, "Words of truth are reliable [קשט]" (Proverbs 22:21). In Aramaic, קושטא is the translation of both "truth" and "justice" (Targum to Deuteronomy 16:20).

9. *Berachot* 5a, based on Psalms 4:5; see also *Igeret HaKodesh* 25. When one sees someone else sinning or about to sin, he may feign anger in order to prevent him from continuing (*Shulchan Aruch HaRav, Orach Chaim* 156:3).

spouse in particular, one must strive to assume[10] the Divine attribute of "infinite patience."[11]

Patience fosters one's ability to wait[12] for conflict to resolve itself,[13] to suspend judgment,[14] and to continuously check one's tendency to respond impulsively. It is the key to avoiding the damage one inflicts on oneself and others when unable to control the responses of one's "first nature."

---

10. It is a *mitzvah* to emulate G-d's attributes. See pp. 216, 353.

11. Exodus 34:7. In Hebrew: ארך אפים. The most literal reading of this idiom is "of long nostrils" (see the commentary of Ibn Ezra *ad loc.*). "Long nostrils" implies "long breath," the power of the soul to calm anger and stress.

Just as the idiom for patience is ארך אפים, so is the idiom for anger קצר אפים, literally, "of short nostrils" (= "of short breath," i.e., quick to anger), as in Proverbs 14:17: "quickness to anger [קצר אפים] results in foolishness." This last-quoted verse implies that patience is the source of wisdom (see *Sefer Yetzirah* 4:3). In the terminology of Kabbalah, the *partzuf* of *keter*, *Arich Anpin* (אריך אנפין, the Aramaic form of ארך אפים) is the source of wisdom, i.e., the *partzuf* of *Abba*, the origin of the right axis of the sefirotic structure, which is referred to (*Tikunei Zohar*, introduction [17a]) as the "long axis" (חד אריך, in contrast to the left, "short" axis and middle, "intermediate" axis).

12. The verb "to wait" in Hebrew (להמתין), is cognate to the word for "loins" (מתנים). Just as the loins give the body its equilibrium, so does the power to wait reflect the inner stability of one's soul.

13. While one continues to work on oneself, according to the principle of "Rectify yourself first" cited above. See below, p. 218.

14. As quoted above, "Do not judge your fellow until you have reached his place."

Prematurity

All the great, archetypal sins recorded in the Torah resulted from a lack of patience:

The primordial sin was the eating of the fruit of the tree of knowledge of good and evil. Had Adam and Eve waited a mere three hours[15] until the onset of Shabbat before eating from the tree,[16] they would have inherited the blessings of Eden for all time. It was their impatience that brought about the fall of that initial pristine reality, the decree of death for mankind and our protracted exile from paradise.[17]

The people of Israel as a whole returned to the Edenic state, freed from the angel of death, upon receiving the Torah at Mt. Sinai. But we forfeited this state with the sin of the golden calf, the idol meant to replace our leader, Moses. We were unable to wait for him to descend from the mountain.[18] Our sages refer to this sin as the archetypal sin of a community.[19]

---

15. *Shemot Rabbah* 32:1.

16. Eating the fruit of the tree of knowledge involved engaging in marital relations, as taught in Kabbalah (*Sha'ar HaKavanot, Derush Rosh HaShanah* 1; see, as well, Ibn Ezra on Genesis 3:6, that the fruit of the tree of knowledge aroused sexual desire).

17. This accords with the general principle that G-d's "behavior" toward man reflects man's own behavior. Man's impatience arouses G-d's impatience, as it were. The Divine decree of death and exile is the expression of this impatience.

18. *Shemot Rabbah, loc. cit.*

19. *Avodah Zarah* 4b-5a.

As we saw above,[20] David and Bathsheba were destined for each other from the beginning of time. They were intended to be the consummate rectification of the primordial couple, Adam and Eve. Yet, David took Bathsheba prematurely.[21] This impulsiveness was the essence of his sin, which our sages refer to as the archetypal sin of an individual.[22]

Both marriage partners need to be constantly vigilant in cultivating patience. Patience depends upon faith and trust in G-d; if we want something and do not receive it, it is because we do not yet deserve it.[23] When spouses realize

---

20. p. 38.

21. It is interesting to note that the idiom used to describe this is "he partook of her before she had ripened," an allusion to and comparison with the sin of eating the fruit of the tree of knowledge of good and evil. See *Likutei Moharan* 2:88.

22. *Avodah Zarah, loc. cit.*

23. In chapter six, we saw that true lowliness is the feeling that one does not (and will *never*) deserve anything. In contrast, infinite patience results from the realization that one does not *yet* deserve what he desires. This latter awareness is necessary in order to motivate improvement and to keep one from expecting the other person to improve before he improves himself.

This patience, nonetheless, does not compromise one's existential lowliness, since the belief that one may eventually fulfill his desires may be based on a belief in predestination (*mazal*) rather than on the hope of ever actually deserving on the basis of merit. One may indeed feel undeserving but nonetheless believe that G-d has some predestined good in store for him for which he must patiently wait. The improvement this motivates is not a means to achieve or deserve one's desires, but rather a way of creating a proper vessel for the predestined good.

Thus, lowliness is the foundation of patience. One first realizes that he deserves nothing; this implies that whatever good may be in

this, they become much more patient with each other. Rather than demanding that their partner be more perfect than they are, they focus on rectifying their own character first, with G-d's help.

With patience comes the ability to transcend one's innate, mortal character and fulfill the commandment to emulate G-d: "Just as He is merciful, so be you merciful.... Just as he is infinitely patient, so be you infinitely patient."[24]

Such was the temperament of Moses, as it says:[25] "And the man Moses was very humble." Rashi defines the word "humble" here as "lowly and patient."[26]

---

store for him is purely due to his *mazal*. To receive this good he must improve himself, but in the meantime, he waits patiently, knowing that any good he may receive is an undeserved gift rather than just deserts he can demand.

In the terminology of Kabbalah, lowliness is the inner property of *malchut*, while patience is associated with *keter*. In *keter*, "the outcome is dependent on *mazal* (predestination) rather than on merit" (*Moed Katan* 28a). See below, footnote 26. *Malchut* and *keter* are the respective "end" and "beginning" of the sefirotic tree; their interdependency is an expression of the Kabbalistic principle: "their end is wedged in their beginning, and their beginning in their end" (*Sefer Yetzirah*).

24. *Shabbat* 133b; see *Mishneh Torah, Deiot* 1:6.

25. Numbers 12:3.

26. In this order, since lowliness is the prerequisite to patience. The two terms "lowly" and "patient" refer to the two states of consciousness that unite as "humility," as described above in footnote 23.

The Land of Israel

Infinite patience is conceptually associated with the nature of the Land of Israel.[27] The Holy Land is frequently referred to in the Bible as "a land flowing with milk and honey,"[28] evoking an image of the sublime tranquility of spirit one would hope to experience in one's home, wherever it is.

Patience can best be acquired in the Holy Land.[29] Israel is the gateway to the garden of Eden,[30] where G-d

---

27. *Likutei Moharan* 1:155

28. Exodus 3:8, etc.

29. The Hebrew for "milk and honey" (**חלב ודבש**) is numerically equal to "infinite patience" (**ארך אפים**, 352).

The initials of the words **ארץ** ("land"), **חלב** ("milk") and **דבש** ("honey") together spell **אחד** ("one"). The Hebrew word for honey—**דבש**—may be seen as an acronym for the names of David and Bathsheba (**דוד בת שבע**), the archetypal couple whose rectification depends on "infinite patience," and whose names together equal **שלום בית** ("domestic tranquility"). Furthermore, the word for milk—**חלב**—may be seen as an acronym for **לבי חלל בקרבי**, "my heart is void within me," King David's statement of consummate *teshuvah* with regard to his sin with Bathsheba (*Likutei Moharan* 2:1:4).

In Kabbalah, milk symbolizes the five states of *chesed* in *da'at* (corresponding to the male), and honey the five states of *gevurah* in *da'at* (corresponding to the female). See above, p. 115.

30. In particular, this is said of the Machpelah cave in Hebron, and secondarily of the city of Tzefat (*Chesed l'Avraham* 3:13, see also 3:3). The patriarchs and matriarchs, buried in the Machpelah cave, are the rectification of Adam and Eve, who, according to our sages (*Sotah* 13a) are also buried there. The sages refer to the patriarchs and matriarchs as "the upright ones" (*Avodah Zarah* 25a). Uprightness implies patience (*Torat Shalom*, p. 178).

had originally intended that the first man and woman live and grow spiritually together, relating to one another with love and infinite patience, thereby meriting eternal bliss.

When one of the *chassidim* of Rabbi Menachem Mendel of Lubavitch[31] asked him whether or not to move to Israel, he answered: "Make the Land of Israel here."[32] In accordance with our above understanding of infinite patience and its relation to the land of Israel, we can see that the implication of this saying is: "wherever you are, learn to be patient." Impatience represents the existential state of living outside Israel, while serene composure manifests the very essence of the land.[33]

Agility with Deliberation

The tolerant attitude fostered by cultivating infinite patience should not, however, make one passive about life. On the contrary, it should enhance one's energetic drive (זְרִיזוּת, "agility") to rectify reality. This is because true patience is based on the awareness that G-d is ever present in one's life and is influencing the outcome of one's endeavors. One thus feels G-d working in and

31. The third Lubavitcher Rebbe, known (after his work of halachic responsa) as the *Tzemach Tzedek*.

32. *Igrot Kodesh Admor HaRayatz*, vol. 1, p. 485; *Likutei Sichot*, vol. 2, p. 621.

33. The land of Israel is called ארץ רחבה ("a wide space," Exodus 3:8); the archetype of the Diaspora is the land of Egypt, whose name in Hebrew (מצרים) means "cramped." The land of Israel in space is thus the analog of patience in time.

through him, and at the same time, orchestrating events from without. He is aware that he is G-d's agent and has a unique and imperative task to fulfill, but paradoxically knows that it is not he himself that is executing the task, but the power of G-d working in him. The balanced condition that such an awareness inspires is referred to by the Ba'al Shem Tov as "deliberate agility" (זְרִיזוּת בִּמְתִינוּת).[34]

From all the above, it is clear that infinite patience is the key to self-rectification. To the extent that one has succeeded in rectifying himself, integrating infinite patience into his very being so that it is reflected in his external demeanor, he can then proceed to rectify others. This he does with sweet and gentle words, as it is said: "The words of the wise [i.e., one who possesses the insight to first rectify himself], when spoken gently, are heeded."[35]

---

34. *Keter Shem Tov*, addendum 169; *Sefer HaSichot 5700*, p. 52.

35. Ecclesiastes 9:17.

10

The Jewish Home

One's Home is One's Wife

We have described husband-wife relationships as being the "spatial" dimension of their love. The most concrete setting in which this dimension is manifest is the couple's home. And indeed, our sages say that "one's home is one's wife."[1]

To consider one's wife one's home is to see her as his anchor in life[2] and the ultimate source of his consciousness of his Divine source. The soul leaves its celestial home and descends to the earthly plane in order to perform its Divinely ordained task: to make this world a dwelling place for G-d.[3] As husband and wife build their earthly

---

1. *Yoma* 2a. see also *Shabbat* 118b.

2. As it is said: "Her husband's heart trusts in her" (Proverbs 31:11). This verse is the second in the alphabetic poem "A woman of valor," recited as part of the Shabbat evening home liturgy, and begins with the letter *beit*. As the word *beit* (בית) means "home" (בית), this verse epitomizes how "one's home is his wife." Remarkably, the only letter common to all the words of this phrase (בטח בה לב בעלה) is *beit*!

3. *Tanya*, ch. 36, based on *Midrash Tanchuma*, *Naso* 16, ed. Buber 24.

home on the foundations of the Torah, they increase the manifestation of Divinity in this world, and thereby fulfill their purpose in life and enhance their awareness of their own original home together above.[4]

Thus, the essence of one's home-consciousness derives from the soul of one's wife. In all his worldly endeavors, she anchors her husband's consciousness in his Divine source and mission in life. For this reason she is referred to as "the foundation of the home."[5]

The spirit of the home and the soul of one's wife are thus intimately linked. The husband, then, should consider his home a dynamic environment with a living spirit that should be treated with respect and sanctity,[6] just as he should treat his wife.

---

4. The *yechidah*, the highest of the soul's five levels, which is bound to the essence of G-d, is manifest in one's home (*Likutei Torah* 4:98d-100b).

In Kabbalah, the five levels of the soul and the five worlds are said to be manifest in the five stages of root (שרש), soul (נשמה), body (גוף), garment (לבוש), and chamber (היכל) (*Etz Chaim* 42:2; *Mavo Shearim, Derush P'nimi uMakif* 1:2). Just as we saw above (p. 17) with regard to the five levels of the soul, these five levels interrelate inversely: the root is manifest in the chamber, and the soul in the garment; the body is left as the central fulcrum of the array. In our context, we see here as well that the root of the soul, the *yechidah*, is manifest in the chamber, or one's home.

5. *Bamidbar Rabbah* 14:8; *Zohar* 1:154a. See additional note at the end of this chapter (p. 233).

6. The couple sanctifies their home by means of the Divine commandments they perform in it (as we say in the blessing before we perform each *mitzvah*, "who has sanctified us by His commandments..."). The word "to sanctify" (קדש) is the same as that for "to betroth" (see *Tanya*, ch. 49).

It is thus important that one invest both spiritually and materially in one's domestic environment with dedication and love.[7] This implies ensuring that the home is physically pleasing to live in, but more important, that it possesses Jewish dignity[8]—as reflected in the *mezuzahs*

---

7. Just as one is bidden to honor his wife "beyond his means" (see above, p. 3, footnote 7).

8. Generally, respecting someone or something is a lower, more mundane way of relating to it than considering it holy. The Hebrew word for "respect" (כבוד) is often used to mean "garments" (which earn one respect by virtue of his outward appearance), and in particular to mean "cleaning" the home (*Semachot* 11:9; *Derech Eretz* 1:7).

Nonetheless, our sages teach us that "good behavior precedes the Torah" (*Vayikra Rabbah* 9:3; *Tana d'vei Eliahu* 1). In other words, respectful behavior in the realm of the mundane is prerequisite to integrated consciousness of holiness; respect precedes sanctity.

The numerical value of this statement (דרך ארץ קדמה לתורה, 1305) equals the word for "woman" (אשה, when the א of אשה is taken to equal 1000), from which we may infer that this principle applies in particular in relation to woman (and, by extension, to one's home, since "one's home is one's wife"). First one must learn to respect one's wife (and home) and thereby become able to sanctify his relation to her (it) in full consciousness.

In contrast, "dignity" in this context means showing respect or exhibiting self-respect based on sanctity. A noble person commands spontaneous respect by virtue of his noble or holy character. The respect one shows an important person who lacks intrinsic nobility or sanctity, however, is artificial.

In the terminology of Kabbalah, intrinsic respect (כבוד נאצל) is a function of *chochmah,* while artificial respect (כבוד נברא) is a manifestation of *malchut* descending into the lower worlds of *Beriah, Yetzirah,* and *Asiyah.*

affixed to its doors, the *kosher* food which one eats, and, especially, the holy books which line its walls.[9]

The Miniature Sanctuary

What makes a place a home is love.[10] G-d created the world in order to have creatures on whom to bestow His

9. The sanctity of the home is undermined by books (or other media) which contain heretical ideas or immoral themes. Their very presence may have a palpably adverse effect on the "home," i.e., the wife (e.g., her physical and spiritual ability to be "pure") and her family. Such books should therefore be removed from the home, in order to safeguard the purity of one's environment and the spiritual development and immunity of one's family.

10. Each of Jacob's four wives had their own tent, but the one Jacob principally resided in was Rachel's (Rashi on Genesis 31:33), since he loved her more than the others.

Still, it is explained in Kabbalah that the relationship of Jacob and Rachel reflects the union of G-d's attributes in the "revealed world" (עלמא דאתגליא), whereas his relationship with Leah reflects the nature of this union in the higher, "concealed world" (עלמא דאתכסיא). Thus, although Rachel's tent was Jacob's "revealed home," Leah's was his "concealed home." In fact, the very word for "tent" in Hebrew (אהל) is a permutation of "Leah" (לאה). From this it follows that each of Jacob's wives' tents was encompassed by the concealed presence of Leah, Jacob's "concealed home."

goodness and love,[11] as it is said: "the world was built[12] through loving-kindness."[13]

Since love is man's primary emotion,[14] and the home is the essential vehicle through which man becomes able to express his love, "a man[15] without a home is not a man."[16] He is unable to realize the depths of his innate love and

---

11. *Etz Chaim*, beginning.

12. According to some sources, the root of the word "house" (בית) is "to build" (בנה). (The alternative opinion is that its root is "to come" [בוא]; see below, p. 322, footnote 21.)

13. Psalms 89:3. Literally, this verse reads: "the world *shall be* built through loving-kindness." Since every individual is a "small world" (*Midrash Tanchuma, Pekudei* 3), this verse also means that the life of every person *shall be* built—i.e., created anew, upon marriage, and rectified throughout married life—by loving-kindness. The essence of this loving-kindness begins with the love of husband and wife.

The Torah begins with the letter *beit*, which means "house." The first word of the Torah (בראשית) may be permuted to read **בית אשר**, "a house of happiness." In the parallel verse which begins the second account of creation (Genesis 2:4), "These are the generations of heaven and earth when they were created," the word for "when they were created" (בהבראם) may be permuted to read **באברהם**, "with Abraham." The verse may then be read: "These are the generations of heaven and earth, that were created with [the attribute of] Abraham," which is love (*Bereishit Rabbah* 12:9).

14. See above, p. 16, footnote 32.

15. The term "man" (אדם) refers to the composite of man and woman (see above, p. 58, footnote 22).

16. See *Yevamot* 63a; *Tosefot ad loc., s.v. she'ein; Vayikra Rabbah* 22:1. "One cannot live without a house for even a moment" (*Likutei Torah* 4:99b)

passion, both for the world in general as well as the passion he feels in the self-fulfillment that comes with creativity.[17]

Originally, the entire world was to be G-d's abode.[18] In the wake of the primordial sin,[19] however, the Divine Presence was forced to withdraw, since the world had become unsuited for its revelation.

Abraham thought the ideal setting for G-d's Presence to dwell again on earth was a mountain. "And Abraham called the place 'G-d will see,' as it is called unto this day, 'the mountain on which G-d will be seen.'"[20] Abraham felt that in order to contact G-d, man must rise out of mundane reality to a higher state of consciousness.

Although this is necessary, Abraham's vision was not complete.

---

17. "A house is built with wisdom; it is established with understanding; the chambers are filled with knowledge, with all pleasant and precious riches" (Proverbs 24:3-4). According to Kabbalah and *Chassidut*, the entire array of man's conscious soul-powers is referred to in these two verses (*Zohar* 3:291a). Thus, all one's potential is expressed through his house.

It is further explained that the ultimate delight of the soul and the expression of one's basic will to live is expressed in the desire to have a home (see *Besha'ah Shehikdimu*, pp. 1096-1130; *Siddur Im Dach*, pp. 183a-184b, 199b-202b, 204b-205a; *Biurei HaZohar (Tzemach Tzedek)*, vol. 2, pp. 788 ff. (quoted in *Sefer HaLikutim, Miluim*, pp. 438 ff.).

18. *Shir HaShirim Rabbah* 5:1; *Bereishit Rabbah* 19:7.

19. And the ensuing sins of the subsequent generations (as listed in the sources cited in the previous footnote).

20. Genesis 22:14.

Isaac communed with G-d in the field. "And Isaac went out to pray in the field."[21] He felt that G-d was most accessible in the setting of nature, away from the distractions and corruption of civilization.

Although there is value in occasional escape and solitude, this vision was incomplete as well.

Jacob envisioned the Divine Presence resting in a home. "And he called the place 'the House of G-d.'"[22] Rather than believing man's union with G-d required transcending or escaping reality, he saw it as a part of everyday life. Excursions to mountains or fields may be helpful for renewing inspiration, but the setting in which man truly brings G-d into his life is his home.

G-d accepted Jacob's vision as complete.[23]

Thus, in order to enable the Divine Presence to dwell once again in this world, G-d commanded the Jewish

---

21. *Ibid.* 24:63.

22. *Ibid.* 28:19.

23. *Pesachim* 88a. In the present context, "one's home is his wife" would thus mean that the goal of one's Divine service should be that the Divine Presence be manifest in his wife's consciousness. In a similar vein, we are taught that the term "the house of Jacob" (Exodus 19:3) refers to the women of Israel in general (*Mechilta* and Rashi *ad loc.*) and "the house of Israel" (Psalms 98:3) refers to the righteous women in whose merit Israel will be redeemed (*Yalkut Shimoni, Ruth* 606). The combined numerical value of these two phrases (**בית יעקב** and **בית ישראל**, 1547) is equal to that of "Happy are those who dwell in Your House, they shall praise You forever" (**אשרי יושבי ביתך עוד יהללוך סלה**, Psalms 84:5).

Abraham signifies love (see above, footnote 13). In the present context, this would mean that love's ultimate goal is to be made manifest in a home.

people to build Him a "home," the Tabernacle (which was later superseded by the Holy Temple). From this point, the Divine Presence is intended to spread outward again into the world.[24] Thus, when G-d gave the commandment to build the Tabernacle, He said: "And they shall make Me a sanctuary, so that I may dwell in their midst."[25] Our sages point out[26] that this verse does not say "in *its* midst" but "in *their* midst," meaning in the heart of each and every Jew. Thus, the ultimate purpose of the Holy Temple is to draw the Divine Presence into the heart of every Jew, wherever, and whenever, he may be.[27]

---

24. Thus the windows of the Temple were built narrow on the inside and wide on the outside, in order for the light of the *Shechinah* to shine outward (1 Kings 6:4; *Menachot* 86b, Rashi *s.v. Shekufim*; *Vayikra Rabbah* 31:7; *Likutei Sichot*, vol. 2, p. 315).

25. Exodus 25:8.

26. *Reishit Chochmah, Ahavah* 6; *Shnei Luchot HaBrit, Sha'ar HaOtioiot, s.v. Lamed, Ta'anit, s.v. MeiInyan HaAvodah*, etc.; *Likutei Torah* 3:20b, etc.

27. In other words, the Holy Temple is the setting for the consummation of the union between the celestial groom and bride, G-d and Israel. Its innermost chamber, the holy of holies, housed the ark of the covenant, on top of which were the two cherubim, symbolizing and expressing the love between G-d and the Jewish people. Thus, the inner chamber of the Temple is called "the bedroom" (*Shir HaShirim Rabbah* 1:2; Rashi on 2 Kings 11:2, Song of Songs 1:16, 2 Chronicles 22:11).

Hence we are taught that "since the destruction of the Holy Temple, the joy of marital relations has been removed and surrendered to the sinners" (*Sanhedrin* 75a). Without the physical expression of Divine love, the intensity of the experience of love on the personal level is impaired accordingly. See below, p. 353.

Together with our assumptions concerning the shifting of reality toward its rectified state as we approach the messianic era, however,

Houses of prayer and Torah study are also considered houses of G-d[28] or "miniature sanctuaries"[29] where He may be sought.[30] Indeed, many of the laws governing the construction of and our conduct in the synagogue are derived from the laws surrounding the Temple.

The ultimate house of G-d, however, is the Jewish home, for it is in their home that each couple expresses their unique and common soul-root and Divine purpose in life.[31]

We have thus identified three levels of "home": the Holy Temple, synagogues around the world, and the

---

we may also assume that the more one cultivates a messianic consciousness, the more one will experience the "joy of marital relations" that was removed from the world as a result of the exile.

28. *Tana d'vei Eliahu Rabbah* 28.

29. Ezekiel 11:16; *Megilah* 29a.

30. See *Bereishit Rabbah* 63:6.

31. Hence the juxtaposition of King Solomon building the Temple (the house of G-d) and his own house (1 Kings 6:37-7:1, 9:10). Building G-d's house is intimately connected with building one's own. This is why it was specifically King Solomon, builder of the Temple, who wrote the Song of Songs, the consummate expression of spousal love.

Furthermore, every Jew is intended to make his home resemble the Temple by practicing in it the three "pillars on which the world stands" (*Avot* 1:2): Torah study, prayer, and charity (*Likutei Sichot*, vol. 25, p. 297 ff.).

Having emulated the Temple by serving to reveal G-d's presence on earth, the synagogues of the Diaspora will, with the advent of *Mashiach*, be transplanted in Jerusalem and become part of the rebuilt third Temple (*Megilah* 29a; *Chidushei Agadot, ad loc.; Sefer HaSichot 5748*, p. 464, fn. 77). To the extent that the private homes will have accomplished this as well, they will be similarly transplanted and become part of the third Temple (*Sefer HaSichot 5752*, vol. 1, p. 154).

Jewish home. In the terminology of Kabbalah, the seminal revelation of the Divine Presence corresponds to the *yud* of the Name *Havayah*. The Holy Temple corresponds to the first *hei*, where the point of Divine indwelling begins to expand. The synagogues around the world correspond to the *vav*, since through them the Divine Presence revealed in the Holy Temple is transmitted (in diminished form[32]) throughout the world. The Jewish home corresponds to the latter *hei*, the final resting-place of the Divine Presence before it expands to fill the world as it did at the outset of creation.

י	revelation of the Divine Presence
ה	the Holy Temple
ו	synagogues
ה	the Jewish home

Hospitality

Another essential element in sanctifying one's home is traditional Jewish hospitality. Our sages teach us that "welcoming guests is greater even than greeting the *Shechinah* [שְׁכִינָה, Divine Presence]."[33]

32. The Kabbalistic term for "diminished form" is זעיר אנפין, corresponding to the *vav* of the Name *Havayah*.

33. *Shabbat* 127a. We learn this remarkable principle from our first forefather Abraham, who interrupted G-d's revelation to him in order to greet guests (Genesis 18:13 and Rashi *ad loc.*).

It would appear that hosting guests and inviting others into their home would infringe on the intimacy enjoyed by husband and wife. In fact, however, they enhance it.

The private intimacy between husband and wife is a form of "greeting the *Shechinah.*" This is firstly because the Divine Presence dwells between the couple when they merit, and secondly because marital relations are likened to the union of G-d's transcendent essence with the *Shechinah,* His immanent Divine Presence.

From this analogy between marital relations and the union of G-d's transcendent and immanent aspects, we see that the *Shechinah* is considered the feminine side of Divinity. During the exile, the *Shechinah* longs to be united with the male side of Divinity, the revelation of G-d's infinite transcendence. Thus, every guest who finds even a temporary resting place in one's house carries a spark of the *Shechinah,*[34] G-d's estranged and exiled Presence which is seeking its home.

To extend hospitality is thus to welcome sparks of spiritual desire into one's home. These sparks awaken and enhance the wife's own holy fire—her passion and desire toward her husband[35]—and increase the couple's potency and fertility.[36]

---

34. The *Shechinah* is compared to fire. See above, p. 111, footnote 4.

35. Thus, the longing and passion characteristic of the exile is superior in its intensity to the consummate fulfillment of redemption exemplified in the normal intimate relations between husband and wife. The Ba'al Shem Tov therefore interprets Psalms 63:3 to mean "would that I sustain the longing for You I feel in exile when the Temple will be rebuilt" (*Likutei Torah* 4:92b, 5:50c; *Sefer HaMa'amarim*

This is evident from the Biblical account of Abraham and Sarah, who were only able to bear a child after they graciously welcomed and hosted the three angelic wayfarers.[37]

Still, the demands of accommodating guests may become too physically and psychologically straining for the wife, no matter how much her husband his helping her.[38] A couple should therefore always decide jointly how much hospitality they can realistically practice at any given time. For, after all, the guests represent the "sparks" of the *Shechinah*, whereas the woman represents the *Shechinah* itself. One may interrupt the "receiving of the *Shechinah*" in order to ultimately enhance her power, but not to cause her to collapse, G-d forbid!

5689, p. 122 and sources cited there, footnote 63; *Likutei Sichot*, vol. 4, p. 1331).

36. As Rabbi Dovber, the Maggid of Mezeritch, told Rabbi Shneur Zalman of Liadi, hospitality facilitates fertility, as it is said: "How shall a youth merit to his path?" (Psalms 119:9), which may be read: "How can one merit a child? By hosting guests."

37. This is the continuation of the story in footnote 33, above.

38. The "woman of valor" is praised as she who "oversees the ways of her household" (Proverbs 31:27). This implies that no matter who actually does the work involved in running a household, it is the wife—who after all embodies the home—who will by her very nature feel the burden of responsibility for and obligation to it.

Additional Note

to page 222.

The word for "home" in Hebrew (בית) is formed by inserting the letter *yud* (י) into the word for "daughter" (בת). This alludes to the following teaching of our sages (*Shemot Rabbah* 52:5):

> At first, the Holy One, blessed be He, called Israel His daughter, as it is said (Psalms 45:11): "Listen, My daughter, and see, lend your ear. Forget now your people and your father's house."
>
> His love for them increased until he called them His sister, as it is said (Song of Songs 5:2): "Open up to Me, My sister, My companion, My dove, My perfect one, for My head is filled with dew, and My locks with the drops of the night."
>
> His love increased further, until he called them His mother, as it is said (Isaiah 51:4): "Hearken to Me, My people, and listen, My nation, for instruction comes from Me, and My statutes will be suddenly a light unto the nations." [The word for "My nation" (לאומי) may be read "My mother" (לאמי).]

We see here three levels of relationship: Father-daughter, brother-sister, and son-mother. In the first, G-d is superior to Israel; in the second, the two are equals; in the third, Israel is superior.

In *Chassidut* (*Torah Or* 37c) we are taught that in the messianic era, the groom (i.e., G-d) will reach a fourth, even higher level of relationship to his bride (Israel), which He will express by again calling her "My daughter." (The word "my daughter" [בתי] is actually a permutation of בית.)

In Kabbalah, "daughter" signifies the *partzuf* of *malchut* (or *Nukvei d'Z'eir Anpin*, see above, p. 123), and the *yud* (of the Name *Havayah*) signifies the *partzuf* of *Abba* (which corresponds to the *sefirah* of *chochmah*). *Abba* is in fact the source of *malchut* (*Zohar* 3:248a, 256b, etc., based on Proverbs 3:19).

The higher level of "My daughter" which will be reached in the messianic era is the revelation of the source of *malchut* in *Abba*. The *yud* (י) of *Abba* permeates the essence of the "daughter" (בת), thereby forming the word for "home" (בית).

In our Divine service, this is reaching the level of ultimate selflessness and the binding of one's finite will to G-d's infinite will.

To summarize:

י	"My daughter"	source of *malchut* in *Abba*
ה	"My mother"	*Ima*
ו	"My sister"	*Z'eir Anpin*
ה	"My daughter"	*Malchut (Nukvei d'Z'eir Anpin)*

11

Living with the Times

Essence and Experience

Of the three frames of reference—space, time, and soul—space is the most palpable, and soul is the most abstract. Time is the intermediate realm, more abstract than space,[1] in which it appears to be garbed,[2] yet more concrete than the soul, whose conscious experience it clothes.[3] Thus, it can be said that one experiences one's soul being drawn into the world of space by means of the intermediate reality of time.

The better attuned a person is to his own sensations and feelings—i.e., the way he reacts to the vicissitudes of time—the more vivid will be his life experience. The

---

1. In the mathematical representation of four-dimensional space-time, the three space-coordinates are "real," whereas the fourth, time, is "imaginary."

2. I.e., we conceive of the events of time occurring on the stage of space.

3. I.e., we conceive of the life of the soul playing itself out in the context of time.

purpose of the spiritual life, however, is not merely to experience one's essential vitality of being, but to utilize that awareness in fulfilling G-d's will. When one does this, he is "living with the times."[4]

The primary time frame that impinges on the life of a couple is that of the wife's menstrual cycle. During her monthly cycle, the patterns of time direct not only a woman's physiology, but her soul and sense of self as well. Here, as in other instances, *Chassidut* teaches us how to use this given as an opportunity for spiritual growth. If the husband is properly in tune with his wife, he can both help her through the psychological and spiritual tides of this process and benefit from her insights and experience as well.

In Hebrew, the word commonly used to denote "experience" (חֲוָיָה) is derived from the name of the first woman, Eve (חַוָּה).[5] Thus, the sensory realm of experience, which unfolds in the conscious dimension of time, is intimately bound up with woman's very identity.

---

4. This expression of Rabbi Shneur Zalman of Liadi is generally interpreted to mean that one should analyze his ongoing life experience in light of the weekly Torah-portion (*Sefer HaSichot 5702*, p. 29 ff.). Here it is taken in its more literal sense.

5. The root חוה, as it appears in the Torah, denotes self-expression, as in Psalms 19:3: "...and night to night expresses [יחוה] knowledge." Self-experience and self-expression are intimately related. As functions of one's inner life, they serve to characterize woman as essentially a subjective creature (whereas man is more objective by nature, as will be discussed presently).

See additional note 1 at the end of this chapter (p. 257).

A man, on the other hand, is by nature associated with abstract essence, which is above time and removed from explicit sensation.[6] Through his wife, however, a husband can experience life in all its rich detail as she helps ground him in a here-and-now awareness of reality. And he—through his inherent detachment and objectivity—can help and support her in making productive use of her experience.[7] Thus, husband and wife complement and balance each other.

In a similar sense, the cosmic groom and bride, G-d and the Jewish people, complement each other. Although G-d's essence axiomatically lacks nothing, we are taught that in the context of creation His delight in the future deeds of the righteous is what motivated Him to create the world.[8] In this sense, man provides G-d with the experiential side of creation that He lacks, so to speak.[9] In turn,

---

6. To a large extent, women are under the direction of time, i.e., they are innately "in tune" with it. For this reason they are exempt from time-bound *mitzvot*. In contrast, man's ideal calling is to direct time. He uses *time* to channel *soul* in order to rectify *space*.

7. Moreover, by adding his sense of abstraction to her experience, he can enable her to free herself from her intrinsic subjection to the constraints of time.

8. See above, p. 27.

9. "Israel sustains their Father in heaven" (*Zohar* 3:7b). This is an example of the principle that "the shell develops prior to the fruit." Each stage of creation may be considered an obstacle relative to the subsequent stage. The previous stage cannot "do" what the next stage is able to, and is thus a state of relative inaction, which in Chassidic thought is synonymous with negativity, apathy, and impurity; the "no" that precedes the "yes." In this context, the world as it exists in G-d's abstract essence is "incomplete" relative to its subsequent, actualized creation.

G-d provides man with the Torah, the instructions that enable him to maximize and properly interpret and respond to his experiences.[10]

The Female Pulse of Time: Run and Return

These essential differences in the nature of man and woman will, of course, affect the dynamics of their marital relationship.

Typically, a wife gives of herself in marital relationships more openly and completely than a husband.[11] This is so because the wife's tendency toward total involvement reflects her innate dynamic of "run and return."

The phrase "run and return" appears in the vision of Ezekiel,[12] in reference to the angels of the Divine Chariot:

---

10. The metaphor of husband and wife can also be used to describe the relationship of the *tzadik* to the *beinoni*. As a *rebbe*, the *tzadik* gives the *beinoni* the objectivity he needs to help him through his ups and downs. This may take the form of advising him how to deal with his situation (this is called התלבשות [*hitlabshut*], "enclothing" himself in the problem), or inspiring him to transcend his natural level (this is called השראה [*hashra'ah*]). In return, the *beinoni* provides the *tzadik* with vicarious experience, which allows the *tzadik* to himself become a *ba'al teshuvah* as he "lives through" the crises of those he helps. As the Ba'al Shem Tov taught, a *tzadik* can only help a *rasha* by finding something akin to the *rasha*'s problem in himself, fixing it, and based on this, instructing the *rasha* how to rectify himself.

11. Though never violating her intrinsic modesty in the process. See p. 196, note 3.

12. Ezekiel 1:14.

וְהַחַיּוֹת רָצוֹא וָשׁוֹב כְּמַרְאֵה הַבָּזָק.

And the angels were running and returning as the vision of a bolt of fire.

The word used here for "angels" (חַיּוֹת) means literally "living beings." In Kabbalah and *Chassidut*, this term is taken to refer to the underlying pulse of all life (חַיּוּת),[13] which alternately runs "upward" out of its body to reunite with its Divine source, and thereafter returns "downward," investing itself with new life force.

In aspiring to total union with her beloved, a wife expresses the natural (albeit not generally conscious) tendency of the soul—the bride of the Song of Songs—and indeed, of all creation, to "run" toward its Beloved and extricate itself from the alienation imposed upon it by the prison of the body.[14]

---

13. See *Keter Shem Tov* 34, 37, 90, 121, 139, 188, 356; *Or Torah* 184; *Or HaTorah, Shavuot*, p. 139 ff., etc.

14. Allied to this idea is the phenomenon that prior to the ban of Rabbeinu Gershom (c. 960-1040), a man was permitted to have more than one wife, whereas a woman is strictly forbidden to have more than one husband. When practiced, polygamy was for the sake of "stabilizing" and guarding the intensity of the each wife's "run"; each wife was, indeed, an individual spark of the husband's true and complete soul mate.

Inasmuch as in the G-d-soul paradigm, the soul assumes the role of the wife and G-d that of the husband, this phenomenon is simply correlate to the fact that G-d creates many creatures, but each creature must recognize only the one G-d; polyandry is thus analogous to idolatry.

Nevertheless, monogamy has always been the usual and recommended practice in Judaism. This would seem to indicate that it is

This run of the soul, if unmitigated by a corresponding return, may have unhealthy consequences. For example, in the famous Talmudic story of "the four who entered paradise,"[15] we read of how Ben Azai died, Ben Zoma went insane, Elisha Ben Avuyah renounced his faith, and only Rabbi Akiva "entered in peace and emerged in peace." *Chassidut* teaches that Rabbi Akiva survived because he set out on his mystical journey with total commitment and surrender to the Divine will. This included the commitment to return to the lower realm after having reached the height of his soul's ascent to cling to G-d. The basis of this commitment is the allegiance to

---

tacitly recognized that a man should ideally concentrate his relational focus on one woman. In the G-d-soul paradigm, this means that G-d concentrates His relational focus on the Jewish people collectively as well as on each individual Jew. Each Jew may thus assume that he enjoys G-d's full attention, so to speak, as if He had no other "spouse." In the words of the Ba'al Shem Tov: every Jew is dearer to G-d than is an only son born to his parents in their old age (*Likutei Sichot*, vol. 3, p. 982; vol. 4, p. 1280).

(In the *tzadik-beinoni* paradigm discussed above [footnote 10], if the *tzadik* assumes the role of a *rebbe*, this principle would mean that a *rebbe* may have many *chassidim*, but each *chassid* should devote himself to only one *rebbe*, and that despite this, each *chassid* is justified in assuming that he enjoys his *rebbe's* full devotion.)

15. *Chagigah* 14a. Rabbi Yitzchak Luria (*Sha'ar Ma'amarei Razal* on *Chagigah* 14b) teaches that the four who entered paradise correspond to the four powers of the mind: *chochmah*, *binah*, the source of love in *da'at*, and the source of fear in *da'at*. Rabbi Akiva, who "entered in peace and went out in peace" personified the source of love in *da'at*. This clearly is the essential mental power for a happy, rectified marriage, since love is obviously the basic emotion of marriage, and knowledge is the unifying power of husband and wife—"and Adam *knew* his wife Eve."

the Divine purpose of creation that man turn this lowly material realm into a "dwelling place" for the Holy One, blessed be He.[16] The other sages did not set out with such a commitment.[17]

It is likewise taught that Nadab and Abihu, the two elder sons of Aaron who were consumed by fire upon volunteering an incense-offering at the inauguration of the Tabernacle—not having been so commanded—were also guilty of running toward G-d with no prior commitment to return.[18]

Nevertheless, *Chassidut* teaches that during the run itself, one must temporarily lose his awareness of his prior commitment to return.[19] This is necessary in order that the

---

16. *Tanya,* ch. 36, based on *Midrash Tanchuma, Naso* 16, ed. Buber 24.

17. In Kabbalah we are taught that the phrase "run and return" (רצוא ושוב) numerically equals "Torah" (תורה = 611). As "run and return" refers in particular to the feminine dynamic of the soul, we may infer from this equality that the Torah referred to here is the oral Torah, which is considered the feminine aspect of Torah relative to the written Torah, which is considered the masculine aspect. "*Malchut* [the feminine principle] is the mouth, and it is called the oral Torah" (*Tikunei Zohar,* introduction [17a]). The number midway between 1 and 611 (i.e., the "middle point" of 611) is 306, the numerical value of the word for "woman" (אשה).

Just as Moses is the "pillar of the written Torah," so is Rabbi Akiva the "pillar of the oral Torah." How appropriate, then, that we learn the proper nature of the "run and return" dynamic from Rabbi Akiva.

18. Leviticus 10:1. See *Or HaChaim* on Leviticus 16:1. Nadab and Abihu offered a "foreign fire" and were consumed by fire. This reminds us of the statement made by Rabbi Akiva with regard to marriage (quoted above, p. 109): "If man and woman merit, the Divine Presence dwells between them. If not, fire consumes them."

19. See *Or Torah* 111 (p. 38b-39a).

intensity of the run not be compromised. If the run is not sufficiently inspired and does not express genuine abandon, it may be expressing nothing more than a selfish search for a spiritual "high." The commitment to return must therefore not be allowed to interfere with the force and passion of the run.

Unconsciously, however, the commitment to return from the most sublime of spiritual states actually serves to facilitate one's journey up "the mountain of G-d,"[20] even as it causes one to turn around upon reaching its peak.

Thus, similar to Rabbi Akiva, a woman must preserve the natural balance of run and return in her marriage. Selfless devotion to her husband must be complimented by a commitment to fulfill her obligations toward herself, her family, and society. These commitments need not undermine her devotion toward her husband, but can and should actually serve to enhance it. Assuming her husband values and encourages the manner in which she fulfills these obligations, by performing them she is in fact fulfilling his will as well. In this way, through physical deed she becomes one with him in essence.

In reference to G-d, it is said that "He and His will are one."[21] In the soul's upward run to G-d, it can never reach His essence, since the very self-awareness and desire driving the run make it impossible for the soul to lose its finite consciousness in G-d's infinity. Only when the soul returns to perform G-d's will on earth does it become

---

20. Psalms 24:3.

21. See *Tanya*, ch. 4

united with His essence. In the words of *Sefer Yetzirah*:[22] "If your heart *runs, return* to the One." The "One"—the manifestation of the absolute union of Creator and creation through the means of the servant Jewish soul—is achieved by the return. Thus, it is paradoxically by retreating from the quest for and the experience of ecstatic union that one consummates the quest and achieves true, essential union.

Moreover, the return itself actually feeds the subsequent run. Just like every guest is a spark of spiritual desire that kindles a wife's passion for her husband, so does every good deed spark a similar desire in her.[23] The hidden union of essence with essence stirs the desire to unite consciously again, and so the cycle of run and return is renewed.

The Male Pulse of Time: Touching and not Touching

In contrast, the husband's dynamic in marriage is referred to as "touching and not touching."[24] This idiom is

22. As quoted in *Tikunei Zohar*, introduction (7a).

23. It is thus customary prior to performing a *mitzvah* to voice or contemplate one's intention to "unite the Holy One, blessed be He, and His *Shechinah*, in the name of all Israel."

24. In Hebrew: נוגע ואינו נוגע (*Y. Chagigah* 2:1; Rashi on Deuteronomy 32:11). The Aramaic translation of and the Kabbalistic term based on this expression is מטי ולא מטי (see *Etz Chaim* 7).

expressed in the Torah[25] by the image of an eagle gently hovering over its nest, careful not to harm its young or disturb the nest's delicate order. The desire to "touch" or alight on the nest indicates the husband's wish to care for his wife and all her needs. At the same time, the restraint reflected in "not touching" indicates his willingness to allow his wife the space necessary to function independently. While not touching, though, the husband never distances himself to the extent that his wife feels abandoned. His love and concern continue to hover over her even as she tends to her own needs and the needs of her household.

This dynamic underlies the process of creation itself. In order to generate finite reality, G-d had to, figuratively speaking, remove His infinite "light" from the arena of creation so that the universe could unfold without disturbance. The first realm to emanate out of G-d's will[26] is endowed with the greatest sense of His immanent proximity. The elements[27] of that world possess a sense of being totally and continuously "in touch" with Divinity (that is, they experience reality as transcending time and space).

In the creation of the subsequent, lower spiritual realms, G-d's distance or not touching becomes more apparent. This lends these successive worlds an increasing sense of independent existence. In truth, of course, G-d

25. Deuteronomy 32:11. Cf. *Likutei Amarim* (of the Maggid of Mezeritch) 99, 137, 162, 184, 225; *Or Torah* 57, 83, etc.

26. This is the world of *Atzilut*.

27. In the terminology of Kabbalah, the "vessels."

never really ceases to touch any part of reality.[28] Nevertheless, experiencing this truth demands a lifetime of devoted effort.

The dynamic of touching and not touching is reflected in the Talmudic dictum that refers to, among other things, raising children: "the left hand pushes away while the right hand draws near."[29] An element of good

---

28. In the words of the Maggid of Mezeritch: "*Atzilut* is here as well." As pointed out, *Atzilut* means "proximity" (from the root אצל, "near"). The insight of the Maggid is that not only is *Atzilut* "near" G-d (i.e., deeply and consummately conscious of Him, which is why the interpretation of *Atzilut* as "near" is considered in *Chassidut* to refer to its inner dimension, whereas the common interpretation of *Atzilut* as "emanation" is seen to refer to its outer dimension), but that it is also "near" and present in the three lower spiritual worlds of *Beriah*, *Yetzirah*, and *Asiyah*, and even our physical world.

Thus, *Atzilut* epitomizes the consciousness of a true *tzadik*, who is depicted in *Chassidut* as being simultaneously אין וועלט אויס וועלט ("in the world and outside the world"). He is always consciously concerned with the needs of lower reality while never removing his consciousness from clinging to G-d. It is told of the Ba'al Shem Tov (the mentor of the Maggid) that he beseeched the Almighty to grant him a level of consciousness that had never yet been attained: that even in the height of an "ascent of soul" (עלית הנשמה, in which the soul temporarily leaves the confines of the body to cling to G-d) he should be able to carry on a seemingly mundane conversation with another, earth-bound soul.

29. *Sotah* 47a. see also *Rut Rabbah* 2:16; *Zohar* 3:177b. The literal reading of this dictum implies that one should use his left (i.e. weaker) hand to "push away" undesired behavior, and his right hand to "draw near," or encourage the expression of positive behavior. Here, we are interpreting it in an almost opposite sense: "push away" to encourage independence; "draw near" to manifest one's presence and care.

"Pushing away" is more characteristic of male behavior, while "drawing near" is more characteristic of female behavior. In the

child rearing is learning when to maintain a certain distance from one's children so that they can become aware of their own independent existence and abilities. At the same time, it is the knowledge that parents are always available and caring that gives children the freedom and security to explore their own capabilities. This paradoxical touching and not touching is the essential context of any healthy growth environment.

There is a verse in the Song of Songs, spoken by the bride about her beloved, that evokes the same imagery: "His left arm is under my head, while his right arm embraces me."[30] The distancing force or "left arm" of her beloved is depicted as supporting her "head," i.e. her consciousness of self.[31] At the same time, the embracing force of his right arm communicates how her entire being—even her back (representing her experience of detachment and separateness)—is encompassed by his love and concern.

In each of the above examples, we see how the ultimate goal of touching is to lead to the subsequent state of not touching. By demonstrating his concern for his wife, the husband shows her that even when he is withdrawn,

---

terminology of Kabbalah, in *Abba*, the *gevurot* are more manifest, while in *Ima*, the *chasadim* are more manifest. The *gevurot* of *Abba* can become the *chasadim* of *Ima* because *Abba* itself is on the right side, and is thus more intrinsically a manifestation of *chesed* than *Ima* herself.

30. Song of Songs 2:6.

31. When rectified, her self-awareness is "lifted" to a state of existential "lowliness," as explained in *Chassidut*.

his concern still embraces her.[32] And by withdrawing, recognizing her independence, the husband inspires his wife to aspire (run) to a fuller degree of unity with him.

Similarly, G-d's omnipresent touching of all levels of creation allows Him to be accessible even at the levels where His Presence is not manifest. A parent's concern for his child is aimed ultimately at giving him the confidence to become an independent individual.

Each spouse thus expresses their love in a unique and profound way: the woman through the more experiential dynamic of run and return, and the man through the subtler dynamic of touching and not touching.[33]

The United Pulse

The male dynamic is thus a "descent for the sake of ascent,"[34] while the female dynamic is an "ascent for the

---

32. Thus we see that when the prophet Elijah set out to win Elisha as his disciple, he merely touched him, and then left. This inspired Elisha to follow him (1 Kings 19:16 ff.).

33. It should be pointed out that while "run and return" resembles an "alternating current" in which each state is experienced independently, "touching and not touching" may occur simultaneously—as in the example of the eagle hovering over its nest—and may thus be likened to a uniform "direct current." The same may be said of the dynamic of "the left hand pushes away while the right hand draws close."

34. *Makot* 7b. In *Chassidut*, this phrase is used to describe the descent of the soul into the body. By successfully facing the challenges of life, a soul earns a higher state of being in the afterlife than it

sake of descent."[35] Yet, when husband and wife unite, their ascents and descents "garb" themselves within each other.

The husband awakens his wife's love for him by "touching" her, revealing to her an aspect of his concern and care for her. This initial arousal inspires her—subconsciously, perhaps—to "run" toward him.[36]

His subsequent withdrawal, empowering her independence, gives impetus to this desire to unite with him. We said above that if the wife's run is not sufficiently intense it can become self-oriented, seeking its own pleasure in capturing a man (or, in the analog of G-d and the Jewish people, in our "capturing" G-d). The husband's not touching reinforces and lifts her run upward, helping it reach its highest peak. The increased force of her run increases the energy and blessing brought down by her return.

On the other hand, we said, if the wife's run is too intense, it can prove destructive. Her husband's not touching helps here, too, serving to objectify her ascent and give it the purpose that will ultimately transform it

---

enjoyed before its descent. Thus, its descent is "for the sake of" an ascent to a higher level of manifest Divinity.

35. This idiom is found in the writings of Rabbi Dovber of Lubavitch.

36. This is analogous to the relationship between G-d and the Jewish people in the month of *Elul*, when the revelation of G-d's thirteen attributes of mercy serve to subconsciously arouse the Jewish people to seek out G-d "on their own" in this month and the following month of *Tishrei* (the month of the High Holy Days). This contrasts with the dynamic of the month of *Nisan* (and its central holiday, *Pesach*), in which G-d openly initiates the relationship by taking us out of Egypt on His own.

into a descent. Like Rabbi Akiva, she will be able to "enter in peace and emerge in peace."

Similarly, whenever G-d reveals Himself in this world, it is in order to elevate the world to a higher plane of spirituality, to coax us out of our materialism and "capture" us for His own. By doing *mitzvot* in this world, we, in turn, are trying to "capture" G-d, so to speak, and reveal His Presence here.

So, sensing that the true union with her husband is in the concrete here and now, the wife returns to focus on herself and her affairs in the world. This reorientation from the abstract to the concrete, however, inspires her husband once again to touch her, to inspire her just enough to arouse her once more from her focus on the experiential. This time, however, his descent is "garbed" in her descent: his desire to coax her out of the experiential world is permeated with a healthy appreciation for the fulfillment possible only in the concrete world. Therefore, his subsequent ascent is not a retreat out of the experiential world into the abstract, but an elevation of the experiential world itself into the sublime consciousness of the higher realms.

We thus note that the only phase that remains subjective is the initial male half-dynamic of descent, since it comes first, by itself. When the husband descends to touch his wife, he is only conscious of his own desire to subsequently inspire her to go after him in his ascent of not touching. He does not become conscious of the ultimate objective, his wife's return, in which they actually unite, until his ascent becomes garbed in hers.

The female half-dynamic of descent, in contrast, has already been objectified by the united run and not touching that preceded it.

It follows that the purpose of a wife's upward run—her expression of devotion—is only to capture her husband so he will focus on her. Her true desire is to unite with his essence in her return. Her ascent is only a means; for her, the true end is her descent.

For the husband, however, the opposite is true: his descent, his touching his wife, is the means, while his ascent, his not touching—inspiring and coaxing her to pursue him—is his end. The general image of the husband descending and the wife ascending thus refers to their *initial* directions of movements, the means towards their respective ends. With regard to their goals, the husband seeks to ascend, and the wife to descend.

In other words: whereas a wife seeks primarily to unite with her husband, a husband seeks primarily to inspire and entice his wife to pursue him. The husband seeks to inspire his wife with abstract infinities; the wife seeks to concretize her husband's dreams in the here and now. The husband seeks challenge; the wife, fulfillment. The husband seeks to inject romance into their relationship; the wife seeks to drive it towards its ultimate consummation.[37]

---

37. If common experience seems to indicate that women are more romance-oriented than men are, it is only because they generally conceive of romance as a means to its fulfillment, the "happily ever-after."

Thus, the husband's and wife's respective dynamics complement each other. The husband's not touching keeps the wife's return from stagnating into an all-consuming preoccupation with the here and now, while the wife's return keeps her husband's not touching from degenerating into a retreat from objective reality.[38]

Thus, we may refer to the union of husband and wife and the merging of their two dynamics as a "descent for the sake of ascent for the sake of descent in turn."[39]

---

38. This accords with our earlier description of the couple's respective experiences of marital relations (see above, p. 128 ff.).

39. In the terminology of Kabbalah and *Chassidut*, the husband's initial touching and not touching is his initial, general "arousal from above" (אתערותא דלעילא בדרך מקיף) which subconsciously inspires the wife's "arousal from below" (אתערותא דלתתא). This arousal from below subsequently causes the husband to respond again with a second, essential and more focused "arousal from above" (אתערותא דלעילא פנימי ועצמי, see *Sefer HaMa'amarim 5689*, p. 82 ff.; see also *Bereishit Rabbah* 68:4, end).

Another image used to describe this is that of the protruding seal (חותם בולט) vs. the indented seal (חותם שוקע). The protruding seal leaves an indented impression in the wax, while the indented seal leaves a raised impression on it. Each seal, then, produces its inverse. In the present context, the husband's touching and not touching may be envisioned respectively as a protruding and indented seal hovering above; the wife's run and return may be envisioned respectively as protruding and indented seal facing up from below. The final, mutual ascent is again an indented seal from above with a protruding seal from below.

If we consider the protruding seal to be the active, "male" dynamic and the indented seal the passive, "female" dynamic, it follows that the husband's not-touching is the female aspect of his dynamic, while the wife's run is the male aspect of her dynamic.

All this is reflected in the form of the Hebrew letter *chet* (ח). The form of this letter portrays the dynamic of run and return.[40] The *chet* is formed of the two letters preceding it in the alphabet, a *vav* (ו) on the right and a *zayin* (ז) on the left, with a thin bridge connecting them above.

The *vav* on the right symbolizes the descending return, while the *zayin* on the left symbolizes the ascending run. The thin, connecting bridge above alludes to the Divine Presence that sustains and regulates the life-dynamic.

In general, the *vav* and *zayin* of the *chet* respectively symbolize the husband (or male force, the downward return) and the wife (or female force, the upward run) under the wedding canopy.[41]

The final ascent of the couple is not a "stage" *per se* but rather the continuous elevation of consciousness that results from the consummation of the third phase.

40. The form of each letter of the Hebrew alphabet portrays a spiritual dynamic of the soul and of the Divine creative process. With regard to the *chet*, see *The Alef Beit*, p. 122 ff. Even the name of the *chet* (חית) means "life force" (חיות, *chayut*).

41. It is significant that both the word for "wedding" (חתונה) and the word for "wedding canopy" (חופה) begin with the letter *chet*.

In our present, more detailed exposition, however, we have described the feminine dynamic as run and return (i.e., first upward and then downward) and the complimentary, male dynamic as touching and not touching (i.e., first downward and then upward). Both dynamics can still be depicted by the *chet*: in the male, the downward force of the *vav* precedes the upward force of the *zayin*, whereas in the female, the upward force of the *zayin* precedes the downward force of the *vav*.

Thus, a man begins from the right side of the *chet* (the *vav*), while a woman begins from the left (the *zayin*).

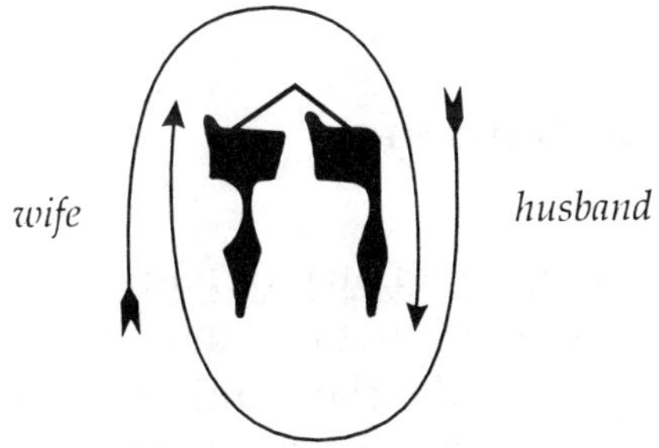

When husband and wife unite, his ascent (or *zayin*, the culmination of his dynamic) unites with hers (her *zayin*, the beginning of her dynamic), and her descent (or *vav*, the culmination of her dynamic) unites with his (his *vav*, the beginning of his dynamic).

The difference is that his ascent becomes enclothed in hers, whereas her descent (being the final stage of the threefold process described above) serves to "inspire" his subsequent descent. On one level, this second descent of the husband is informed by the wife's return, and its accompanying ascent is the mutual ascent of the couple into infinite levels of simultaneous transcendence and consummation.

On another level, his descent may be seen as a renewal of the cycle from its beginning. The consummation of the couple's union inspires the husband to seek to capture his wife on yet higher and deeper levels, so he begins the cycle anew.

We thus envision the dynamic of run and return as manifest between the two components of the letter *chet* itself (from the *vav* to the *zayin* and back to the *vav*).

The Bracelet of Marriage

When the complementary dynamics of husband and wife—touching and not touching and run and return—are considered independently, their union can be pictured as the union of two *chets* (חָח), which form the Hebrew word for "bracelet." Bracelets were the first articles of jewelry that the righteous women of Israel donated toward the construction of the Tabernacle:[42]

42. Exodus 35:22.

וַיָּבֹאוּ הָאֲנָשִׁים עַל הַנָּשִׁים, כֹּל נְדִיב לֵב
הֵבִיאוּ חָח וָנֶזֶם, וְטַבַּעַת וְכוּמָז, כָּל כְּלִי זָהָב...

And the men came together with the women,
every generous person,
bringing bracelets and nose rings,
finger rings and chastity belts,
all manner of golden ornaments....

The complimentary, cyclic dynamics of husband and wife thus constitute a "bracelet" which binds their lives into a unified whole.

The word for "together with" (עַל) used in this verse means literally "upon."[43] The verse can thus be understood to mean that the inspiration to donate "descended" from the men *onto* the women. The women's generosity then reinforced the men's philanthropic spirit; the descending inspiration ascended back to its source, following the paradigm of "descent for the sake of ascent."

Alternatively,[44] the verse may be understood to mean that the men donated because they were inspired by the women to do so; the inspiration "ascended" from the women to the men. The ascending inspiration thereafter descended to reinforce the philanthropic spirit of the women. In this way, we see the inspiration ascending and then flowing down, following the paradigm of "ascent for the sake of descent."

---

43. See Rashi on this verse, and additional note 2 at the end of this chapter (p. 258).

44. Taking the word על to mean על ידי ("by means of"), as is the case, for example, in Malachi 3:24 (see Rashi *ad loc.*).

Having explored the differing natures of man and woman and how they interact in married life, we can now analyze the specific effect that the woman's menstrual cycle has on a couple's relationship, and how it is meant to benefit their joint spiritual growth.

Additional Notes

1

to page 236.

Eve is called the "mother of all life" (אם כל חי, Genesis 3:20), which can also be interpreted to mean "the source of all 'living'" or "all 'being alive,'" thereby portraying the woman as the origin of all life experience.

This idea is supported by the following remarkable numerical phenomena. The numerical value of the concluding verse of the account of the six days of creation (Genesis 1:31),

וַיַּרְא אֱלֹהִים אֶת כָּל אֲשֶׁר עָשָׂה, וְהִנֵּה טוֹב מְאֹד, וַיְהִי עֶרֶב
וַיְהִי בֹקֶר יוֹם הַשִּׁשִּׁי,

And G-d saw all that He had made, and behold it was very good, and it was evening and it was morning, the sixth day,

is 3065 = 5 · 613. (613 is the total number of commandments in the Torah. The Torah was given on the sixth day of Sivan, which our sages say is alluded to by the phrase "the sixth day" in this verse [*Avodah Zarah* 3a].) The phrase **אם כל חי**, "mother of all life," also equals this number, when each of its six letters is squared:

$$\text{א}^2 + \text{ם}^2 + \text{כ}^2 + \text{ל}^2 + \text{ח}^2 + \text{י}^2 = 1^2 + 40^2 + 20^2 + 30^2 + 8^2 + 10^2$$
$$= 1 + 1600 + 400 + 900 + 64 + 100$$
$$= 3065.$$

Thus, we conclude that, Eve, "the mother of all life," represents the sum total of all (Divine) experience of Creation.

Furthermore, when each one of the six letters of אם כל חי is "triangled":

$$\Delta\text{א} + \Delta\text{ם} + \Delta\text{כ} + \Delta\text{ל} + \Delta\text{ח} + \Delta\text{י} = \Delta 1 + \Delta 40 + \Delta 20 + \Delta 30 + \Delta 8 + \Delta 10$$
$$= 1 + 820 + 210 + 465 + 36 + 55$$
$$= 1587.$$

1587 = 3 · 529. 529 is the numerical value of the word **תענוג** ("pleasure"). Thus, the average value of the three words for "the mother of all life" is that of the word for "pleasure." In addition, the numerical value of the word for "pleasure" itself (**תענוג**, 529) = 23^2; 23 = **חדוה** ("joy").

"Pleasure" is understood to be synonymous with "life experience," as in the verse: "for with You is the source of life" (Psalms 36:10), which is interpreted: "for with You is the source of all pleasure." In Kabbalah, we are taught that the full manifestation of pleasure is in the *partzuf* of *Ima* ("mother").

2

to page 255.

The word "upon" (**על**) equals 100 = 10^2. The number 100 alludes to the perfect inter-inclusion of the ten *sefirot*, each of the ten being manifest in all ten. (In general, squaring a number signifies the manifestation of its full "inter-inclusion," each individual element of its primary being reflecting and manifesting the full array of all its elements. Furthermore, male-female union [for the sake of procreation] is conceived in Kabbalah as a "multiplication" process [the secret of "be fruitful and *multiply*"], rather than a simple addition. The perfect multiplication is a square.)

Though here the word for "together with" is על, the usual word for "together" in Hebrew is יחד. In the beginning of the final Torah-portion, וזאת הברכה, we read (Deuteronomy 33:5):

וַיְהִי בִישֻׁרוּן מֶלֶךְ בְּהִתְאַסֵּף רָאשֵׁי עָם,
יַחַד שִׁבְטֵי יִשְׂרָאֵל.

And there will be a king in Jeshurun
when the heads of the nation gather,
the tribes of Israel together.

Our sages interpret this to mean that only when all the tribes of Israel (beginning with the leaders) gather together, in love of Israel and commitment to serve G-d, does G-d accept Israel's coronation of

Him as King (see Rashi *ad loc.*). Both the idiom for "commitment" (קבלת על, literally: "accepting the *yoke*") and that for "appointing" a king (שום תשים עליך מלך, "you shall surely place a king *upon* you," Deuteronomy 17:15) employ and emphasize the word על. Thus, we may conclude that על depends on יחד, and יחד depends on על.

The word יחד equals 22. The periphery of a strip of 10 · 1 (whose area is 10) is 22. The number 22 represents the twenty-two letters of the Hebrew alphabet, which are said in Kabbalah to "garb" ("encompass," "hold") the 10 *sefirot*.

Although the word יחד does not appear explicitly in the above cited verse, it is repeatedly alluded to. the Torah-portion in which our verse appears is *Vayakhel* (ויקהל), the *22nd* Torah-portion; our verse is the *22nd* verse in this Torah-portion; and it possesses 22 words!

The first word (and the name) of this Torah-portion, ויקהל ("And he gathered *together*" = 151), when added to the first word of our verse, ויבאו ("And they came" = 25), equals 176 = 8 · 22 (as in ch. 119 of Psalms, the largest chapter—with respect to the number of verses—in the entire Bible, which possesses 176 verses, 8 verses for—and beginning with—each of the 22 letters of the alphabet).

The full spelling of the letter *chet* itself (חית) equals 418 = 22 · 19. 19 = חוה, Eve, whose name begins with a ח, and who was named for "life"—"for she was the mother of all life" (Genesis 3:20).

The primordial union of husband and wife is that of Adam (אדם = 45) and Eve (חוה = 19), whose names added together equal 64 = 8 · 8, ח times ח, the letter *chet* "squared" (in the secret of the word חח, the "bracelet of marriage")!

12

The Cycles of Marital Intimacy

The Monthly Cycle—a Spiral of Spiritual Growth

"Family Purity" is the name of the area of *halachah* (הֲלָכָה, "Jewish law") that addresses the circumstances under which a couple are allowed to engage in marital relations. As will be described presently, the axis around which these laws revolve is the wife's menstrual cycle.

A couple who lives by the laws of Family Purity can truly be considered to be "living with the times." The wife's menstrual cycle enables them to be acutely sensitive to the patterns of time in creation[1] and to apply the understanding of the significance of these patterns to their service of G-d.

---

1. Since the menstrual cycle is related to the lunar cycle. The Jewish calendar is primarily lunar, although it is adjusted in order to accord with the solar cycle as well. This indicates that the experience of time in Judaism centers primarily on the feminine consciousness. See additional note at the end of this chapter (p. 275).

One of the most fundamental teachings of the Ba'al Shem Tov is that every complete act in the service of G-d entails three phases: submission, separation, and sweetening.[2] In accordance with the principle of inter-inclusion[3] true for every integral set of concepts or experiences in Divine service, each of these three stages manifests all three within itself. When thus articulated in full, the three stages expand into nine levels of spiritual experience.

As a woman goes through her monthly cycle and experiences the bodily changes that accompany it, she and her husband can construct a model of Divine service that follows each of these stages.

---

2. In Hebrew: הכנעה, הבדלה, המתקה, respectively. *Keter Shem Tov* 28. The three stages of submission, separation, and sweetening reflect the model of *chash-mal-mal* ("silence, circumcision, speech"), for "silence" is the submission of one's ego; "circumcision" is the separation of the impure foreskin from the body; and "speech" is the power to sweeten reality.

mal	speech	המתקה	sweetening
mal	circumcision	הבדלה	separation
chash	silence	הכנעה	submission

3. In Hebrew: התכללות.

Days of Seeing, Days of Cleanliness, Days of Purity

The onset of menstruation and its attendant emotional changes focus a woman's attention on herself. During her period, she is preoccupied with the biological and emotional reality of her physical condition and therefore cannot fully direct her attention to another person. Since she cannot, at this time, fully feel the serenity in which marital relations are meant to take place, marital relations are forbidden.[4]

As we have discussed above,[5] over-self-consciousness and awareness are considered states of "impurity" and "defilement" in Jewish thought, impediments to spiritual orientation and growth. Therefore, menstrual blood is considered an impure state from which a wife must ritually purify herself before she and her husband may resume marital relations.

In Jewish law, the menstrual cycle is divided into three stages: the "days of seeing," the "days of cleanliness," and the "days of purity."

The days of seeing are the period of time during which a woman experiences her menstrual flow. This

---

4. The term used in the Torah for the woman's seeing blood is הרגשה, which means "feeling," "experiencing," or "sensing." Rachel said to her father, Laban: "I cannot get up, for the way of women is with me" (Genesis 31:35). Although the plain meaning of this is that she was unable to physically get up, it may be understood allegorically to refer to the feeling of gravity and emotional moodiness that accompanies menstruation.

5. See, in particular, p. 54, and footnote 14 there.

period lasts either five days or until the woman stops bleeding, whichever is longer.

The days of cleanliness, always numbering seven, immediately follow the days of seeing. During this period, the woman "recuperates" and cleanses herself from the psychological gravity of the days of seeing.[6] Therefore, although no blood is seen, the body is still considered spiritually impure from the previous flow. During these first two periods, all manner of physical contact between husband and wife is forbidden.

Following the woman's immersion in a *mikveh* (מִקְוֶה, a ritual pool) at the end of the seventh clean day, the days of purity begin. Husband and wife are then permitted to resume physical intimacy until the re-appearance of menstrual blood.

<table>
<tr><td>days of purity (≈ 18)</td><td>period following immersion in mikveh</td><td>marital relations permitted</td></tr>
<tr><td>days of cleanliness (7)</td><td>week following cessation of menstrual flow</td><td rowspan="2">marital relations forbidden</td></tr>
<tr><td>days of seeing (≈ 5)</td><td>period of menstrual flow</td></tr>
</table>

6. The "gravity" and "feeling down" of the impure state is contrasted with the elation and feeling of being uplifted that accompanies purity.

As is taught in Kabbalah and *Chassidut*, there are seven emotions of the heart. These were "defiled" by the egocentricity of menstruation, and therefore seven days are required to cleanse them of its defilement (i.e., to forget the self-orientation of the days of seeing).

These three periods of the physical menstrual cycle parallel the three stages of Divine service mentioned above:

The days of seeing correspond to submission. Upon her initial sight of impure blood, the involuntary physical estrangement of the wife from her husband reminds them of the existential distance of the soul from G-d, imprisoned as it is in its "impure" (i.e., unrectified) body. The couple experiences the same existential humility a servant does when told to leave the king's presence.

They know, however, even in the depth of the estrangement, that it is only temporary. Being distant from one's beloved gives rise to an intense longing to draw closer to him.[7]

The sincere desire for and faith in the eventuality of reunion, together with trust in G-d's providence and benevolence even in the present moment of distance, protects one from sinking into the depression of feeling severed and estranged, which may further degenerate into despair and apathy. The bitterness that one does experience can actually spur him to change his behavior in ways that promise to resolve the source of the discontent.

The days of cleanliness correspond to the spiritual work of separation. Each day during this period, the woman scrupulously checks herself for signs of a

---

7. Thus, the imposition of physical separation fosters emotional, mental, and spiritual closeness. The menstrual cycle therefore serves as the catalyst that elevates a couple from the "spatial" level of relationship to the "temporal" level of togetherness. The true test of togetherness is physical separation; if a couple can feel together despite physical separation, they are truly together. See above, p. 72.

continued or resumed menstrual flow. Spiritually, this process teaches the couple to examine whether or not they have properly separated themselves from thoughts, feelings or behavior that may perpetuate their distance from G-d. In the verse "turn from evil and do good,"[8] this level of Divine service corresponds to the fulfillment of "turn from evil."

On a deeper level, the daily checking serves to enhance the woman's mounting anticipation of future reunion with her husband, and the couple's rapprochement with G-d. Each blood-free day is counted, and when seven consecutive days accrue, the woman may immerse herself and once again become spiritually cleansed. This hopefulness and expectation for the future balances her meticulous concern over the possibility of residual blemish or impurity.

Finally, the woman immerses herself in a *mikveh* and so begins the days of purity, corresponding to the service of sweetening. The preoccupation with past and future characterizing the recent days of cleanliness gives way to an unadulterated joy in the present moment that achieves its consummation in the physical union, in sanctity and purity, of husband and wife. Their marital relations are the absolute sweetening of the longing and desire which they both felt. On the spiritual plane, the couple learns from this to experience the unmitigated joy of union with G-d afforded by performing His *mitzvot*. This is the ultimate fulfillment of the Divine command "and do good."

To summarize:

---

8. Psalms 34:15. See above, p. 51, footnote 8.

cycle of Family Purity	stage of spiritual growth	aspect of Divine service
days of purity	sweetening	union with G-d in the performance of *mitzvot*; "...and do good"
days of cleanliness	separation	examination of one's behavior; "turn from evil..."; anticipation of reunion with G-d
days of seeing	submission	awareness of existential distance from G-d

Nine Levels of Inter-inclusion

Let us now examine in greater detail these three phases of passage from impurity to purity, contemplating the elements of inter-inclusion within each:

THE DAYS OF SEEING

1 Submission within Submission

The first appearance of menstrual blood is experienced as a fall of spirit. Concomitant to falling away from one another, the couple senses apparent alienation from Divine grace, which fills them with humility and an attitude of surrender to G-d's will as it manifests itself in the cycles of nature.

2 Separation within Submission

This level of service, reflecting the couple's willing acceptance of the laws prohibiting physical contact, prevents the initial feelings of lowliness from degenerating into despair, G-d forbid. The couple finds substitute attachment and identification in their collaborative effort to meticulously observe these laws. Their mutual concern for upholding the Torah's discipline and adhering to halachic imperatives focuses them more on their spirit and intellect than on their bodily natures and emotions. Feelings of despair quickly give way to a humble acceptance of G-d's will, and a readiness to carry out the mandates of that will as expressed through the Torah.

Having reconciled themselves to temporary separation, the couple can begin anticipating the promise of renewed physical intimacy. The experience of separation must inevitably lead to an increased desire for the state of purity identified with holy conjugal union. This desire and the spiritual benefit that it provides continue to grow until the days of purity are reached.

3 Sweetening within Submission

This stage is inspired by the determination that the woman's menstrual flow has ceased—the *hefsek taharah* (הֶפְסֵק טָהֳרָה, "cessation [of bleeding, indicating] purity")[9]

---

9. The word *taharah* (purity) in this expression implies the inter-inclusion of the days of purity (and the general state of sweetening to come) within this present level of submission.

Let us note that the word *taharah* (טהרה, "purity") comes from the root טהר, which is one of the thirteen synonyms in Hebrew for "light," as in the phrase (Exodus 24:10) "as the essence of the heavens—purely radiant [טהר, i.e., the cloudless sky]." All experience of light is one of sweetening, as stated in the verse "for light is sweet" (Ecclesiastes 11:7). In Kabbalah, we are taught that the experience of טהר relates to the *partzuf* of *Ima,* whose womb is the source of the waters of the *mikveh.* At an even deeper level, the very vacuum (מקום פנוי) created by the initial contraction (צמצום) of G-d's infinite light, which signals the end of the days of seeing. When this is achieved, there is reason for the couple to modestly rejoice, although they must remain aware that the process is only partially complete and submission is still in order.

THE DAYS OF CLEANLINESS

4 Submission within Separation

During the seven days of cleanliness, the woman examines herself each morning and afternoon (before sunset) to be sure that her flow has indeed ceased. One suspects that perhaps a residue of impure blood remains, that one may regress and fall once more into a state of existential distance from G-d.

Both wife and husband are well aware that a state of ritual impurity still exists. The discipline of two daily examinations helps to preserve the feelings of humility and surrender to G-d elicited by the days of seeing.

---

the "womb" of all created reality, is called the טהירו, for though it may appear dark in contrast to the infinite light that disappears within it, it is nonetheless a "brilliant sky" encompassing all subsequent reality.

From here we may understand that טהר is actually that level of light that possesses varying, descending degrees of intensity. For instance, Kabbalah speaks (in reference to the initial contraction) of the טהירו עילאה and the טהירו תתאה, the "higher pure-brilliance" and the "lower pure-brilliance." All these degrees are experienced in the feminine psyche: they are all degrees of "womb." Thus, even at this lowest general level of submission, the inter-inclusion of sweetening within submission implies a degree of purity (טהרה).

5 Separation within Separation

This is the essence of the couple's experience during the days of cleanliness. Together with the attention they maintain with regard to the laws of separation inherited from the days of seeing, their primary experience is now the growing anticipation of the reunion about to consecrate a period of renewed purity. This primary expression of this anticipation is the wife's counting of the seven days.[10]

The hopefulness generated by this anticipation must nevertheless remain mute, as though covered by the laws of separation. Even as preparations for immersion in the *mikveh* begin, toward nightfall at the end of the seventh clean day, the increased excitement and expectation does not compromise the attention to halachic detail necessary in order to ensure a valid immersion.[11]

6 Sweetening within Separation

The culminating event of these days, the ritual immersion, represents the sweetening moment that concludes the period of separation. All the joy suppressed throughout this period of meticulous examination can now emerge in the euphoric moment of immersion in the waters of the *mikveh*.

---

10. See below, p. 280.

11. These preparations are called *chafifah* (חפיפה). The word *chafifah* in Hebrew also means "overlap" or "intersect." In the intense cleaning (that no foreign matter remain on the body) and bathing process of the *chafifah*, the two levels of separation within separation and sweetening-within-separation overlap.

Jewish law stipulates that immersion must be total; not even one hair may remain outside the waters of the *mikveh*. Spiritually, a "hair" represents a fleeting thought; not even the smallest part of one's consciousness may refuse to enter the pleasant waters of the *mikveh*-"womb." One's previous, impure state of being becomes nullified, and one becomes reborn as a new, pure being.[12]

---

12. The word in Hebrew for "immersion" (טבל) is a permutation of the word for "self-nullification," (בטל), as taught in Kabbalah and *Chassidut* (see *Siddur Im Dach* 159d). The very power inherent in self-nullification is the ability to permute letters, the "building blocks" of creation, into new words, i.e., new states of reality (*Sefer HaSichot 5697*, p. 197; *Keter Shem Tov*, addendum 3 [the fifth teaching received from the Ba'al Shem Tov]).

This is expressed in the verse: "Who can give pure from impure, if not the One?" (Job 14:4). The sages (*Bamidbar Rabbah* 19:1) interpret this verse as a reference to Abraham, the son of Terach, the pure soul born from the impure. From here we learn that becoming pure through immersion in the *mikveh* is like the absolute metamorphosis of conversion from the impurity of idolatry (the practice of Terach) into the purity of perfect faith in one G-d (the faith of Abraham).

THE DAYS OF PURITY[13]

7 Submission within Sweetening

After immersion in the *mikveh*, the woman is once again rendered spiritually pure, and the couple may resume physical contact and marital relations. Yet, here too, there remains an aspect of submission. Though no longer forced to separate, the couple is still bidden to conduct their relations with modesty. Marital relations are required by Jewish law to be conducted in an atmosphere of mystery and awe. The laws of modesty remind both husband and wife that G-d is ever present, and that one must "walk modestly"[14] before Him.

8 Separation within Sweetening

At this level of spiritual service, the couple sanctifies their marital relations by concentrating—both before and

---

13. Until this point, the stages in the ninefold process have occurred one at a time. As the cycle progresses, however, the intensity accelerates, and the final three stages occur essentially simultaneously; the sequential process is preserved only in thought.

Thus, modesty, though only the seventh stage, occurs at the end of the process (together with the eighth and ninth stages), and can thus be considered to follow the principle of "the end is wedged in the beginning." The submission within sweetening is wedged in the submission within submission. "All sevenths are beloved" (*Vayikra Rabbah* 29:11); this stage of modesty is thus the innermost dimension of even the final, ninth stage (see below, p. 280, footnote 12).

14. Micah 6:8. See at length below, ch. 15.

during relations—on proper thoughts.[15] These include the intention and heartfelt prayer to the Almighty to bring G-d-fearing children into the world,[16] or the desire, springing from the innate goodness of one's soul, to bring true pleasure and fulfillment to one another.[17]

Yet higher levels of intention involve meditating on the omnipresence of G-d. As we have said, contemplating the teachings of the Torah's inner dimension elevates a couple to a level of consciousness at which they experience their physical union below as a true model and expression of the union of G-d and the *Shechinah* above.[18]

Further sanctification of marital relations is achieved by synchronizing them with spiritually conducive occasions.[19]

---

15. The word for "sanctity" (קדושה) implies separation from all forms of mundane consciousness and activity. Thus, the sanctity of the marital union corresponds to the level of separation-within-sweetening.

16. See below, p. 349 ff.

17. See below, p. 339 ff. Pleasure is "true" only when one experiences the union of the spiritual and the physical. When the couple experience this true pleasure, it reflects the same phenomenon happening universally, for the Jewish soul (experience) corresponds to the inner Divine life force of all creation. The attribute of "truth" (אמת) refers, in Kabbalah and *Chassidut*, to the *sefirah* of *yesod*, the unifying force in marital relations.

18. The effect of observing G-d's commandments and fulfilling His will is to unify the Holy One, blessed be He, with His *Shechinah* (יחוד קודשא בריך הוא ושכינתיה), i.e., G-d's infinite, transcendent light with His immanent light. See below, p. 353 ff.

19. See below, p. 342 ff.

9 Sweetening within Sweetening

The essence of sweetening is experienced in the marital union itself. When the couple has successfully ascended through the prior stages of spiritual service and preparation, having neutralized their selfish and animalistic desires, they stand to merit an experience of great, uplifting force as their bodies and souls unite. In their experience of profound joy and closeness to G-d, the couple ascend to pure spiritual heights. The children of this union will be pure in soul and embody G-d's truth and benevolence.[20]

To summarize:

sweetening	days of purity	sweetening	joy of marital relations
		separation	proper thoughts during relations
		submission	modest conduct during relations
separation	days of cleanliness	sweetening	ritual immersion in *mikveh*
		separation	anticipation of reunion
		submission	daily examinations
submission	days of seeing	sweetening	*hefsek taharah*
		separation	observance of laws of separation
		submission	appearance of menstrual flow

20. This experience is the consummate *experience* of the first two *intentions* (as well as the last, see above, footnote 18) described in regard to the previous level (separation within sweetening).

The couple conceive spiritual "children" even when they cannot conceive physically (see below, p. 352).

Additional Note

to page 261.

There are three pairs of names for the sun and moon in Hebrew, corresponding to the essential male and female archetypes of the three lower worlds:

	sun		moon	
Beriah	שמש	*shemesh*	ירח	*yareiach*
Yetzirah	חמה	*chamah*	לבנה	*levanah*
Asiyah	חרס	*cheres*	סהר	*sahar*

The combined numerical value of the three names of the moon (the female archetype) is 570, which equals $30 \cdot 19$, 19 being the value of **חוה** (Eve). The average value of the three names is 190, which equals **צלע** (the "side" or "rib" from which Eve was created); this number is the triangle of 19, **חוה**. The average menstrual cycle (עונה בינונית) is 30 days long.

The combined numerical value of the three names of the sun (the male archetype) is $961 = 31^2$, and 31 is the value of G-d's Name *Kel* (**אל**), which is associated with the *sefirah* of *chesed* ("loving-kindness"). *Chesed* is the male principle, as it is said: "He remembered His loving-kindness" (Psalms 98:3); the word for "remembered" (זכר) also means "male."

The sun is called the "great luminary" (Genesis 1:16). As explained above (p. 140, footnote 10), the attribute of "greatness" is identified with the *sefirah* of *chesed*, the male principle symbolized by the sun. When each letter of the word for "great" (גדול) is squared, the sum $(3^2 \perp 4^2 \perp 6^2 \perp 30^2)$ is $961 = 31^2$, the numerical value of the sun's three names.

13

From Exile to Redemption[1]

The Cosmic Marriage

Our sages refer to the giving of the Torah at Mt. Sinai as the marriage of the Jewish people to G-d.[2] The events leading up to the giving of the Torah can thus be correlated to the stages leading to the union of husband and wife that we have described above.

The exile of Egypt is the prototype for all the exiles the Jewish people have suffered,[3] as well as for all

---

1. The exposition presented in this chapter is based on *Reshimot* 10 (p. 22) and 98 of the Lubavitcher Rebbe and *Etz Chaim* 39:9. The marriage dynamic and the exodus-to-Redemption dynamic parallel, in turn, the personal process of ongoing spiritual redemption of each individual from his relative states of estrangement from G-d. Although we have not discussed this parallel explicitly, it is implicit in the exposition and is discussed at length in Chassidic sources (see, *inter alia, Magen Avot* 7:73a ff.).

2. *Ta'anit* 26b.

3. "All the nations [which subdue Israel] are called 'Egypt' [מצרים], since they all oppress [מצירות] Israel" (*Bereishit Rabbah* 16:4).

personal states of alienation from G-d that any individual may experience. Egypt is identified as the seat of spiritual impurity[4] and in this context can be seen to symbolize the days of seeing, which we have identified with the spiritual state of submission.

The descent of Jacob's household into Egypt—the existential fall of the Jewish people into exile[5]—corresponds to the first sight of menstrual blood, the experience of submission within submission.

Throughout the Egyptian exile, the Jewish people retained their unique identity. They did not change their names, language, or clothing. In addition, they carefully observed all the laws of Family Purity, which the patriarchs and matriarchs had taught them.[6] Moreover, their faith in the promised redemption never waned.[7] The

---

4. See above, p. 95, footnote 46.

5. Although the severe physical oppression of the Egyptian exile began only 124 years later (86 years before the exodus), the *spiritual* oppression began as soon as the Jews left their natural, holy environment—the land of Israel—and descended to Egypt, the seat of spiritual impurity.

6. See *Midrash Tehilim* 114:4; *Vayikra Rabbah* 32:5; *Shir HaShirim Rabbah* 4:24, etc.; *Pesikta Zotarta*, Exodus 6:6.

7. The strength of one's faith in redemption is dependent on his observance of the laws of Family Purity. The psychological root of the conscious, ever-growing anticipation of reunion—separation-within-separation—is in this level of separation within submission. At the level of separation within separation, one anticipates the joy of the holy marital union itself, which parallels the giving of the Torah at Mt. Sinai. At the level of separation-within-submission, one possesses faith (whether conscious or unconscious) in the imminent redemption from Egypt, the cessation of the days of "seeing" and the beginning of the days of cleanliness.

period of exile thus corresponds to the level of separation within submission.

The exodus from Egypt symbolizes the cessation of menstrual bleeding and the *hefsek taharah,* the level of sweetening within submission.[8]

Even after the exodus, the Jewish people feared that they might be pursued by the Egyptians and forced back into exile. They therefore counted the days that had elapsed from their exodus, in effect "pinching" themselves to be sure that their liberation was real.

Although the physical threat of pursuit ceased when G-d drowned the Egyptian army in the sea, the possibility of returning to the slave mentality of Egypt (and even voluntarily returning to the land of Egypt) remained.[9] For this reason, each of the forty-nine days from the exodus to the receiving of the Torah is considered an additional step in leaving Egypt. This mental state corresponds to the state of submission within separation.

The intent of this counting, however, was related not to the past (the flight from Egypt) but to the future (the giving of the Torah).[10] From day to day the Jewish people's anticipation of meeting and "marrying" G-d at Mt. Sinai

---

8. *Magen Avot, loc. cit.*

9. This can be seen from the fact that on many occasions during their sojourn in the desert, the Jews lost heart, lamented leaving Egypt, and even suggested returning (Exodus 13:17, 14:10-12, 17:3; Numbers 11:5, 11:20, 14:3-4, 20:5, 21:5).

10. This counting was subsequently transformed into the *mitzvah* of counting the *Omer* (Rabbeinu Nissim, *Commentary on Sefer HaHalachot,* end of *Pesachim*).

grew. The *Zohar*[11] parallels this seven-week period of counting to the seven days of cleanliness that precede the ritual immersion in the *mikveh*. This corresponds to the level of separation within separation.

The immersion of the Jewish people in the *mikveh* prior to receiving the Torah parallels the wife's immersion prior to uniting with her husband and corresponds to the level of sweetening within separation.

Three days before giving the Torah, G-d commanded Moses to fence off Mt. Sinai and forbid the people to approach the mountain. This was in order to imbue the people with a sense of modesty and restraint when they would consummate their relation with G-d.[12] This corresponds to the level of submission within sweetening.

During these three days of restriction, the Jewish people were commanded to abstain from marital relations. This was so that when receiving the Torah they would be pure both in mind and body.[13] This purity allowed them to

---

11. 3:97b. The day of the giving of the Torah is the holiday of *Shavuot*, whose name means "weeks," indicating that the essence revealed on that day is a direct consequence of the spiritual service that led up to it, the anticipation of counting the days and weeks.

12. Moses was here the emissary of the people, who through him spoke with G-d and received the Torah from Him "face to face." As will be explained in ch. 15, the innermost points of a couple's souls approach and meet one another in virtue of their modest conduct during marital relations. Similarly, Moses, the innermost point of the collective soul of the Jewish people, ascended to meet G-d on the mountain, as G-d Himself descended to give to Moses the innermost point of His own being, as it were, the Torah (see below, footnote 17).

13. Marital relations impart a degree of ritual impurity to the couple (Leviticus 15:16-18), which prevents either of them from

concentrate solely on their Divine groom[14] while His voice spoke to them from all the directions (and dimensions) of reality.[15]

The day before the three days of restriction, they had exclaimed to Moses: "we desire *ourselves* to behold our King"[16] (and not to receive the Torah by way of a mediator). Now, at the giving of the Torah, their request was granted. This corresponds to the level of separation within sweetening.

In the giving of the Torah, G-d gave us, as it were, the seed of His essence, just as in marital relations the husband conveys his essence to his wife.[17] At that moment, the wife's very being merges with her husband's, and she begins to integrate the seed of his being into herself. Here, the Divine groom and bride, G-d and Israel, reach the peak of ecstasy in their holy union; the Jewish people become "the people in whose heart is My Torah."[18] This corresponds to the level of sweetening within sweetening.

To summarize:

---

entering the Temple precincts or eating certain categories of food until nightfall, after immersion in a *mikveh*. See below, p. 303, footnote 59.

14. In particular, this refers to the concentration of all their marital energies, their *da'at*.

15. Exodus 20:14; Rashi *ad loc.*

16. *Mechilta, Yitro* 19:9.

17. The first word spoken by G-d to the people of Israel at Sinai, the first word of the Ten Commandments—"I" (אנכי)—is an acronym for אנא נפשי כתבית יהבית, "I have written and conveyed [to you] My very Self" (*Pesikta Zotarta, Yitro* 20; *Midrash Tanchuma*, ed. Buber, *Yitro* 16, etc.). see also *Likutei Torah* 4:93d ff.

18. Isaiah 51:7.

			the cycle of marital relations	**the exodus from Egypt**
sweetening	days of purity	sweetening	joy of marital relations	receiving the Torah
		separation	proper thoughts during relations	purity of body; focusing on G-d
		submission	modest conduct during relations	restriction from ascending Mt. Sinai
separation	days of cleanliness	sweetening	ritual immersion in *mikveh*	purification in *mikveh*
		separation	anticipation of reunion	counting the days to Mt. Sinai
		submission	daily examinations	threat of Egyptian pursuit
submission	days of seeing	sweetening	*hefsek taharah*	exodus from Egypt
		separation	observance of laws of separation	adhering to Jewish identity
		submission	appearance of menstrual flow	descent into Egyptian exile

Adorning the Bride

Between the immersion in the *mikveh* (the conclusion of the separation phase) and the modesty of the couple in their marital relations (the beginning of the sweetening phase), there is an intermediary stage, in which the wife prepares herself for relations with her husband. This stage is a rehearsal for the coming union. By imagining and preparing for the various facets of the encounter, she sets in motion the spiritual forces that will determine the quality and mood of what is to come.

This stage is necessary since it is difficult for most people to pay attention to the intentions motivating (and therefore determining the quality of) an action while engaged in the action itself. This is true with regard to the performance of all *mitzvot*, and for that reason we are taught that the time to concentrate on the meaning one wishes to infuse into a *mitzvah* is *before* beginning it.[19]

The three stages of this preparatory phase parallel the three facets of marital relations.

In the first stage, the wife readies herself physically, beautifying and adorning herself in order to express and accentuate her natural grace and charm. The dominant sense that should pervade these preparations is that of modesty.

---

19. *Tanya*, ch. 41 (58b). The Ba'al Shem Tov goes so far as to say that the *main* aspect of the spiritual dimension of performing a *mitzvah* is the preparatory stage, since it is what determines the quality of the deed that follows.

The difference between intentions at the preparation stage and at the execution stage is that the former are pervaded by a sense of anticipation and yearning, while the latter are pervaded by concern that the *mitzvah* be performed correctly. In the case of marital relations, this means concern that the *mitzvah* of *onah* is properly fulfilled, that no seed is inadvertently spilled, and in general that the act be performed successfully.

Actually, we can identify three phases of *kavanah*: of concepts expressed by the deed (*chabad*), of emotions expressed by the deed (*chagat*), and of the technical details of the deed's performance (*nehi*). The *mitzvah* of marital relations can been seen as the archetype for all others in this sense, since in it the way one progresses through these three stages of *kavanah* is most evident.

It may seem contradictory that a woman's mind should be focused on modesty while she is making herself physically attractive. But the Torah teaches us that "the glory of the princess is within."[20] There is a tendency in married life to put on one's best self only when going out, letting one's familiarity with one's spouse degenerate into laxity and inattentiveness to appearance and behavior. Although it is certainly important for a couple to feel relaxed together, excessive familiarity can backfire, undermining the couple's perception of each other as the main focus of their lives.

Rather, the Torah teaches that one's best self, and one's innermost beauty, should be reserved for one's private relationship with one's spouse.[21] Modesty and attractiveness are therefore interdependent: a wife's modesty enhances her attractiveness to her husband, and her attention to her attractiveness for her husband's sake is an eloquent expression of her modesty.[22]

By dressing up for her husband in a spirit of modesty, the wife ensures that their marital relations will be conducted modestly, and in a spirit of mystery and awe, as we described above.

---

20. Psalms 45:14. All Jews are princes (and Jewesses princesses), as noted below, p. 351, footnote 111.

21. See *Mishneh Torah, Nedarim* 12:1, that beautifying oneself with jewelry is considered exclusively a matter "between a man and his wife."

22. This subject is developed at length in ch. 15.

Physical preparation is an act of submission, in that the wife must pay scrupulous attention to the laws of modest attire even while she is making herself attractive.[23]

Besides refreshing and relaxing her, attention to grooming and personal hygiene allows the wife to put aside the other parts of her life and concentrate on the imminent reunion with her husband. Thus, her physical preparation catalyzes the next stage, her psychological preparation. Here, she thinks about what she think about during marital relations, and reviews all the sublime thoughts with which she wishes to imbue their physical union, as described above. By focusing on her husband, she is separating or isolating her consciousness from anything else that may vie for her attention.

The third phase of preparation is her creation of an atmosphere of intimacy, particularly by speaking to her husband with affection and charm. This inspires him to focus all the more on her. This phase of preparation corresponds to the act of marital relations itself, since speech is a metaphor (and euphemism) for marital relations, as we have noted.

To summarize:

---

23. The interdependence between beauty and humility is seen in the parallel construction of the two verses: "A graceful woman will obtain honor" and "the humble in spirit will obtain honor" (Proverbs 11:16, 29:23). Also: "He will give grace to the humble" (*ibid.* 3:34). The beauty which radiates from modesty is called "ענות חן" (based on the previously cited verse).

	phase of preparation	corresponding phase of marital relations
sweetening	creating an intimate atmosphere; words of affection	joy of union in marital relations
separation	focusing her attention on her husband	proper thoughts during marital relations
submission	physical adornment	modesty in marital relations

The wife's preparations and overtures parallel the three days of preparation preceding the giving of the Torah.[24]

G-d commanded the people to wash their clothes during the three days of restriction.[25] This corresponds to the wife's grooming and dressing, the first stage of her preparations.[26] Clothing both enhances one's appearance and is an expression of modesty. G-d was thus intimating here to the Jewish people that they should both summon their best selves for the imminent occasion while simul-

24. Above, we noted that during the three days of preparation G-d commanded the people not to ascend Mt. Sinai and to abstain from marital relations. There, however, the reference was to how they were told during this period not to ascend the mountain or be in a state of ritual defilement *during the giving of the Torah*. Here, we are discussing the events of the three preparatory days as ends in themselves.

25. Exodus 19:10.

26. In Kabbalah, the custom of reading the beginnings and ends of the twenty-four books of the Bible on the night of *Shavuot* is called spiritually "adorning" the Divine bride with the twenty-four ornaments enumerated in Isaiah 3:18 ff. With these Israel "enters the *chupah*" the following morning (*Zohar* 3:98a).

taneously emptying themselves of any selfhood that would jeopardize their openness to the new consciousness they were about to receive. This is particularly evident when we recall that in Kabbalah and *Chassidut*, the soul's "garments" are its modes of expression: thought, speech, and action.[27]

As we mentioned above, the purity of mind introduced by the Divine command to abstain from marital relations allowed the people to focus exclusively on their Divine groom. The intensity of this focus increased until it reached its climax at the receiving of the Torah.

The culmination of the preparatory period was on the day before the revelation, when the people offered a sacrifice to G-d at the foot of Mt. Sinai[28] and unconditionally surrendered themselves to Him, exclaiming: "We will do and we will hear."[29] This declaration expressed the epitome of self-sacrifice to G-d. There are no more intimate words of

---

27. *HaYom Yom*, 5 Sivan.

28. In Hebrew, the word for "sacrifice" (קרבן) comes from the root "to come near" (קרב).

See additional note 1 at the end of this chapter (p. 309).

29. Exodus 24:7. In particular, the sacrifice expressed our unmitigated abnegation of selfhood in our desire to be completely consumed by Divinity ("take me"); saying "we will do" expressed the dedication of our lives to G-d's will; saying "we will hear" expressed our preparedness to internalize the message of the Torah. The chief expression of the selflessness implied in the sacrifice is the dedication to G-d's will implied in saying "we will do." This dedication to living one's life according to the Torah constitutes the chief preparation for a Jew's role in the world, i.e., applying the written Torah to life through the aegis of the oral Torah.

affection and devotion than those that express one's love and joyful surrender to one's spouse.

To summarize:

	the marital cycle	the exodus from Egypt
sweetening	creating intimate atmosphere through words of affection, etc.	offering sacrifice; exclaiming "we will do and we will hear"
separation	focusing her attention on her husband	abstaining from marital relations
submission	physical adornment; modesty	washing their clothes; restricted access to mountain

The third stage of preparation—words of affection/ offering sacrifice—can be broken down into a further triplet:

An animal (or other object) becomes halachically designated as a sacrifice and assumes the attendant sanctity when its owner orally dedicates it before he brings it to the Temple. Later, just before he offers the sacrifice, he verbally confesses his sins (in the case of a sin offering or burnt offering) or expresses his thanksgiving and joy (in the case of other offerings) to G-d.[30] Lastly, he

30. *Mishneh Torah, Ma'aseh HaKorbanot* 3:14-15. The text of the confession is: "I have sinned, committed iniquity, and wantonly transgressed, having done such and such. I have now repented and returned to You, and this [sacrifice] is my atonement." The confession thus contains both regret for past misdeeds and a statement of resolution and commitment for the future.

slaughters the animal,[31] thereby expressing his commitment to serve G-d in the future.[32]

Similarly, when they stood at the foot of Mt. Sinai, the Jewish people dedicated their sacrifice and thus demonstrated how their affection for G-d consumed even the

---

31. A non-priest is allowed to slaughter his sacrifice himself (*ibid., Bi'at HaMikdash* 9:6). Even if a priest performs the slaughtering, he is, of course, merely the agent of the offerer. The offerer or priest slaughters the animal immediately after and in the same place as the offerer makes his confession or utters his words of praise (*ibid., Ma'aseh HaKorbanot* 3:12). This indicates that the sacrifice is to be considered the concretization of the sentiments expressed by the preceding confession or praise.

32. As mentioned, a sacrifice is an expression of one's desire to come close to G-d. By offering an animal, an individual is offering his own animal soul, i.e., reorienting his animal impulses—which caused him to sin or enervated his relationship with G-d—toward holiness. Thus transformed, these impulses, instead of being obstacles in his relationship with G-d, become an integral part of it (see *Likutei Torah* 2:2b ff.; *Sefer HaMa'amarim 5710,* p. 112ff.). The sacrifice thus neutralizes the cause of the previous sin.

The three modes of expression employed in the sacrificial process correspond to the progressive ascent of *malchut* (the feminine principle in general and the power of speech in particular) from the three lower worlds into the Divine world of *Atzilut*:

By sanctifying an object that was hitherto mundane, one rectifies the lower world of *Asiyah* (the world of Action).

By expressing the depth of one's emotions when bringing his sacrifice to the Temple, one rectifies the world of *Yetzirah* (the world of Formation, which corresponds to the emotions of the soul).

By expressing his unconditional commitment to serve G-d in the future—the realm of the unknown—one rectifies the world of *Beriah* (the world of Creation, which is referred to in Kabbalah as the state of formless matter, pure mental energies that will only find their realization in the future).

mundane realm. They then confessed their sins and articulated their thanksgiving to G-d. Finally, they avowed their commitment to Him, saying "we will do and we will hear."

These three stages of expression are paralleled in the bride's words of affection to her groom before marriage. While they are meeting, she may feel an innate affinity to her suitor as they converse. As she reflects on her feelings, she becomes more emotionally involved as they talk. Finally, she articulates her commitment to their relationship by accepting his proposal.

Having consciously expressed her devotion and become engaged, the bride subsequently ascends to a state of consciousness that transcends selfhood and self-expression. Thus, the bride does not speak at all during the marriage ceremony held under the *chupah* (חֻפָּה, "wedding canopy").[33] Having surrendered her independent selfhood, she now reaches a state of transcendent consciousness that precludes self-expression.[34] Only in the messianic era will we hear both "the voice of the groom and the voice of the bride."[35] The bride will then ascend to a yet higher level,[36] in which her existential "nothingness" is transformed into true, essential "somethingness"; her lost voice will return and even transcend that of her groom.

---

33. She remains silent as the groom places the ring on her finger and declares his only words in the marriage ceremony: "Be betrothed unto me by this ring according to the laws of Moses and Israel."

34. I.e., she has entered the state of *bitul* that characterizes the world of *Atzilut*.

35. Jeremiah 7:34; 16:9; 25:10; 33:11.

36. The level of *Adam Kadmon*, higher than the world of *Atzilut*.

In terms of the sacrificial offerings, the stage of non-expression corresponds to when the Temple priests silently perform the sacrificial rites as the owner of the sacrifice watches. At this stage, the human participants (the owner and his representative, the priest) are relatively passive, as the Divine fire descends from heaven to consume the offering.

We are taught that "even though fire descends from heaven [to devour the sacrifice], we are [nonetheless] commanded to bring natural fire as well."[37] In the future, this lower, man-made fire will reveal its true Divine source. It will soar upwards as its existential "nothingness" manifests its essential "somethingness," transcending the heavenly fire itself.

Similarly, when we heard and saw G-d speaking to us at Mt. Sinai, we were like the bride under the *chupah* and were silent. But in the messianic future, we will speak again, as the union of G-d and Israel is manifest in the new revelations of Torah we will express.[38]

These stages are also reflected in a wife's expressions of affection for her husband in preparation for marital relations. She first expresses her love and affection through the tone underlying their mundane conversation. The love within her words sanctifies and elevates her speech. This done, she can then openly confess the depth of her emotions toward him, and finally, surrender her state of separate being in words of devotion.

---

37. *Eiruvin* 63a.

38. See above, p. 175.

During marital relations one's consciousness ascends to a state of true selflessness. One "loses" one's voice as one silently, in complete modesty, clings to one's spouse.

The "new song" that husband and wife will sing with the coming of *Mashiach* will express the secret of their conception of the "new souls" that will then be drawn down. This "new song" is, as well, the secret of the "new Torah" that *Mashiach* will reveal, the Divine words that will issue from the mouths of all Israel.

To summarize:[39]

marriage ceremony	marital relations	rite of sacrifice	exodus from Egypt
messianic voice of the bride; true "somethingness"	drawing down the souls of the future	ultimate manifestation of lower fire	the new Torah of the future
silence of the bride under the *chupah;* "nothingness"	silence in marital relations	the silent service of the priests	seeing and hearing G-d at Mt. Sinai
the bride's deliberate expression of total commitment to her groom	the wife's expression of total commitment to her husband	the act of sacrifice and avowal of commitment to G-d	"We will do and we will hear"
the bride experiencing her emotions	the wife expressing her emotions to her husband	confession or expression of thanksgiving	confession or expression of thanksgiving
innate sense of affinity	mundane words spoken with affection	dedication of sacrifice	dedication of sacrifice

Aroused by the Jewish people's consummate expression of self-sacrifice, G-d "suspended the mountain

39. See additional note 2 at the end of this chapter (p. 311).

over them."[40] This is interpreted in *Chassidut* to mean that G-d caressed His bride, embracing her with His "right arm" of all-encompassing love.

וַיְהִי בַיּוֹם הַשְּׁלִישִׁי בִּהְיֹת הַבֹּקֶר
וַיְהִי קֹלֹת וּבְרָקִים
וְעָנָן כָּבֵד עַל הָהָר
וְקֹל שֹׁפָר חָזָק מְאֹד...
וְכָל הָעָם רֹאִים אֶת הַקּוֹלֹת וְאֶת הַלַּפִּידִם
וְאֵת קוֹל הַשֹּׁפָר וְאֶת הָהָר עָשֵׁן....

And on the third day, as it became morning,
there was thunder and lightening,
and a heavy cloud upon the mountain,
and the powerful blast of the shofar....
And the people saw the thunder and the flaming torches,
the shofar blast and the smoking mountain....[41]

These preparations are how G-d "kissed" and aroused His bride before and during the giving of the Torah. The thunder, lightning and flaming torches correspond to the kissing which precedes marital relations, which is meant to express one's desire to unite. This arouses one's spouse and readies her for physical union.

The *shofar* blast corresponds to the kissing which takes place during marital relations themselves.[42] This is meant to express one's pleasure in uniting with one's

---

40. *Shabbat* 88a. This event followed the declaration "we will do and we will hear" (*Tosefot ad loc.*).

41. Exodus 19:16; 20:15.

42. See *Etz Chaim* 29:9.

spouse,[43] the feeling that their relationship has reached consummation. We explained above that kissing expresses a unity that cannot be put into words. It is explained in *Chassidut* that blowing the *shofar* expresses a yearning for G-d that originates in the innermost point of the heart and is also inexpressible in words.

The caressing and kissing which precedes and extends into marital relations may thus be seen to also comprise three levels:

the marital cycle	receiving the Torah
kissing during relations	the *shofar* blast
kissing before relations	the thunder and torches
caressing	suspending the mountain

All these physical acts are for the sake of focusing on and feeling the soul of the spouse. They therefore correspond to separation.[44]

Since we have now examined the cycle of marital intimacy in great detail, let us reiterate that the purpose of doing so is, as we said, to help a couple understand their own marital experience in terms of the corresponding spiritual levels. In daily life, the spontaneity of any relationship will demand occasional deviations and/or

43. The kissing before relations is an expression of the will (רצון) of the couple to unite; the kissing during relations is an expression of the pleasure (תענוג) of the union. The experience of pleasure within that of will is called "desire" (חפץ, *Likutei Torah* 3:38c, etc.).

44. See above, p. 285.

variations from the general pattern[45] (except, of course, where specific behaviors and their sequence are dictated by Jewish law).

To summarize:[46]

---

45. As Rabbi Yitzchak Isaac of Homil reported in the name of his mentor, Rabbi Shneur Zalman of Liadi, the intricate patterns of intention and meditation detailed in Kabbalah are meant to be studied and integrated into one's consciousness, but thereafter serve to inspire one in his Divine service—as ideals realized by the great souls of the past—rather than dictate patterns of practice for the present. This is alluded to in the verse, "And such was the practice in Israel" (Ruth 4:7); the word for "and such" (וזאת) refers in Kabbalah to the ascent of the *sefirah* of *malchut*, the collective soul of Israel in its Divine service.

46. The fifteen levels in the cycle of marital intimacy are now grouped into *five* sets of submission, separation, and sweetening. These five can be clearly associated with the five supernal *partzufim* and the corresponding five levels of the soul:

Arich Anpin	*yechidah*	marital relations
Abba	*chayah*	caressing and kissing
Ima	*neshamah*	preparation for marital relations
Z'eir Anpin	*ruach*	days of cleanliness
Malchut	*nefesh*	days of seeing

Malchut is the level of "acceptance of the yoke of the kingdom of heaven." *Z'eir Anpin* is the level of emotions and yearning. The stages corresponding to *Ima* are those of preparation, while the stages corresponding to *Abba* are those of focusing on one's mate. One's concentration at the level of *Ima* is in contemplation (התבוננות and עיון); at the level of *Abba* it is in pure mutual experience ("gazing at the countenance of the King," which is an experience of "touching and not touching"). This is already the beginning of relations. The level of *Arich Anpin* is that of pure clinging or "super-touching."

sweetening	days of purity	sweetening	marital relations	sweetening	joy of marital relations	receiving the Torah
				separation	proper thoughts during relations	abstention from marital relations; focusing concentration on G-d
				submission	modest conduct during relations	restriction of the people from ascending Mt. Sinai
		separation	caressing and kissing	sweetening	kissing during relations	the *shofar* blast
				separation	kissing before relations	the thunder and torches
				submission	caressing	suspending the mountain
		submission	preparation for marital relations	sweetening	words of devotion	offering sacrifices; "We will do and we will hear"
				separation	concentration on spouse	abstention from marital relations
				submission	beautification	washing clothes
separation	days of cleanliness	sweetening			ritual immersion in *mikveh*	purification in *mikveh*
		separation			anticipation of reunion	counting the days to Mt. Sinai
		submission			daily examinations	threat of Egyptian pursuit
submission	days of seeing	sweetening			*hefsek taharah*	exodus from Egypt
		separation			observance of laws of separation	adhering to Jewish identity
		submission			appearance of menstrual flow	descent into Egyptian exile

In general, the stage of beautification and the subsequent stages which reflect the ascending flame of love of the Jewish soul for G-d express the soul's existential "run" to become one with His infinite light. With the caress of G-d's "right hand," before the actual union of the giving of the Torah, begins the "return" of the soul, "sweetened" with Divine light. The soul continues to ascend in its experience of love and affection for G-d, while conscious, from this point on, that it is G-d Himself who is lifting it up.

Eight Stages of Affection

Upon examining the above paradigm, we can identify eight ascending stages in a wife's expression of affection for her husband:

1. The first sight of menstrual blood interrupts the wife's previous state of ongoing physical intimacy with her

---

In addition, it will be recalled that 15, the number of levels we have developed in our analysis, is the numerical value of the Divine Name *Kah* (יה), the "Divine Presence" that dwells between the couple who so merit (above, p. 114). The entire process can thus be viewed as the way the Divine Presence manifests itself in the couple's romantic life.

Further analysis reveals that the first five levels are states of impurity, while the remaining ten are states of purity. The complete process reflects the transcendent wholeness of "whole and half" discussed above (p. 132); the completeness of purity being complemented by the imperfect, incomplete impurity.

The ten stages of purity begin with the wife's ecstasy of immersion and end with the couple's ecstasy of marital relations.

husband. With this, the physical focus of her life naturally shifts to her other pursuits. In this context, they may be viewed as distractions to her attention on her husband.[47] When she is able to perform a *hefsek taharah*, she experiences her first psychological release or "redemption" from this "bondage" to the mundane world.

2. Her longing to reunite with her husband increases during the seven days of cleanliness, which she counts in anticipation of their reunion.
3. This longing culminates with her immersion in the *mikveh*.[48]
4. She then beautifies herself in order to inspire her husband's love.
5. She concentrates all her attention on him, in order to arouse him.

---

47. The word "Pharaoh" (פרעה), the title of the monarch of Egypt and oppressor of Israel, comes from the root פרע, which means "disturbance" or "distraction" (הפרעה).

Although physical contact is prohibited, the couple still remain "trusted friends" (ch. 8) and may, for example, share intimate conversation and study the Torah together (see above, p. 264, footnote 7). Similarly, the wife is allowed and encouraged to dress nicely in her husband's presence so that he not feel psychologically disassociated from her (*Ketubot* 65b; *Shulchan Aruch, Yoreh Deah* 195:10).

48. As mentioned above (p. 271, footnote 12), the word for "immersion" (טבל) is a permutation of the word for "self-nullification," (בטל). In immersing, the finite, individual consciousness of the soul becomes null in the infinite "living waters," the Divine all-encompassing source of the souls of Israel. Just as the revelation of one's all-encompassing soul-root purifies the consciousness of the soul garbed in a physical body, so does a woman, upon immersing in the *mikveh*, become purified of (i.e., transcend) her previous state of partial consciousness, in order to unite with her husband.

6. She addresses him with words of affection and devotion.
7. They caress and kiss.
8. They join in the union of marital relations.[49]

As we have seen, each of these stages parallels an event or level in the ascent of the Jewish people from the exodus to the receiving of the Torah.[50]

	marital union	giving of the Torah
8	marital relations	receiving the Torah
7	caressing and kissing	suspending the mountain, thunder and torches and *shofar* blast
6	words of affection	"We will do and we will hear"
5	concentration on husband	refraining from marital relations
4	beautification	washing clothes and dressing
3	immersion in the *mikveh*	immersion in the *mikveh*
2	counting seven clean days	counting the days to Mt. Sinai
1	*hefsek taharah*	exodus from Egypt

It may appear from this that the woman is the active force in the marital dynamic, and that the male is

49. See additional note 3 at the end of this chapter (p. 312).

50. It will be noted that the following chart includes all the levels of the preceding chart except for the two lowest. (The two highest levels, marital relations and caressing and kissing, have been collapsed from their subdivision into three each into their original iteration of one level each. The exodus and the threat of Egyptian pursuit have also been combined into one, since the exodus was not complete until this threat had been eliminated at the splitting of the sea.)

relatively passive. This seems to contradict the normal conception of the male as the active force.

When G-d created the world, He did so solely on His own initiative,[51] since there was obviously no one to elicit or deserve[52] any Divine revelation. But thereafter, G-d desired that humanity elicit all Divine revelation. The ability to do this characterizes the essence of the Jewish soul. We possess the power to arouse G-d, as it were, as a wife does her husband. This is the essence of the Divine parable of the Song of Songs.

The love between husband and wife is only considered rectified when the revealed (yet modest, for only a woman is able to reveal passion garbed in modesty) flame of passion ascends from the wife to her husband.[53] Though both husband and wife possess holy fires,[54] the husband's is like water relative to his wife's and serves to quench her flame.[55] It is at this point that the husband becomes the active partner in the union, and the wife becomes relatively passive.

In all the stages of ascending affection described above, the husband is only involved indirectly, overseeing and directing, as it were, his wife's progressive steps

---

51. The Aramaic term is "arousal from above" (אתערותא דלעילא).

52. "Arousal from below" (אתערותא דלתתא).

53. As it is written, "...and your passion shall be directed toward your husband" (Genesis 3:16).

54. See above, ch. 5.

55. See *Sha'arei Ahavah v'Ratzon*, p. 26.

toward him.[56] Though always aware of and sensitive to his wife's ongoing emotional ascent, it is only at the seventh[57] and eighth levels of affection that the husband begins to take the initiative.

Continual Renewal

We shall conclude this discussion by considering why G-d created woman in such a way as to necessitate the repetition of the process described above every month.

The menstrual cycle divides approximately into just under a week of submission (actual flow), one week of separation (examination for cleanliness), and just over two weeks of sweetening (permissible relations). Thus, just under half the month is spent in abstinence and the other just-over-half in sharing physical intimacy.

---

56. The husband's indirect involvement is most felt in the *hefsek taharah*, which he must encourage her to do, since "all beginnings are difficult" (*Mechilta* to Exodus 19:5). Similarly, G-d Himself had to wrest the Jewish people out of Egypt (*Shemot Rabbah* 2:5; *Mechilta* to Exodus 12:12 and 12:29); after this initial effort, His involvement was relatively indirect, until the giving of the Torah on Mt. Sinai. The initial assistance of the groom in each case is the "arousal from above" which precedes and precipitates the "arousal from below"; the subsequent ascent of the bride on her own is the "arousal from below."

57. Actually, Rabbi Yitzchak Luria states (*Etz Chaim* 39:9) that the wife initiates the embrace, while the husband initiates the pre-relations kissing. This is in order that husband and wife be balanced in their expression of passion and enter physical union equally. Only thus can a couple unite consummately.

This symmetry applies as well to the internal process the couple experiences during the first two weeks of separation and the final two of reunion. The experience of dejection that accompanies the first sight of blood is counter-balanced by the elation that a woman experiences on the night of her immersion in the *mikveh* approximately two weeks later. Furthermore, we find that just as the intensity of dejection wanes over the first two weeks, so does the intensity of elation experienced in the couple's first re-embrace decrease over the final two weeks of the cycle. As it is said, "continuous pleasure is not pleasure."[58]

Consequently, it becomes necessary to revitalize the relationship by beginning a new cycle of longing and fulfillment. The period of abstention allows a couple to relive the romantic anticipation they experienced when they were engaged, and the monthly immersion in the *mikveh* becomes a reenactment of their wedding night.

---

58. *Toldot Yaakov Yosef, Tazria* 2 (p. 312; quoted in *Keter Shem Tov* 121); see *Nidah* 31b; *Imrei Binah* 44d. The psychological phenomenon that "continuous pleasure is not pleasure" is reflected, on the physical plane, by the waning of the moon (the symbol of the Jewish people in general and the feminine soul in particular) after reaching its high point on the eve of the full moon.

The entire lunar cycle can be compared to a woman's monthly cycle. The disappearance of the moon reflects the psychological fall of the couple upon the first sight of impure blood. Their subsequent spiritual commitment to abide by the *halachah,* assured of the "reconstruction" of their intimate relationship, corresponds to the "birth" of the new moon (the *molad*). The waxing of the moon reflects the ever-growing anticipation of the couple approaching the night of the *mikveh,* which corresponds to the night of the full moon.

Taking this thought to a deeper level, one can appreciate the need for the monthly repetition by recognizing that during and after marital relations, each partner inevitably experiences feelings of self-satisfaction.[59] Over the two-week period of purity, these egocentric feelings tend to grow; a couple tends to lose, to a certain degree, the selfless ecstasy of the *mikveh* night. Spiritually, this necessitates renewed submission to G-d, in order to begin the submission-separation-sweetening process anew.

The heightened feeling of closeness to G-d the couple felt on the *mikveh* night, however, makes their sense of dejection at the next sight of blood more profound than it had been last time.[60] Thus, their sense of submission

---

59. Even when one performs a commandment or good deed that does not involve direct physical gratification, "there is no *tzadik* on earth that does good and does not sin" (Ecclesiastes 7:20). The Ba'al Shem Tov explains this to mean that every act of good, no matter how pure one's intentions at the outset, becomes slightly tainted at its conclusion with a feeling of self-gratification. Instead of rejoicing in having merited by G-d's grace to perform a *mitzvah*, one takes a bit of pride in oneself (see *Keter Shem Tov* 393). This is due to the bite of the primordial snake at man's heel, for "heel" (עקב) in Hebrew also means "end," i.e., the experience of self, the "fall" from Divine consciousness, that comes at the end of an act. (This is another way in which the *rasha* is inter-included in the *tzadik*; see above, p. 82, footnote 16, and p. 90, footnote 34.) How much more so, then, with regard to marital relations, the epitome of physical pleasure (for which reason marital relations render a couple halachically impure with regard to touching or eating sacred objects, as mentioned above, p. 280, note 13).

60. "All before Him are considered naught" (*Zohar* 1:11b). Rabbi Shneur Zalman of Liadi interprets this to mean, "the closer one is to Him, the more one becomes (or should feel) naught (*Igeret HaKodesh* 2). In the present context, this would imply that the greater the

becomes deeper than it was before, and this in turn leads to an even greater sense of closeness to G-d when the process reaches its next climax.

With every cycle, then, a couple is brought to a more profound experience of the nine components of inter-inclusion described above.[61] The cyclical repetition is thus transformed into a spiraling ascent.

A second reason for the repetition of the menstrual cycle is that with every repetition, the couple experiences each of the progressive stages in a more profound way. They thus become more and more attuned to the levels' inherent inter-relationship and inter-inclusion, and their experience of them becomes more and more homogeneous. The nine levels subdivide into twenty-seven (3^3), and so on, *ad infinitum*.[62] This accords with the teaching of the Ba'al Shem Tov that the higher one's level of consciousness, the higher the "frequency" and the shorter the "wavelengths" in his cycle of submission, separation, and sweetening.[63] One approaches the "steady-state,"

---

experience of holy elation and Divine unity on the *mikveh* night, the greater the sense of self-abnegation at the next sight of blood.

61. As will be explained later (p. 398 ff.), this spiraling experience of renewal occurs also in the relationship of the couple to each other psychologically, and grants ongoing freshness to their spiritual relationship as well as their physical one.

62. The fifteen levels detailed above are simply a conceptual expansion of the basic nine levels.

63. As we mentioned earlier (p. 27, footnote 58), the sense that corresponds to *chochmah* is sight (or light), whereas hearing (or sound) corresponds to *binah*. Thus, as one ascends from *binah* to *chochmah*, his "velocity" increases from the speed of sound to the speed of light,

limiting point at which submission, separation and sweetening are all experienced as one.[64]

One of the great Chassidic masters, the Maggid of Kozhnitz,[65] said that at the beginning of one's Divine service, the way is rough. As one progresses and matures, the way becomes smoother, so that one almost loses a sense of motion. So does the way of a couple in marriage become smoother and smoother as time proceeds and their monthly experiences spiral upward.

A third (and essentially physical) reason the menstrual cycle must repeat itself is that the return of the woman's period (as it affects the consciousness of the couple) serves to emphasize the fact that the true objective of marital relations—becoming pregnant—has not yet been achieved. The realization that the holy seed has not been absorbed and integrated causes a deep sense of submission before the Creator, who commanded mankind to "be fruitful and multiply, fill the world and conquer it."[66] Here again, the husband is intended to identify with

---

from a relative state of infrared light to one of ultraviolet light. See *Sod HaShem Lireiav*, pp. 105-6.

64. As we saw above (p. 271, footnote 13), this simultaneity exists originally only at the level of sweetening.

65. Rabbi Yisrael Hofstein (1736-1814).

66. Genesis 1:28. Filling the earth and conquering it is the extended image of the woman becoming pregnant (full). Having children increases the manifestation of G-d's image on earth (see below, p. 349).

The word for "conquer" (רדו) is cognate to that for the word "descend," alluding to its use in this sense in the verse: "Behold, I have heard that there is food in Egypt, descend there and buy us some…" (Genesis 42:2). Our sages state that the word רדו in this verse

the state of his wife. If she has not absorbed the seed physically, neither have they, on a spiritual level, absorbed the Divine seed of procreation, which enables them to spread Divine consciousness throughout creation.

If the wife *does* become pregnant, the couple's life together gains a new focus: that of the child growing within her. This mutual reorientation towards the developing manifestation of their oneness[67] serves to neutralize the egocentricity that typically increases after the immersion night and necessitates a renewal of the menstrual cycle. This focus on the infant continues throughout the nursing period, during which as well the wife usually does not menstruate. The couple are therefore able to maintain a high level of spirituality in their marital relations throughout this period.[68]

These three motifs underlying the need for continual renewal of a couple's submission, separation, and sweet-

---

alludes to the 210 years (the numerical value of רדו) of servitude the Jewish people suffered in Egypt (*Bereishit Rabbah* 91:2).

In this sense, we may say that if the couple fails to fulfill the directive to "conquer," they will have to "descend" to the exile, symbolized by Egypt. Once in Egypt, they can learn how to fulfill the directive in its intended sense, as it is written: "And the children of Israel were *fruitful*, and increased abundantly, and *multiplied*, and grew exceedingly mighty…" (Exodus 1:7).

Similarly, our sages state that "any woman who has abundant blood will have an abundance of children" (*Ketubot* 10b).

67. As pointed out above (p. 68), in the Biblical verse "Therefore shall a man leave his father and mother, and cleave to his wife, and they shall become one flesh," the phrase "one flesh" refers to their common child.

68. Regarding menopause, see below, p. 314.

ening can themselves be seen to correlate to the paradigm of Divine service, as follows:

The realization and experience of failure to become physically/spiritually pregnant reflects the state of submission in the soul. The clarification process—the realization that one must continuously refine one's emotions and desires, cleansing them from the taints of the ego—corresponds to the state of separation in the soul. The experience of ever-increasing inter-inclusion between the varying levels of one's Divine service—thus approaching a true sense of inner unity in all the seemingly heterogeneous experiences of life[69]—corresponds to the state of sweetening in the soul.

To summarize:

sweetening	ever-increasing inter-inclusion
separation	the clarification process
submission	the sense of failure

In the messianic future, the spirit of impurity will be removed from the world.[70] This means that there will no longer be any sense of independent selfhood, and therefore no one will ever feel estranged from G-d. The

69. Thereby fulfilling the precept expressed by King David in Psalms 16:8: "I have placed G-d before me at all times." The Ba'al Shem Tov interprets the word for "I have placed" (שויתי) to mean "I relate equally" (שויתי from שוה, "equal"; *Tzeva'at HaRibash* 2). All of one's experiences become equally Divinely inspired when he keeps "G-d before me at all times."

70. Zechariah 13:4.

physical correlate of this is that women will no longer experience menstrual bleeding. Marital relations will spiral continuously upward in spiritual intensity. Thus, we are told, "women will give birth every day"[71] (without the pain of childbirth). The constancy of marital bliss will reflect the continuous union of the cosmic couple, G-d and Israel,[72] and the constant flow of Divine revelation that will "fill the earth and subdue it."[73]

---

71. *Shabbat* 30b.

72. See additional note 4 at the end of this chapter (p. 313).

73. The submission of the future is submission to intrinsic good, while the three levels of submission-separation-sweetening of the present are merely the dialectic process by which good is extricated from evil. The submission of the present is the first stage of *leaving* exile (the final stage, the sweetening, is the experience of revelation, the consummation of redemption from exile); the submission of the future is the experience of *entering* the Promised Land. Therefore, the submission of the future is higher than even the sweetening of the present (see *Keter Shem Tov* 28).

This future submission serves as inspiration for the entire current process of submission-separation-sweetening, but in particular, the promise it holds raises the submission in every new cycle higher than the sweetening of the cycle preceding it.

Additional Notes

1

to page 287.

This sacrifice concluded the existential "conversion" process the Jewish people had to undergo in order to enter the covenant of marriage with G-d.

Until the giving of the Torah, the Jewish people had the halachic status of non-Jews, and they were not required to observe all 613 commandments. True, the forefathers fulfilled the Torah before it was given (*Vayikra Rabbah* 2:10), but this observance was voluntary.

At the giving of the Torah, when we fully accepted the Torah as an obligation, we were "converted" into Jews in the legal sense, and the latent Jewish spirituality and super-rational commitment to G-d's will we inherited from our forefathers became activated. For this reason, on the holiday of *Shavuot*, we read the book of Ruth, the righteous convert.

In preparation for his conversion, *halachah* requires that the convert-to-be be circumcised, immerse in a *mikveh*, and (when the Temple is standing) offer a sacrifice to G-d. Similarly, the Jewish people, before receiving the Torah, underwent this three-stage conversion process. First, they circumcised themselves immediately prior to and in order to merit the exodus (the circumcision of a man can be compared to the *hefsek taharah* of a woman, which, as we have noted, corresponds to the exodus itself). While in the desert, they immersed in a *mikveh*, and finally offered their sacrifice to G-d at the foot of Mt. Sinai.

These three stages of our conversion process are summarized in G-d's words to Israel before He gave us the Torah (Exodus 19:4):

אַתֶּם רְאִיתֶם אֲשֶׁר עָשִׂיתִי לְמִצְרָיִם;
וָאֶשָּׂא אֶתְכֶם עַל כַּנְפֵי נְשָׁרִים וָאָבִא אֶתְכֶם אֵלָי.

You have seen what I did to Egypt;
how I lifted you upon the wings of eagles
and brought you to Me.

As the Lubavitcher Rebbe explains (*Reshimot* 10, p. 22), "You have seen what I did to Egypt" refers to the plagues inflicted on the Egyptians, which crushed their power and neutralized their dominion over the Jewish people. This is similar to the circumcision of the impure foreskin, which conceals and obstructs the male reproductive organ.

"I lifted you up on the wings of eagles" refers to the elating experience of shedding one's past identity and "becoming" one's true self, the experience of immersion in the *mikveh*.

"I brought you to Me" refers to the experience of approaching the essence of G-d and giving oneself freely to Him. This was expressed by the sacrifice.

To summarize:

sacrifice	at the foot of Mt. Sinai	"I brought you to Me"
mikveh	in the desert	"I lifted you up on the wings of eagles"
circumcision	immediately prior to exodus	"You have seen what I did to Egypt"

The initial step, circumcision, is itself a three-stage process. It is possible to correlate these three stages with those of the conversion process, and thus identify the threefold process of conversion within its first stage, as follows:

The first step, *milah* (מילה), cutting off the coarse, outer foreskin, corresponds to the *hefsek taharah*.

The second step, *periah* (פריעה), tearing off the thin, inner membrane, by which the "crown" (the glans) of the male reproductive organ (the essential holiness and purity of the Jewish body) is revealed, corresponds to the woman's immersion in the *mikveh*. Just as a woman purifies her body by immersing, so does the purification of a man's body come with the act of *periah*.

The third and final stage of circumcision is *metzitzah* (מציצה), the extraction of a drop of blood from the organ. This aspect of the circumcision symbolizes the offering of a sacrifice to G-d, as taught by our sages.

To summarize:

<table>
<tr><td>sacrifice</td><td></td><td></td></tr>
<tr><td>immersion</td><td></td><td></td></tr>
<tr><td rowspan="3">circumcision</td><td>metzitzah</td><td>sacrifice</td></tr>
<tr><td>periah</td><td>immersion</td></tr>
<tr><td>milah</td><td>hefsek taharah</td></tr>
</table>

2

to page 292.

Based on the Kabbalistic correspondences we have made, the five levels of this chart may be associated with the five worlds in ascending order, as follows:

G-d's Name	world	marriage ceremony	marital relations	sacrifice	exodus
thorn of י	*Adam Kadmon*	voice of bride	future souls	source of lower fire	new Torah
י	*Atzilut*	silence of the bride	silence in marital relations	service of priests	perceiving G-d at Mt. Sinai
ה	*Beriah*	bride's commitment	wife's commitment	commitment to G-d	"We will do and hear"
ו	*Yetzirah*	bride's emotions	wife's emotions	confession; thanksgiving	confession; thanksgiving
ה	*Asiyah*	sense of affinity	mundane words	dedication of sacrifice	dedication of sacrifice

Adam Kadmon is the realm of true existence (יש האמיתי); *Atzilut* is the realm of the consciousness of nothingness (אין); *Beriah* is the realm of relative (i.e., created) existence (יש הנברא). Becoming married under a *chupah* is thus the transition from creature-consciousness to Creator-consciousness; as a potential parent one becomes a creator of new worlds. It is the vessels of the world of *Atzilut* that express the Creator's power to create (*Igeret HaKodesh* 20); since the woman is a manifestation of the vessels (while the man is a manifestation of the lights), this is experienced more in the bride than in the groom.

3

to page 299.

These eight stages of affection correspond, in Kabbalah, to the ascent of *malchut* (the feminine principle within creation) out of its exile in the lower worlds into and through the Divine world of *Atzilut*. All these steps proceed along the middle axis of the sefirotic tree:

With the *hefsek taharah* the woman is "redeemed" from the distraction (impure blood) of the lower worlds and ready to ascend into the Divine realm of *Atzilut*.

The actual ascent to the level of the *malchut* of *Atzilut* is achieved by the yearning that characterizes the counting of the seven clean days.

Immersion in the *mikveh* lifts a woman to the level of the *yesod* of *Atzilut*, which is referred to as the "fountain of living waters."

The wife's beautification to enamor her husband corresponds to the *tiferet* ("beauty") of *Atzilut*.

Her loving concentration on her husband corresponds to the *da'at* ("knowledge," the power of concentration) of *Atzilut*.

As will be explained in ch. 15, *keter* subdivides into three "heads": will, pleasure and faith. With words of affection and devotion spoken to her husband, a wife rises to the level of "will" (the power inherent in words of devotion, or "reconciliation").

Caressing and kissing continues to elevate the emotional experience of the wife to the level of pleasure.

The marital union itself elevates a couple to the supreme level of faith, where G-d's absolute essence, as it were, resides.

To summarize:

ascent to faith	marital relations
ascent to pleasure	caressing and kissing
ascent to will	words of devotion
ascent to *da'at*	concentration
ascent to *tiferet*	beautification
ascent to *yesod*	immersion in *mikveh*
ascent to *malchut*	counting seven clean days
readiness to ascend from the lower worlds	*hefsek taharah*

4

to page 308.

As we mentioned above (p. 123), G-d's Name *Havayah* represents two levels of union: the first two letters (*yud-kei*) that of the father- and mother-principles, and the latter two letters (*vav-kei*) that of the son- and daughter-principles. The union of the latter two letters is only intermittent during the exile, since it depends on the deeds of mortal man. In contrast, the union of the initial two letters does not depend on our deeds and is therefore constant. We are told that with the coming of *Mashiach*, "G-d shall be one and His Name one" (Zechariah 14:9). In Kabbalah, the words for "G-d *shall be*" (יהיה יהו-ה) are interpreted to mean that the letters ו-ה of the Name *Havayah* (יהו-ה) will rise to the level of the letters יה. In other words, the lower, occasional union alluded to in the final two letters of the Name *Havayah* shall rise to the level of the higher, constant union alluded to in the first two letters.

Husband and wife in our world generally manifest the state of "lower union." When they merit to have the light of the "higher union" shine on them, "the *Shechinah* dwells between them" (as represented by the holy Name יה, the י of איש and the ה of אשה, the letters of the "higher union"). In the future, they themselves will become one with the light of the *Shechinah*, and the "lower union" will rise to the level of the "higher union" forever.

The constant union of the two letters *yud-kei* is somewhat reflected on our physical plane even now, after the woman has reached menopause. In this stage of their lives, it is never forbidden for husband and wife to engage in marital relations. Using the metaphor mentioned previously (p. 304, footnote 63), the couple at this stage has reached the spiritual "ultraviolet" state, in which they experience submission, separation, and sweetening all at once. This is the ultimate, absolute experience of sweetening (but unlike its true source, which will be revealed in the future, post-menopausal relations cannot produce physical children).

14

Marital Union—the Mystery of the Sabbath

The Day of Holiness

Marital relations are profoundly related to the holiness of the Sabbath.

As mentioned above,[1] Adam and Eve were originally intended to wait until Shabbat before engaging in marital relations. It is explained in Kabbalah that the essence of the sin—which precipitated the fall of all reality from the idyllic state of paradise—was that they did not wait for the proper time to consummate their marriage.

Their process of "return" to G-d (*teshuvah*) after the fall began that very Shabbat, for Shabbat possesses the power to rectify spiritual blemishes caused by the breaching of the holy covenant of marriage.[2] From all this

---

1. p. 214.

2. One of the meanings of the word Shabbat (שבת) itself is "to return." In addition, **שבת** permutes to spell **תשב**, "you cause to return," as in the verse, "You cause man to return [תשב] until he is

we may understand that Shabbat in general represents the rectified state of marital union.

The verse:

וְשָׁמְרוּ בְנֵי יִשְׂרָאֵל אֶת הַשַּׁבָּת

The children of Israel shall keep the Shabbat[3]

contains the acronym בִּיאָה (literally, "coming"),[4] one of the three primary idioms in Hebrew for marital relations.[5] The four words whose initial letters make up this acronym literally read: "the children of Israel [together with] the Shabbat." This implies that the marital union alluded to

---

broken, and say 'return, O mankind!'" (Psalms 90:3). From this we learn that the beginning of *teshuvah* is "returning" to the experience of being broken, i.e., the state of existential lowliness in which one's innate egocentricity dissolves. See above, p. 80, footnote 10.

It has been noted that the word for "broken" (דכא) in this verse is an acronym for the three things that our sages say broaden man's mind and enhance his consciousness: a beautiful home (דירה נאה), beautiful vessels (כלים נאים), and a beautiful wife (אשה נאה, *Berachot* 57b). This teaches us that if a person merits it, G-d brings him to realize the depths of his depraved, unconscious desires by *providing* him with these three beautiful entities. Out of deep gratitude to G-d, he returns to Him on his own. This is the true *teshuvah* of Shabbat, the day of Divine pleasure. See above, p. 92.

3. Exodus 31:16. This verse and the one immediately following it (which will be discussed presently) constitute the central theme of the Shabbat morning liturgy and are also recited before the Shabbat-day *kiddush*.

4. *Siddur Beit Yaakov, Hanhagot Leil Shabbat* 1:2.

5. This and the other two common idioms will be discussed presently.

here is that of the Jewish people and the Divine sanctity of Shabbat. And indeed, our sages teach us that Shabbat is the spiritual bride of Israel,[6] and the Jewish people's delight in the Sabbath is the consummation of their union.[7]

Thus, while the Jewish people are G-d's *bride*, as we have mentioned, we are Shabbat's *groom*. When Israel unites in holiness with the Shabbat, the Shabbat-bride herself becomes the "sign" of the union between G-d the groom and Israel the bride.[8]

This is alluded to in the verse following the one just cited:

בֵּינִי וּבֵין בְּנֵי יִשְׂרָאֵל אוֹת הִוא...

It is a sign between Me and the children of Israel...

This phrase contains the same acronym (**בִּיאָה**), also spelled by the initial letters of four consecutive words.

---

6. *Bereishit Rabbah* 11:9. This provides insight into the Talmudic injunction prohibiting non-Jews from observing Shabbat, on penalty of death (*Sanhedrin* 58b), for this would constitute an act of spiritual adultery (adultery being a capital offense for non-Jews as well as Jews).

7. The first word of the verse, "and they shall keep" (ושמרו), refers to the transcendent light which "surrounds" and "protects" the holy union of Shabbat. Spiritually, this becomes manifest in our anticipation of this union, since the verb שמר ("to keep") means as well "to watch or wait in anticipation" (See Rashi on Genesis 37:11; *Keter Shem Tov*, beginning, in interpretation of the verse, "One who keeps [שומר] a *mitzvah* will know no evil" [Ecclesiastes 8:5]).

See additional note 1 at the end of this chapter (p. 359).

8. Similarly, the Jewish people are seen as the groom of the land of Israel (see above, p. 197, footnote 8).

Here, the union referred to is that "between Me and the children of Israel"; G-d is the groom, Israel the bride, and Shabbat the "sign" of their union.

In this light, it is clear why the Shabbat night is considered the most propitious time for marital relations.[9] There can be no better day to consummate marital union than the day which itself expresses the cosmic union the earthly couple is meant to manifest. In fact, since all creation ascends on Shabbat in tandem with the Jewish people, all types of pleasure and joy, both spiritual and physical, are sanctified and elevated, through them, to a level of Divine consciousness on Shabbat.

Furthermore, the holy souls of Israel are themselves sparks of the holy light of Shabbat. In addition to being the bride of the collective souls of the Jewish people, Shabbat is also the collective origin of each individual Jewish soul.[10]

---

9. *Ketubot* 62b. As pointed out above in our discussion of the relationship between speech and kissing (p. 169, footnote 92), kissing reflects the principle of inter-inclusion. Inter-inclusion is the hallmark of holiness; therefore, Shabbat, the day of holiness and union, is also the day of inter-inclusion. As our sages say, "all things of Shabbat are double" (*Midrash Tehilim* 92:1). Thus, we can understand that the relation of Shabbat to the weekdays parallels the relation of kissing to speech. The world was created in six days by G-d's speech. On Shabbat, He rested from speech, but "kissed," as it were, His creation with the blessing and sanctity of Shabbat, as it is said: "And G-d blessed the seventh day and sanctified it" (Genesis 2:3). Our sages have even said that "it is barely permitted to speak even words of Torah on the Sabbath" (*Y. Shabbat* 15:3). The words of Torah that we do speak reflect the level of the Torah that will be revealed by *Mashiach*, which is the ultimate experience of "kissing," as we said above.

10. See additional note 2 at the end of this chapter (p. 359).

Thus, Shabbat is the day of peace and holy union between G-d and Israel, between husband and wife, and between spirituality and materiality. This is why we greet each other on Shabbat with the words "*Shabbat Shalom,*" "Sabbath peace."[11]

Even when a couple engages in marital relations during the week, they should try to infuse their intimacy with the holiness of Shabbat.[12] Since the holiness of Shabbat is in essence above time, it can be drawn into one's consciousness during the week, as well.[13]

Three Levels of Shabbat

Besides expressing the unity of G-d with the Jewish people (and through them, with creation at large), Shabbat expresses a couple's common soul-root.

---

11. This custom is most likely based on the greeting recorded in the Talmud (*Shabbat* 12b): "Enjoy the Sabbath rest in peace."

12. See *Likutei Moharan* 1:11:5 ff.

13. The fourth of the Ten Commandments, which begins: "*Remember* the Sabbath day to sanctify it...," implies that one should consciously prepare for Shabbat the whole week. In the *Zohar* (2:63b; see *Sefer HaMa'amarim Kuntresim*, vol. 1, p. 20a) it is stated that "from Shabbat, all the days of the week are blessed." The holiness of the Sabbath is drawn into the week by means of the weekday prayers (see *Torah Or* 88a). Before the recital of the "Song of the Day" in the morning liturgy, we emphasize that "Today is the first [second, etc.] day of [lit., 'in'] *Shabbat*." This accords with the usage of our sages, in which the term "*shabbat*" may mean "a whole week."

Shabbat is divided into three periods, each of which possesses its own degree of spirituality.[14] These periods reflect the threefold dynamic of Divine service we have discussed above: submission, separation, and sweetening.

In the evening, we "welcome" the Shabbat. The central motif is the cessation from work and the experience of the completion of creation. This is reflected in the opening words of the Sabbath-evening *kiddush*: "And the heavens and the earth and all their hosts were completed…." During the workweek, we are intended to assume responsibility for refining the world, which implies an awareness of ourselves and our power to impose our imprint on reality. In this first stage of Shabbat-consciousness, however, we are bidden to surrender this role,[15] and orient ourselves instead to receiving the revelation of Divinity that is descending upon the world.[16]

---

14. This is reflected in the fact that the central blessing of the *Amidah*-prayer is different for each of the three chief prayer services of Shabbat, which is not the case on other days of the week. (The *Musaf* prayer must be seen in this context as extra-categorical, since the text of its central blessing does not express the unique spirituality of its time frame but rather of the day as a whole.)

15. In the words of our sages, on Shabbat one must act as if all his work has been completed (*Mechilta, BeChodesh, Yitro* 7).

16. In the terminology of Kabbalah and *Chassidut*, our weekday role is to separate good from evil (עבודת הברורים), while on Shabbat we are to unify the consciousness of the world with its inherent holiness (עבודת היחודים). The former process entails direct involvement (התלבשות, "enclothing") in unrectified reality, while the latter is simply the assumption of a higher, more profound perspective on the nature of reality.

Having shed our consciousness of refining the physical world, we proceed to become aware of our true identity—our soul-root in Divinity—on Shabbat morning.[17] This is when a couple recognizes their common, single root, before their souls separated[18] and descended to earth.

Finally, on Shabbat afternoon, the epitome of the Shabbat experience, our consciousness ascends to its ultimate state, that of unity with G-d.[19] G-d's ultimate will in creation—to cling to and become one with it– then finds expression in the Jewish soul. Just as G-d's unity with creation is revealed, so is that of the married couple.

sweetening	Shabbat afternoon	oneness with G-d
separation	Shabbat morning	awareness of soul-root
submission	Shabbat evening	shedding orientation toward refining the physical world; experiencing the completion of creation

17. In the terminology of Kabbalah, the ascent of the *partzuf* of *Z'eir Anpin* to its root in *Atika Kadisha*.

18. Paradoxically, the Divine service of "separation" in marital union is that the couple senses their common, single soul-root, before their souls "separated" to descend to earth.

19. In the terminology of Kabbalah, this time is called "the will of wills" (רעוא דרעוין). The word for "will" in Aramaic (רעוא) is cognate to the word for "companion" (רֵעַ) in Hebrew. At this time, a couple reaches the highest spiritual level of "the two *companions* that never separate" (*Zohar* 3:4a).

These three levels of consciousness are reflected in the three most common synonyms for marital relations in Rabbinic literature: "coming" (בִּיאָה, *biah*), "mating" (זִוּוּג, *zivug*), and "joining" (חִבּוּר, *chibur*).[20]

The first idiom, "coming" (or "entering"), suggests submissive conduct. As we have mentioned, one's wife is compared to (and in essence is synonymous with) one's home. Our sages have pointed out the potentially harmful effects of entering one's home unexpectedly, and that one must therefore politely knock before entering.[21] Psychologically as well, one must calm any egocentric excitement or notions he might be suffering from before one enters one's home. Entering abruptly is considered a lack of good manners (דֶּרֶךְ אֶרֶץ), which our sages identify with the attribute of humility or submission.

Analogously, before marital relations with one's wife, one must calm his impetuosity in order not to

---

20. The sum of the numerical values of the three idioms for marital union—**ביאה** (18), **זווג** (22), and **חבור** (216)—is $256 = 16^2 = 4^4 = 2^8$.

256 is the value of the name Aaron (**אהרן**), the High Priest, whose task it was to make peace between husband and wife (*Pirkei d'Rabbi Eliezer* 17).

Marital union is the secret of the "powers of two." The ultimate "power of two" is to become absolutely one. This is alluded to by the above relation, $256 = 4^4$, for it is taught in Kabbalah that the secret of the large *dalet* (**ד** = 4) of the word **אחד** (in the verse: "Hear O Israel, *G-d* is our G-d, *G-d* is *one* [**אחד**]") is "four *dalets*," or "four to the fourth power."

21. *Pesachim* 112a; *Vayikra Rabbah* 21:8. Cf. Song of Songs 5:2: "The voice of my beloved knocks...." According to certain opinions, the primary root of **בית**, "home" is **בוא**, "to come," "to enter." (According to other opinions, its root is "to build" [**בנה**]; see above, p. 225, footnote 12.)

intimidate her and inspire her appropriately ("knock") before proceeding.

Thus, on Shabbat night, we call the Shabbat bride to enter: "*Come*, O bride; *come*, O bride."[22] We also invite the ministering angels to enter: "Greetings to you [*Shalom aleichem*], ministering angels.... *Come* in peace, angels of peace...."[23]

The second idiom, "mating," implies the ability of a couple to identify in one another their true soul mate and be conscious of belonging to one another as a preordained pair (זוּג). This exemplifies the state of separation in the marital union, for by identifying someone as one's unique soul mate, one singles her out as the exclusive focus of his marital attention. This sense of "separation" is the meaning of sanctity or holiness (קְדֻשָּׁה) in Hebrew.

The third idiom, "joining," reflects the state of sweetening in the marital union, the absolute unity of husband and wife. This state is referred to in the verse: "and he shall cling to his wife and they shall become one flesh."[24]

These three levels clearly reflect the triad of levels of relationship we have discussed above:[25] relationship, togetherness, and oneness.

---

22. *Shabbat* 119a. This has been incorporated into the liturgical poem *Lecha Dodi*, recited in the prayers for welcoming the Sabbath.

23. Shabbat evening liturgy in the home; based on *Shabbat* 119b.

24. Genesis 2:24; see above, p. 67. This verse refers to the ideal state of Adam and Eve before the primordial sin.

25. p. 70.

To summarize:

"joining"	sweetening	oneness
"mating"	separation	togetherness
"coming"	submission	relationship

The three periods of Shabbat described above are three stages in the soul's ascending experience of mystical union with G-d. This union is the apex of the soul's weekly journey through the levels of consciousness.

The soul expresses itself through three "garments": thought, speech, and action. The soul itself, however, transcends expression; its experience of its own essence is simply its intrinsic union with G-d.

Although the soul experiences its own essence and expresses itself through its three garments at all times, on each day of the week a different one of these aspects is dominant. The three days before Shabbat, the soul's consciousness ascends through its three garments; on Shabbat, it transcends expression and experiences its mystical union with G-d;[26] and during the three days after Shabbat, it descends again through its three garments.[27]

---

26. As it is said, "I have taken off my robe; how shall I put it on?" (Song of Songs 5:3). This is akin to the concept of "divestment of the physical" (התפשטות הגשמיות). On this experience, see commentaries of Rabbis David Kimchi and Levi ben Gershon on 1 Samuel 19:24; of Rabbi David Kimchi on 2 Kings 9:11; *Zohar* 2:116b; Maimonides, *Commentary on the Mishnah*, introduction to ch. 10 of *Sanhedrin*, 7th principle, introduction to *Avot*, ch. 7; *Mishneh Torah, Yesodei HaTorah* 7:6; *Moreh Nevuchim* 2:41. On the term, see *Arba Turim*

To illustrate:

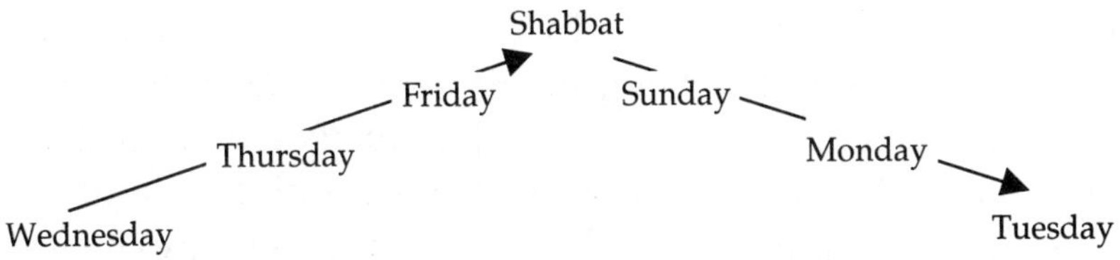

Wednesday	Thursday	Friday
ascent through action	ascent through speech	ascent through thought

Shabbat	Sunday	Monday	Tuesday
mystical union	descent through thought	descent through speech	descent through action

The Moment above Time

In addition to expressing the soul-root of the married couple, Shabbat expresses the soul-root of the child conceived in their marital relations.

---

and *Shulchan Aruch, Orach Chaim* 98; *Keter Shem Tov* 199, 284; *Shulchan Aruch HaRav, Orach Chaim* 98 and *Hilchot Talmud Torah* 4:5; *Kuntres Acharon* 4; *Sefer HaMa'amarim 5710*, p. 118. On the connection between this concept and Shabbat, see *Pri Etz Chaim, Sha'ar HaShabbat* 3.

27. See additional note 3 at the end of this chapter (p. 362).

There are three critical moments in the descent of a soul into a body:[28] that of conception,[29] that of formation,[30] and that of birth.[31] These three moments are transition-points in the soul's development, when it ceases to exist in its former state and is about to begin its existence in its next state. At each of these moments, a child's soul-root (*mazal*) must shine strongly, in order to ensure its safe passage into the next phase.[32]

---

28. These are referred to by Rabbi Avraham Abulafia as "the three moments."

29. The moment of conception can occur within the three days following marital relations, this being the "life span" of the sperm in the womb, during which time it is able to fertilize an ovum.

30. Forty days from conception, when the clear differentiation of the fetus' major limbs and its sex occurs (*Nidah* 30a).

31. The optimal time from conception to birth is 271 days (this number is the numerical value of the word for "pregnancy," הריון). Since conception can take place on the same day as marital relations or on either of the two days following (as above, footnote 29), this optimal time, when calculated from the day on which a couple had marital relations, can be either the 271st, 272nd, or 273rd day.

32. In the terminology of *Chassidut*, these "moments" are states of "nothingness" (אין) between the former and future states of "somethingness" (יש). When a soul is passing through this state of nothingness, it could, G-d forbid, remain there, or emerge from it in an undesirable way. It is therefore necessary for its *mazal*, the hidden purpose of its existence, to be revealed, since this directs the soul toward the fulfillment of its mission on earth.

Similarly, Rabbi Yitzchak Luria states that if one has completed a certain aspect of his mission on earth, he is judged—when his soul ascends at night during sleep—as to whether he should remain in heaven (i.e., die) or descend to earth in order to proceed to the next phase of his mission (or begin a new mission altogether).

At these three moments, the soul acquires the three modes of expression we have discussed.[33] At conception, it becomes prepared to receive the faculty of thought, for thought is the inception of a new reality. At the moment of formation, when its sex is determined, it becomes prepared to receive the faculty of speech. This is because speech is the primary mode of communication, which, as we have explained, is an essentially sexual act.[34] At birth, when it becomes fully vested in a physical body, the soul becomes prepared to receive the faculty of action.[35]

Marital relations transcend these three moments and correspond to the heavenly state of the soul-root's origin.[36]

---

33. The physical fetus, of course, is not aware of all this and becomes conscious only at birth.

34. And, as explained above, "speech" itself is a euphemism for marital relations.

35. These three moments correspond to the three lower worlds, *Beriah*, *Yetzirah*, and *Asiyah*:

The moment of conception is when the initial point of new existence (the living fetus) is "created" *ex nihilo* and thus corresponds to the world of *Beriah* ("Creation").

The moment of formation, when the fetus' form becomes apparent, is called "the formation of the child" (יצירת הולד) and corresponds to the world of *Yetzirah* ("Formation").

The moment of birth, which occurs once fetal development is complete, corresponds to the world of *Asiyah* ("Action"), inasmuch as the word for "to do" in Hebrew (לעשות) means also "to complete" (see Rashi on *Bereishit Rabbah* 11:6). At this moment, a baby's individual and independent self is born, and therefore, it is when his *mazal* shines the strongest (see above, p. 21, footnote 41).

36. I.e., the consciousness of the world of *Atzilut* ("Emanation"). To summarize:

As we have said, this is both the consciousness of the soul on Shabbat and the essential state of consciousness a couple should aspire to reach during marital relations. Here we have another perspective on why Shabbat is the most propitious time for marital relations: it is appropriate that the heavenly inception of a new human being's consciousness occur on the day that itself embodies this level of consciousness.

Furthermore, as we said above,[37] Shabbat is essentially above time. Time implies process; since conception, formation, and birth are all phenomena of process, they are moments in time. In contrast, marital relations in their purest sense do not involve consciousness of a temporal process, but are rather an essential act of union. Marital relations are oriented upward, transcending the barriers of time and space, whereas the three moments of conception, formation, and birth are oriented downward; they are three moments within an evolutionary process intended to reveal man on earth. The "moment" of marital relations, therefore, the secret of Shabbat,[38] is above time.

The world of *Atzilut*	moment of marital union
The world of *Beriah*	moment of conception
The world of *Yetzirah*	moment of formation
The world of *Asiyah*	moment of birth

37. p. 30.

38. And the consciousness of the Divine world of *Atzilut*. Rabbi Shneur Zalman of Liadi used to refer to the world of *Atzilut* as "above" (אויבן in Yiddish) and the three lower worlds as "below" (אונטן, *Besha'ah Shehikdimu*, p. 11).

We may now expand the previous paradigm of the descent and ascent of consciousness through the soul's garments from Shabbat to Shabbat to encompass the entire life of a person, as follows:

The first Shabbat, as we said, is the existence of the soul prior to conception, when it is an undifferentiated part of Divinity. This is the transcendent "moment" of the parents' marital relations.

Sunday, in the "week" of life, would thus correspond to the child's conception; Monday, to its formation; and Tuesday, to its birth.

After birth, a child begins to acquire higher and higher levels of consciousness, in correspondence to those levels of consciousness through which his soul descended on its way into the body.[39] His Torah-education proceeds from "action" (obedience to G-d's commandments) to "speech" (Torah study) to "thought" (meditation in prayer). These three stages correspond to the ascent of Wednesday, Thursday, and Friday. If he reaches the summit of this ascent, he returns to the origin of his soul

---

This is the true experience of "the pleasure of Shabbat" (ענג שבת). We are taught in Kabbalah that the word for "pleasure" (**ענג**) is an acronym for "Eden, river, garden" (**עדן נהר גן**), alluding to the verse: "And a *river* went forth from *Eden* to water the *garden*" (Genesis 2:10). This alludes to the marital relations between the father (Eden, the realm of *chochmah*) and the mother (the garden, the realm of *binah*) as they experience the soul-root of their child-to-be as the power which unites them (the river, the realm of *da'at*). See above, p. 129.

39. The Maggid of Mezerich said that G-d created the world "from nothing to something" in order that the righteous souls of Israel—in their Divine service—cause all created reality to "return" to G-d "from something to nothing" (see *HaYom Yom*, 29 *Adar* 2).

in the Divine consciousness.[40] This second Shabbat, a state of constant meditative union with G-d, can be sustained only by the very righteous.[41]

To illustrate:

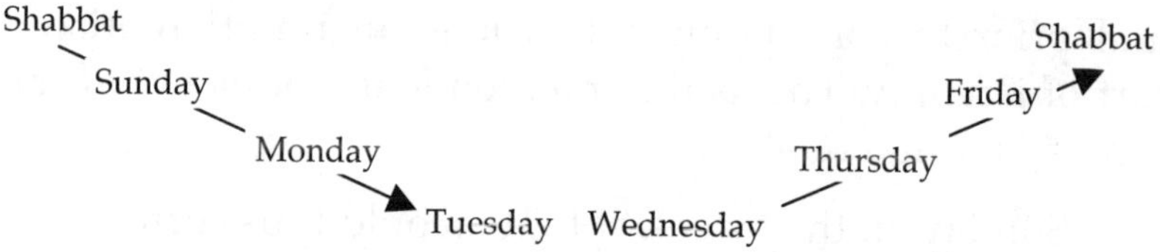

Shabbat	Sunday	Monday	Tuesday
moment of marital union	moment of conception	moment of formation	moment of birth

Wednesday	Thursday	Friday	Shabbat
ascent in action	ascent in speech	ascent in thought	mystical union with G-d

This sheds greater light on the saying of our sages cited above: Were Israel to keep two successive Sabbaths, the true and complete Redemption would come. The first Shabbat corresponds to the holiness of the marital union, before the descent of the soul into the body; the second to the soul's return to its Divine source, the experience of mystical union with G-d.

---

40. See additional note 4 at the end of this chapter (p. 363).

41. See *Tanya*, ch. 39 (53a), where *tzadikim* are described as serving G-d "far above even the fear and love derived from the understanding and knowledge of the greatness of G-d," and that "we cannot comprehend hidden things, i.e., the [level of these] great *tzadikim*."

***Kavanah* in Marital Relations**

The meditative intention of the mind and heart with which one performs a *mitzvah* is called *kavanah* (כַּוָּנָה, plural: *kavanot*). Although *kavanah* is an important element of the performance of any *mitzvah*, it plays a particularly central role in the *mitzvah* of marital relations.

The Ba'al Shem Tov teaches[42] that the use of the plural (*mitzvot*) in the verse "the wise of heart will take *mitzvot*"[43] alludes to the fact that every *mitzvah* possesses two dimensions. The outer dimension is the deed itself, while the inner dimension is the *kavanah*. He calls the outer dimension the "lower *mitzvah*" and the inner dimension the "higher *mitzvah*." The higher and deeper the consciousness of the *kavanah* (the "higher *mitzvah*") the greater is the refinement of the deed (the "lower *mitzvah*"). The "wise of heart" is one who knows how to bind the "lower *mitzvah*" to the "higher *mitzvah*" in every *mitzvah* he performs.

In the blessing recited before performing a *mitzvah*, we say: "...who has sanctified us with His *mitzvot*," in the plural. This, too, alludes to the two dimensions (deed and *kavanah*) inherent in every *mitzvah*.

In general, the relation of Shabbat to the weekdays is that of *kavanah* to deed.[44] As marital relations reflect the

---

42. *Keter Shem Tov* 9. See *Sod Hashem Lireiav*, ch. 28 (p. 398 ff.).

43. Proverbs 10:8.

44. Above, we noted how the weekdays manifest the three "garments" of the soul—thought, speech, and deed—while Shabbat manifests the soul's intrinsic union with G-d. Relative to the essential

secret of Shabbat, it is clear that *kavanah* is an essential and intrinsic element of this *mitzvah* especially. In virtue of the "additional soul"[45] all Jews receive on Shabbat, we all rise to the level of "the wise of heart";[46] we intuitively recognize the two levels of each *mitzvah* and know how to unite them.[47]

The various *kavanot* pertaining to marital relations are discussed in several sacred texts.[48] There are four general levels of these *kavanot*,[49] which we will now discuss. Shabbat consciousness finds its expression in the highest of these.

1 *Calming One's Passions*

The lowest level of *kavanah* in marital relations is in order to calm one's sexual passions.

---

union experienced on Shabbat, all three "garments" are activities ("deeds") of the soul, as opposed to its essential, intrinsic self-experience.

45. *Beitzah* 16a.

46. In the terminology of Kabbalah, on Shabbat we receive *mochin d'Abba*.

47. As we have mentioned, on Shabbat, every aspect of reality ascends to unite with its higher correlate. Therefore, on Shabbat, the passion of the "lower *mitzvah*" is to rise and unite with the "higher *mitzvah*," just as the wife's holy passion is to unite with her husband in the true love and peace of Shabbat.

48. See *Ba'alei HaNefesh; Igeret HaKodesh; Menorat HaMaor* (Abuhav); *Reishit Chochmah, Sha'ar HaKedushah*, ch. 16; *Siddur Beit Yaakov, Hanhagot Leil Shabbat*, etc.

49. These can be associated with the four "worlds," or levels of consciousness described in Kabbalah, as we will explain.

"You shall guard yourself from all evil things."[50] Our sages teach us that this refers to guarding one's thoughts with regard to sexual passion and doing all one can to calm the erotic urges of his animal soul. The detrimental effect of unrectified sexual imagination on a person's life has been noted above.

It is especially important for a man to curb his sexual passions, for, as the Torah states,[51] if he does not, he will inevitably become defiled by emission of vital seed.[52]

The first line of defense against erotic desire is simple non-indulgence. The more one successfully checks and diverts these thoughts, the less they will plague him. As our sages say: "Man possesses a small organ, which if satiated, hungers, but if starved, is satisfied."[53]

When attacked by the evil inclination of base sexual passion, one should first try to calm and diffuse it by studying Torah. As our sages teach us, "if the 'debased one' meets you, drag him to the house of study...."[54] The

50. Deuteronomy 23:10.

51. In the verse following the one just cited (*ibid.*, 11): "If there will be among you someone who is not pure due to a nocturnal emission...."

52. The fact that the Torah considers the emission of seed outside the context of marital relations a sin renders any man educated in accordance with the Torah's teachings somewhat obsessed with the fear of "spilling seed." A woman is, of course, spared this obsession. This sheds additional light on the fact, to be explained presently, that a woman's body is more in tune with "mother nature," and that her natural passions need not be checked or repressed to the extent that a man's must.

53. *Sukah* 52b.

54. *Ibid.*; *Kidushin* 30a.

Torah's grace and charm make it, for a Jew, even more beautiful and attractive than women.[55]

Secondly, our sages generally recommend that one marry young in order to avoid the psychological and physical ill effects of being a mature person unable to express his sexual drives in a positive and permissible manner. A healthy and balanced marital life is the surest way to prevent both sexual frustration and excess.

Finally, when a husband is feeling sexually aroused and is unable to calm himself in any other way, it is permissible for him to ask[56] his wife (provided she is halachically permissible to him) to engage in marital relations.

In such a case, the husband should try to sense his existential fall (reflected by his inability to subdue his physical passions in any other manner[57]), while doing his utmost to transcend this state.

Although the dynamic of fall-and-return that has characterized human life ever since the primordial sin and the expulsion from Eden applies to all facets of consciousness, it affects most intensely one's *kavanah* in marital relations. In order to begin to return one must first be conscious of having fallen.

---

55. This thought is the underlying motif of the entire book of Proverbs. In particular, see Proverbs 5:19 and *Mishneh Torah, Isurei Biah* 21:19, 22:21.

56. He may not engage her in marital relations without her consent (*Eiruvin* 100b).

57. See additional note 5 at the end of this chapter (p. 364).

It is related in the Talmud[58] that at times, even great sages were unable to overcome their passions. For these great men, such an experience was usually necessary only once in a lifetime, in order to firmly impress upon them the realization of man's existential lowliness.

As the Rambam teaches,[59] even when one's evil inclination overcomes him with passion or anger, one can at the same time sustain a positive, refined emotion and intention that come from his good inclination. Thus, even at this lowest level of *kavanah* during marital relations, one should attempt to connect to higher levels of intention.

Perhaps the worst part of succumbing to physical passion is that by doing so one uses his spouse to gratify his own egocentric desires. This causes a husband and wife to become spiritually distant from one another, which is the antithesis of the true intent of marital relations. The only way to rectify this, albeit to a limited extent, is to follow the Rambam's advice and "springboard" to a higher level of *kavanah* even while temporarily overcome by one's evil inclination. The "used" spouse must, of course, try to sympathize with her partner, and through understanding his present state of motivation, help him rise to higher levels of *kavanah*.[60]

---

58. See *Kidushin* 81a.

59. *Commentary on the Mishnah, Berachot* 9; see above, p. 193, footnote 23.

60. Overall, this level of *kavanah* corresponds to the consciousness of the lowest spiritual world, *Asiyah* ("action"). This world has split and fallen away from the higher worlds. (The three lower worlds are alluded to in the verse: "All who are called by My Name, whom I have created, formed, even made..." [Isaiah 43:7]. The verb "I have

It should be noted that the sexual passion of the wife's animal soul is not as reprehensible[61] as that of the husband. This is because her body is more in tune with the Divine statutes engraved in the fabric of nature than is his. While G-d created Adam outside the garden of Eden and only subsequently placed him there, He created Eve *in* the garden.

The garden of Eden is the epitome of rectified nature, where the marital relations of husband and wife reflect no more and no less than their absolute, unadulterated love for one another. Inasmuch as the correlate of the garden of Eden in space[62] is Shabbat in time, this means that a woman's body is closer to the ideal state of Shabbat,[63]

---

made," which alludes to the world of *Asiyah,* is separated from the previous verbs by the adverb "even.") Its state of consciousness is thus predominantly evil. The little good it possesses is the *kavanah* of the *mitzvah* of the Torah to "guard oneself from all evil things," as explained above.

61. Or "*post facto*" (בדיעבד). See *Eiruvin* 100b.

62. Above (p. 217), we have noted that the garden of Eden is also associated with the land of Israel.

63. The woman, *malchut*, is the secret of the seventh day, the Sabbath "bride" and "queen."

Upon first seeing Eve, Adam exclaimed: "This time, a bone of my bones, and flesh of my flesh...!" (Genesis 2:23). The two words used here to describe the origin of Eve in the being of Adam, "bone" (עצם = 200) and "flesh" (בשר = 502), together equal "Shabbat" (שבת = 702).

Just as woman's very body is more "in tune" with the secret of Shabbat than is man's, so we may infer that with regard to any given *kavanah* in marital relations, the wife's consciousness is on a higher plane than the husband's. This means that in order to be "equal," the husband must assume an even higher level of consciousness and *kavanah* than that of his wife.

when physicality and spirituality become one. Since her physicality is *a priori* more rectified, she is more allowed and encouraged to follow its cue. It is therefore, ideally, her function to know when and how to physically arouse her husband, and then to do so.

With his fall and expulsion from the garden, man's consciousness became polluted; his motivations became subject to his passion for sensual self-gratification. Since the woman also participated in the primordial sin, and in fact was the first to eat the forbidden fruit, she too suffered a fall. The sin entailed overt expression of passion while engaging in martial relations; thus G-d said to Eve, in pronouncing her punishment: "you shall passionately desire your husband, but he shall rule over you."[64] The implied curse is that the wife is no longer allowed to verbally request marital relations from her husband, but must rather intimate her desire for relations non-verbally.[65]

---

64. Genesis 3:16.

65. Rashi *ad loc.*; *Eiruvin* 100b. Articulating her desire, in the present order, would constitute a breach of modest conduct and defile the innate purity of the desire itself.

Notwithstanding, the wife is both allowed and encouraged to articulate her desires obliquely. We are taught that when the Jewish people were enslaved in Egypt, "when the husbands were tired from the hard labor, their wives would bring them food and drink and induce them to eat. They would then take their mirrors, each one gazing at herself in her mirror together with her husband, saying endearingly to him, 'See, I am more beautiful than you!' Thus they awakened their husband's affection, and in this way became the mothers of many children. And so it is written, 'I awakened your love under the apple trees' [Song of Songs 8:5]" (*Midrash Tanchuma, Pekudei*; Rashi on Exodus 38:8). The mirror, the reflection of the couple in a common frame, represents the image of their common soul-root.

But although she may no longer articulate her natural passions, she may and should still be sensitive to them. Not so her husband: as *Chassidut* teaches,[66] if he expresses the same degree of physical passion toward her as she does toward him, he suffers a further fall and the situation reverses. "You shall passionately desire your husband, but he shall rule over you"; but if he passionately desires you, you shall rule over him![67]

This, of course, is not to say that women are immune to sexual aberrations (again, let us remember that she was the first to fall). In fact, her innate subjectivity makes her

---

66. As Rabbi Menachem Mendel of Kotzk once reproached one of his *chassidim*.

67. The husband becomes elated when he feels that his wife is *physically* impassioned toward him. This draws him "down" to her. For the wife, on the other hand, her deepest desire is fulfilled when she senses that her husband is enamored of her not only physically but, primarily, *spiritually*. As our sages say (*Yevamot* 63a), the word for "groom" (חתן) is derived from the word for "descend" (נחת), and we are also taught (*Likutei Torah* 5:1a) that the word for "bride" (כלה) alludes to the "yearning [כלות] of the soul" to rise and unite with its groom on the spiritual plane.

In the terminology of *Chassidut*: every *sefirah* is composed of light and vessel. The vessel yearns to unite with the light; the light, recognizing that the origin of the vessel in the Divine essence is higher than its own, becomes elated and aroused by sensing the vessel's passion for it.

When the wife senses that her husband is primarily impassioned with her on the physical plane, this makes her, as it were, the spiritual leader of the couple, thereby reversing the order of nature.

This explains in greater depth why physical passion is more permissible to the wife than to the husband.

more prone to assess reality inaccurately;[68] this may even lead her passion—in extreme cases—to degenerate into a lust for adultery.[69]

Notwithstanding, the Torah sanctions[70] a wife's physical passion for marital relations as a legitimate motivation, since it is more natural to her than to her husband.

2 *Gladdening one's Spouse*

The most basic of the approved and recommended *kavanot* for a husband to have in marital relations is to want to please and "gladden his wife."[71] Seeing this as the foundation of happy married life, the Torah exempts a man from military service for the whole first year of his marriage in order that he devote himself to this end.[72] Likewise, the wife should intend to please her husband.[73]

---

68. Woman is less able to withstand temptation than man (due to the nature of her *da'at* [*Shabbat* 33b]).

69. *Sotah* 3a. From *her* the sages learn that, in general, "no one sins unless a spirit of folly enters him." See *Tanya*, ch. 24 (p. 30a).

70. Albeit as the lowest level of *kavanah* for her as well (the difference being that for her it is considered permissible *de jure* [לכתחילה]—as the base point, as it were, for higher levels of *kavanah*—whereas for him it is permissible only *de facto* [בדיעבד]).

71. Deuteronomy 24:5.

72. In Hebrew, "to gladden" is a verb form of the common word for "happiness" or "joy" (שמחה). See additional note 6 at the end of this chapter (p. 366).

73. This being the state of the world to come, as is explained in additional note 6.

For the man, this is the first positive step toward the rectification of the primordial sin, whose effect was to pollute his consciousness with gross desire for self-gratification, as discussed above.[74]

This *kavanah* is an integral element of the husband's *mitzvah* of satisfying his wife's conjugal rights.[75] He is commanded to satisfy her in this regard just as he is commanded to provide her with food and clothing.[76] He

---

74. This level of *kavanah* is associated with the second world from below, *Yetzirah* ("formation"), the domain of the emotions. Its state of reality is termed "half good and half evil." The "half evil" refers to the self-consciousness of the beings of this world. (Even when intending to satisfy someone else, human nature is such—especially in the context of marital relations—that in order to give pleasure one must receive pleasure as well.) The "half good" refers to the emotional sensitivity of one to the other as expressed in the genuine desire to "gladden one's spouse."

75. Exodus 21:10. The Torah obligates a husband to have marital relations with his wife throughout their married life (*Mishneh Torah, Ishut* 14; *Shulchan Aruch, Even HaEzer* 76).

76. The three categories of food, clothing, and conjugal rights (שאר כסות עונה)—listed in the Torah in this order—correspond, in their root, to the three mental powers of *chochmah* ("wisdom"), *binah* ("understanding"), and *da'at* ("knowledge"). Thus, a husband is obligated to provide all three categories of mental life force to his wife.

As explained in *Chassidut*, "food" refers to the spiritual sustenance of the Torah, which was given from the *sefirah* of *chochmah*, the "father"-principle (the imagery being that of a father teaching his son).

"Clothing" refers to the performance of *mitzvot*, which "garb" the soul and protect it from evil. Similarly, the *sefirah* of *binah*, the "mother"-principle, hovers over her children, the emotional attributes, protecting and clothing them (the imagery being that of a mother clothing, protecting, and educating her children to be good and upright Jews and perform G-d's will in all avenues of life).

thereby endows full legitimacy to her natural need for physical intimacy.[77]

"Conjugal rights" refers to the direct experience of Divinity in creation, or *da'at*. *Da'at* is also used to mean marital relations, the direct knowledge and experience of husband and wife. Of the revelation of the future, with the *coming* of *Mashiach* (just as the *coming* of husband to wife), it is said: "for the earth will be full of the knowledge of G-d as water covers the seabed" (Isaiah 11:9; *Mishneh Torah, Melachim* 12:5). In the performance of the *mitzvah* of *onah*, the *da'at* or "knowledge" which the husband gives his wife is the knowledge that he loves and cares for her.

food	*chochmah*	Torah
clothing	*binah*	*mitzvot*
conjugal rights	*da'at*	direct experience of Divinity

It is significant that the three categories of food (**שאר** = 501), clothing (**כסות** = 486), and conjugal rights (**עונה** = 131) together equal 1118 = **שמע ישראל יהו־ה אלהינו יהו־ה אחד** ("Hear O Israel, *G-d* is our G-d, *G-d* is one"). This teaches us that by fulfilling one's Torah-responsibilities in marriage, one merits to cling to and become one with his spouse ("And he shall cling to his wife, and they shall become one flesh" [Genesis 2:24]) ever conscious (with all three mental powers of *chochmah, binah,* and *da'at*) of G-d's absolute unity (as reflected in the unity of husband and wife).

77. In Kabbalah and *Chassidut* we are taught (*Likutei Torah* 4:10d, *et al.*) that the three necessities of life—food, clothing, and shelter (home)—correspond to "inner consciousness," "close surrounding consciousness," and "distant surrounding consciousness" (see above, p. 14), respectively.

As the first two of the responsibilities of husband to wife—to provide her with food and clothing—are the same as the first two basic necessities, it follows that the third, her conjugal rights, corresponds to the third of life's basic necessities, shelter.

The Hebrew term for this *mitzvah, onah* (עוֹנָה), literally means "time," in the sense of "frequency." This teaches us that the beginning of rectified consciousness with regard to marital relations is learning to recognize their appropriate time and frequency.[78]

The first consideration in determining the proper timing for marital relations is, of course, whether or not they are halachically permitted.[79]

---

basic necessity	responsibility of husband to wife	level of consciousness
shelter	conjugal rights	distant surrounding consciousness
clothing	clothing	close surrounding consciousness
food	food	inner consciousness

Just as from the outset of marriage "one's home is one's wife," so does the husband throughout marriage provide his wife with spiritual shelter and inspire her to fully manifest the fact that she is his "home" by uniting with her in sanctity according to *halachah*.

In performing the *mitzvah* of conjugal rights, one draws down the infinite "distant surrounding consciousness" of the Divine Presence that dwells between the couple who merit.

As mentioned above (footnote 76), the three responsibilities of husband to wife—food (שאר, 501) clothing (כסות, 486) and conjugal rights (עונה, 131)—equal together "Hear, O Israel, *G-d* is our G-d, *G-d* is One" (שמע ישראל יהו־ה אלהינו יהו־ה אחד, 1118). In our proclamation of G-d's absolute unity, we unite the three levels of consciousness (inner, close surrounding, and distant surrounding) to become one. And so, in living up to the responsibilities and challenges of marriage, we unite the three levels of consciousness and manifest G-d's unity on earth.

78. As explained in ch. 11, the state of consciousness necessary for a happy marriage is "living with the times."

79. The woman's menstrual cycle and its attendant ritual impurity originated at the time of the primordial sin. "Living with the

Within the period when relations are permitted, the most important time is the night of the wife's immersion in the *mikveh*.[80] This night is considered a private holiday for the couple,[81] a re-experience of their wedding night. On this night, marital relations are not only most timely, but halachically obligatory.[82] On this occasion, the husband should summon all his love and attention for his wife, in recognition of the fact that, in her devotion to him, she has prepared herself for this night with great effort over an extended period of time.

Throughout the remainder of the days of purity, when relations are permitted, the oral Torah—taking into consideration the individual dispositions and circumstances of each couple and the norms of each generation—has established guidelines for the frequency of relations.[83]

On occasion, however, a couple may be aroused beyond the recommended frequency. Here again, if it is

---

times" (of the woman) thus can be understood to constitute an essential element in the rectification of the primordial sin.

Aside from the woman's menstrual cycle, there are specific days of the year when marital relations are forbidden (*Shulchan Aruch, Orach Chaim* 210:12, 554:1, 615:1; *Yoreh Deah* 383:1) or discouraged (*cf. Taharat Yisrael* 240:11).

80. Witness is borne to this by the fact that if the night of the wife's immersion falls on one of the days when marital relations are otherwise forbidden (see the preceding footnote), Jewish law in many such cases considers marital relations not only permissible but *obligatory*.

81. Since Shabbat and *Yom Tov* are considered propitious times for marital relations.

82. *Shulchan Aruch, Even HaEzer* 76:4.

83. *Ketubot* 61b; *Shulchan Aruch, Even HaEzer* 76; *Igrot Moshe, Even HaEzer* 3:28, end.

the husband that is aroused to additional intimacy (not in response to his wife's overtures), he should try to calm his physical desire by learning Torah, performing *mitzvot*, and so forth. If, on the other hand, it is the wife who desires intimacy beyond the recommended frequency, the couple may view it positively. Her husband should consider it as a sign of Divine providence that now is a proper time for relations, and respond to her overtures.[84]

Nonetheless, should the husband see that his wife's additional arousal is becoming more "regular" than "occasional" (and these terms are relative for each couple), he should gently and diplomatically try to calm her passions. She should herself, of course, develop a sensitivity to her own physical desires and know when to curb them. The sages have warned that excessive indulgence in

84. *Pesachim* 72b, *Rashi ad loc.*; *Shulchan Aruch, Orach Chaim* 240:1. In general, Divine providence, in the sense of "the [exceptional] call of the hour" (הוראת שעה), especially with regard to marital relations, becomes manifest through the wife, who, in Kabbalah, represents the *sefirah* of *malchut*, which is referred to as חיי שעה, "the life of the hour." (The husband represents the *partzuf* of *Z'eir Anpin*, referred to as חיי עולם, "eternal life," meaning the commitment to abide by the eternal rulings of the Torah.) Thus, the husband should take his cue as to what G-d considers to be "the call of the hour" from his wife. (See *Teshuvat HaShanah*, p. 251 ff., where woman, as the "mother"-figure, is related to "sin for the sake of heaven," which according to our sages [*Nazir* 23b] is greater than a "*mitzvah* not for the sake of heaven.")

marital relations is detrimental to a couple's spiritual[85] and physical health.[86]

The *mitzvah* of *onah* entails satisfying one's wife not only physically but also emotionally. Clearly, if a wife senses that her husband is only performing the physical act and ignoring its emotional side, she will interpret his affections as nothing more than an attempt to satisfy his own physical urges or minimum halachic obligations. In such a case, she may feel used—or even abused—by her husband, the exact opposite of what he should be attempting to accomplish!

It is the husband's responsibility, therefore, to lovingly prepare his wife for physical intimacy, in word and in deed. He must be cognizant of the fact that she is aroused more slowly than he is, and he should adjust his physical pace to hers both before and during relations.

This is one of the reasons that night is the preferred time for marital relations.[87] We have had occasion to note above that the husband is symbolized by the day and the wife by the night.[88] At night, the pace of life slows down and the hubbub of the day subsides. Our sages point out that one cannot hear as well in the daytime as at night, for

---

85. See *Berachot* 22a: "...for scholars should not be as accustomed to have relations with their wives as regularly as roosters." The word for "rooster" (תרנגול) is etymologically related to the word for "habit" (התרגלות).

86. *Mishneh Torah, Deiot* 4:19.

87. *Shabbat* 86a; *Shulchan Aruch, Orach Chaim* 240:11, *Even HaEzer* 25:5.

88. p. 32, footnote 69; p. 236, footnote 5.

there is too much noise.[89] Relative to each other, day is the time of seeing while night is the time of hearing. While "seeing" in Hebrew carries the meaning of direct, objective perception, "hearing" carries the meaning of indirect, subjective understanding; the time of hearing is a time of understanding one another. In fact, the word for "night" (לילה) is a synthesis of the two words for "mine is hers" (לי לה).[90] Fully sensitive to his wife and her needs, the husband devotes himself to his wife at night.

The pace of life continues to slow down until midnight, when it becomes totally quiet and one's power of hearing becomes most acute. After reaching its apex at midnight, the night-consciousness begins to become conscious of the next day. In the idiom of Kabbalah, at midnight the gates of paradise open and the light of "tomorrow" begins to shine into the world.

Thus we are taught that marital relations should ideally be conducted not only at night, but after midnight.[91] By prescribing marital relations after midnight,

---

89. *Yoma* 20b. The sense of sight tends to overshadow and obstruct the experience of the other senses and one's sensitivity to spirituality. By conducting relations in a darkened room, one can be better attuned both to the sensuality of touch and hearing and to the spiritual dimension of marital relations. See *Sefer HaMa'amarim 5720-22*, p 29.

90. This recalls what Rabbi Akiva said to his students in praise of his wife Rachel, who had sent him away for decades to learn Torah: "All that is mine and yours is hers" (*Ketubot* 63a). (On the spiritual plane, he had continually been giving of himself to her—by knowing that "mine is hers"—all the time he was away.)

91. Jewish *law* insists only that a couple engage in marital relations in a darkened room, whether by day or by night (*Pesachim*

the Torah is in effect teaching that although they should be conducted on the woman's level, she should be fully conscious of and sensitive to her husband's level.[92]

112b; *Shulchan Aruch, Orach Chaim* 240:11), for reasons of modesty. At night, the preferred time is the middle part of the night (*ibid.*, 240:7; *Even HaEzer* 25:3), for the same reasons.

According to Kabbalah, however, marital relations should be conducted only after midnight (*Zohar* 3:81a; *Sha'ar HaMitzvot, Bereishit, s.v. Iyan HaZivug; Ta'amei HaMitzvot, Bereishit, s.v. BeInyan HaZivug; Sha'ar HaKavanot, Inyan HaShulchan, s.v. Inyan HaZivug* [73a in 5662 edition; p. 88 in Brandwein edition]; *Pri Etz Chaim* 16:11, *s.v. Sod HaZivug beChatzot HaLailah* [p. 339 in Brandwein edition only]; *cf. Mishneh Torah, Isurei Biah* 21:10, *Deiot* 5:4).

92. The level of sensitivity of each spouse to the other reflects his level of humility. The word **עוֹנָה** is cognate to the word **עֲנָוָה** ("humility") (and numerically equals **מצא**, see above, p. 3 footnote 19). As each spouse represents one *onah*, one state of humility, the two together become ענוים, two "humble ones." The Midrash (*Yalkut Shimoni*, Isaiah 499) states that in the year that *Mashiach* comes, he will stand on the roof of the Holy Temple and declare to Israel: "O humble ones, the time of your redemption has arrived." The *Mashiach* addresses the Jewish people as "humble ones" in accordance with the verse (Isaiah 61:1): "Since [יען, cognate to ענוה] G-d has anointed [**משח**, the root of **משיח**, *Mashiach*] me to bring tidings to the humble," from which our sages learn that humility is the greatest of all attributes—"humility is the greatest of them all" (*Avodah Zarah* 20b). The numerical value of the declaration "O humble ones, the time of your redemption has arrived" (**ענוים הגיע זמן גאולתכם** = 861) is equivalent to that of the phrase "the Holy Temple" (**בית המקדש**).

When each of the two spouses manifests his level of time (עונה) and humility (ענוה), together they build a Holy Temple (בית המקדש) for G-d, and the Divine Presence resides between them. The *Mashiach*, who stands on the roof of the Temple, alludes to the soul of their child-to-be. He addresses them from the roof of their Temple (the crown of their common soul-root) and says: "O humble ones, the time of your redemption has arrived." "The time of your redemption"

Here, a husband's sensitivity to his wife parallels the Jewish people's sensitivity to its collective "soul mate," Shabbat. With the coming of Shabbat, we slow our pace and rest from labor, in order to become one with her on her "longer wavelength."

The importance of tranquility and calm was conspicuous as well in the ancient rite of anointing kings.[93] The kings of Israel were anointed next to the placid Shiloach spring, just outside Jerusalem.[94] Of its gentle flow it is said: "...the waters of the Shiloach which flow slowly...."[95] The tranquillity and stillness associated with this setting reflects the mood and tone one should strive for in marital relations.

By learning to control his own impulses and strive instead for mutuality, a husband joins his wife in lifting the entire experience to a level of consciousness conducive to receiving the Divine light of Shabbat, the day of peace and tranquility.

All of this is alluded to in the word *onah* itself, since it is cognate to the verb "to answer" (ענה). The husband

---

alludes to the hour of the marital union, referred to in the Torah as the hour of פקידה, a synonym for "redemption."

As will be explained presently, an further reason for conducting marital relations after midnight is because this is a propitious time for drawing down a holy soul into the child conceived.

93. The association between marital relations and the anointing of kings is given below, p. 351.

94. *Mishneh Torah, Melachim* 1:11; 1 Kings 1:45 (the Gichon is synonymous with the Shiloach; see Targum to 1 Kings 33:38).

95. Isaiah 8:6; the Targum *ad loc.* states that the "waters of the Shiloach" refer to the kings of the house of David. see also *Sanhedrin* 94b.

must fulfill the commandment in a way that responds sensitively to both his wife's physical desires and her emotional needs.

3 *Be Fruitful and Multiply*

The next, higher level of *kavanah* in marital relations is to fulfill the *mitzvah* to "be fruitful and multiply."[96] Although some sages are of the opinion that this *mitzvah* is equally incumbent on husband and wife, the halachic ruling is that it devolves solely on the husband.[97] The wife, however, should intend to be her husband's partner in his fulfillment of this *mitzvah* (which he cannot, of course, perform without her!).[98] Though the Torah encourages one to bring as many children into the world as possible[99] (each child being an additional "Divine image"[100] on earth and a hastening of the advent of *Mashiach*), the minimal halachic requirement is to have at least one son and one daughter.[101]

On a deeper level, this level of *kavanah* includes the conscious desire and heartfelt prayer to conceive *holy* children, to bring *holy* souls into the world. The sacred texts explain that the purity of the parents' thoughts and behavior during marital relations determine the nature of

---

96. Genesis 1:28, 9:2.

97. *Mishneh Torah, Ishut* 15:2; *Shulchan Aruch, Even HaEzer* 1:13.

98. See *Likutei Sichot*, vol. 20, p. 138 ff.

99. *Mishneh Torah, Ishut* 15:16; *Yevamot* 62ab, based on Ecclesiastes 11:6. See additional note 7 at the end of this chapter (p. 368).

100. *Yevamot* 63b.

101. *Mishneh Torah, Ishut* 9:4; *Shulchan Aruch, Even HaEzer* 1:5.

their offspring.[102] Although their *kavanah* may have no bearing on the essence of their child's soul,[103] it does effect the "garment"[104] of the soul they draw down. This "garment" comprises the mental, emotional, and physical means the newborn soul will have at its disposal to express its innate Divinity.[105] Parents who wish their children to have minds and bodies receptive to and in tune with their Divine natures will concentrate on wholesome and holy thoughts during relations.[106]

---

102. *Siddur Beit Yaakov, Hanhagot Leil Shabbat* 2:2, etc.

103. As is taught by Rabbi Yitzchak Luria, exceptionally holy children can be born to quite ordinary (or even less than ordinary) parents.

104. *Tanya*, ch. 2, citing *Zohar* 1:90b, 1:112a, 3:80a, *Zohar Chadash* 11a, and *Ta'amei HaMitzvot, Bereishit, s.v. Periah uReviah.*

105. The "mental means" is the "intellectual soul" (נפש השכלית); the "emotional means" is the "natural soul" (נפש הטבעית); the "physical means" is the physical body (*Cf. Kitzurim VeHe'arot leSefer Likutei Amarim*, p. 75; *Biurei HaZohar - Admor HaEmtza'i* 117b). The soul's "innate Divinity" is the "Divine soul" (נפש האלקית) of every Jew.

Note that here, the word "garment" (לבוש) is used in a slightly different sense than the more common usage of the term "garments" (לבושים), which refers to the three "servants" of the soul's powers: thought, speech and action.

106. See above, p. 272.

This level of *kavanah* is associated with the highest of the three lower worlds, *Beriah* ("creation"), the domain of the intellect. Its state of reality is termed "mostly good." Here, self-consciousness, though present, is minimal. The desire and intention that predominates in *Beriah* is to become a partner with G-d in creation. The very fact that a wife intends to be her husband's partner in fulfilling the Divine command of procreation inspires *both* husband *and* wife to consider themselves partners with their Creator in *His* creative process.

This is another reason why the most propitious time for marital relations is after midnight.[107] After midnight, the gates of paradise (the spiritual abode of souls waiting to be born) are fully open, and a couple can elicit a soul of the highest order.[108]

The intent of drawing down a holy soul is associated as well with the ancient rite of anointing the kings of Israel.[109] The effect of this ritual was to draw the kingly soul of the king-to-be into his consciousness; prior to this he was completely incognizant of this aspect of his soul.[110] Inasmuch as "all Jews are kings,"[111] a couple's *kavanah*

Beriah, continual re-creation, is the consciousness of "something from nothing." The greater the awareness of the Divine "nothing," the origin of the "something," the more the couple merit to draw down a holy, Divine soul.

The soul-root (*mazal*) of every Jew is the Divine nothing, as taught by the Ba'al Shem Tov in his reading of "there is no [אַיִן] *mazal* for Israel" (*Shabbat* 156a): "The Divine nothing [אַיִן] is the *mazal* of Israel" (*Meor Einaim, Likutim, s.v. KesheRatzah Avraham* [Jerusalem, 1976 ed.: p. 277a]; *Likutei Amarim* [the *Maggid*] 137, 172; *Or Torah* 147, 191).

107. See above, p. 346, footnote 91 and end of footnote 92.

108. The spirituality of a weekday after midnight is comparable to that of Shabbat night before midnight; Shabbat after midnight is on an even higher level (sources cited above, p. 346, footnote 91).

109. In practice, anointment was performed only when the new king did not inherit the title from his father, or there was some controversy surrounding which candidate would inherit the throne (*Mishneh Torah, Melachim* 1:12).

110. *Cf. Sefer HaMa'amarim 5710*, pp. 95 ff.

111. *Zohar* 2:26b; *Tikunei Zohar*, introduction (1b). In the Talmud (*Shabbat* 67a), all Jews are said to be princes.

during relations should resemble the intention that accompanied the anointing ritual.[112]

In marital relations, the husband symbolizes the prophet anointing the king, who is symbolized by his wife,[113] since it is she who will develop his seed into a new "kingdom."

The *kavanah* of drawing down a holy soul is relevant even when a couple is physically unable to conceive, for it is taught that spiritual offspring result from every act of holy marital relations.[114] These spiritual "offspring" can be the souls of future converts, thoughts of *teshuvah* which inspire fellow Jews to enhance their own relationships

---

A Jew is a king by virtue of his mission to conquer and subjugate the earth to the service of G-d. This mission first appears as the culmination of G-d's blessing and command to Adam and Eve to "be fruitful and multiply, fill the earth and conquer it, and rule..." (Genesis 1:28). After their fall, this mission became reserved for the Jewish people alone (*Yevamot* 61a), who then became entrusted with the Divine mission of realizing G-d's kingdom on earth. The Hebrew word for "mission" (שליחות) is related to the name of the Shiloach spring (שלוח).

112. Inasmuch as the sin of David and Bathsheba was essentially that of haste (as was explained above, p. 215), we may presume that the Davidic kings were anointed at the tranquil Shiloach spring in order to rectify this flaw.

113. In this analogy, the oil of anointment is the husband's seed. (The Hebrew word for "oil," *shemen* [שמן], the essential extract of the olive, is reflected in the English word *semen*, the essential "extract" of the man.) The woman is the personification of the *sefirah* of *malchut*, "kingship."

114. *Sha'ar HaMitzvot, Bereishit; Or HaChamah* on *Zohar* 3:90a; *Chesed L'Avraham* 2:66.

with G-d, or simply psychological sensations of warmth and goodness which spread through reality.

4 *Emulating the Divine*

The highest level of *kavanah* in marital relations is to emulate or effect the union of the Divine "couple," the Holy One, blessed be He, and the *Shechinah* (which is the collective source of the souls of the Jewish people). A couple, expressing their love for each other during marital relations, becomes a reflection of the cosmic love relationship between G-d's transcendent, infinite light and His indwelling, immanent Presence, or its manifestation in this world, the souls of Israel.

At this level of consciousness, the couple is performing the *mitzvah* of "you shall walk in His ways."[115] Our sages illustrate this commandment by saying: "just as He is merciful, be you merciful; just as He is compassionate, be you compassionate; just as He is patient, be you patient...."[116]

Furthermore, the couple can intend through their union not only to emulate the Divine union but to actually effect and enhance it. Through our sins, we negatively influence the "relationship" of the Divine couple, causing the estrangement, as it were, of the *Shechinah* from the Holy

---

115. Deuteronomy 28:9.

116. *Shabbat* 133b; see *Mishneh Torah, Hilchot Deiot* 1:6. As will be explained, this is the consciousness of *Atzilut*, i.e., not just to act as a (finite) partner with (the infinite) G-d but to emulate Him and His Divine (infinite) attributes in essence.

One, blessed be He. This is known as the "exile of the *Shechinah*," and results in our own, physical exile from our homeland. So, too—and all the more so[117]—our good deeds, beginning with the expression of true love and compassion between husband and wife as reflected in their marital relations, cause the reconciliation and reunification (on successively higher levels) of the Divine couple.[118]

---

117. For "the recompense for good deeds is greater than that for evil" (*Sotah* 11a).

118. This level, the consciousness of the world of *Atzilut*, is "all good" and all Divine.

There are two, complimentary facets of this consciousness, which are termed in *Chassidut* "G-d is all" and "all is G-d" (*Likutei Diburim* 36 [p. 1322]). "G-d is all" means that nothing exists but G-d. "All is G-d" means that *all* that does exist is in essence G-d. These two sides of the same coin are the origin of the consciousness of the husband and wife, respectively.

In marital union itself, we are taught in Kabbalah and *Chassidut* that each of the partners manifests the consciousness of the other (see *Likutei Torah* 2:19c). Specifically, it is the female within the male that unites with the male within the female.

At the level of consciousness of *Atzilut*, the male dimension of the Divine union ("G-d is all") becomes conscious of "all is G-d," while the female dimension ("all is G-d") becomes conscious of "G-d is all." And so the Divine couple is drawn to unite with one another.

The coin that Abraham minted had his and Sarah's picture on one side, and Isaac and Rebecca's on the other (*Bava Kama* 97b and Rashi *ad loc.; Bereishit Rabbah* 39). In the imagery of Kabbalah, Abraham and Sarah allude to the higher consciousness of *Abba* and *Ima* proper (that of "G-d is all"), while Isaac and Rebecca allude to the lower consciousness of *chochmah* and *binah* (that of "all is G-d"), known as *Yisrael Saba* and *Tevunah*. Relative to each other, these two levels of consciousness are male and female, respectively. Thus, the pictures on each side of the coin allude to the inter-inclusion of the male and female levels of consciousness.

The ultimate manifestation of the Divine union will come with the Redemption of the Jewish people (and through them, the world at large) from its physical and metaphysical exile, with the coming of *Mashiach*.[119]

The intention to emulate the Divine can also become an adjunct to the couple's *kavanah* in conceiving children, since Adam and Eve were told to procreate in order to "fill the earth, subdue it, and rule over it."[120] By increasing the presence of the Jewish people on earth (through the fulfillment of the *mitzvah* to procreate), we fill reality with our unique Jewish consciousness of G-d's absolute oneness. This is the essence of the revelation of the messianic era, as it is said: "for the earth will be full of the knowledge of G-d as water covers the seabed."[121] We thus bring the world closer to the coming of *Mashiach*,[122] who will bring all mankind to serve G-d together, and rule over all worldly creatures, elevating them to a state of Divine consciousness.

male	*chochmah*	"G-d is all"	*Abba*	"G-d is all"	Abraham
			Ima	"all is G-d"	Sarah
female	*binah*	"all is G-d"	*Yisrael Saba*	"G-d is all"	Isaac
			Tevunah	"all is G-d"	Rebecca

119. This is alluded to by the fact that the above-mentioned term for marital relations (ביאה) is used also to refer to the "coming" of *Mashiach* (ביאת המשיח).

120. Genesis 1:28.

121. Isaiah 11:9.

122. And so are we taught: "The son of David will not come until all the souls have been emptied from the body" (*Yevamot* 62a). The term "body" here refers to the celestial storehouse of Jewish souls. In Kabbalah, this is identified with the "womb" of the *sefirah* of *malchut*.

On Shabbat, we experience a "taste of the world to come."[123] As we have said, though G-d commanded Adam to procreate on the day He created him (the sixth day of the primordial week), the intention was that he should wait until Shabbat in order to fulfill this commandment. Had he done so, he and Eve would have given birth, on the very first Shabbat, to *Mashiach*.[124]

Similarly, on each Sabbath, we are given the opportunity to fully rectify the primordial sin, give birth to *Mashiach*, and taste the world to come.

We may summarize these four levels of *kavanah* as follows:[125]

kavanah	***mitzvah* performed**	**orientation of consciousness**
emulating the Divine union	"You shall walk in His ways"	"G-d is all and all is G-d"
becoming partners with G-d in procreation	"Be fruitful and multiply"	awareness of continual re-creation—something from nothing
gladdening one's spouse	"He shall not diminish her conjugal rights"	emotional sensitivity to satisfy the other
calming one's passions	"You shall guard yourself from all evil things"	consciousness of one's existential "fall"

123. *Berachot* 57b.

124. Rabbi Yitzchak Luria teaches that the word Adam (אדם) is an acronym for Adam (אדם), David (דוד), *Mashiach* (משיח, *Sefer HaGilgulim* 62; *Torah Or* 46d). Had Adam and Eve not sinned, Adam would have retained his true identity as Adam, Eve would have manifested the level of King David, and their son would have been *Mashiach*.

125. See additional note 8 at the end of this chapter (p. 369).

A Continuum of Consciousness

Previously, we followed the developing soul of a child-to-be through its four "moments"—its parents' marital relations, its own conception, formation, and birth—in terms of how the soul traverses the continuum of consciousness from absolute unity with G-d to thought, speech, and finally independent action. A similar journey occurs in the consciousness of the parent couple.

As we have explained,[126] the intensity and height of marital relations tends to wane during the wife's days of purity. An impression of the serene experience of marital relations lingers in the couple's consciousness until their child is conceived. As we have noted, conception may occur either simultaneously with marital relations or up to three days later.[127] Thus, if the wife conceives on the night of her immersion, the couple may actually experience the consciousness of marital relations (as it descends to unite with the experience of thought) whenever they engage in martial relations, for up to three days.

Conception brings the couple fully into the consciousness of procreation. The impression of this consciousness remains until the formation of their child in the mother's womb. During the conception-period, they may experience

---

126. Above, p. 302.

127. Above, p. 326, footnote 29. In Kabbalah, the two worlds of *Atzilut* and *Beriah* (the states of consciousness associated with the moments of marital union and conception, respectively) correspond to the two *sefirot* of *chochmah* and *binah*, or *Abba* and *Ima*, which are called "the two companions that never separate" (*Zohar* 3:4a).

the consciousness of being partners with G-d in the creation of their child.[128]

From the moment of formation to that of birth, they may experience the consciousness of formation. Our sages teach us that when a husband pleases his wife in marital relations it enhances the development of the fetus.[129] Therefore, by pleasing one another in marital relations, the couple may experience the consciousness of formation.

At the moment of birth, the wife's bleeding renders her halachically impure and marital relations cease. This itself prevents a couple's consciousness from falling to the lowest, base-level of *kavanah*, where one's primary concern is with satisfying himself. Instead, their newborn child now becomes their rectified, common, Divinely oriented ego, as it were.[130]

---

128. In Kabbalah, this corresponds to the consciousness of the world of *Beriah*, the continual experience of the re-creation of the universe.

129. This corresponds to the consciousness of the world of *Yetzirah*, the realm of the emotions.

130. Thus:

Atzilut	marital/Divine union	relations to conception
Beriah	partners with G-d in creation	conception to formation
Yetzirah	pleasing one's spouse	formation to birth
Asiyah	consciousness of newborn	after birth

Additional Notes

1

to page 318.

There are three aspects to the observance and experience of Shabbat: the cessation from work (and all mundane activity), the experience of delight (both physical and spiritual), and the ultimate experience of rest (the elevation of the soul to communion with the Divine). Inasmuch as Shabbat in general corresponds to the spiritual state of sweetening, these three aspects of its observance may be seen to correspond to the threefold process of submission, separation, and sweetening within sweetening, as well as to the three aspects of union between husband and wife.

The cessation from work, when devoid of any motivation other than obedience to the will of G-d, is an act of submission. Refraining from work and considering "all your work to be done" (*Mechilta* to Exodus 20:9) is the modest submission of one's own creative will to the will of G-d the Creator (submission within sweetening; see above, p. 272).

Experiencing delight, either physically, through festive meals and the like, or spiritually, through prayer and Torah study, expresses the level of separation within sweetening. One has graduated from the sense of release afforded by the cessation of work and is now focused on the Divine experience of Shabbat itself. As such, this aspect of Shabbat observance may be compared to the couple's kissing and caressing before and during marital relations—actions that focus the spouses' attention on one another, as we have explained.

The essential experience of rest (as opposed to the rest implied in simple cessation from work) is the absolute communion with G-d. This is the consummate sweetening of the Sabbath experience (sweetening within sweetening) and corresponds, of course, to the sense of soul-union that crowns a couple's marital relations.

These three aspects of Shabbat observance also correspond to the three historical foci of Shabbat: creation, revelation, and redemption. Shabbat celebrates G-d's resting from the "work" of creating the world, and in this sense directs our attention to the past, enabling us to reconnect with the Divine origin of everything. Since the Torah was given on Shabbat, Shabbat also celebrates the giving of the Torah, and thus directs our attention to our task in the present to rectify the world via the study and observance of the Torah. Finally, Shabbat is a "taste of the world to come" and thus focuses us on the consummation of creation and revelation, the final Redemption, when the purpose of creation will be accomplished and the essence of the Torah will be revealed.

As will be explained later (in ch. 15), there are three levels of the super-conscious dimension of the soul (its *keter*): faith, pleasure, and will. (Faith, in this context, is the presently unknowable pleasure of the future.) These three aspects of Shabbat-observance exemplify the ascent through these three levels of consciousness, as well.

To summarize:

aspect of Sabbath observance and experience	**process of spiritual ascent**	**Level of Shabbat**	**level of the soul**
the ultimate experience of rest	sweetening within sweetening	Shabbat of the future	faith
the experience of delight on physical and spiritual planes	separation within sweetening	Shabbat of the present	pleasure
cessation from work and all mundane activity	submission within sweetening	Shabbat of the past	will

2

to page 318.

Shabbat is synonymous with delight, as it is said: "and you shall call the Sabbath a delight" (Isaiah 58:13). The souls of the Jewish people originate in G-d's delight, as we have mentioned (p. 24; see also Jeremiah 31:19). (The higher level of Shabbat is the infinite light preceding the *tzimtzum* [*Likutei Torah* 2:41a ff.; *Pelach HaRimon, Shemot,* p. 244 ff.]. The origin of Shabbat is the "sublime delight" [עונג הנעלם] of G-d's essence [*Pelach HaRimon* 19b]). Shabbat is called a "gift" (*Shabbat* 10b), just as the service of G-d achieved by *tzadikim* ("love of delights") is referred to as a "gift" (Numbers 18:7; *Sha'ar HaYichud veHaEmunah,* introduction; *Tanya,* ch. 40), a foretaste of the world to come.

Moreover, inasmuch as Shabbat is the day of delight, it is appropriate that the couple engage in their primary delight, marital relations, on this day. It is because their small children remind parents of the delight they experienced in conceiving them (consciously or unconsciously, see *Vayikra Rabbah* 2:3) that they enjoy playing with them. Babies are called טף since their parents sense in them the seminal drop (טפה) from which they developed. This is the mystical reason why children are the legal responsibility of their parents: in the parents' consciousness, the child is just a reflection of themselves.

In the terminology of Kabbalah, Shabbat represents the ascent of the lower *hei* (*malchut*) of the Name *Havayah* to the level of the first two letters (*yud-hei, chochmah* and *binah*), which are in a constant state of union. *Chochmah* and *binah* were G-d's "delights day by day" (Proverbs 8:30), which our sages interpret to refer to the two "days" (millennia) before the creation of the world (*Midrash Tanchuma, VaYeishev* 4). The Jewish people, as well, arose in this level of delight (*Bereishit Rabbah* [ed. Theodor-Albek] 1, *s.v. Bereishit*).

Shabbat and the origin of the Jewish people are the infinite light of G-d shining inwards toward Himself, while the source of the world is the infinite light shining outward.

This is alluded to by the fact that the full spelling of *Shabbat* (שין בית תו) equals 1178, the sum of "Israel," "Torah," and "G-d" (ישראל תורה יהו־ה), the triad that existed as one before creation. In the *Zohar* (2:204a), the word *Shabbat* is seen to allude to the three forefathers (in the three arms of the ש) and the souls of the rest of the Jewish people (בת, their "daughter"). See above, p. 31, footnote 66.

3

to page 324.

In the terminology of Kabbalah: on the three days before Shabbat, one ascends through the three lower worlds, from the world of *Asiyah* ("Action") on Wednesday, to the world of *Yetzirah* ("Formation") on Thursday, and to the world of *Beriah* ("Creation") on Friday. On Shabbat, one reaches the Divine world of *Atzilut* ("Emanation"). On the three days following Shabbat, one descends through the three lower worlds, from the world of *Beriah* on Sunday, to the world of *Yetzirah* on Monday, to the world of *Asiyah* on Tuesday.

For this reason, Rabbi Yitzchak Luria teaches that the ideal days for physical labor are Tuesday and Wednesday, when one is spiritually in the world of Action; the ideal days for speech are Monday and Thursday (which, for this reason, are the two weekdays on which the Torah is read in the synagogue and on which the court sits to hear testimony); and the ideal days for thought are Sunday and Friday.

At the end of the Song of the Day for Wednesday, the liturgy appends the first three verses from the following psalm, which also opens the liturgy for Welcoming the Sabbath (*Kabbalat Shabbat*) on Friday night. Wednesday is thus clearly the beginning of the upward swing toward Shabbat.

To summarize:

Wednesday	**Thursday**	**Friday**
ascent from *Asiyah*	ascent from *Yetzirah*	ascent from *Beriah*
action	speech	thought

Shabbat	**Sunday**	**Monday**	**Tuesday**
the Divine world of *Atzilut*	descent to *Beriah*	descent to *Yetzirah*	descent to *Asiyah*
mystical union	thought	speech	action

This entire weekly process is reflected in the dream of Jacob: "He dreamt, and behold: a ladder was standing on earth, and its head reached the heavens. And behold: angels of G-d were ascending and descending it. And behold: [the Presence of] G-d stood upon it" (Genesis 28:12-13). According to our sages, Jacob's ladder possessed four rungs, in direct correspondence to the four worlds, and the ladder's summit (upon which G-d's Presence stood) corresponded to the Divine world of *Atzilut*.

The numerical value of Jacob (**יעקב** = 182) itself is 7 times 26. 26 is the value of G-d's essential Name *Havayah*. Jacob (a collective name for the Jewish people) experiences G-d's Presence, Divine providence, and unity at each of the seven levels of his ascent and descent on the seven days of the week. In particular, he experiences G-d's providence in all the events of the six weekdays (and psychologically, in all of his own thoughts, words, and actions) and His absolute unity on Shabbat, in mystical union with Him.

4

to page 330.

In the terminology of Kabbalah:

Shabbat	**Sunday**	**Monday**	**Tuesday**
Atzilut	*Beriah*	*Yetzirah*	*Asiyah*
moment of marital union	moment of conception	moment of formation	moment of birth

Wednesday	**Thursday**	**Friday**	**Shabbat**
Asiyah	*Yetzirah*	*Beriah*	*Atzilut*
ascent in action	ascent in speech	ascent in thought	mystical union with G-d

From another perspective, we may say that the moment of "action" (in ascent, Wednesday) is the moment of the child's circumcision (the moment when the child's body is completely "made" in holiness). (We are taught that females are considered circumcised from birth [*Avodah Zarah* 27a]; her "Tuesday" and "Wednesday," as it were, occur simultaneously.)

The moment of "formation" (in ascent, Thursday) can be seen as the moment of *bar-mitzvah* (or *bat-mitzvah*), the day when all his spiritual "limbs" (248 limbs corresponding to the 248 positive commandments of the Torah, and 365 major blood-vessels, corresponding to the 365 negative commandments of the Torah) become clearly differentiated and permeated with the life force of *da'at* (the mental power and inner soul of the emotive attributes of "formation," which one receives upon becoming *bar-mitzvah*).

One's moment of "creation" (in ascent, Friday) can be seen as his wedding day (before the actual marital union), when a groom sanctifies his bride, just as in the moment of conception, his vital seed fertilizes hers.

To summarize:

Shabbat	**Sunday**	**Monday**	**Tuesday**
Atzilut	*Beriah*	*Yetzirah*	*Asiyah*
moment of parent's marital union	moment of conception	moment of formation	moment of birth

Wednesday	**Thursday**	**Friday**	**Shabbat**
Asiyah	*Yetzirah*	*Beriah*	*Atzilut*
circumcision	*bar-* (or *bat-*) *mitzvah*	wedding	moment of marital union with spouse

5

to page 334.

In the original commandment to "be fruitful and multiply, fill the earth and conquer it, and rule over the fish of the sea and the birds of the heavens, and over all the animals that swarm on earth," the word for "and conquer *it*" (וְכִבְשֻׁהָ) is interpreted by our sages [because of the lack of the expected *vav* after the *shin*] to read, as well, "and conquer *her*" (וּכְבָשָׁהּ). The meaning of this with regard to the rectification of the psyche is that through the rectification of one's approach toward marital relations, one gains the power to subdue, conquer, and check his yet-unrectified passion toward his wife.

In the terminology of *Chassidut*: the two verbs "be fruitful and multiply" refer respectively to the *sefirot* of *chochmah* and *binah*. "Fill the earth" refers to *da'at* and the emotions it produces, as in the verse (Proverbs 24:4) "the chambers are filled with knowledge." "Conquer it" refers to *yesod*, the seat of sexuality ("Who is valorous? He who conquers his animal instincts" [*Avot* 4:1]). "Rule" refers to *malchut*. If one's *chochmah* and *binah*—his attitude—is correct, he will be able to proceed correctly through the subsequent levels and conquer his sexuality. To the extent that he conquers his sexuality, he will be able to rule over and rectify the rest of his animal psyche (alluded to by the mention of the animals that man is meant to rule over). This, in turn, will enable him to rule over the rest of reality.

However, as our sages tell us, if one does not merit, he will be unable to rule and will fall (ירדו carries both meanings: "rule" [רדיה] and "fall" [ירידה]) under the spell of this world's enticements (beginning with his own wife's sexuality).

Rectifying one's attitude toward marital relations means chiefly focusing one's passion inwardly, that is (1) solely on one's wife, and (2) on her inner self rather than her external appearance. In general, rectifying one's emotions (of which there are seven, as taught in Kabbalah and *Chassidut*) is seen as the spiritual correlate of the commandment to conquer the seven Canaanite nations.

As we said above, "to conquer it" can be read "to conquer *her*." Our sages interpret this to mean that the husband is instructed to control and limit his wife's forays outside her natural environment (*Bereishit Rabbah* 8:12). Since "it is the way of man to wage war, but not of woman" (*Kidushin* 2b), it is the man that naturally undertakes to conquer foreign powers. If the husband answers his calling and rectifies his emotions, his wife will feel no need to venture forth into the world to conquer evil. If, on the other hand, he neglects this, she, being his other half, will feel called to the world without.

On the other hand, as we have previously noted (see above, p. 164, footnote 77), the status of men and woman begins to reverse with the approach of the messianic era. Thus, in our times, women are more called upon to assume the role of the conqueror, albeit in ways that in no way compromise their femininity and modesty (*HaYom Yom*, 21 *Shevat*).

With the primordial sin, man lost his ability to naturally "conquer *her* [in himself]." Nowadays, he can only conquer her by first rectifying his attitude toward marital relations, as we have described.

There are thus three levels of the *mitzvah* of procreation: (1) the procreation of proper attitudes, (2) the procreation of children, and (3) the procreation of the knowledge of G-d in the world (see above, p. 352). These three levels may be seen to correspond to the three stages of consciousness we have discussed, submission, separation, and sweetening:

One must empty one's consciousness of self-assured preconceptions in order to elicit new insights from his super-conscious mind. This is an act of submission.

The procreation of children, like all other *mitzvot*, entails deliberate separation between the forbidden and the permitted.

Spreading Judaism and the consciousness of G-d in the world is an act of sweetening.

sweetening	spreading the knowledge of G-d
separation	procreation of children
submission	cultivating proper attitudes

6

to page 339.

The full phrase in the Torah reads: "...he shall be 'clean' [i.e., released from military service] for his home for one year and he shall gladden his wife" (נקי יהיה לביתו שנה אחת ושמח את אשתו). This phrase of eight words numerically equals 2864, which equals 8 times

358 (the average value of the eight words). 358 equals *Mashiach* (משיח), which permutes to spell "he shall gladden" (ישמח). In Kabbalah, *Mashiach* is the secret of the number 8, which indicates the transcendence of nature. (*Mashiach* is associated with the number 8 in many ways: for example, he will play a harp of 8 strings). The eighth *sefirah* in ascent from *malchut* (the kingdom of *Mashiach*) is *binah*, which as a *partzuf* is the "mother" image, of whom it is said: "the *mother* of children is joyous" (Psalms 113:9).

In Kabbalah, it is explained that the relation between husband and wife parallels that between Shabbat pleasure (ענג) and holiday joy (שמחה). *Pleasure* is the feeling of being one with one's source (i.e., G-d), while *joy* is the feeling of belonging (i.e., to the community). Joy is dependent on pleasure: mere "lateral" belonging without also being "upwardly" connected leaves the feeling of belonging meaningless. Thus, one's optimal experience of the joy of the Jewish holidays is dependent on his connection to G-d as manifest in his observance of Shabbat. In a similar way, a husband must devote himself to laying the foundation of his wife's happiness during their first year of marriage.

Ideally, by the end of this first year, the wife has become a "joyful mother of children"; it is now her children who sustain this heightened level of happiness. Subsequently, "reflecting light" (אור חוזר) shines from her to her husband, and her joy can enhance his, just as the feeling of community fostered by holiday observance can enhance one's feeling of connection to G-d as manifest on Shabbat.

Similarly, we are taught that in this world it is the husband that gladdens his wife, whereas in the world to come (when the wife rises above her husband, to the consummate level of "the woman of valor" who is "the crown of her husband" [Proverbs 12:4]), it is the wife who will gladden her husband. As the Hebrew for "the world to come" (עולם הבא) implies that its light and inspiration are "coming," in the present, these two states are in fact, coexistent ("this world" without and "the world to come" within).

In this world, it is the sublime point of pleasure (of Shabbat) that shines and expands (externally) to express itself as manifest joy (on the holidays). In the world to come, the essential point of pleasure "widens" infinitely by the power of joy. (In the terminology of *Chassidut*, this state is referred to as the revelation of מרחב העצמי, "the essential, infinite, Divine breadth.")

7

to page 349.

The verse containing the commandment to be fruitful and multiply begins: "And G-d *blessed* them, and G-d *said* to them, 'Be fruitful, and multiply....'" Thus, before G-d *commanded* them to be fruitful and multiply, He *blessed* them to be fruitful and multiply. Though the commandment, according to *halachah*, devolves solely on the husband, the blessing is for both. We may further infer that as the commandment is primarily the husband's, so is the blessing primarily the wife's.

Rashi (on Genesis 1:22) explains the phrase "be fruitful and multiply" as follows: "had it only said 'be fruitful,' one [person] would have only one child. The addition of the word 'and multiply' means that each shall have many children." In Kabbalah, the power to "be fruitful" is associated with *Abba* ("father") whereas the power to "multiply" is associated with *Ima* ("mother"); the consciousness of *Abba* is one of singularity, whereas that of *Ima* is one of plurality. Thus, since throughout the Torah, "blessing" implies plenitude, it becomes clear why the *blessing* of "be fruitful and multiply" relates to the woman in particular.

As the Torah prescribes a minimum of one son and one daughter, this would certainly suffice for the *Abba*-consciousness (as is said, "the [letter of the law of the] Torah derives from wisdom [*Abba*]"). It is the *Ima*-consciousness, "unbounded" by the finite measure set by *halachah*, which motivates a couple to have as many children as possible.

As is explained elsewhere (*Muda'ut Tivit*, ch. 2, addendum 2), the male or *Abba*-consciousness, is one of "commanded and does," whereas the female or *Ima*-consciousness is one of "not commanded yet [nonetheless] does." In this world, the first level of consciousness is higher than the second, whereas in the world to come, the opposite shall be the case.

The Targum translates "be fruitful and multiply" (פרו ורבו, Genesis 1:28) as "increase and become great" (פושו וסגו). This implies that of all the Torah's commandments, constant increase is most intrinsic to this one.

On the other hand, procreation is historically the first *mitzvah* given to man in the Torah. Since "everything is determined by the beginning" (*Pirkei d'Rabbi Eliezer* 42), it is thus considered the archetypal *mitzvah*. Therefore, since its essence is increase, it follows that *all mitzvot* are intended to be ever increasing (*Likutei Torah* 5:38d).

Rabbi Shneur Zalman of Liadi generalizes the scope of procreation, the first *mitzvah*, to mean that it is the primary responsibility of every Jew to manifest the *Jewishness* of his fellow Jew: "the primary axiom in Torah and in a Jew's life is that a Jew should make another Jew" (*Sefer HaSichot 5684*, p. 56, 82; *Sefer HaSichot 5691*, p. 262; *Sefer HaSichot 5696-5700*, p. 119; *Likutei Sichot*, vol. 1, p. 114, vol. 10, p. 187; see below, p. 352).

Procreation and brotherly concern are thus both included in the first *mitzvah* of the Torah.

The fact that the written Torah only obligates one to have a son and a daughter, while the oral Torah prescribes that one have as many children as he can, itself illustrates how the phenomenon of the oral Torah, relative to the written Torah, is one of increase (see *Shir HaShirim Rabbah* 6:2, based on Song of Songs 6:8).

8

to page 356.

To summarize the correspondences between these four levels of *kavanah* and the four spiritual worlds:

emulating the Divine union	*Atzilut*	"all good"
becoming partners with G-d in procreation	*Beriah*	"mostly good"
gladdening one's spouse	*Yetzirah*	"half good, half evil"
calming one's passions	*Asiyah*	"mostly evil"

As noted above, the Torah applies the first level of *kavanah*—"you shall guard yourself from all evil things"—to someone serving in the military, at battle with the evil forces of this world and both spiritually and physically away from home. The world of *Asiyah*, both objectively and subjectively predominantly evil, is the chief theater of battle in the war between good and evil.

In the world of *Yetzirah*, though one's people are objectively at war, one is subjectively exempt from participating. His responsibility toward G-d and his people is to gladden his wife. His being home serves to anchor his people's consciousness with the promise that all the soldiers will return home in peace.

In the world of *Beriah*, there is no active state of war, but its possibility is not *a priori* excluded. One is in a state similar to that of Adam and Eve before the primordial sin, where they were commanded to procreate, "fill the earth, conquer it, and rule...." They were intended to conquer reality by filling it. (This applies also to the level of the mind, the general state of the world of *Beriah*: a wise sage "conquers" reality by filling it with his insights.)

In the world of *Atzilut*—the world where all is considered to exist within the "private domain," the Divine "home" and holy sanctuary, where all becomes one—eternal and *absolute* peace rules. This is the state of the messianic era and the world to come, a taste of which we receive on Shabbat.

Atzilut	absolute peace	the all-encompassing "home"	becoming one
Beriah	at peace	making the world "home"	creating together
Yetzirah	exempt from war	at home; drawing others home	satisfying the other
Asiyah	at war	away from home	guarding oneself

15

Modesty and Mystery

The Meaning of Modesty

The union of the married couple, articulated so eloquently in their marital relations, is expressed most fully in their modesty.

Our sages teach:[1]

הֲדַר תּוֹרָה חָכְמָה;
הֲדַר חָכְמָה עֲנָוָה;
הֲדַר עֲנָוָה יִרְאָה;
הֲדַר יִרְאָה מִצְוָה;
הֲדַר מִצְוָה צְנִיעוּת.

The splendor of Torah is wisdom;
the splendor of wisdom is humility;
the splendor of humility is awe;
the splendor of awe is [a] mitzvah;
the splendor of [a] mitzvah is [its] modesty.

---

1. *Derech Eretz Zuta* 5.

The Biblical source of the concept that modesty is the apex of Divine service is the well-known verse from the prophet Micah:[2]

הִגִּיד לְךָ אָדָם מַה טּוֹב
וּמָה ה׳ דּוֹרֵשׁ מִמְּךָ:
כִּי אִם עֲשׂוֹת מִשְׁפָּט וְאַהֲבַת חֶסֶד
וְהַצְנֵעַ לֶכֶת עִם אֱלֹהֶיךָ.

It has been told you, O man, what is good,
and what G-d asks of you:
Only that you do justice, love kindness,
and walk modestly with your G-d.

Commenting on this verse, our sages say: "Six hundred and thirteen *mitzvot* were given through Moses.... Micah came and established them on [i.e., encapsulated them into] three."[3]

Why is the splendor of a *mitzvah* its modesty, and why is modesty the apex of Divine service? To understand this, let us first examine the meaning of both *mitzvot* and modesty.

The root of the word *mitzvah* (צוה) means "attachment" or "connection."[4] There are two general categories of *mitzvot*: one's duties to G-d, and one's duties to one's fellow man. A *mitzvah* between man and G-d connects the

2. 6:8.

3. *Makot* 24a.

4. *Likutei Torah* 2:45c; *Likutei Sichot*, vol. 7, p. 30 ff. and sources cited in footnote 7 there.

soul to G-d; a *mitzvah* between man and man connects one's soul to the soul of his fellow.[5]

It is customary to think that modesty (צְנִיעוּת, *tzeniut*) is expressed by the way one dresses. Although this is true, it is not the whole picture. As we have pointed out, the three modes of expression—thought, speech, and action—are called the "garments" of the soul. Thus, modesty is also expressed by the way one "dresses" himself in these,

---

5. The numerical value of the phrases for these two categories of *mitzvot* (בין אדם למקום בין אדם לחברו) equals $676 = 26^2$. 26 is the value of G-d's essential Name *Havayah*. Thus, the consummate revelation of G-d (the significance of *squaring* the value of His Name) depends on both levels of attachment. All the *mitzvot* are referred to as the *mitzvot* of *Havayah* (see *Sod Hashem Lireiav*, ch. 28).

The four letters of the word *mitzvah* (מצוה) itself correspond to the four letters of the Name *Havayah*: The first two letters of *Havayah*—יה—transform in the "reflective" alphabetic transformation system of *atbash* to מצ, the first two letters of מצוה. The second two letters of both *Havayah* and *mitzvah* are identical: וה. Thus, the first two letters of *mitzvah* conceal their corresponding letters of the Name *Havayah*, while the second two letters of *mitzvah* reveal their corresponding letters. This accords with the general principle in Kabbalah that the first two letters of the Name *Havayah* are intended to be concealed, whereas the last two are revealed. This principle is alluded to in the verse: "The concealed matters are G-d's, and the revealed matters are ours and our childrens'..." (Deuteronomy 29:28). The term "concealed matters" refers to the *kavanot* of the *mitzvot*; "revealed matters" refers to the performance of the *mitzvot*.

The principle of inter-inclusion applies to the categories of "between man and G-d" and "between man and fellow." We perform *mitzvot* between man and G-d "in the name of all Israel," and *mitzvot* between man and fellow with the intention to please G-d, our Father in heaven, by showing Him that His children behave lovingly to one another. This is an additional way of understanding the verse "the wise of heart will take *mitzvot*" (see above, p. 331).

his spiritual garments.[6] Modesty in action means taking care to move[7] in a way that does not attract undue attention to oneself. Modesty in speech means taking care not to overtly refer to oneself (whether in pride or in scorn). Modesty in thought means not exaggerating one's self-image in his own mind. The "upper limit" of this is the state of consciousness wherein one does not think of oneself at all. The ultimate expression of modesty, thus, is in the way one thinks.

The negation of self-focus that characterizes modesty, however, is not something that one deliberately imposes on his way of thinking, talking, acting, or dressing. The deliberate attempt to nullify one's self-orientation is an act of humility (עֲנָוָה, *anavah*) rather than modesty. In other words, the difference between modesty and humility is that whereas a humble person *nullifies* his ego, a modest one *transcends* it.[8]

There are four basic stages in the nullification of the ego: the sense of lowliness, the sense of subservience to a superior, unpretentiousness, and selflessness.[9] The common

---

6. Physical and spiritual garments are closely related: the way one dresses affects the way one moves, talks, and even thinks.

7. The word **הצנע** ("modestly," from Micah 6:8) can be read as a *notrikun* for **הצ**[דיק] **נע**, "[the way] the *tzadik* moves."

8. In the five-rung ladder of ascent in the levels of splendor, humility (*anavah*) is reached by the second ascent—"the splendor of wisdom is humility," whereas modesty culminates all five levels—"the splendor of [a] *mitzvah* is [its] modesty."

9. See at length *Lev LaDa'at*, p. 17 ff. The four levels of humility correspond to the four letters of G-d's Name *Havayah* and to the four worlds, as follows:

denominator of all of these, however, is that one is focused on oneself and one's ego, even if only in order to nullify it; they are all levels of humility.[10]

י	*Atzilut*	בטול	*bitul*	selflessness
ה	*Beriah*	ענוה	*anavah*	unpretentiousness
ו	*Yetzirah*	הכנעה	*hachna'ah*	subservience
ה	*Asiyah*	שפלות	*shiflut*	lowliness

10. There is a higher level of *bitul,* at which one is "existentially nullified" (בטול במציאות) altogether, and is so consumed within Divinity that he has no conscious awareness of himself as an entity distinct from his Divine source. At this stage, it is no longer necessary to actively nullify one's ego; this has already been accomplished. This level is the province of *tzadikim,* whose process of self-refinement is essentially behind them and who have reached a steady-state type of Divine service. Thus, in the *Tanya* (ch. 15), the *beinoni* is referred to as "one who is actively engaged in the service of G-d" (עובד אלהים), in contrast to the *tzadik,* who is referred to as "the servant of G-d" (עבד אלהים). We are here discussing the service of the *beinoni,* and therefore the *bitul* we refer to is the type that must be actively imposed (בטול היש).

Nonetheless, although the *beinoni* cannot on his own reach existential nullification or absolute self-annihilation (בטול במציאות), he can be so focused on Divinity that it appears as if he has. This is the level of modesty. In the terminology of Kabbalah, a *tzadik* possesses the consciousness of *Atzilut,* or absolute *bitul,* while the *beinoni* possess the consciousness of *Beriah,* or possible existence (אפשריות המציאות). The *beinoni could* "be there" but is not, because he is focused on what is above him, whereas the *tzadik* is "not there" *a priori.* A *tzadik* experiences the aspect of *reisha d'lo ityada* that reflects the essence of *bitul* (שם מ"ה), while the *beinoni* experiences the aspect of *reisha d'lo ityada* that reflects a state of "existent" *bitul* (שם ב"ן).

We must therefore qualify our previous statements to the effect that modesty is the apex of Divine service: modesty is the apex of the Divine service *of the beinoni.* Similarly, the reason why modesty and not *bitul* is the "the splendor of a *mitzvah*" is because *mitzvah* refers to

Cultivating modesty, in contrast, means rising above the spiritual conflict involved in the process of actively refining one's lower self and expressing instead one's earnest, sincere connection to G-d.[11] By virtue of this simple devotion, one's entire array of soul powers becomes oriented toward Divinity. This is what is meant by transcending one's ego.[12]

---

the "connection" between man and G-d, as we said, and any connection implies two distinct parties, not one that has been absorbed into the other.

11. This sincerity is termed *temimut* (תמימות, see *Besha'ah Shehikdimu*, pp. 155-8; *Torat Shalom*, p. 180). In this context, *temimut* may be considered an encompassing soul-power (כח מקיף). As such, it possesses both characteristics of modesty: it transcends (surrounds) and covers (encompasses) that which is below and within it. *Hod*—which, as we have noted (page 157, footnote 57), is associated with *temimut*—is associated with the inner dimension of *keter* (*Besha'ah Shehikdimu*, p. 236-8).

12. As we shall explain, all levels of modesty are levels of "clothing" (i.e., levels of "rectification"; see above, p. 47, footnote 1). We may identify four levels of modest "clothing" that "garb"/rectify the four levels of humility enumerated above, as follows:

world	level of humility		level of modesty
Atzilut	*bitul*	selflessness	not thinking of oneself
Beriah	*anavah*	unpretentiousness	modest thought
Yetzirah	*hachna'ah*	subservience	modest speech
Asiyah	*shiflut*	lowliness	modest motion

Thus, we see that the relationship between humility and modesty is one of "body" to "clothing," or in the more abstract terms of Kabbalah, of "lights" to "vessels." It is axiomatic in Kabbalah that the origin of the vessels is higher than the origin of the lights. We can

"The Unknowable Head"

Transcending the ego and thereby cultivating modesty is an expression of the highest super-conscious level of the soul.

As taught in Kabbalah, the soul possesses three levels of super-consciousness.[13] These are called "the three heads" of *keter* (the "crown"). Just as a crown rests *upon* the head, the super-conscious mind transcends the conscious mind.

The lowest level of the super-conscious is its will. This is the source of our instinct for self-preservation, and the source of our desire to enhance and improve our lives and actualize all our potentials.[14] As the soul descends from its source and vests itself in the body, this is the first point at which it experiences itself as an independent entity, with its own interests and drives.

Inasmuch as the super-conscious powers of the soul are not localized in any specific part of the body, they hold sway over the conscious powers. This is particularly

---

therefore understand why modesty (and not humility) is regarded as being rooted in the unknowable head of *keter*.

13. *Zohar* 3:288a. Since man is created in the Divine "image," these three levels of super-consciousness are a reflection of the spiritual worlds. See above, p. 15, that all three "heads" (will, pleasure, and faith) are part of the highest level of the soul, the *yechidah*.

14. When properly rectified, this survival instinct becomes the desire to lead a meaningful life, making every day count (see *Likutei Sichot*, vol. 3, p. 772 ff.; see below, footnote 16). Afterwards, it expands to become a desire for eternal life, and is therefore the motivation for *teshuvah*, by which one merits one's portion in the world to come.

observable with regard to the will, which can direct and focus the intellect and the emotions, and control their expression. Thus, in Kabbalah, this level of *keter* is called "the long head"[15]—"long" because it reaches and controls all conscious aspects of the soul.[16]

When allowed to reach its ultimate conclusion, the soul's quest for self-fulfillment and self-actualization leads paradoxically to its self-abnegation. When one becomes aware that all his transient wills and drives reduce to the simple will to be, and that the only true existence is G-d's, he willfully surrenders his sense of independent self in order to be absorbed into the greater reality of Divinity.[17]

Thus, the next, higher level of the super-conscious is called "the head of nothingness."[18] This is the sense that G-d is everything while one's self is existentially nothing. Freed from the "weight" of ego and its subservience to materialism, one experiences at this level a spiritual "weightlessness."[19] This serene nothingness is an experience

---

15. In Hebrew: *reisha d'arich* (רישא דאריך). This level is synonymous with the *partzuf* of *Arich Anpin*, the external dimension of *keter*.

16. "Long" also in that it is the source of the will to survive, the will for longevity (see above, footnote 14).

17. Compare the statement of the Maggid of Mezeritch quoted above, that G-d creates the world "something from nothing," and the righteous reverse the process, transforming themselves and their portion in the world from "something to nothing" (see *HaYom Yom*, 29 *Adar* 2).

18. In Hebrew: *reisha d'ayin* (רישא דאין). This level is synonymous with the *partzuf* of *Atik Yomin*, the inner dimension of *keter*.

19. Many non-Jewish spiritual disciplines consider this egolessness (or "nirvana" experience) the highest level of consciousness attainable, and therefore assume that the goal of Divine service is

of infinite delight and contentment as well as ultimate fulfillment.[20]

Again, if this sense of selflessness is pursued to its conclusion, it is replaced altogether by the awareness of G-d.[21] This is the highest level of super-consciousness

---

simply to overcome the independent will (*reisha d'arich*) and reach this level. This reflects a lack of the highest level of *keter*, *reisha d'lo ityada*, which inspires one experiencing nothingness and delight (*reisha d'ayin*) to descend into *reisha d'arich* in order to give birth to a new, higher will (see below, p. 406). To remain at this penultimate level of abstract bliss is to succumb to an illusion, which is likened to "an alien woman...whose house inclines to death, and her paths to the dead. None that go to her return, nor do they regain the paths of life" (Proverbs 2:16-19). (In contrast, Western religion *has* adopted the Jewish ideal of purpose, albeit in a distorted fashion.) When one rises to this level of egolessness, the nothingness he attains derives from the *reshimu*, the impression of Divine light that remains in the void created by the *tzimtzum*.

20. To be more precise, the abstract experience of pleasure (תענוג פשוט) here described is the consciousness of the intellect of *Atik Yomin*. (This consciousness is referred to as "essential delights" [שעשועים עצמיים].) The pleasure found in something specific (תענוג מורכב), which gives rise to will, is the consciousness of the *midot* of *Atik Yomin*. As will be explained, the faith that resides in *reisha d'lo ityada* (at the level of *keter* of *Atik Yomin*) directs the essential, abstract pleasure into compound pleasure, then to be vested in *reisha d'arich* as will.

21. Herein lies the difference between the authentic Jewish experience of being "at one with G-d" vs. that of the "nirvana"-oriented spiritualist (described above, footnote 19). The former is an experience of reaching up beyond the *tzimtzum* to the unknowable Divine light (since nothing beyond the *tzimtzum* can be known). The latter, as we have noted, is an experience of blending into the *reshimu*, the "backdrop" of Divine light that permeates the void in which creation occurs.

possessed by the soul as a being discrete from G-d Himself. Of course, as long as the soul retains its identity, it *ipso facto* cannot "know" G-d directly but only believe that He exists:[22] G-d is infinite and unbounded, while the intellect is finite and limited. It is thus said that "the summit of knowledge is to know that we cannot know."[23]

Nonetheless, from this radical awareness that we cannot intellectually know G-d springs true experiential awareness of Him. Once one has exhausted his intellect in pondering the essence of Divinity, he can truly know that his intellect is and will forever remain incapable of grasping Him.[24] Divested of the notion that his conscious mind will ever succeed in connecting him to G-d, one can submit himself to G-d willingly and unconditionally. This allows the axiomatic reality of G-d's being to become his operative consciousness.[25] His awareness of G-d continuously

---

22. Above (footnote 12), we noted that modesty is the origin of the vessels. "Vessel" in Aramaic (מנא) is cognate to "faith" in Hebrew (אמונה, see above, p. 113, footnote 10).

23. *Bechinat Olam* 13:45. In the words of the *Zohar*, "no thought can grasp You at all" (*Tikunei Zohar*, introduction [17a]). *Chassidut* explains that this includes even the primordial thought of *Adam Kadmon*, which in man corresponds to the source of the soul after the *tzimtzum*. However, *Chassidut* adds, G-d *can* be grasped by "the will of the heart" (רעותא דליבא) and by observing the Torah and its commandments. (*Tanya*, ch. 4; *Torah Or* 27a; *Likutei Torah* 3:81d, *Or HaTorah*, *Bereishit*, p. 256. These two are the "run" and "return" of the nullification of the self to G-d, respectively.)

24. See *Keter Shem Tov* 3 and accompanying endnote quoting the explanation of Rabbi Hillel of Paritch.

25. The verse "G-d appeared to me from afar" (Jeremiah 31:2) can be interpreted to mean: "It is specifically out of my sense of being far from G-d that He can appear to me." The numerical value of this

creating the world *ex nihilo*, sustaining and directing it, as well as of His omnipresence and transcendence, becomes so acute and absolute that it overtakes his consciousness entirely.

Thus it is said that "You are a G-d that hides Himself."[26] G-d's essence is absolutely inaccessible to our conscious minds and can only be felt, sensed, or grasped when we shed our selfhood and make the ontological quantum leap of surrendering ourselves to Him.

This highest level of super-consciousness is therefore called "the unknowing and unknowable head."[27] Here, the

---

verse (מרחוק ה' נראה לי) is 26^2, which signifies the fullest revelation of G-d, as we have mentioned above (p. 373, footnote 5). Similarly, King Solomon said, "I said 'I shall become wise,' but it was far from me" (Ecclesiastes 7:23).

26. Isaiah 45:15.

27. In Hebrew: *reisha d'lo yada v'lo ityada* (רישא דלא ידע ולא אתידע), usually abbreviated to *reisha d'lo ityada*. When considered to correspond to the simple faith of the Divine soul (which transcends even the "essential delight"), it is synonymous with the *keter* of *Atik Yomin*, as mentioned above, footnote 20. See *Besha'ah Shehikdimu*, p. 327.

Rabbi Yitzchak Luria (*Commentary on Sifra d'Tzniuta*, cited in *Sha'ar Ma'amarei Rashbi* p. 29c) refers to *reisha d'lo ityada* as חביון עוז העצמות, "the hiding place of the might of G-d's essence." Alternatively, this phrase may be translated "the hidden might of G-d's essence." These two interpretations express the two sides of the paradox inherent in *reisha d'lo ityada*, which we will discuss presently.

(The expression חביון עוז is taken from Habakkuk 3:4. In *Sefer HaLikutim, Ki Tisa, s.v. uMoshe lo Yada* #2 [43c (204b in Brandwein edition)], this expression is said to allude to "the hidden transcendence of knowledge and *zivug*.")

To this level, the *Zohar* (3:288b) applies the verse (Numbers 24:11), "flee now to your place." "You" here is the Divine soul, the essence of the soul is "unknowing" because it cannot know its true object of consciousness, G-d, and "unknowable" because one's entire being is focused not on himself[28] and there is therefore, in effect, no one to be known to anyone else.[29]

As we said, this is the highest super-conscious level of the soul. There is a higher aspect of the soul, however, which is for all intents and purposes a part of G-d Himself[30] and as such possesses no independent con-

---

"portion of G-d"; its "place," its origin, is *reisha d'lo ityada*, where it is manifest. (see also *Zohar* 2:177a [in *Sifra d'Tzniuta*], and commentary of R. Eliahu of Vilna *ad loc.* [p. 35a of Jerusalem, 1986 ed.].)

The ontological distinction between the three heads of *keter* may be summarized as follows:

reisha d'lo ityada	concealed and non-existent within the super-conscious	העלם שאינו במציאות
reisha d'ayin	concealed, yet existent within the super-conscious	העלם שישנו במציאות
reisha d'arich	existent within the super-conscious	ראשית המציאות

28. And, as the Ba'al Shem Tov taught, "a person is where his will is focused" (*Torat Shmuel, Mayim Rabim* 113; *Sefer HaMa'amarim, Kuntresim*, p. 818). Thus, by focusing completely outside oneself, he empties himself of his own selfhood.

29. One would think that if one cannot know the object of his consciousness, no one else can, either. Yet, we are told that the Ba'al Shem Tov would send his disciples to observe the simple faith of unlearned Jews, who were not aware of the extraordinary communion with G-d they had achieved. This was possible, however, only because these disciples possessed a sensitivity and existential affinity to this level.

30. The Jewish soul is an "actual portion of G-d above" (Job 31:2; *Tanya*, ch. 2: the word "*actual*" is added in the *Tanya*).

sciousness (or even super-consciousness) *per se* whatsoever.[31] At this point, the subject-object dichotomy between the soul and G-d vanishes.

Thus, we are presented here with the ultimate paradox: the soul is focused on G-d, whom it can only

---

31. Relative to the *yechidah*, this aspect of the soul is the *yachid*, or "spark of the Creator which afterwards becomes a creature." (*Etz Chaim*, 42:1; *Nahar Shalom*, beginning; *Sefer HaMa'amarim 5679*, p. 308 ff.; *Sefer HaMa'amarim 5719*, p. 630 ff.). The *yechidah* is a name of the soul, and thus only a level of its manifestation, not its essence. It is a "garb" that the soul dons in order to manifest itself. Still, because *reisha d'lo ityada* is the dissolution of the subject-object dichotomy between the soul and G-d, it is compared to "the snail, whose garment emerges from and is part and parcel of itself" (*Bereishit Rabbah* 21:5; *Tanya*, ch. 21 [27a]; *Sha'ar HaYichud VeHaEmunah*, ch. 7 [84b]). The Aramaic word for "snail" in this expression (קמצא) is related to the name of the vowel (קמץ) associated in Kabbalah with *keter*, which in turn is an acronym for the terms used in the *Zohar* (*Tikunei Zohar* 69 [115b], 70 [128a, 135b]) to refer to the three levels of light in *keter* (אור קדמון, אור מצוחצח, אור צח) which are the origin of the three heads of *keter*.

In particular, we may identify three degrees to which the soul-essence is clothed in its manifestations, corresponding to how it is enclothed in physicality:

reisha d'lo ityada	soul-essence present in its essential manifestation	blood	the viable soul so present in the blood that it is identified with it
soul-powers: delight and below	the soul-essence enclothed in its powers	body	the viable soul enclothed in the body
garments: thought, speech and deed	powers further enclothed by their means of expression	clothing	the body further enclothed by clothing, which express the soul

believe in but not know directly, but at the same time, it itself is a part of G-d.[32] In other words, it reaches up beyond itself, but the object it is trying to reach and which existentially eludes it is in fact itself. Its true essence is its own insoluble mystery.

Thus, a Jew's search for G-d leads him to his own unknowable essence. He cannot know G-d unless he knows his own innermost self. But since his innermost self is a part of G-d, he can never know it.

Therefore, the soul at this level can neither know itself nor be known to anyone else. It is an eternal enigma; its true essence is forever hidden. This is the essence of modesty.

Thus, the root of modesty, the highest of the three precepts of Micah, is faith in G-d.[33] And thus our sages say,

---

32. This follows from the Chassidic doctrine that the *tzimtzum* described in Kabbalah is to be understood non-literally, i.e., the created world's consciousness of G-d is withdrawn, but not His essence.

33. The three pillars of Divine service into which Micah encapsulated the six hundred and thirteen *mitzvot*—"to do justice, love kindness, and walk humbly with your G-d"—correspond to the three supernal "heads" of *keter* in ascending order:

level of Divine service	**three heads of *keter***	**inner life force**
"to walk humbly with your G-d"	*reisha d'lo ityada*	simple faith, self-sacrifice, instinct to do *teshuvah*
"to love kindness"	*gulgalta*	*chesed* of *Atik Yomin*
"to do justice"	*mocha stima'ah*	*gevurah* of *Atik Yomin*

continuing the statement quoted above: "Habakkuk came and established them on [i.e., encapsulated them into] one, as it is said, 'the righteous one shall live by his faith.'"[34]

On the other hand, the soul's experience of itself at this level as both the knower and the known (or rather, the unknower and the unknown) means that just at this irreducible point of absolute essence, the soul exists as a duality, a two-faced coin. These two faces of the soul's essence are the two soul-roots of the married couple. The soul's experience of itself as the "unknower" is the root of the husband, and its experience of itself as the "unknown" is the root of the wife.

This is the mystical reason why true completeness (שְׁלֵמוּת) is possible only in the context of married life.[35] The ascent to one's essence, as we have said, is the discovery of the soul-root of one's spouse. This is what he has "found"; this is why "one's wife is one's home."[36] There is

---

Here, the three heads are identified according to the nomenclature of *Etz Chaim*, rather than that which we generally employ, which is that of *Emek HaMelech*.

34. Habakkuk 2:4. See above (footnote 10), where we pointed out that *tzeniut* is the highest level a *beinoni* can attain, while a *tzadik* can attain *bitul bimtziut*.

35. The sin of "blemishing the covenant" (i.e., sexual aberration) blemishes one's "completeness" (*Torat Shalom*, pp. 172-3).

36. Thus, the idealized essence of a man is his wife, and the idealized essence of a woman is her husband. Similarly, the week may be conceived of as "dreaming" of Shabbat. During the week we are to "remember the Sabbath day to sanctify it" (Exodus 20:8); "to sanctify" (לקדש) is the same verb used to mean "betroth."

an "I" and a "she":[37] one's "I" is what one transcends (i.e., "cannot be known"), and the "she" is what one transcends to (i.e., "seeks to know but cannot"). To find my real self, I must transcend myself and find my spouse, for she is the real me. But at the same time, I cannot know her except by knowing my innermost self.[38]

If one's ego prevents him from reaching *reisha d'lo ityada*, he lacks this vision of his own self-perfection being dependent on joining with a soul mate of the opposite sex. Focused on himself, he will seek perfection through the expansion of his one-sided incompleteness, in effect trying to project and replicate himself. This is the spiritual root of homosexuality. The fact that this sin is rooted in such a radical character flaw is testified to by the disproportionately large number of remedies for it found among Rabbi Yitzchak Luria's prescriptions (*tikunim*) for rectifying various types of sin. Furthermore, as we mentioned above, egocentricity will lead men to consider women "more bitter than death," which will also cause them to view the opposite sex as the enemy rather than as the path to perfection.

We have mentioned previously (p. 159) that it is natural not to want to waste oneself. If a man perceives women negatively, he may consider investing his seed in her as a form of self-destruction. Thus, the legitimate fear of spilling seed in vain becomes distorted into a fear of relations with a woman, leading again to homosexuality and true waste of oneself.

37. In popular parlance, the relationship changes from "I-it" to "I-thou" (see above, p. 8, footnote 15).

38. This is the mystical reason why, though both men and women are required to be modest, modesty is usually associated with women. Throughout the oral Torah, modesty is considered to be the most praiseworthy attribute of righteous women. While a praiseworthy man is generally called a "righteous man" (איש צדיק), a praiseworthy woman is generally called a "modest woman" (אשה צנועה).

(The relationship between the oral and written Torah is compared to that of a wife to her husband. In Kabbalah, the oral Torah is associated with the *sefirah* of *malchut* [the feminine manifes-

This is why modesty is the essential mystery of marriage. Above, we quoted our sages' statement that "the splendor of [a] *mitzvah* is [its] modesty," and explained that *mitzvah* means connection. Marital relations, of course, are the most intense form of connection and are therefore termed the greatest of *mitzvot*.[39] Thus, the above statement—"the splendor of a *mitzvah* is its modesty"—implies, in particular, that the beauty of marital relations lies in their modesty. In other words, the modesty that characterizes a couple's marital relations creates an even stronger bond (*mitzvah*) between them than does their physical contact itself.

It may seem paradoxical that modesty can foster deeper mutual identification than can marital relations alone. Nonetheless, inasmuch as man and woman are of opposite natures, their true union can only occur through

---

tation of Divinity], whereas the written Torah is associated with the *sefirah* of *tiferet* [the masculine manifestation of Divinity].)

This is so because the ultimate origin of the female soul, the *sefirah* of *malchut*, is *reisha d'lo ityada*. The male soul, in contrast, which corresponds to the *sefirah* of *tiferet* (the central point of the emotive attributes of the heart) is rooted in *reisha d'ayin* (which becomes manifest as the great, essential loving-kindness of the *gulgalta*).

The fact that the origin of *malchut* is *reisha d'lo ityada* accords with the general principle in Kabbalah that "the end is wedged in the beginning." Here, "the end" is *malchut*, the last of the ten *sefirot*, which corresponds to the female soul; the beginning is *reisha d'lo ityada*, the absolute "beginning" of *keter* itself.

Of course, men must also be modest and women righteous. But by being so, they are manifesting their feminine and masculine sides, respectively.

39. In the context of procreation. (*Tosefot* on *Shabbat* 4a, *s.v. Vechi*; and on *Gitin* 41b, *s.v. Lo Tohu*).

paradox.[40] Through the care they take to preserve modesty even in their most intimate and self-exposing moments, each spouse connects to the other's deepest and most private realms of being and becomes able to perceive the most sublime beauty of the other's soul.

The Source of Blessing

The fact that modesty is the quintessential means of expression of "the unknowable head" is illustrated by the story of the ten blessings that Isaac bestowed on Jacob the first time he blessed him.[41]

וְיִתֶּן לְךָ הָאֱלֹהִים מִטַּל הַשָּׁמַיִם
וּמִשְׁמַנֵּי הָאָרֶץ,
וְרֹב דָּגָן,
וְתִירֹשׁ.
יַעַבְדוּךָ עַמִּים,
וְיִשְׁתַּחֲוֻ לְךָ לְאֻמִּים.
הֱוֵה גְבִיר לְאַחֶיךָ,
וְיִשְׁתַּחֲווּ לְךָ בְּנֵי אִמֶּךָ.
אֹרְרֶיךָ אָרוּר,
וּמְבָרְכֶיךָ בָּרוּךְ.

---

40. Significantly, the Hebrew verb for marriage, נישואין, has the same root as the verb used to express "paradox"—נשיאת הפכים (literally, "the carrying of opposites"). For this reason, marriage—נישואין—is referred to as a "covenant" (ברית), implying the union of opposites, as well. See *Pelach HaRimon*, *Shemot* 296a.

41. Genesis 27:28-29. Isaac blessed Jacob again later (*ibid*. 28:1-4).

May G-d give you of the dew of heaven,
and the fats of the earth,
and an abundance of grain,
and wine.
May peoples serve you,
and nations bow down to you.
Be a master over your brother,
and may your mother's sons bow down to you.
May those who curse you be cursed,
and those who bless you be blessed.

We are taught in Kabbalah and *Chassidut* that these blessings are the highest and greatest of all the blessings of the patriarchs. They are understood to be the Divine "intermediate" linking the ten sayings of creation to the Ten Commandments of the Torah.[42]

---

42. See *Pirkei d'Rabbi Eliezer* 32; *Pelach HaRimon, Bereishit* 10c ff. The Ten Commandments correspond to the ten sub-*sefirot* of *chochmah* of *Atzilut*, while the ten sayings of creation correspond to the ten sub-*sefirot* of *malchut* of *Atzilut*. *Chochmah* and *malchut* of *Atzilut* are referred to as "Eden" and the "garden of Eden," respectively (compare above, p. 328, footnote 38). "And a river went forth from *Eden* to water the *garden*" (Genesis 2:10). The ten blessings of Isaac correspond to the river that joins Eden with the garden.

(When Isaac dug his final well, he called it *Rechovot* [literally, "wide spaces"], "and he said: 'for G-d has now made room for us, and we shall be fruitful [ופרינו] in the land'" [*ibid.* 26:22]. "Fruitful" is the literal translation of "Euphrates" [פרת], the name of the fourth river to branch out from the original river which watered the garden of Eden [*ibid.* 2:14]. Our sages state that this branch is in fact the reappearance of the original river itself [*Bechorot* 55b; *Bereishit Rabbah* 16:3]. In addition to this, the name *Rechovot* itself is elsewhere associated with the Euphrates [*ibid.* 36:37, see Targum *ad loc.*].)

Any intermediate must contain two dimensions, each of which connects to one of the entities it is intended to unite. In this way, the intermediate reflects the common source of the entities it connects, which transcends both of them. In our case, Isaac's blessings reflect the common source in G-d's essence of His relatively immanent power

---

The seventh of these ten blessings is to "be a master over your brother." Jacob and Esau personify the good and evil inclinations, respectively. The ability given the good inclination to subdue the innate, evil inclination is the basis of free choice and Torah observance. Once subdued, the evil inclination will eventually reorient itself toward holiness and be subsumed within the good inclination. This is why these blessings are the intermediary between the ten sayings of creation (i.e., nature) and the Ten Commandments (i.e., Torah).

An intermediary can serve as such only because its source is higher than either of the entities it bridges. Thus, the ultimate source of Isaac's blessings is higher than either the ten sayings of creation or the revelation of the Ten Commandments.

The two tablets of the Ten Commandments may be conceived of as addressing the two twins, Jacob and Esau, the good and evil inclinations. The commandment to honor parents is found on the first tablet, since Esau apparently did a better job of honoring his parents than Jacob did (*Bereishit Rabbah* 65:16): "Isaac loved Esau, for he provided him with venison" (Genesis 25:28); "Joseph was separated from his father Jacob for twenty-two years, as punishment for the twenty-two years during which Jacob was separated from his father Isaac and could not perform the duty of honoring him" (Rashi on *ibid.* 28:9). The commandment to honor parents (Exodus 20:12; Deuteronomy 5:16: כבד את אביך ואת אמך) begins with the letters **כב**, which equal 22; the second rendering of this commandment (*ibid.*) contains 22 words.

The Ten Commandments were given on Shabbat, and the Sunday of each week begins the reenactment of the ten sayings of creation. It is therefore customary to recite the ten blessings of Isaac on *Motzaei Shabbat* as a link between the Ten Commandments of Shabbat and the ten sayings of the week.

inherent in creation and His relatively transcendent power manifest in the Torah.

In the terminology of the Ba'al Shem Tov,[43] the ten sayings of creation reflect the level of "Worlds," the Ten Commandments reflect the level of "Divinity," and these blessings reflect the level of "Souls" (the Divine souls of the Jewish people), which links "Divinity" with "Worlds."[44]

But Isaac gave these blessings to Jacob thinking that he was Esau! In the words of the Torah:

וְלֹא הִכִּירוֹ
כִּי הָיוּ יָדָיו כִּידֵי עֵשָׂו אָחִיו שְׂעִרֹת
וַיְבָרְכֵהוּ.

And [Isaac] did not recognize [Jacob],
for his hands were hairy like the hands of Esau,
and he blessed him.[45]

Rebecca knew that the power embodied in these blessings was too sublime to be received directly. Only by

---

43. See *Keter Shem Tov* 1; *The Hebrew Letters*, introduction.

44. The soul, as we said before, is an "actual portion of G-d above," whereas "Divinity" refers only to manifestations of G-d in the world rather than G-d Himself. On the revealed plane, the soul is on a lower level than Divinity, but when it serves as an intermediary it manifests its inner origin which is higher than the revelation of Divinity in the world.

In the words of the sages, "the power of the son exceeds that of the father" (*Shavuot* 48a). This reads literally: "the power of the son is better from within the power of the father," meaning that the power of the son is greater because it manifests the *inner* power of the father, which the father himself cannot manifest. See *Sod Hashem Lireiav*, p. 181.

45. Genesis 27:23.

elevating Jacob to the level of the "unknowable head," by negating his awareness of himself as himself, would he be able to receive them.[46] She therefore dressed Jacob in Esau's clothes,[47] for nothing can be as concealing as clothing oneself in one's *opposite*.[48] By donning Esau's physical

---

46. Sarah was "of beautiful appearance" (יפת מראה, Genesis 12:11). Rebecca was "of exceedingly goodly appearance" (טובת מראה מאד, *ibid.* 24:16). Rachel was "of beautiful form and beautiful appearance" (יפת תאר ויפת מראה, *ibid.* 29:17). The word "beautiful" used in reference to Sarah and Rachel (יפה) refers to external beauty, while that used in connection with Rebecca (טוב) refers to modest, hidden beauty (see *The Hebrew Letters*, p. 138). In this sense, Rebecca was the most modest of the matriarchs, and therefore the one most sensitive to the unique power of modesty to elicit transcendent blessing.

Modesty is a form of restraint, and is therefore a function of *gevurah*, the left side of the sefirotic tree, associated with Isaac and Rebecca.

As we will note later (p. 397), in the world to come, modesty will reveal as well as conceal. We are taught that in the world to come, Isaac will be seen as the most essential of the three forefathers (*Shabbat* 89b). His very name (יִצְחָק) is the future tense of the basic form (קַל) of the verb "to laugh." The full expression of laughter will occur in the world to come, as it is said: "When G-d will return the captives of Zion...*then* will our mouths be filled with laughter" (Psalms 126:1-2). When Isaac and Rebecca were in the land of the Philistines, "after he had been there for a long while, Abimelech, the king of the Philistines, looked through his window, and he saw Isaac amusing Rebecca his wife" (Genesis 26:8). The word for "amusing" (מְצַחֵק) is the *present* tense of the intensive form (פִּעֵל) of the verb "to laugh," which here refers to his engaging in marital relations with Rebecca. Thus, the alliteration "Isaac amusing" (יִצְחָק מְצַחֵק) means that he brought the laughter of the future into the present. The yet-unrectified world (personified by Abimelech), however, watched from "without" their Edenic state, thereby somewhat defiling its sublime nature.

47. This was besides covering his arms and neck with goatskins.

48. This idea is the basis for the Jewish custom to dress up in costumes on Purim. On Purim one is enjoined to drink "*until he does*

clothes, Jacob was to a certain extent garbing himself in Esau's personality as well, and was thus able to identify with him and say to their blind father, "I am Esau, your firstborn."[49]

From this we see that by hiding one's true identity in existential modesty one becomes worthy to receive the greatest of blessings, those that derive from "the unknowable head"—the abode, so to speak, of G-d's essence. And indeed, it is the innate modesty of the souls of Israel that allows them to join, as in a marriage, the relatively female level of "Worlds" to the relatively male level of "Divinity."

To summarize:

Divinity	the Ten Commandments of the Torah	the Divine groom
Souls	the ten blessings of Isaac to Jacob	the uniting power of modesty
Worlds	the ten sayings of creation	the existential bride

---

not know the difference between 'cursed be Haman' and 'blessed be Mordechai'" (*Megilah* 7b). The phrase "until he does not know" (עד דלא ידע) may be seen as an allusion to "the unknowing and unknowable head"; on Purim we are to ascend to the level where all dichotomies lose their reality. This elicits the highest blessing, the revelation of the essential unity of G-d and the Jewish people, which in turn brings "light, joy, gladness and honor" (Esther 8:16).

Still, even on Purim, men are forbidden to dress up as women and women as men (Deuteronomy 22:5; *Shulchan Aruch, Yoreh Deah* 182:5). The deepest aspects of life are borderline cases, and if they are taken even slightly too far they cross into sin.

49. Genesis 27:19.

An End to Hiding

Thus, the true purpose of modesty is not to conceal but to reveal the hidden dimension of one's spouse's inner essence. This essential paradox of modesty will be ultimately resolved and revealed only in the messianic future.

Had Eve merited, she would have epitomized the attribute of modesty. But she naïvely felt that the fact that G-d had created her and her husband naked meant there was nothing wrong with open nakedness. Forgetting that G-d placed them in the garden to *perfect* reality, she[50] fell into the ideological trap of simply aspiring to be one with G-d's creation as it was.[51] She understood G-d's directive to "cling and become one flesh" superficially; therefore, although she sought to unite with her husband, she was oblivious to the need for modesty as an acknowledgment of their essential, unknowable selves, their transcendent

---

50. Although both Adam and Eve were guilty of this, the rectification of reality by keeping it from overstepping its bounds is primarily a female function. (*Zohar* 1:48b, 2:92a: "It is written, '*Remember* the Sabbath day' [Exodus 20:8] and '*Guard* the Sabbath day' [Deuteronomy 5:12]. 'Remember' is for the male; 'guard' is for the female." The word "remember" [זכור] is cognate to the word for "male" [זכר].)

51. Thus, the sin of Adam and Eve was that they wanted to go directly from submission (recognizing the dependency of creation on G-d) to sweetening (consummating the unity of all creation together) without first undergoing the intermediate stage of separation (distinguishing between proper and improper behavior). As will be mentioned below (p. 407, footnote 85), this is the fundamental misconstruction of non-Jewish spirituality.

unity. She and Adam therefore cohabited in the open;[52] they were aware of being observed by the animals[53] but felt there was nothing wrong with this.

Her fall continued with her immodest conversation with the snake, who then pushed her to touch the tree of knowledge—a descent into even further immodesty (that of action)—until she finally ate the forbidden fruit. By the power of her free will, she could have stopped the fall at any time by asking G-d, the omnipotent One, to "catch" her in midair and not let her "crash."[54]

The beginning of the rectification of the primordial sin was when G-d clothed Adam and Eve, indicating that they must learn modesty. Immediately upon eating the forbidden fruit, "the eyes of both of them were opened, and they knew that they were naked, so they sewed fig leaves and made themselves sashes."[55] After pronouncing their punishment, G-d Himself clothed them: "And G-d

---

52. Cohabiting while naked, an expression of the couple's true union, is not only not frowned upon but is in fact required by Jewish law (*Shulchan Aruch, Even HaEzer* 76:13; see *Tikunei Zohar* 58). However, the couple must be covered by a sheet or blanket (sources cited in *Taharat Yisrael* 240:8:66), and, of course, may not cohabit in public. This dual behavior of complete immodesty (being naked) and modesty (being covered and in private) expresses the paradox of the union at the level of "unknowing and unknowable."

53. See *Nidah* 17a.

54. As it is said: "Even when he falls he shall not be let go [to crash to the ground], for G-d supports his hand" (Psalms 37:24).

55. Genesis 3:7.

made for Adam and his wife tunics of skin and clothed them."[56]

A further stage of rectification of the sin was when G-d first appeared to Moses and He "hid" Himself in the burning bush. Moses was thus presented with the opportunity to gaze at the Divine Presence, alluringly veiled in a cloak of modesty. He responded by hiding his own face, in order not to behold the Divine Presence.[57] According to one opinion, this was proper; he did not make the same mistake as Eve and knew that to look immodestly at the Divine face would be a denial of the higher knowledge expressed by modesty.[58]

According to another opinion, however, G-d would have preferred that Moses look at Him.[59] As the redemption was beginning, He was hinting to him that the primordial sin was now in the process of being rectified,

---

56. *Ibid.*, 3:21. Above (p. 47, footnote 1), we noted that the Aramaic word for "vessel" (מנא) is also used to mean "clothing," and (p. 113, footnote 10) that this root is related to the word for "faith" (אמונה).

After their sin, Adam and Eve were somewhat aware that their lack of modesty had caused their downfall, as indicated by the fact that they covered themselves partially. It remained for G-d, however, to teach them the complete meaning of modesty, as reflected in being fully clothed.

57. Exodus 3:6. Note the juxtaposition of "appearing" and "hiding."

58. Moses was a reincarnation and rectification of Abel. (Moses' three principle incarnations are alluded to by the letters of his name, *Moshe* [משה]: *Moshe* [משה], *Shet* [שת, Seth], *Hevel* [הבל, Abel].) Abel who incurred the death penalty because he gazed at the *Shechinah* when G-d accepted his offering (*Tikunei Zohar* 69 [102a]).

59. *Berachot* 7a.

and that it was time to put aside external modesty. He wanted him to put an end to the hiding.

Moses did not understand this hint until after the sin of the golden calf, when he prayed: "Please show me Your glory."[60] But by then it was too late; by sinning, the Jewish people had fallen spiritually and were no longer capable of receiving a direct revelation of G-d.[61] G-d replied: "You cannot behold My face, for no one [now] can behold My face and live."[62] In the words of our sages: "When I wanted, you did not want; now that you want, I do not want."[63] Instead, G-d hid His "face," and revealed only His "back" to Moses. This reflects the paradox of simultaneous revelation and concealment, the secret of modesty.

One's "back" is the part of oneself he cannot see. It therefore alludes to one's super-conscious self, or the

---

60. Exodus 33:18.

61. According to the opinion that it was proper for Moses to hide his face at the burning bush, in this merit his face later shone (Exodus 34:28-35). "Come and see how great is the power of sin! For before they sinned, 'the sight of the glory of G-d was like a devouring fire atop the mountain in the eyes of the children of Israel' [*ibid.* 24:17], yet they were not afraid and did not tremble. But after they made the golden calf, they recoiled and trembled even at the sight of the rays of glory shining from Moses' face!" (*Sifrei* to Numbers 5:3). Just as he was ashamed to look at G-d's face, so were the people ashamed to look at his face.

"And Moses *did not know* that his face shone...and he put a veil over his face." Moses here was at the level of *reisha d'lo ityada*, the essential source of modesty; he was not aware of the level he had achieved. Putting the veil on (after he saw the people recoil and thus became aware that his face was shining) was an act of modesty.

62. *Ibid.* 33:19.

63. *Berachot, loc. cit.*

source of one's spouse. Of course, G-d does not have a super-conscious, but He does have a super-rational desire for His "spouse," the Jewish people; this is His "back."

By telling Moses "you will see My back," G-d was telling him: "you must relate to My innermost desire, which is you. From this, you will understand that to see My face, you must look at *your* back—*your* innermost super-conscious desire. There, you will see Me."

The ultimate rectification of the sin will be in the messianic future, when "your Teacher will cloak Himself no more, for your eyes shall behold your Teacher."[64] The paradox of the future is that although modesty will remain, it will reveal as well as conceal.

Boaz and Ruth

The intimate paradox of the knowable and the unknowable and its messianic resolution is reflected in the story of Ruth. When she came to gather crops in Boaz's field, he gave her special attention. She asked him: "Why

---

64. Isaiah 30:20. Before the creation of the world, G-d's finite power was not revealed; it was hidden within His infinite power. By creating the world, G-d hid His infinite power within His finite power. In the future, the infinite will be revealed within the finite. The *tzimtzum* will remain, but it will reveal instead of conceal. This is analogous to the idea, mentioned above (p. 290), that in the future the voice of the bride will be heard together with the voice of the groom.

have I found favor in your eyes that you should recognize me, being that I am a stranger?"[65]

In Hebrew, the word "stranger" (נָכְרִי) and the word "recognition" (הַכָּרָה)[66] share the same root (נכר).[67] Rationally, one cannot recognize a stranger, since a stranger is by definition a person one does not know. Thus, we may interpret her words as an expression of wonder: "How could you know me, when I am by nature unknowable? How did you succeed in resolving the paradox of my existence?"

Only at the super-rational level of "the unknowable head" do "recognition" and "strangeness" share a common root. At that level, the paradox, while remaining a paradox, becomes resolved. Even in her existential state as a

---

65. Ruth 2:10.

66. *Chassidut* explains that "recognition" (הכרה) is the inner dimension of "knowledge" (דעת). Just as "knowledge" alludes to marital relations, so do our sages interpret the word הכרה in Ruth's statement to mean that she prophetically sensed that Boaz was going to marry her (*Rut Rabbah* 5:2).

67. As is the case with many Hebrew roots, a concept and its antithesis often share the same root. (Similarly, a word and its antithesis often share the same *gematria*.)

In this case, the two-letter sub-root of **נכר** ("stranger") and **הכרה** ("recognition") is **כר**, the same as that of **כתר** (*keter*, "crown"). The initially super-conscious, "unrecognizable" ("strange") level of *keter* becomes known and "recognized" at the level of *da'at*. This accords with the general principle that "when one 'counts' [concentrates on] *keter*, one does not count *da'at*; when one counts *da'at*, one does not count *keter*." *Keter* and *da'at* are two sides of one existential reality, and in general cannot be envisioned simultaneously.

"stranger," her innate modesty,[68] Ruth's *true*, Divine Jewish soul[69] was visible to Boaz.

Ruth was the ancestress of King David.[70] Resolving the paradox of true identity by reaching the ultimate, essential Divine identity of the Jewish soul is the essence of *Mashiach*.[71]

---

68. Ruth's modesty is described in *Rut Rabbah* 4:8; *Rut Zuta* (Buber) 2:3.

69. And the fact that she was a potential "mother of royalty" (*Bava Batra* 91b; 1 Kings 2:19), the progenitor of the Davidic line. This is alluded to by the fact that the sum of the numerical values of Ruth (רות, 606) and David (דוד, 14) is the numerical value of *keter*, "crown" (כתר, 620), the "crown of kingdom" (Esther 1:11, 2:17, 6:8).

70. Ruth 4:10, 21-22.

71. The soul of *Mashiach*, more than that of any other soul of Israel, reflects the level of *reisha d'lo ityada*. This is alluded to in the final verse of the song Hannah sang in praise to G-d for giving her a son, Samuel: "G-d will judge the ends of the earth; He will give strength to His king, and power to His anointed" (1 Samuel 2:10). "His king" refers to King Saul and "His anointed" refers to King David, the two kings Samuel anointed (commentary of Rabbi Levi ben Gershon *ad loc.*). Samuel actually saw King Saul reign in his lifetime, but died before David became king. Thus, the "anointed" (the literal meaning of *mashiach*) in this song is a king who has been anointed but not yet crowned. He has to wait patiently, as David did, before he can rule. If we understand the ritual of anointment to reflect G-d's "anointment" of the king—His election of the king's soul to rule—it is possible for a king to be "anointed" without his conscious knowledge. He doesn't know he's king until he is crowned. This, in fact, is the case with regard to *Mashiach*: he does not know that he is the *Mashiach* until he actually begins to redeem Israel. Not knowing his true identity, he is the quintessential reflection of *reisha d'lo ityada*.

The culmination of a king's election comes when he actually begins to rule. There are thus three stages in the process of the election of a king: anointment, coronation, and commencement of

Modesty and Romance

When one is not conscious of oneself, he is also not conscious of his merits or sins.[72] His usually "exposed" shortcomings and failings are "covered" by the cloak of his modesty. And inasmuch as his sense of self has dissolved into G-d's, he sees everyone else—particularly those closest to him—as part of the same collective self. Thus, by "covering" himself, he "covers" and becomes oblivious to the sins of others, as well.[73]

---

rule. These are manifestations of the three levels of the super-conscious, and in addition, correspond to the three meanings of the word *keter* ("to wait" or "anticipate," "crown," and "to surround," see *Pardes Rimonim, Sha'ar Erkei HaKinuyim, s.v. keter*; *Besha'ah Shehikdimu*, pp. 1-127):

stage in election of the king	**level of the super-conscious tapped**	**corresponding meaning of *keter***
anointment	*reisha d'lo ityada*	"wait," "anticipate"
coronation	*reisha d'ayin*	"crown"
ruling	*reisha d'arich*	"surround"

72. Cf. *Likutei Sichot*, vol. 16, p. 271 ff.

73. As we have explained, the moon is a symbol for the Jewish people. We mark the monthly renewal of the moon with special prayers and celebrations. On *Rosh HaShanah*, however, the prayers and celebrations of the new year eclipse those of the new moon, and virtually almost no mention of it is made in the liturgy. Our sages take this "hiding" of the moon on *Rosh Hashanah* to allude to the way in which G-d covers over all our sins on this day, thereby wiping them away forever (see *Midrash Tehilim* 81:5; beginning of *Sefer Hama'amarim 5670*).

At the same time, he becomes truly altruistic. When one's own self occupies no place in one's consciousness, only the "other" exists. One's sole delight then comes from ensuring the other's pleasure. Each partner of a truly united couple will thus seek the gratification and fulfillment of the other in all areas of marital life.[74]

Paradoxically, however, it is precisely at this point of total self-abnegation that one's *true* self shines through. What we normally identify as our "self," as "I," is merely the face of one's unrectified animal soul. Once all the superficial aspects of selfhood have been neutralized, the true Divine self—one's soul-essence—can be revealed.

The Divine self cannot, of course, express itself in the same way that its lower counterpart does, inasmuch as it lacks the consciousness of existing as anything other than a part of G-d.[75] It therefore remains in the paradoxical position of representing both a negation of man's ability to be known, and an affirmation of the only true "self" that can be known. In this state, it forever retains its essential purity.

Herein lies the lesson the Torah teaches us with regard to modest conduct—especially as it concerns husband and wife, both within and without the context of marital relations.[76] If one assumes that he can "know" his spouse, then their relationship automatically becomes

74. See *Mivchar HaPeninim, Sha'ar HaTzeniut*.

75. See above, note 30.

76. See *Shabbat* 53b.

reduced to superficial and mundane familiarity.[77] But if one realizes that as much as he knows his spouse, there always remain aspects of her that he can never touch, that there are facets and depths of her soul that he has yet to plumb, their relationship stays eternally fresh and new. The sense of wonder in their marriage is never exhausted.

Although, as we have discussed, there is a rational side to marriage, it is its super-rational aspect that affords it its infinite depth. Only the recognition that marriage is a miracle wrought by G-d for His own inscrutable reasons can imbue a marital relationship with this profound sense of mystery.

The secular notion of romance is the tension preceding and leading to the consummation of love. Once this tension is resolved, boredom sets in, and even hostility may follow[78]; artificial means must therefore be found to reinstate the tension and renew the challenge. As we mentioned above, a Jewish marriage is spared this need by the laws of Family Purity. The romantic dynamic of tension and fulfillment is built into these observances, which constantly refresh the couple's romantic love on the physical plane. On the metaphysical plane, however, the intensity of romance is preserved by the couple's modesty.

---

77. Similarly, to presume to know G-d would be to belittle Him and reduce Him to the realm of the mundane.

When "Adam *knew* his wife, Eve," he was relating to her on all levels save that of *reisha d'lo ityada,* since they lacked the proper sense of modesty, as was discussed. In other words, he *knew* her, but did not succeed in achieving the paradox of simultaneously *not knowing* her.

78. The classic example of this is Amnon and Tamar (2 Samuel 13:1-15; *Avot* 5:16).

By virtue of their mutual acknowledgement of their unknowable essences, they remain forever virgin to one another. No matter how well they know each other, there is always a dimension to the other's soul that the one has yet to touch; on this level, every shared encounter is their first.[79]

Modesty Attracts

This is why modesty attracts. The unknown side of one's spouse beckons and entices him to reveal and know it.

When one of the angels who visited Abraham asked him, "Where is Sarah your wife?" he responded: "Behold, she is in the tent."[80] Our sages teach us that the angel's question was intended to call Abraham's attention to Sarah's modesty[81] and thereby to arouse his attraction toward her.

---

79. *Ani L'Dodi V'Dodi Li*, p. 21. According to the Ba'al Shem Tov, this spiraling experience of mutual virginity is alluded to in the verse: "Then shall the virgin rejoice in her dance" (Jeremiah 31:12; see *Keter Shem Tov*, addendum 40). see also above, p. 303; *Sefer HaSichot 5703*, p. 180, on the verse: "The Torah of G-d is unblemished, restoring the soul" (Psalms 19:8).

80. Genesis 18:9.

81. Rashi *ad loc*. From this we see that it is good to be aware of one's wife's modesty.

Abraham was not initially so conscious of modesty, since the angel had to point Sarah's modesty out to him. In order to father Isaac, the embodiment of modesty, Abraham had to first attain modesty-consciousness (see following footnote).

In general, mystery attracts. Something is kept secret and guarded because it is deemed too unique for common knowledge or benefit; it is reserved for the benefit of the select and privileged. The secrecy both conveys the intrinsic worth of what is being hidden and challenges and beckons the outsider to prove himself worthy of being privy to it. This is why a concealing manner and modest dress is in fact attractive and arousing. This is also why people can dupe others into thinking something is worthwhile simply by surrounding it with an artificial aura of secrecy. The reverse also applies: if something possesses intrinsic worth, treating it with respect and awe generates sensitivity to this aspect of it.

True, the popular notion is that one dresses modestly in order *not* to be attractive and arousing. And indeed, if a woman's modest dress is a reflection of her inner modesty—which expresses itself in the way she thinks, talks, and moves—her modest dress will not prove alluring to men other than her husband. This is a further paradox of modesty: it renders one attractive (to her spouse) and not attractive (to others) at the same time.[82]

In marriage, a delicate balance must be struck between the frankness a couple displays as each other's most trusted friends and the mystery they must preserve

---

82. In this sense, modest comportment may be compared to vesting a very sublime or complex idea in a parable. Whereas those familiar with the recondite concepts discussed in the parable will understand its allusions, all others will simply appreciate the parable at its face value. This is the essence of the spiritual garment known as the *chashmal*, which both conceals and reveals (see *Ma'amarei Admor Ha-Zaken, Ethalech-Liozhna*, p. 23 (cited in *Keter Shem Tov*, addendum 35).

through the modesty surrounding even their most intimate contact. Even when openness is called for, there must always be an underlying awareness of each other's essential mystery. This is afforded by the couple's growing sensitivity to "the unknowing and unknowable" side of their souls. To the extent that they internalize the inherent paradox of their super-conscious essence, they can be both frank and modest, knowing and not knowing, knowable and not knowable.[83]

The Mystery of Conception

The belief that there is a G-d who created the world with a purpose and a promise for its future is what reorients one's sense of delight from the floating serenity of the eternal present toward the greater pleasure of future consummation. Moreover, together with the sense of G-d's purpose in creation comes an awareness of one's unique role in helping realize it, the "memory" that it was G-d's vision of His people manifesting His presence in the world which inspired Him to create.[84]

Once one has ascended to the plane at which all self-awareness is lost and one's sole focus is Divinity, one

83. Specifically, not-knowing is the experience of *reisha d'lo ityada per se*, while knowing is the experience within *reisha d'lo ityada* of the origin of all the levels below it.

Of course, this sense of mystery should never serve as an excuse or reason for a breakdown in communication.

84. See above, p. 24.

becomes a transparent conduit for Divinity in the world. Lacking any ego to interpose itself between G-d and lower reality, the "unknowing and unknowable" individual serves to establish a perfect rapport between G-d and His creation.

As such, one becomes a true "partner with G-d in the work of creation." The seminal expression of the soul's drive-powered-by-delight-inspired-by-faith to participate with G-d in creation and infuse reality with Divinity is the desire to have children.[85]

At the heart of the secrecy surrounding a couple's union lies the mystery of conception. Although conception occurs in the context of their most intimate moments, it takes place in the hidden recess of the womb. Although procreation is the primary reason for engaging in marital relations, physical conception occurs without the couple's

---

85. Thus, another example of the aversion to married life that results when one stops short of *reisha d'lo ityada* would be the description given above of the acme of non-Jewish spirituality. If seen as an end, rather than as a means, the pleasure of egolessness becomes ironically the epitome of egocentricity. One so revels in the experience of his own nothingness that he is loath to surrender it in order to accomplish G-d's purpose on earth. This is why, outside of Judaism, celibacy is almost universally considered the corollary to the spiritual life (see above, p. 104, footnote 65, with reference to the verse "and the unimpassioned [of the flock] were Laban's"). One who strives to be "a partner of G-d in the work of creation," must have a spouse. This is the inner meaning of why G-d's Name is in the plural (בראשית ברא אלהים, "In the beginning, G-d created," etc.) throughout the account of creation, and Himself speaks in the plural in the context of the creation of man (נעשה אדם, "Let us make man"). (Note that only in the context of the creation of man is the *verb* in the plural, indicating that only man can evince the true idea of partnership.)

conscious intention. Conception is thus a concrete expression of the knowledge/mystery paradox of the "unknowable head."

Inasmuch as the mystery of conception is a reflection of a couple's modesty, the moment in which G-d consecrates a couple's union with new life is intrinsically linked to the degree of modesty they demonstrate. We have noted above how a couple's *kavanah* during marital relations influences the nature of their children. In addition, modest behavior facilitates conception in general, and in particular is prerequisite to drawing down a holy soul.

Giving birth to a child means, in a sense, giving birth to one's true self. To have a child is to participate with G-d in the act of creation; just as G-d created man "in His image, after His likeness," so do latent traits of one's own character become manifest in his progeny.[86] In this sense, one's child is a more genuine revelation of oneself than one can ever be on one's own. This is the ultimate paradox of procreation, the paradox of the union of husband and wife in modesty.

The first Jewish couple, Abraham and Sarah, epitomized the attribute of *tzeniut*.[87] Because of this, they

---

86. *Mei HaShiloach* throughout, e.g., p. 15c. This is the inner meaning of our sages' statement cited above (footnote 44): "the power of the son exceeds that of the father," i.e., the child is more the parent than is the parent.

87. The first reference to marital *tzeniut* in the Torah is to Abraham and Sarah. When they went down to Egypt, Abraham turned to Sarah and said: "Now I know that you are a beautiful woman" (Genesis 12:11). According to the Midrash (*Midrash Tanchuma, Lech Lecha* 5; *cf. Midrash HaGadol, Lech Lecha* 11), their modesty had not allowed him to notice her physical beauty earlier;

merited to be the progenitors of the Jewish people, i.e., to bear children like them, who embodied the Divine essence hidden in the "unknowable head."

We are taught in Kabbalah that in these latter generations, there is not so great a spiritual relationship between the souls of parents and those of their children. Indeed, the souls of parents and children may nowadays derive from different soul-roots altogether.[88] Still, the greater the modesty of the parents in marital union, the greater the likelihood that their child will indeed reflect their true selves, their "unknowable head."

There was once a woman named Kimchit who had seven sons, all of whom served as high priests in the Holy Temple. The sages asked her: "What have you done to merit this?" She replied: "The beams of my house have not seen the plaits of my hair or the lining of my robe my whole life." They applied to her the verse: "The glory of the princess is within."[89]

Mysteries of the Torah

Marrying and having children, then, reveals a dimension of reality that was previously hidden, whether in oneself, one's spouse, or one's children.

---

only now, when they were crossing a river, he accidentally saw her reflection in the water and became aware of how beautiful she was. see also above, p. 404.

88. *Sha'ar HaMitzvot, Yitro, s.v. Mitzvat Kibud Av v'Eim.*

89. Psalms 45:14; *Vayikra Rabbah* 20:11. Cf. *Yoma* 47a.

In this sense, the mystery of the marital relationship is similar to the mystery of unraveling the secrets of the Torah. This is why, according to some authorities, one should not begin the study of Kabbalah until he is married.[90] Before marriage, one should devote himself primarily to the study of the revealed dimension of the Torah, the *halachah,* that teaches one how to rectify the revealed dimension of reality through one's deeds. Only after marriage can one experience the Divine mystery and intention underlying creation, G-d's desire for the union (or "marriage") of His transcendent essence to His immanent Presence as manifest in His chosen people, Israel.

The next stage of life, after marriage, is the pursuit of a livelihood.[91] Here, one tries to reconcile life's physical and spiritual demands by elevating the former to the latter, thereby preparing the material realm to receive the

---

90. This applies specifically to the study of Kabbalah; *Chassidut,* in contrast, was revealed in an idiom suitable for all. As such, *Chassidut* evinces something of the ultimate modesty that will characterize the Divine revelations of the messianic era and the world to come. G-dliness will then be both *fully* revealed (i.e., completely, and for all creatures as public knowledge) and *fully* concealed (i.e., it will not overwhelm reality, thereby allowing it to exist).

91. According to *Avot* 5:22: "...at eighteen one should marry, at twenty pursue livelihood...." Full maturity comes only at the age of twenty, the age of conscription (the connection between pursuing a livelihood and serving in the army is indicated by the common root of the words for "bread" (לחם) and "war" (מלחמה). *Halachah* considers a person responsible enough to sell his father's inheritance only at the age of twenty. In Kabbalah, this is so because only at the age of twenty does one acquire *mochin d'Abba.* At the age of thirteen one acquires *mochin d'Ima.* Only at twenty can one achieve the state referred to in *Chassidut* as being "*in* and *out* of the world simultaneously" (in the original Yiddish: *in velt ois velt,* אין וועלט אויס וועלט).

Divine secrets one has been able to reveal. And so one fulfills the purpose of creation, by making the physical world a "dwelling place" for G-d[92] and facilitating the ultimate "marital harmony," that between G-d and Israel, in the context of our physical world.

By studying the inner dimension of the Torah, one develops one's sensitivity to the mystery and holiness of life, which in turn inspires him to seek out the inner essence of his own soul, his relationship with G-d and the world, particularly with his spouse. By relating to each other in modesty, reflecting the super-rational aspect of their common soul-root, and dedicating their lives to consummating G-d's will, a husband and wife merge into one true entity.

This is the essence of the mystery of marriage.

---

92. *Tanya*, ch. 36, based on *Midrash Tanchuma, Naso* 16, ed. Buber 24.

Appendix 1

The Hebrew Alphabet, Numerology, "Filling," and Substitution Systems

The Hebrew Alphabet—known after its first two letters, *alef-beit* (אָלֶף-בֵּית)—comprises twenty-two letters, five of which possess a secondary form used at the end of a word. These letters are all consonants. Vowels are generally indicated as diacritical marks underneath, above, or after the letters; however, four of the twenty-two consonants indicate vowel-sounds as well, as will be explained.

	letter	name		sound
1	א	אָלֶף	*alef*	'
2	ב	בֵּית	*beit*	b, v
3	ג	גִּימֶל	*gimel*	g
4	ד	דָּלֶת	*dalet*	d
5	ה	הֵא	*hei*	h
6	ו	וָו	*vav*	v
7	ז	זַיִן	*zayin*	z
8	ח	חֵית	*chet*	ch
9	ט	טֵית	*tet*	t
10	י	יוּד	*yud*	y
11	כ, ך	כָּף	*kaf*	k, ch
12	ל	לָמֶד	*lamed*	l
13	מ, ם	מֶם	*mem*	m
14	נ, ן	נוּן	*nun*	n
15	ס	סָמֶך	*samech*	s
16	ע	עַיִן	*ayin*	'
17	פ, ף	פֵּא	*pei*	p, f
18	צ, ץ	צָדִי	*tzadi*	tz
19	ק	קוּף	*kuf*	k
20	ר	רֵישׁ	*reish*	r
21	ש	שִׁין	*shin*	sh, s
22	ת	תָּו	*tav*	t

Gematria

Each letter possesses a numerical value. Thus, Hebrew words and phrases can be compared based on their numerical values. This technique is called *gematria* (גִּימַטְרִיָּא). There are several systems of *gematria*:

1. The system most generally used is the **absolute value** (מִסְפָּר הֶכְרֵחִי) or **normative value**. The letters are assigned numerical values in order, first the ones (1-9), then the tens (10-90), and then the hundreds (100-400). The final forms have the same values as their regular forms.

כ, ך	י	ט	ח	ז	ו	ה	ד	ג	ב	א
20	10	9	8	7	6	5	4	3	2	1

ת	ש	ר	ק	צ, ץ	פ, ף	ע	ס	נ, ן	מ, ם	ל
400	300	200	100	90	80	70	60	50	40	30

In a variation on this system, the five final forms are assigned the remaining hundreds, so that the last, twenty-seventh letter equals 900:

ס	נ	מ	ל	כ	י	ט	ח	ז	ו	ה	ד	ג	ב	א
60	50	40	30	20	10	9	8	7	6	5	4	3	2	1

ץ	ף	ן	ם	ך	ת	ש	ר	ק	צ	פ	ע
900	800	700	600	500	400	300	200	100	90	80	70

In this scheme, the thousands are indicated again from *alef* (which actual *means* "a thousand"), and thus the *alef-beit* becomes a complete cycle.

2. In the **ordinal value** system (מִסְפָּר סִדּוּרִי), each of the twenty-two letters is given a value from one to twenty-two, in order.

3. In the **reduced value** system (מִסְפָּר קָטָן, "modulus 9" in mathematical terminology), each normative value of 10 and over is reduced to a figure of one digit by ignoring the zeros of its normative value.

In both of these systems, just as in the case of the absolute value system, the final letters are sometimes considered to have the same numerical values as the regular forms and sometimes to possess their own numerical values.

ל	כ	י	ט	ח	ז	ו	ה	ד	ג	ב	א	**letter**
12	11	10	9	8	7	6	5	4	3	2	1	**ordinal value**
3	2	1	9	8	7	6	5	4	3	2	1	**reduced value**

ץ	ף	ן	ם	ך	ת	ש	ר	ק	צ	פ	ע	ס	נ	מ
27	26	25	24	23	22	21	20	19	18	17	16	15	14	13
9	8	7	6	5	4	3	2	1	9	8	7	6	5	4

4. In the **integral reduced value** system (מִסְפָּר קָטָן מִסְפָּרִי), the total value of a *word* (if more than 9) is reduced to one digit by repeatedly adding the integers of its value according to the normative, ordinal or reduced value systems (the same result will be obtained in each case). For example, the word for "peace," שלום = 376 in the normative system (300 ⊥ 30 ⊥ 6 ⊥ 40), 52 in the ordinal system (21 ⊥ 12 ⊥ 6 ⊥ 13), and 16 in the reduced system (3 ⊥ 3 ⊥ 6 ⊥ 4). The integral reduced value is obtained by adding either 3 ⊥ 7 ⊥ 6 = 16 and then adding again 1 ⊥ 6 to give 7; by adding 5 ⊥ 2 = 7; or by adding 1 ⊥ 6 = 7.

Reducing the full value of a letter or word to a smaller number is a process of *tzimtzum* ("contraction"), projecting the original range of meaning onto a lower level of consciousness. In the absolute system, the letters are assigned their full values. In the ordinal system, each letter still possesses a unique value, but the fundamental principle of consciousness reflected by the "base ten" ("decimal") system has disappeared. In the reduced system, the numbers are still calculated independently, but each letter no longer possesses a unique value. In the integral reduced system, the letters lose their independent identity altogether and disappear into the integral value of the word.

Thus, the four systems of *gematria* correspond to the four successive archetypal levels of consciousness of the four worlds, as follows:

In *Atzilut*, the *sefirot* are manifest in their fully developed and revealed form. Inasmuch as the *sefirot* are ten (*Sefer Yetzirah* 1:4: "ten and not nine, ten and not eleven"), the notion of assigning letters values based on the full decimal system is intrinsic to this world.

In *Beriah,* the lights of the *sefirot* (in which inhere the intrinsic principle of "ten and not nine...") disappear from view, leaving consciousness only of their vessels, in the form of a linear series of 22 letters. Awareness is thus no longer based on the decimal system. The letters are the building blocks of the words and constructs of thought.

In *Yetzirah,* the letters lose their unique values and become grouped into nine categories or species. Still, the letters retain their unique identities and thus there is awareness of creation being dependent on the Divine letters that make up the name of the creature.

In *Asiyah,* this awareness is also lost and the only force life seems dependent upon is the laws of nature, as represented by numbers *per se.*

absolute or normative value system	*Atzilut*
ordinal value system	*Beriah*
reduced value system	*Yetzirah*
integral reduced value system	*Asiyah*

There are also more complex systems of *gematria.* An example of these is the progressive system (מִסְפָּר קְדְמִי), in which the value of each letter is equal to the sum of the values of all the letters up to and including itself in the normative system. For example, the word for "water" (מים) = (1 ⊥ 2 ⊥ 3 ⊥ 4 ⊥ 5 ⊥ 6 ⊥ 7 ⊥ 8 ⊥ 9 ⊥ 10 ⊥ 20 ⊥ 30 ⊥ 40) ⊥ (1 ⊥ 2 ⊥ 3 ⊥ 4 ⊥ 5 ⊥ 6 ⊥ 7 ⊥ 8 ⊥ 9 ⊥ 10) ⊥ (1 ⊥ 2 ⊥ 3 ⊥ 4 ⊥ 5 ⊥ 6 ⊥ 7 ⊥ 8 ⊥ 9 ⊥ 10 ⊥ 20 ⊥ 30 ⊥ 40) = 145 ⊥ 55 ⊥ 145 = 345. This is the same as the value of the word for "Moses" (משה) in normative *gematria.* "And she called him 'Moses,' as she said: 'for I drew him out of the water" (Exodus 2:10).

"Filling"

The "filling"—or, in Hebrew, *milui* (מִלּוּי)—of a word is obtained by spelling out the letters used to spell its name. The additional letters used to spell out the letters of the original word are considered to be "pregnant" within them. Once spelled out, the numerical value can then be calculated of the entire *milui.*

For example, the *milui* of the word for "grace," **חן**, is **חית נון**, which adds up to 524.

The names (*milui*) of some letters have variant spellings. The system of spellings given above is considered the simplest system, although it not necessarily the most frequently applied in Kabbalah. The most common variants are for the letters *hei* (הא, הה, הי), *vav* (וו, ואו, ויו), *pei* (פא, פה, פי), *tav* (תו, תאו, תיו), and *tzadi* (צדי, צדיק).

Substitution Systems (or Transformation Algorithms)

Words may also be analyzed by interchanging their letters with others according to certain specific substitution schemes. These schemes are identified by the first two pairs or triplets of the system. The principal substitution systems are:

1. ***Atbash*** (אַתְבַּ"שׁ): the simple reflective transformation. The first letter of the alphabet is paired with the last, the second with the second-to-last, and so on. These letters of these pairs may then be interchanged.

כ	י	ט	ח	ז	ו	ה	ד	ג	ב	א
ל	מ	נ	ס	ע	פ	צ	ק	ר	ש	ת

2. ***Albam*** (אַלְבַּ"ם): the simple linear transformation. The *alef-beit* is split into two groups of eleven each, and then the first letter of the first group is paired with the first letter of the second group, the second with the second, and so on. The letters of these pairs may then be interchanged.

כ	י	ט	ח	ז	ו	ה	ד	ג	ב	א
ת	ש	ר	ק	צ	פ	ע	ס	נ	מ	ל

3. ***Achbi*** (אַכְבִּ"י): the double reflective transformation. The *alef-beit* is split into two groups of eleven each, in each group of which the first letter is paired with the last letter, the second with the second-to-last, and so on. The letters of each pair may then be interchanged. Note that the middle letter of each original group of eleven remains unpaired and therefore does not transform.

<table><tr><td rowspan="2">פ</td><td>ע</td><td>ס</td><td>נ</td><td>מ</td><td>ל</td></tr><tr><td>צ</td><td>ק</td><td>ר</td><td>ש</td><td>ת</td></tr></table>

<table><tr><td rowspan="2">ו</td><td>ה</td><td>ד</td><td>ג</td><td>ב</td><td>א</td></tr><tr><td>ז</td><td>ח</td><td>ט</td><td>י</td><td>כ</td></tr></table>

These three algorithms together form a "ring" of transformations, in which the application of any two to a given letter will yield the same result as applying the third. For example: א in *atbash* is ת, ת in *albam* is כ, but א in *achbi* is also כ. Again: א in *achbi* is כ, כ in *albam* is ת, but א in *atbash* also ת. (Note that the only pair that is identical in *atbash* and *albam* is פ-ו; these letters therefore cannot be paired with any other letters in *achbi* in order for this "ring"-phenomenon to work.)

4. ***Atbach*** (אַטְבַּ"ח): the triple reflective transformation. The *alef-beit* is first split into three groups (the integers, tens, and hundreds according to normative *gematria*), and then the first letter of each group is paired with the last, the second with the second-to-last, and so on. The letters of these pair may then be interchanged. (The second line is an alternative version of the third group formed when the final forms of the letters are considered independently.)

<table><tr><td>ר</td><td>ק</td></tr><tr><td>ש</td><td>ת</td></tr></table>

<table><tr><td rowspan="2">נ</td><td>מ</td><td>ל</td><td>כ</td><td>י</td></tr><tr><td>ס</td><td>ע</td><td>פ</td><td>צ</td></tr></table>

<table><tr><td rowspan="2">ה</td><td>ד</td><td>ג</td><td>ב</td><td>א</td></tr><tr><td>ו</td><td>ז</td><td>ח</td><td>ט</td></tr></table>

<table><tr><td rowspan="2">ך</td><td>ת</td><td>ש</td><td>ר</td><td>ק</td></tr><tr><td>ם</td><td>ן</td><td>ף</td><td>ץ</td></tr></table>

Note that the sums of each pair in the first group are all 10, in the second group, 100, and in the third group, 500 (if the final forms are not included) or 1,000 (if they are). The letters that do not pair spell הנך, "here you are," alluding to Psalm 139:8.

5. ***Ayik Becher*** (אַיְ"ק בְּכָ"ר): the triple linear transformation. The *alef-beit*—including the final forms of the letters—is split into three groups of nine letters, which are then aligned in order. Any letter of any triplet may then be interchanged with either of the other two.

ט	ח	ז	ו	ה	ד	ג	ב	א
צ	פ	ע	ס	נ	מ	ל	כ	י
ץ	ף	ן	ם	ך	ת	ש	ר	ק

Note that in this system, the members of each triplet possess the same reduced value in *gematria*.

6. ***Achas Beta*** (אַחַ"ס בֵּטַ"ע): a variation on the triple linear transformation. The *alef-beit*—this time without the final forms—is split into three groups of seven letters, which are then aligned in order. Any letter of any triplet may then be interchanged with either of the other two.

ז	ו	ה	ד	ג	ב	א
נ	מ	ל	כ	י	ט	ח
ש, ת	ר	ק	צ	פ	ע	ס

The "odd" letter here is the *tav*, which may be considered to be either a member of the זנש"ת quadruplet (and interchangeable with any of these letters), or an addition to the initial triplet אח"ס (as the first and only letter of the fourth row; the four letters אחס"ת are equidistant). Alternatively, it may be considered outside the system altogether (and not interchangeable).

The first, second, and sixth of these systems are mentioned in *Shabbat* 104a (the first also in *Sanhedrin* 22a), the third is one of the 231 "gates" in *Sefer Yetzirah* 2:4-5, the fourth is mentioned in *Sukah* 52b, and the fifth in *Zohar Chadash* 59b.

In Kabbalah, these six systems are identified with the six principal *partzufim*, as follows:

ayik becher	*Arich Anpin*
albam	*Abba*
atbash	*Ima*
achbi	*da'at:* soul of *Z'eir Anpin*
achas beta	*Z'eir Anpin*
atbach	*Nukvei d'Z'eir Anpin*

Additional transformation schemes exist in which letters can be interchanged based on their common phonetic origins, the common number of crowns they take in scribal writing, the similarity of their forms, etc.

Appendix 2

The Names of G-d

G-d's essence is beyond any Name or referent. His Names refer to the various ways in which He reveals Himself in creation. (The partial exception to this is the Name Havayah, *see further.) This is why there are a number of Names for G-d in the Bible and in Rabbinic and Kabbalistic literature.*

Due to their sanctity, these Names are not pronounced as they are written except in the course of prayer, when reciting a full Biblical verse, or when teaching someone else how to pronounce them. The Name Havayah, *due to its exceptional sanctity, is not pronounced as written even under these circumstances; only in the Holy Temple is it pronounced as written. Similarly, the Name* Havayah *is written hyphenated or abbreviated (or, in some books, spelled with* kufs *or* dalets *instead of* heis*), except in sacred texts.*

In this book and in this appendix, G-d's Names are referred to as they are pronounced in common parlance.

Havayah (יהו־ה), also known as the Tetragrammaton ("four-letter Name"). Due to its great sanctity, this Name may only be pronounced in the Holy Temple, and its correct pronunciation is not known today. When one is reciting a complete Scriptural verse or liturgy, it is read as if it were the Name *Adni*; otherwise one says *Hashem* (הַשֵּׁם, "the Name") or *Havayah* (הֲוָיָה, a permutation of the four letters of this Name).

Havayah is the most sacred of G-d's Names. Although no name can fully express G-d's essence, the Name *Havayah* in certain contexts *refers* to G-d's essence. In these cases it is called "the higher Name *Havayah*" and is termed "the essential Name" (שֵׁם הָעֶצֶם), "the unique Name" (שֵׁם הַמְיֻחָד), and "the explicit Name" (שֵׁם הַמְפֹרָשׁ).

Otherwise, the Name *Havayah* refers to G-d as He manifests Himself through creation. In these cases it is called "the lower Name *Havayah*," and its four letters are seen to depict in their form the creative process and allude to the worlds, ten *sefirot*, etc., as follows:

		creation	worlds	*sefirot*
קוצו של י	upper "thorn" of the *yud*	will to create	*Adam Kadmon*	*keter*
י	*yud*	contraction	*Atzilut*	*chochmah*
ה	*hei*	expansion	*Beriah*	*binah*
ו	*vav*	extension	*Yetzirah*	the six *midot*
ה	*hei*	expansion	*Asiyah*	*malchut*

The lower Name *Havayah* appears on several levels. It is first manifest as the light within all the *sefirot*. It thus possesses on this level ten iterations, which are indicated as ten vocalizations—each using one of the ten vowels. (These are only meditative "vocalizations," since it is forbidden to pronounce the Name *Havayah* with any vocalization, as we have said.) For example, when each of its four letters is vocalized with a *kamatz*, it signifies the light within the *sefirah* of *keter*; when they are each vocalized with a *patach*, it signifies the light within the *sefirah* of *chochmah*. The other Names of G-d (including the subsequent manifestations of the Name *Havayah*) refer to the vessels of the *sefirot*. In the world of *Atzilut*, where these Names are principally manifest, both the vessels and the lights of the *sefirot* are manifestations of Divinity.

The second manifestation of the lower Name *Havayah* is as the vessel of the *sefirah* of *chochmah*. (This is alluded to in the verse, "*Havayah* in *chochmah* founded the earth" [Proverbs 3:19].)

Its third manifestation is as the vessel of the *sefirah* of *binah*. This manifestation is indicated by the consonants of the Name vocalized with the vowels of (and read as) the Name *Elokim* (for example, Deuteronomy 3:24, etc.).

The most basic manifestation of the lower Name *Havayah* is in the *sefirah* of *tiferet*, whose inner experience is mercy. The Name *Havayah* in general is associated with "the principle of mercy," since mercy is the most basic emotion through which G-d relates to His creation. In this, its most common sense, it is vocalized with the vowels of (and read as) the Name *Adnut*.

Ekyeh (אֶהְיֶה, "I will be"). This Name appears only in Exodus 3:14, when G-d is charging Moses with the mission of redeeming the Jewish people from Egypt. It signifies the revelation or "birth" of Divinity into reality ("I will be"), which occurs by means of the spiritual birth of the Jewish people, i.e., their redemption from exile.

In this verse, *Ekyeh* appears in a double form ("I will be that which I will be"). In Kabbalah, the first *Ekyeh* in this form is associated with (the vessel of) *keter*, whereas the second *Ekyeh* with (the vessel of) *binah*.

Kah (יָהּ). This Name is composed of the first two letters of the Name *Havayah* and appears throughout the Bible (twice in the five books of Moses and frequently in the Prophets and Writings). It signifies the Divine essence of the vessel of *chochmah*.

As they do in the Name *Havayah*, the two letters of this Name signify *chochmah* and *binah*, but as they exist within *chochmah* (i.e., *Abba Ila'ah* and *Ima Ila'ah*).

The Name *Kah*—when seen as the first two letters of the Name *Havayah*—is also referred to as the concealed dimension of this Name, in contrast to its final two letters, which are termed its revealed dimension. This implies that the Divine providence deriving from the Name *Kah* expresses a type of good which is so great that it is (at least initially) unfathomable to the human mind and therefore may be mistaken for bad (see *Tanya*, ch. 26).

Akvah (אהוה). This hidden Name of G-d never appears explicitly in the Bible, but it does appear "encoded" in the initial or final letters of many Biblical phrases. The first and most fundamental allusion to it is in the phrase את השמים ואת הארץ ("the heavens and the earth," Genesis 1:1). It thus signifies the Divine power to unite spirituality (heaven) and physicality (earth), and therefore also the vessel of the *sefirah* of *da'at*. Just as *da'at* is the hidden unifying force within the ten *sefirot* from *keter* to *malchut*, so is the Name *Akvah* hidden throughout the Torah. In other contexts, it signifies the vessel of the *sefirah* of *yesod*.

Kel (אֵל). This Name signifies the Divine essence of the vessel of the *sefirah* of *chesed*, as it is written, "the *chesed* of *Kel* is [manifest] all day" (Psalms 52:3). The two letters of this Name as a verbal root mean "strength." This Name thus signifies G-d's strength as manifest by

His continuous loving-kindness in creating and sustaining the world, as it is written, "the world is built through *chesed*" (Psalms 89:3).

When joined with the Names *Shakai, Havayah,* and *Adnut,* this Name signifies the revelation of Divine creative force and providence in the three lower worlds, as follows:

Kel Shakai	*Beriah*
Kel Havayah	*Yetzirah*
Kel Adnut	*Asiyah*

Elokah (אֱלוֹהַּ). This Name generally signifies the Divine essence of the vessel of the *sefirah* of *chesed*, as does the Name *Kel* (which itself is the first two letters of *Elokah*). Also like the Name *Kel*, it is sometimes considered a "meta-Name," i.e., as referring to (though not expressing) G-d's essence that transcends any specific Name.

Elokim (אֱלֹהִים). This name generally signifies the Divine essence of the vessel of the *sefirah* of *gevurah*, or in the idiom of the sages, G-d's "attribute of strict judgment."

In particular, however, this Name is manifest in three *sefirot*: In *binah*, G-d is called "the living G-d" (אלהים חיים), the source of all life force. In *gevurah*, G-d manifests His strict judgment of creation, as mentioned above. In *malchut*, G-d is manifest through this Name as the inner essence of nature and its laws (the numerical value of **אלהים** being the same as that of **הטבע**, "nature").

Tzevakot (צְבָאוֹת, "hosts"). This Name signifies the Divine essence of the vessels of the *sefirot* of *netzach* and *hod*. It always appears following another Name; when it follows the Name *Havayah*, the combined Name refers to *netzach*; when it follows the Name *Elokim*, the combined Name refers to *hod*. This Name does not appear in the Five books of Moses as a Name of G-d; its first appearance in this sense is in Samuel 1:11.

Shakai (שַׁדַּי, "the Almighty"). This name signifies G-d's power to limit creation's *a priori* tendency to expand endlessly and to His power to make His Divinity consciously accessible to each of His creatures, regardless of their spiritual state or place in the hierarchy of creation. It generally signifies the Divine essence of the vessel of the *sefirah* of *yesod*. It often appears prefaced by the Name *Kel*.

Adnut or ***Adni*** (אֲדֹנָי, "my Master"). This Name generally signifies the Divine essence of the vessel of the *sefirah* of *malchut*, inasmuch as its plain meaning, "My Master" is equivalent to "My King." Signifying G-d's immanence, it serves to reflect (or "garb") G-d's transcendence, which is signified by the Name *Havayah*. This is why we pronounce the Name *Havayah* as if it were the Name *Adnut*.

To summarize:

keter	
Ekyeh	אהיה

chochmah	
Kah	יה

binah	
Havayah vocalized as *Elokim*	הוי׳ בניקוד אלהים □

da'at	
Akvah	אהוה

chesed	
Kel	אל

gevurah	
Elokim	אלהים

tiferet	
Havayah vocalized as *Adnut*	הוי׳ בניקוד אדני □

netzach	
Havayah Tzevakot	הוי׳ צבאות

hod	
Elokim Tzevakot	אלהים צבאות

yesod	
Shakai	שדי

malchut	
Adnut	אדני

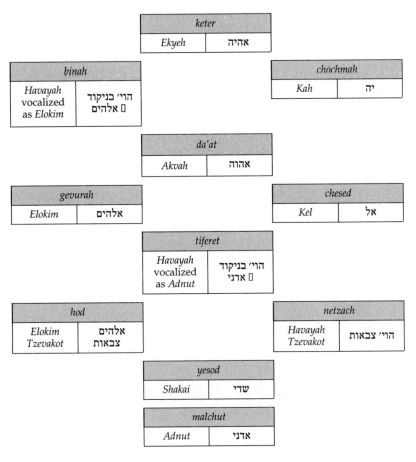

Essential Names: The explicit Names *Havayah*, *Ekyeh*, *Kah*, and the hidden Name *Akvah* are all composed solely of the "vowel-letters" of the Hebrew alphabet (אהו״י). Inasmuch as the source of speech is the plain voice articulated through vowels, these letters are considered the essential "origins" of Hebrew. (This is also indicated by the fact that the sum of their numerical values is 22, the number of letters in the *alef-beit*, and that they are the first, last, and middle of the first ten letters of the *alef-beit*, which represent the first iteration of the ten *sefirot*, the "souls" of the Hebrew letters.) The Names of G-d composed solely of these consonants are therefore considered His "essential" Names.

Glossary

Note: all foreign terms are Hebrew unless otherwise indicated. Terms preceded by an asterisk have their own entries.

Abba (אַבָּא, "father" [Aramaic]): the **partzuf* of **chochmah*.

Adam Kadmon (אָדָם קַדְמוֹן, "primordial man"): the first *world.

Akudim (עֲקֻדִּים, "bound," "striped"): the first stage in the development of the *world of **Atzilut*.

Akvah: see Appendix 2.

Albam: see Appendix 1.

Amidah (עֲמִידָה, "standing"): the central core and highest point of every prayer service. It is recited as a silent devotion while standing, feet together, facing Jerusalem. The weekday version consists of nineteen blessings; the Sabbath and holiday versions consist of seven, and the version of the **Musaf* of *Rosh HaShanah* consists of nine.

Anavah (עֲנָוָה, "humility"): unpretentiousness; the third of the four stages in the nullification of the ego. See p. 374.

Arich Anpin (אֲרִיךְ אַנְפִּין, "the long face" or "the infinitely patient one"): the external **partzuf* of **keter* (the inner dimension is **Atik Yomin*). In psychological terms, it is synonymous with will. It possesses its own *keter* (the **gulgalta*), and its own **chochmah* (**mocha stima'ah*).

Arvit (עַרְבִית, "evening"): the night prayer service. Also called *Ma'ariv* (מַעֲרִיב, "causes to become dark"), after the main word in the opening blessing of this service.

Asiyah (עֲשִׂיָּה, "action"): the lowest of the four *worlds.

Atbash: see Appendix 1.

Atik: short for **Atik Yomin*.

Atik Yomin (עַתִּיק יוֹמִין, "the ancient of days" [Aramaic]): the inner **partzuf* of **keter*.

Atika Kadisha (עַתִּיקָא קַדִּישָׁא, "the holy ancient One" [Aramaic]): in some contexts, this term is a synonym for **Atik Yomin*; in others, for **keter* in general.

Atzilut (אֲצִילוּת, "Emanation"): First and highest of the four *worlds emanating from **Adam Kadmon*.

Av (אָב, "father"): the fifth month of the Jewish calendar.

Ayik Becher: see Appendix 1.

Ba'al Shem Tov (בַּעַל שֵׁם טוֹב, "Master of the Good Name [of G-d]"): Title of Rabbi Yisrael ben Eliezer (1698-1760), founder of the Chassidic movement (**Chassidut*).

Ba'al Teshuvah (בַּעַל תְּשׁוּבָה, "one who returns"): one who returns to the ways of Judaism and adherence to Jewish law after a period of estrangement. Often used in contrast to a **tzadik*, who has not undergone such a period. The *ba'al teshuvah* strives continually to ascend, return and become subsumed within G-d's essence; the *tzadik* strives primarily to serve G-d by doing good deeds and thus drawing His light into the world. Ideally these two paths are meant to be inter-included, i.e. that every Jew should embody both the service of the *ba'al teshuvah* and that of the *tzadik*, as well. see also *teshuvah*.

Bar-Mitzvah (בַּר מִצְוָה, "one [who is obligated to perform the] commandment"; fem. בַּת מִצְוָה, *bat-mitzvah*): the status of coming under full obligation to perform all *mitzvot*. A Jewish man attains this status at the age of thirteen, a woman at the age of twelve.

Bashert (באַשערט, "predestined" [Yiddish]): 1. as an adjective, refers to anything clearly occurring as a result of Divine providence. 2. as a noun, one's predestined soul mate.

Bat-Mitzvah: feminine of **Bar-Mitzvah*.

Beinoni (בֵּינוֹנִי, "intermediate"; pl. בֵּינוֹנִים, *beinonim*): someone who still possesses an evil urge but controls it and does not sin. There are many levels of *beinonim*, from the one who is in a continuous conscious state of battle in order to overcome his evil inclination, to the one so engrossed in his Divine service of Torah and *mitzvot* that he is virtually unaware of the evil inclination dormant in him. See *tzadik*, *rasha*.

Beinonim: plural of **Beinoni.*

Beriah (בְּרִיאָה, "creation"): the second of the four *worlds.

Berudim (בְּרֻדִּים, "patterned," "speckled"): the third, final stage in the development of the *world of **Atzilut*. Synonymous with the world of **Tikun*.

Biah (בִּיאָה, "coming"): an idiom for marital relations.

Binah (בִּינָה, "understanding"): the third of the ten **sefirot*.

Birur (בֵּרוּר, "separation," "choosing," or "refinement"): a type of **tikun* in which one must work to separate good from evil in any given entity, and then reject the evil and accept the good. This may be done actively or in one's consciousness. See **yichud*.

Bitachon (בִּטָּחוֹן, "confidence"): 1. the feeling of confidence in one's G-d-given power to take initiative and succeed in one's mission in life. See **emunah*. 2. The inner experience of the **sefirah* of **netzach*. 3. ("trust"): the feeling that G-d will orchestrate events in accord with the greatest revealed good. This passive *bitachon* is associated with the *sefirah* of *hod*.

Bitul (בִּטּוּל, "annihilation"): any of a number of states of selflessness or self-abnegation. The inner experience of the **sefirah* of **chochmah*.

Chabad (חַבַּ"ד), acronym for **chochmah*, **binah*, **da'at* (חָכְמָה בִּינָה דַּעַת, "wisdom, understanding, knowledge"): 1. the first triad of **sefirot*, which constitute the intellect (see *Chagat*, *Nehi*). 2. the branch of **Chassidut* founded by Rabbi Shneur Zalman of Liadi (1745-1812), emphasizing the role of the intellect and meditation in the service of G-d.

Chafifah (חֲפִיפָה, "washing"): the cleansing a woman must perform prior to immersion in a **mikveh*.

Chagat (חַגַ"ת), acronym for **chesed*, **gevurah*, **tiferet* (חֶסֶד גְּבוּרָה תִּפְאֶרֶת, "loving-kindness, strength, beauty"): the second triad of **sefirot*, which together constitute the primary emotions (see *Chabad*, *Nehi*).

Chasadim: plural of **chesed* (second sense).

Chassid (חָסִיד, "pious one," "kind one"; pl. חֲסִידִים, *chassidim*): an adherent to the teachings of **Chassidut*; specifically, the follower of a chassidic leader (**rebbe*).

Chassidim: plural of **chasid*.

Chassidut (חֲסִידוּת, "piety" or "loving-kindness"; also called "Chassidism"): 1. An attribute or way of life that goes beyond the letter of the law. 2. The movement within Judaism founded by Rabbi Yisrael Ba'al Shem Tov (1648-1760), the purpose of which is to awaken the Jewish people to its own inner self through the inner dimension of the Torah and thus to prepare the way for the advent of **Mashiach*. 3. The oral and written teachings of this movement.

Chavruta (חַבְרוּתָא, "friendship" [Aramaic]): a pair of students who study together. This is the primary method of Torah-study, enabling each student to hone his understanding of the subject matter by questioning and answering his partner dialectically.

Chayah (חַיָּה, "living one"): the second highest of the five levels of the *soul.

Chesed (חֶסֶד, "loving-kindness"; pl. חֲסָדִים, *chasadim*): 1. the fourth of the ten **sefirot*. 2. a manifestation of this attribute, specifically in **da'at*.

Chesed Chinam (חֶסֶד חִנָּם): "undeserved **chesed*."

Chibur (חִבּוּר, "joining"): an idiom for marital relations.

Chochmah (חָכְמָה, "wisdom" or "insight"): the second of the ten **sefirot*.

Chupah (חֻפָּה, "canopy"): the canopy under which the Jewish wedding ceremony takes place.

Da'at (דַּעַת, "knowledge"): 1. the unifying force within the ten **sefirot*. 2. the third *sefirah* of the intellect, counted as one of the ten *sefirot* when *keter*, the superconscious, is not counted.

Deduction: the process of reasoning from the general to the specific.

Deveikut (דְּבֵקוּת, "clinging"): a state of union wherein two parties lose awareness of themselves as separate entities and experience themselves as one undifferentiated essence. *Deveikut* may occur both between the soul and G-d, as it is written, "and you who cling unto *G-d* your G-d..." (Deuteronomy 4:4) and between husband and wife, as it is written, "...and cling unto his wife" (Genesis 2:24).

Din (דִּין, "judgment"; pl. דִּינִים, *dinim*): 1. a synonym for **gevurah*. 2. a manifestation of this attribute. 3. a synonym for **kal vechomer*.

Dinim: plural of *din* (second sense).

Divinity: The highest of the three dimensions in which everything exists, as taught by the Ba'al Shem Tov. See Souls.

Ekyeh: see Appendix 2.

Emunah (אֱמוּנָה, "faith" or "belief"): 1. the belief that no matter what G-d does, it is all ultimately for the greatest good even if it does not appear so to us presently. See **bitachon*. 2. the inner experience associated with **reisha d'lo ityada*.

Gedulah (גְּדֻלָּה, "greatness"): a synonym for **chesed*.

Gematria (גימטריא, "numerology" [Aramaic]): see Appendix 1.

Gevurah (גְּבוּרָה, "power" or "strength"; pl. גְּבוּרוֹת, *gevurot*): 1. the fifth of the ten **sefirot*. 2. a manifestation of this attribute, specifically in **da'at*.

Gevurot: plural of **gevurah* (second sense).

Gezerah Shavah (גְּזֵרָה שָׁוָה, "equal category"): one of the thirteen hermeneutic methods of the Torah, in which two concepts or cases are compared on the basis of terminology common to both.

Gulgalta (גֻּלְגַּלְתָּא, "the skull" [Aramaic]): the **keter* of **Arich Anpin*. In psychological terms, the interface between pleasure and will, which serves as the origin of the super-conscious will.

Haftarah (הַפְטָרָה, "conclusion"): the Sabbath or Holiday reading from the Prophets accompanying the Torah-reading.

Halachah (הֲלָכָה, "way" or "walking"): 1. the entire corpus of Jewish law. 2. a specific Jewish law.

Havayah: see Appendix 2.

Hefsek Taharah (הֶפְסֵק טָהֳרָה, "cessation [of bleeding, indicating] purity"): an examination through which a woman determines that her menstrual bleeding has ceased.

Hod (הוֹד, "splendor," "thanksgiving," "acknowledgment"): the eighth of the ten **sefirot*.

Ima (אִמָּא, "mother" [Aramaic]): the **partzuf* of **binah*.

Induction: the process of reasoning from the specific to the general, or abstracting an archetype or distilling an essence from a specific case or idea.

Kabbalah (קַבָּלָה, "receiving" or "tradition"): the esoteric dimension of the Torah.

Kabbalat Shabbat (קַבָּלַת שַׁבָּת, "welcoming the Sabbath"): the series of psalms and hymns, etc. recited as a prelude to the Friday night prayer service to mark the onset of the Sabbath.

Kah: see Appendix 2.

Kal veChomer (קַל וָחֹמֶר): one of the thirteen hermeneutic methods, in which conclusions are reached by reasoning *a fortiori*.

Kav (קַו, "line"): the ray of light beamed into the vacated space created in consequence of the **tzimtzum*.

Kavanah (כַּוָּנָה, "intention," pl. כַּוָּנוֹת, *kavanot*): 1. the intention or ideas with which one meditatively imbues his actions. 2. a specific idea so used.

Kavanot: plural of **kavanah* (second sense).

Kel; Kel Shakai: see Appendix 2.

Keter (כֶּתֶר, "crown"): the first of the ten **sefirot*.

Ketubah (כְּתֻבָּה, "written [document]"): the Jewish marriage contract.

Kiddush (קִדּוּשׁ, "sanctification"): a ritual performed before Sabbath and festival meals, consisting of a liturgical text recited over a full cup of wine, which is then drunk.

Kittel (קיטל, "small coat" [Yiddish]): a white linen robe worn on **Yom Kippur*.

Kosher (כָּשֵׁר): "fit," used of anything in the sense of "proper" or "good"; in reference to food, used to mean complying with the requirements of Jewish dietary laws.

Lamed-vavnik (ל"ווניק [Yiddish]): one of the thirty-six **tzadikim* in every generation in whose merit the world exits. The numerical value of the two Hebrew letters *lamed* and *vav* (לו) is thirty-six.

Lecha Dodi (לְכָה דוֹדִי, "Come, my beloved"): a hymn recited as part of **Kabbalat Shabbat*.

Lights: see *Sefirah*.

Lubavitch (ליובאוויטש, "City of Love" [Russian]): the town that served as the center of the **Chabad* movement from 1812 to 1915; the movement became known also after the name of this town.

Lubavitcher (ליובאוויטשער): 1. someone from the town of *Lubavitch. 2. [someone or something] belonging to or of the **Chabad* movement.

Malchut (מַלְכוּת, "kingdom"): the last of the ten **sefirot*.

Mashiach (מָשִׁיחַ, "anointed one," "messiah"): the prophesied descendant of King David who will reinstate the Torah-ordained monarchy (which he will head), rebuild the Holy *Temple, and gather the exiled Jewish people to their homeland. This series of events (collectively called "the Redemption") will usher in an era of eternal, universal peace and true knowledge of G-d, called "the messianic era." There is also a prophesied messianic figure called *Mashiach ben* Joseph, who will rectify certain aspects of reality in preparation for the advent of *Mashiach ben* David.

Mazal (מַזָּל, pl. מַזָּלוֹת, *mazalot*): 1. a spiritual conduit of Divine beneficence (from the root נזל, "to flow"). 2. specifically, the thirteen tufts of the "beard" of *Arich Anpin.* 3. a physical embodiment of such a spiritual conduit, such as a star, planet, constellation, etc. 4. specifically, the twelve constellations of the zodiac. 5. According to our sages, the Jewish people are not under the influence of the *mazalot* (*Shabbat* 156a). The Ba'al Shem Tov teaches that the Divine "nothingness" itself is the true *mazal* of the Jewish people (see above, p 350, footnote 106).

Melaveh Malkah (מְלַוֶּה מַלְכָּה, "escorting the queen"): a meal or celebration held on **Motzaei Shabbat* in honor of the departing Shabbat.

Menorah (מְנוֹרָה, "candelabrum"): the seven-branched candelabrum that was lit daily in the sanctuary of the *Tabernacle and, afterwards, in the Holy *Temple.

Metzitzah (מְצִיצָה, "extraction"): the third phase of the rite of circumcision (**milah*). See *milah, periah.*

Mezuzah (מְזוּזָה, "doorpost"): the ritually-written parchment, affixed to the doorpost of the Jewish home, on which are written the first two paragraphs of the **Shema.*

Midah (מִדָּה, "measure" or "attribute," pl. מִדּוֹת, *midot*): 1. an attribute of G-d. 2. specifically, one of the **sefirot* from **chesed* to **malchut,* in contrast to the higher *sefirot* of the intellect. 3. one of the thirteen attributes of mercy, which are part of the revelation of **keter.*

Midot: plural of **midah.*

Midrash: see Bibliography.

Mikveh (מִקְוֶה, "gathering [of water]"): a specially constructed pool used for immersion as a stage of ritual purification. See *tumah* and *taharah.*

Milah (מִילָה, "circumcision"): 1. the rite of circumcision, performed on a Jewish boy on the eighth day after his birth. 2. specifically, the first phase of this rite in which the foreskin is cut. See *metzizah, periah.*

Minchah (מִנְחָה, "offering"): the afternoon prayer service.

Mishnah: see Bibliography.

Mitzvah (מִצְוָה, "commandment"; pl. מִצְוֹת, *mitzvot*): one of the six hundred thirteen commandments given by G-d to the Jewish people, or seven commandments given by G-d to the nations of the world, at Mt. Sinai. 2. one of the seven commandments instituted by the sages. 3. idiomatically, any good deed.

Mitzvot: plural of **mitzvah*.

Mocha Stima'ah (מוֹחָא סְתִימָאָה, "the hidden brain" [Aramaic]): the **chochmah* of **Arich Anpin*. In psychological terms, the power to generate new insight (כֹּחַ הַמַּשְׂכִּיל).

Mochin d'Abba (מוֹחִין דְּאַבָּא, "brains of **Abba*" [Aramaic]): a state of consciousness, mentality, or cognitive life force in which one experiences **chochmah*, or insight.

Mochin d'Ima (מוֹחִין דְּאִמָּא, "brains of **Ima*" [Aramaic]): a state of consciousness, mentality, or cognitive life force in which one experiences **binah*, or understanding or rationality.

Molad (מוֹלָד, "time of birth"): the time when the moon begins its monthly cycle.

Motzaei Shabbat (מוֹצָאֵי שַׁבָּת, "the outgoings of the Sabbath"): the night after the termination of *Shabbat; Saturday night.

Musaf (מוּסָף, "additional"): the additional prayer service recited on *Shabbat, **Rosh Chodesh*, and **Yom Tov*.

Nachamu (נַחֲמוּ, "console"): 1. the **haftarah* recited on the *Shabbat following **Tishah b'Av*, so called after the first word of the passage recited (Isaiah 40:1-26). 2. the Shabbat on which this *haftarah* is recited.

Nefesh (נֶפֶשׁ, "creature," "soul"): 1. the soul in general. 2. the lowest of the five levels of the *soul.

Nehi (נֶהִ"י), acronym for **netzach*, **hod*, **yesod* (נֶצַח הוֹד יְסוֹד, "victory, splendor, foundation"): the third triad of **sefirot*, which together constitute the attributes of behavior (see *Chabad*, *Chagat*).

Nekudim (נְקֻדִּים, "dotted," "spotted"): the second stage in the development of the *world of **Atzilut*.

Neshamah (נְשָׁמָה, "soul"): 1. the soul in general. 2. the third of the five levels of the *soul.

Nesirah (נְסִירָה, "sawing off"): the process of separating Adam and Eve (who were initially created connected back to back) or their spiritual antecedents, **Z'eir Anpin* and **Nukvei d'Z'eir Anpin*, in order that they may unite as a couple.

Netzach (נֵצַח, "victory," "eternity"): the seventh of the ten **sefirot*.

Notrikun (נוֹטָרִיקוֹן, "acronym"): a method of interpretation in which a word is seen as comprising the initials or main consonantal letters of another word or phrase.

Nukvei d'Z'eir Anpin (נוּקְבֵיהּ דִזְעֵיר אַנְפִּין [Aramaic]): the **partzuf* of **malchut*.

Omer: see *Sefirat HaOmer*.

Onah (עוֹנָה, "time"): 1. a season, a period of time, a full night or a full day. 2. the obligation of the husband to fulfill his wife's conjugal rights.

Or makif karov (אוֹר מַקִּיף קָרוֹב, "close surrounding consciousness"): the general level of consciousness corresponding to the **chayah* of the *soul.

Or makif rachok (אוֹר מַקִּיף רָחוֹק, "distant surrounding consciousness"): the general level of consciousness corresponding to the **yechidah* of the *soul.

Or pnimi (אוֹר פְּנִימִי, "inner consciousness"): the general level of consciousness corresponding to the three lower levels of the *soul.

Parashah (פָּרָשָׁה, "section"; pl. פָּרָשִׁיּוֹת, *parashiot*): 1. a paragraph in the written Torah according to the Masoretic text. These *parshiot* are either "open" (followed by a blank space which extends to the end of the line) or "closed" (followed by a blank space equal to the width of nine letters). 2. also *sidrah* (סִדְרָה, "order"): one of the fifty-four sections into which the Five Books of Moses are divided for the purpose of reading one of them in the synagogue each *Shabbat. Thus, the entire Torah is read in full in the course of a year (it is sometimes necessary to read two on the same Sabbath). The *parshiot* are known by one or two of their opening words.

Partzuf (פַּרְצוּף, "profile"; pl. פַּרְצוּפִים, *partzufim*): the third and final stage in the development of a **sefirah*, in which it metamorphoses from a tenfold articulation of sub-*sefirot* into a human-like figure possessing the full set of intellectual and emotional powers. As such, it may thus interact with the other *partzufim* (which could not occur before this transformation. This stage of development constitutes the transition from **Tohu* to **Tikun* (or from *Nekudim* to *Berudim*, see under Worlds).

The *sefirot* develop into a primary and a secondary array of *partzufim*, as follows:

sefirah	**primary *partzufim***		**secondary *partzufim***	
keter	עתיק יומין *Atik Yomin*	"The Ancient of Days"	עתיק יומין *Atik Yomin*	[The male dimension of] "the Ancient of Days"
			נוקביה דעתיק יומין *Nukvei d'Atik Yomin*	[The female dimension of] "the Ancient of Days"
	אריך אנפין *Arich Anpin*	"The Long Face"	אריך אנפין *Arich Anpin*	[The male dimension of] "the Long Face"
			נוקביה דאריך אנפין *Nukvei d'Arich Anpin*	[The female dimension of] "the Long Face"
chochmah	אבא *Abba*	"Father"	אבא עילאה *Abba Ila'ah*	"Supernal Father"
			אמא עילאה *Ima Ila'ah*	"Supernal Mother"
binah	אמא *Ima*	"Mother"	ישראל סבא *Yisrael Saba*	"Israel the Elder"
			תבונה *Tevunah*	"Understanding"
the midot	זעיר אנפין *Z'eir Anpin*	"The Small Face"	ישראל *Yisrael*	"Israel"
			לאה *Leah*	"Leah"
malchut	נוקביה דזעיר אנפין *Nukvei d'Z'eir Anpin*	"The Female of *Z'eir Anpin*"	יעקב *Yaakov*	"Jacob"
			רחל *Rachel*	"Rachel"

Both of the secondary *partzufim* of *Atik Yomin* and *Arich Anpin* exist within the same figure. There are thus actually only ten distinct secondary *partzufim*.

Within any particular *partzuf*, the *sefirot* are arranged along three axes, right, left and middle, as follows:

left axis	center axis	right axis
	keter	
binah		*chochmah*
	da'at	
gevurah		*chesed*
	tiferet	
hod		*netzach*
	yesod	
	malchut	

In this arrangement, there are three triads of related *sefirot*: *chochmah-binah-da'at* (the intellect), *chesed-gevurah-tiferet* (the primary emotions) and *netzach-hod-yesod* (the behavioral attributes).

Parashat: construct of **parashah*.

Periah (פְּרִיעָה, "peel back"): the second phase of the rite of circumcision, in which the membrane is peeled back after the foreskin has been cut off. See *metzitzah, milah*.

Pesach (פֶּסַח, "Passover"): the seven-day **yom tov* (eight days in the Diaspora) commemorating the liberation of the Jewish people from Egyptian slavery.

Rachamim (רַחֲמִים, "mercy"): the inner experience of the **sefirah* of **tiferet*.

Rasha (רָשָׁע, "wicked one," pl. רְשָׁעִים, *resha'im*): one who succumbs to his urge to do evil and commits a sin. He retains this status until he does *teshuvah, at which point he becomes a **ba'al teshuvah*.

Reisha d'Arich (רֵישָׁא דַאֲרִיךְ, "the head of **Arich [Anpin]*" [Aramaic]): the lowest of the three "heads" of **keter*, synonymous with the **partzuf* of **Arich Anpin*. In psychological terms, super-conscious will.

Reisha d'Ayin (רֵישָׁא דְאַיִן, "the head of nothingness" [Aramaic]): the middle of the three "heads" of **keter*, related to the emotions of the **partzuf* of **Atik Yomin*. In psychological terms, super-conscious pleasure.

Reisha d'lo Ityada (רֵישָׁא דְלָא אִתְיַדַע [Aramaic]): the highest of the three "heads" of **keter*, related to the *keter* and intellect of the

**partzuf* of **Atik Yomin*. In psychological terms, super-conscious belief in G-d.

Resha'im: plural of **rasha*.

Rebbe (רַבִּי, "my teacher"): 1. a term used to describe or address a teacher of Torah. 2. leader of a branch of the Chassidic movement.

Reshimu (רְשִׁימוּ, "residue," "impression"): the residual impression of the infinite Divine light that G-d withdrew from the vacated space resulting from the **tzimtzum*.

Rosh Chodesh (ראש חֹדֶש, "new month"): the first day of a Jewish month, a day of celebration.

Rosh HaShanah (ראש הַשָּׁנָה, "beginning of the year"): the Jewish New Year, commemorating the creation of man on the sixth day of creation, a day of universal judgment.

Ruach (רוּחַ, "spirit"): a level of the *soul.

Sabbath: see Shabbat.

Sefirah (סְפִירָה, pl. סְפִירוֹת, *sefirot*): a channel of Divine energy or life force. It is via the *sefirot* that G-d interacts with creation; they may thus be considered His "attributes."

There are altogether eleven *sefirot* spoken of in Kabbalistic literature. Inasmuch as two of them (*keter* and *da'at*) are two dimensions of a single force, the tradition generally speaks of only ten *sefirot*. Each *sefirah* also possesses an inner experience, as discussed in **Chassidut*. The order of the *sefirot* is depicted in the chart on the following page.

Originally emanated as simple point-like forces, the *sefirot* at a certain stage develop into full spectrums of ten sub-*sefirot*. Subsequent to this, they metamorphose into **partzufim*.

Sefirot are composed of "lights" and "vessels." The light of any *sefirah* is the Divine flow within it; the vessel is the identity that flow takes in order to relate to or create some aspect of the world in a specific way. Inasmuch as all reality is created by means of the *sefirot*, they constitute the conceptual paradigm for understanding all reality.

name			inner experience	
keter	כֶּתֶר	"crown"	1. אֱמוּנָה 2. תַּעֲנוּג 3. רָצוֹן	1. "faith" 2. "pleasure" 3. "will"
chochmah	חָכְמָה	"wisdom", "insight"	בִּטּוּל	"selflessness"
binah	בִּינָה	"understanding"	שִׂמְחָה	"joy"
da'at	דַּעַת	"knowledge"	יִחוּד	"union"
chesed	חֶסֶד	"loving-kindness"	אַהֲבָה	"love"
gevurah	גְּבוּרָה	"strength," "might"	יִרְאָה	"fear"
tiferet	תִּפְאֶרֶת	"beauty"	רַחֲמִים	"mercy"
netzach	נֵצַח	"victory," "eternity"	בִּטָּחוֹן	"confidence"
hod	הוֹד	"splendor," "thanksgiving"	תְּמִימוּת	"sincerity," "earnestness"
yesod	יְסוֹד	"foundation"	אֱמֶת	"truth"
malchut	מַלְכוּת	"kingdom"	שִׁפְלוּת	"lowliness"

Sefirat HaOmer (סְפִירַת הָעֹמֶר, "counting the *Omer*"): an *omer* is a dry measure mentioned in the Torah, and it refers specifically to the measure of barley offered in the *Temple on the second day of **Pesach*. Beginning with this day, the Jew is commanded to count the next forty-nine days, after which, on the fiftieth day, falls the holiday of **Shavuot*.

Sefirot: plural of **sefirah*.

Shabbat (שַׁבָּת, "Sabbath"): the day of rest beginning sunset on Friday and ending at nightfall on Saturday.

Shacharit (שַׁחֲרִית, "morning"): the morning prayer service.

Shavuot (שָׁבוּעוֹת, "weeks"): the **yom tov* celebrating the wheat harvest and commemorating the giving of the Torah at Mt. Sinai.

Shechinah (שְׁכִינָה, "indwelling"): the immanent Divine Presence that inheres within the universe, corresponding to the *sefirah* of *malchut*, the "feminine" aspect of Divinity.

Shema (שְׁמַע, "hear"): a compilation of three Biblical passages (Deuteronomy 6:4-9, 11:13-21, Numbers 15:37-41) beginning with this word, or sometimes, the first verse alone. The first verse is the fundamental profession of monotheism, "Hear O Israel, *G-d* is our G-d, *G-d* is one." We are commanded to recite the *Shema* twice daily, and it has been incorporated into the morning and evening services as well as the prayer said upon retiring at night. When reciting the first sentence, we are intended to consider ourselves ready to give up our lives rather than deny the oneness of G-d.

Shemini Atzeret (שְׁמִינִי עֲצֶרֶת, "the eighth-day gathering"): the **yom tov* immediately following **Sukot*, marking the end of the high-holiday season.

Shiduch (שִׁדּוּךְ, "match"): a match made between a man and woman.

Shofar (שׁוֹפָר, "ram's horn"): the *shofar* was blown (by G-d) at the giving of the Torah, is blown (by man) every **Rosh HaShanah* in fulfillment of G-d's commandment, expressing contrition and penitence, and will be again blown (by G-d) at the beginning of the Redemption to herald the arrival of **Mashiach*.

Soul: the animating life or consciousness within man (or any other creature, see *Sha'ar HaYichud VehaEmunah*, ch. 1). The Jew possesses an additional "Divine soul" which is focused on G-d's concerns in creation.

The essence of the soul possesses five manifestations ("names"), as follows:

name			experience
yechidah	יְחִידָה	"unique one"	unity with G-d
chayah	חַיָּה	"living being"	awareness of G-d as continually creating the world
neshamah	נְשָׁמָה	"breath"	vitality of intelligence
ruach	רוּחַ	"spirit"	vitality of emotion
nefesh	נֶפֶשׁ	"creature"	physical vitality

Souls: The Ba'al Shem Tov taught that everything exists in three dimensions: Worlds, Souls, and Divinity. "Worlds" is the lowest, the physical dimension; "Souls" is the middle, the spiritual dimension; "Divinity" is the highest, G-dly dimension.

Sukot (סֻכּוֹת, "huts," "booths"): the **yom tov* celebrating the ingathering of the harvest and commemorating the clouds of glory that accompanied the Jewish people on their desert trek after the exodus from Egypt.

Tabernacle (Hebrew: מִשְׁכָּן, "dwelling"): the temporary, portable version of the *Temple the Jewish people used during their journey in the desert from Egypt to the land of Israel and continued to use in the land of Israel until the Temple was built.

Taharah (טָהֳרָה, ritual "purity"): the spiritual state in which one is purified from a specific degree of **tumah* (or from *tumah* altogether) and is thus allowed to enter areas or touch, be touched by, or consume things or food he otherwise may not. In general, the process of attaining *taharah* involves some type of reaffirmation of life, such as immersion in a **mikveh*. The spiritual correlate to *taharah* is optimistic elation or joy in the service of G-d. See *tumah*.

Talmud: see Bibliography.

Targum: see Bibliography.

Temimut (תְּמִימוּת, "sincerity"): 1. earnestness and sincerity, either in one's conduct with his fellow man or in his connection to G-d. 2. The inner experience of **hod*.

Temple (or "Holy Temple"; Hebrew: בֵּית הַמִּקְדָּשׁ, "house of the sanctuary"): The central sanctuary in Jerusalem which serves as the physical abode of the indwelling of G-d's Presence on earth and as the venue for the sacrificial service. The Temple is the focal point of one's spiritual consciousness. The first Temple was built by King Solomon (833 BCE) and destroyed by the Babylonians (423 BCE); the second Temple was built by Zerubabel (synonymous, according to some opinions, with Nehemiah, 353 BCE), remodeled by Herod and destroyed by the Romans (68 CE); the third, eternal Temple will be built by *Mashiach*.

Teshuvah (תְּשׁוּבָה, "return"): the return of the individual (or community), after a period of estrangement, to a state of oneness with and commitment to G-d and His Torah. See **Ba'al Teshuvah*.

Tevunah (תְּבוּנָה, "comprehension"): the lower of the two secondary **partzufim* which develop from the *partzuf* of **Ima*, the higher one being *Ima Ila'ah* (אִמָּא עִלָּאָה).

Tiferet (תִּפְאֶרֶת, "beauty"): the sixth of the ten **sefirot*.

Tishah b'Av (תִּשְׁעָה בְּאָב, "the ninth of **Av*"): fast day commemorating the destruction of the two Temples, which occurred on this day.

Tikun (תִּקּוּן, "rectification," pl. תִּקּוּנִים, *tikunim*): 1. a state of perfection and order. 2. "The world of *Tikun*" is the *world that first manifests this state, which is synonymous with the world of *Atzilut* (and *Berudim*, see Worlds). 3. the spiritual process of liberating the fragments of Divine light trapped within the material realm, unconscious of G-d's presence, thereby restoring the world to its initially intended state of perfection. This is accomplished through the performance of **mitzvot*. 4. a remedy prescribed against the effects of committing a specific sin.

Tikunim: plural of **tikun* (fourth sense).

Tohu (תֹּהוּ, "chaos"): 1. the primordial, unrectified state of creation. 2. "The world of *Tohu*" is the *world which manifests this state; it is synonymous with the initial, premature form of the world of **Atzilut*. The world of *Tohu* itself develops in two stages: a stable form (*Akudim*) followed by an unstable form (*Nekudim*, see Worlds). The world of *Tohu* is characterized by "great lights" entering premature "vessels," resulting in the "breaking of the vessels" (שְׁבִירַת הַכֵּלִים). See *Tikun*.

Torah: see Bibliography.

Tumah (טֻמְאָה, ritual "impurity"): a spiritual state contracted by someone or something under various circumstances and to various degrees, in which he is prohibited from entering various holy areas or touching, being touched by, or consuming various holy objects or foods. In general, the sources of *tumah* are in some way associated with death (or a missed chance for potential life) and the purification process involves some type of reaffirmation of life. The spiritual correlate to *tumah* is depression or despair. See *taharah*.

Triangle: the sum of all integers from 1 to a specific number. For example, the triangle of five (Δ5) is 1 ⊥ 2 ⊥ 3 ⊥ 4 ⊥ 5 = 15.

Tzadik (צַדִּיק, "righteous" person; pl. צַדִּיקִים, *tzadikim*): someone who has fully overcome the evil inclination of his animal soul (and converted its potential into good). See *beinoni, rasha.*

Tzadik in peltz (צַדִּיק אין פעלץ, "a righteous man in furs" [Yiddish]): depreciative term for someone who tends to his own spiritual well being while remaining oblivious to the spiritual needs of others.

Tzadikim: plural of **tzadik*.

Tzeniut (צְנִיעוּת, "modesty"): the norms of modest behavior, attitude, and dress prescribed by the *Torah.

Tzimtzum (צִמְצוּם, "contraction"): the contraction and "removal" of G-d's infinite light in order to allow for creation of independent realities. The primordial *tzimtzum* produced the "vacated space" (חָלָל) devoid of direct awareness of G-d's presence. See *Kav* and *Reshimu*.

Wedding Canopy: see *chupah*.

Vessels: see *sefirah*.

Vowel-letters: The four Hebrew letters אהו״י, which can serve as vowels as well as consonants. As the source of speech is the plain voice articulated through vowels, these letters are considered the essential "origins" of Hebrew, and the Names of G-d composed solely of these consonants are considered His "essential" Names. See Appendix 2.

World (Hebrew: עוֹלָם): a spiritual level of creation, representing a rung on the continuum of consciousness or awareness of G-d. In general, there are four worlds: **Atzilut*, **Beriah*, **Yetzirah*, and **Asiyah*. In particular, however, these four worlds originate from a fifth, higher world, **Adam Kadmon*. All ten **sefirot* and twelve **partzufim* are manifest in each world; however, since there is a one-to-one correspondence between the worlds and the *sefirot*, a particular *sefirah* dominates in each world.

The world of *Atzilut* is fundamentally different from the three subsequent worlds in that in it there is no awareness of self *per se*, while the three lower worlds are progressive stages in the development of self-awareness.

The worlds correspond to the Name *Havayah* and the **sefirot* as follows:

the Name *Havayah*	**World**	**dominant *sefirah***	**level of consciousness**
קוצו של י	אדם קדמון *Adam Kadmon* "Primordial Man"	*keter*	Divine will to create and plan of creation
י	אצילות *Atzilut* "Emanation"	*chochmah*	solely of G-d; no self-awareness
ה	בריאה *Beriah* "Creation"	*binah*	potential existence; formless substance
ו	יצירה *Yetzirah* "Formation"	*midot*	general existence: archetypes, species
ה	עשיה *Asiyah* "Action"	*malchut*	particular existence; individual creatures

In particular, the world of *Atzilut* develops out of *Adam Kadmon* in three stages (the names of which are taken from Genesis 30:10):

World		**developmental stage**	**description**	
עקודים *Akudim*	"bound," "striped"	ten lights in one vessel	stable chaos	תהו *Tohu*
נקודים *Nekudim*	"dotted," "spotted"	ten lights in ten vessels, unstable	unstable chaos, collapse	
ברודים *Berudim*	"patterned," "speckled"	ten lights in ten inter-included vessels; stable	stable, mature rectification	תקון *Tikun*

Whenever unqualified reference is made to the world of *Atzilut*, its final, mature stage is meant. It should be noted as well that our physical universe is *below* and "enclothes" the final two *sefirot* (**yesod* and **malchut*) of the spiritual world of *Asiyah* referred to above.

Worlds: The lowest of the three dimensions in which everything exists, as taught by the Ba'al Shem Tov. See Souls.

Yechidah (יְחִידָה, "single one"): the highest of the five levels of the *soul.

Yesod (יְסוֹד, "foundation"): the ninth of the ten **sefirot*.

Yetzirah (יְצִירָה, "formation"): one of the four *worlds.

Yichud (יִחוּד, "unification"; pl. יִחוּדִים, *yichudim*): a type of **tikun* in which one does not need to separate good from evil but rather focus one's consciousness on the inherent spiritual unity between two apparently disparate concepts. See **birur*. 2. a specific spiritual exercise of this nature.

Yisrael Saba (יִשְׂרָאֵל סַבָּא, "Israel the Elder" [Aramaic]): the lower of the two secondary **partzufim* which develop from the *partzuf* of **Abba*, the higher being *Abba Ila'ah* (אַבָּא עִלָּאָה, "the higher *Abba*").

Yom Kippur (יוֹם כִּפּוּר, "Day of Atonement"): the holiest day of the Jewish year, marked by fasting and **teshuvah*, particularly through confession of sin.

Yom Tov (יוֹם טוֹב, "good day" or "holiday"): a festive holiday on which, with certain exceptions, weekday work is prohibited just as on *Shabbat.

Z'eir Anpin (זְעֵיר אַנְפִּין, "the small face" [Aramaic]): the **partzuf* of the **midot*, corresponding to the emotive faculties of the soul. In general, the concept of "finitude" or "finite power" is identified with *Z'eir Anpin*.

Zivug (זִווּג, "coupling"): an idiom for marital relations.

Zohar: see Bibliography.

Bibliography

Note: Words preceded by an asterisk have their own entries.

Biblical texts are cited by chapter and verse. If a post-Biblical text is divided into chapters, sections, or the like, it is cited accordingly. Otherwise, it is cited according to its pagination. There are two systems of pagination used in post-Biblical texts. The classic system is that of the Talmud, in which the page number refers to the physical page ("leaf" or "folio"), which is followed by a letter which refers to the column of the page. This usually means that column "a" is on the front side ("recto") of the page, and column "b" on the back ("verso"), but if there are two columns on a page, columns "a" and "b" will be on the front, and columns "c" and "d" on the back. This system was abandoned in later works, which are paginated in the modern fashion, each side of the page having its own number. In citations, then, "43c" means page 43, column 3 of a work paginated in the Talmudic fashion, and "p. 43" means simply page 43 of a work paginated in the modern fashion. References to Talmudic pagination are not preceded by "p.," since the letter following the number makes it clear that the reference is to a page and not a section. References to modern pagination, however, are preceded by "p." in order to distinguish them from references to sections.

Ani L'Dodi V'Dodi Li (אֲנִי לְדוֹדִי וְדוֹדִי לִי, "I am My beloved's and My Beloved is Mine" [Song of Songs 6:3]): Rabbi Yitzchak Ginsburgh. Gal Einai: Rechovot, 1998.

Amos: a book of the *Bible.

Avodah Zarah (עֲבוֹדָה זָרָה, "Idolatry"): a tractate of the *Talmud.

Avot (אָבוֹת, "Fathers"): a tractate of the *Talmud.

Ba'alei HaNefesh (בַּעֲלֵי הַנֶּפֶשׁ, "Possessors of the Soul"): Rabbi Avraham ben David (c. 1120-c. 1197). Laws of Family Purity and philosophy of marital relations.

Bamidbar Rabbah (בַּמִּדְבָּר רַבָּה): the *Midrash on the book of *Numbers.

Bava Batra (בָּבָא בַּתְרָא, "The Last Gate"): a tractate of the *Talmud.

Bava Metzia (בָּבָא מְצִיעָה, "The Middle Gate"): a tractate of the *Talmud.

Bechorot (בְּכוֹרוֹת, "Firstborn"): a tractate of the *Talmud.

Beit HaBechirah (בֵּית הַבְּחִירָה, "The Chosen House"): Rabbi Menachem HaMeiri (c. 1249-c. 1306). Commentary on the *Talmud. Jerusalem, 1968.

Beitzah (בֵּיצָה, "Egg"): a tractate of the *Talmud.

Ben Porat Yosef (בֵּן פֹּרָת יוֹסֵף, "Joseph is a Graceful Son" [Genesis 49:22]): Rabbi Yaakov Yosef of Polnoye (1704-1794). Sermons on the *Torah, containing the earliest recordings of the teachings of Rabbi Yisrael Ba'al Shem Tov (1698-1760).

Berachot (בְּרָכוֹת, "Blessings"): a tractate of the *Talmud.

Bereishit Rabbah (בְּרֵאשִׁית רַבָּה): the *Midrash to the book of *Genesis.

Besha'ah Shehikdimu (בְּשָׁעָה שֶׁהִקְדִּימוּ, "When [Israel] Preceded" [*Shabbat* 88a]): Rabbi Shalom Dovber of Lubavitch (1860-1920). Series of Chassidic discourses. Brooklyn: Kehot, 1991.

Bible: the written *Torah. The Bible comprises twenty-four books, divided into three sections: (1) the Torah (תּוֹרָה, "teaching"), comprising the five books of Moses; (2) the eight books of the Prophets (נְבִיאִים, the first and second books of Samuel and Kings are considered one book, as are the twelve "minor" prophets); (3) the eleven books of the Writings (כְּתוּבִים, the books of Ezra and Nehemiah are considered one book, as are the two books of Chronicles). The Bible is therefore known in Hebrew as the *Tanach* (תַּנַ"ךְ), the abbreviation formed by the first letters of the names of these three sections.

All the books of the Bible are authored by G-d, though transmitted through prophecy via the souls of the various prophets, who are known as the "authors" of the books themselves. Thus, every aspect of these texts contains infinite levels of meaning. If properly studied, they yield the profoundest insights available in any field of knowledge.

Although the division of the Bible into chapters and verses is of medieval, non-Jewish origin, its use has become standard in all Jewish books. The traditional division is into non-numbered paragraphs (*parashiot*, sing. *parashah*) and verses. In addition, the Torah is divided into 54 sections (also *parshiot*), at least one of which is read each week in the synagogue.

Bikurim (בִּכּוּרִים, "First Fruits"): a tractate of the *Talmud.

Binah LaItim (בִּינָה לָעִתִּים, "Understanding for the Times" [1 Chronicles 12:33]): Rabbi Azariah ben Ephraim Figo (1579 1647). Sermons. Venice, 1648.

Biurei HaZohar (Mitteler Rebbe) (בֵּאוּרֵי הַזֹּהַר - אַדְמוֹ"ר הָאֶמְצָעִי, "Explanations of the *Zohar* by the *Mitteler* Rebbe"): Rabbi Dovber of Lubavitch (1773-1827). Chassidic discourses on the *Zohar. Kapust, 1816.

Biurei HaZohar (Tzemach Tzedek) (בֵּאוּרֵי הַזֹּהַר - אַדְמוֹ"ר הַצֶּמַח צֶדֶק, "Explanations of the *Zohar* by the *Tzemach Tzedek*"): Rabbi Menachem Mendel of Lubavitch (1789-1866). Chassidic discourses on the *Zohar*. Brooklyn: Kehot, 1968.

Chagigah (חֲגִיגָה, "The Festival Offering"): a tractate of the *Talmud.

Chanah Ariel (חָנָה אֲרִיאֵל, "The Camp of Ariel" [cf. Ezra 8:15-16]): Rabbi Yitzchak Isaac HaLevi Epstein of Homil (c. 1770-1857). Chassidic discourses. Berdichev, 1902-3.

Chesed l'Avraham (חֶסֶד לְאַבְרָהָם, "Loving-kindness to Abraham" [Micah 7:20]): Rabbi Avraham Azulai (1570-1643). Kabbalah. Salzbach, 1685.

Chidushei Agadot (חִדּוּשֵׁי אֲגָדוֹת, "Novella on the Aggadah"): Rabbi Shmuel Eidels (1555-1631). Commentary on the *Talmud, published 1627-32. Cited according to Talmudic passage discussed.

Chovot HaLevavot (חוֹבוֹת הַלְּבָבוֹת, "Duties of the Heart"): Rabbi Bachya ibn Pakudah (early 11th century). Ethics. Naples, 1490.

Chulin (חֻלִּין, "Profane [Food]"): a tractate of the *Talmud.

Chronicles: a book of the *Bible.

Commentary on ****Sefer HaHalachot***: Rabbi Nissim ben Reuven (c. 1290-c. 1375). Appears in standard editions of the *Talmud.

Commentary on **Sefer Yetzirah*: Rabbi Eliahu, the *Gaon* of Vilna (1720-1797). Grodno, 1806.

Commentary on **Sha'ar HaYichud*: Rabbi Hillel Malisov of Paritch (1795-1864). First published in *Likutei Biurim,* Warsaw, 1868; published in *Ner Mitzvah v'Torah Or (Sha'ar HaEmunah & Sha'ar HaYichud),* New York: Kehot, 1995.

Commentary on **Sifra d'Tzniuta*: Rabbi Yitzchak Luria (1534-1572). Printed in **Sha'ar Ma'amarei Rashbi,* pp. 23c-32d.

Commentary on the *Bible: Rabbi Avraham Ibn Ezra (1089-1164). Cited according to Biblical passage discussed. Naples, 1488.

Commentary on the *Bible: Rabbi David Kimchi (Radak, 1160-1235). Cited according to Biblical passage discussed. Lemburg, 1868.

Commentary on the *Bible: Rabbi Levi ben Gershon (Ralbag, Gershonides, 1288-1344). Cited according to Biblical passage discussed. Amsterdam, 1724.

Commentary on the *Bible: Rabbi Moshe ben Nachman (Ramban, Nachmanides, 1194-1270). Cited according to Biblical passage discussed. Rome, before 1480.

Commentary on the *Bible: Rabbi Shlomo ben Yitzchak (Rashi, 1040-1105). Cited according to Biblical passage discussed. First printed in Italy, 1475.

Commentary on the **Mishnah*: Rabbi Moshe ben Maimon (Maimonides, 1135-1205). Cited according to Mishnaic passage discussed. Naples, 1492.

Commentary on the **Mishnah*: Rabbi Ovadiah of Bartinura (c. 1440-c. 1516). Cited according to Mishnaic passage discussed. Venice, 1549.

Commentary on the *Talmud: Rabbi Shlomo ben Yitzchak (Rashi, 1040-1105). Cited according to the Talmudic passage discussed. Printed on the same page as the Talmudic text from the latter's first printing (Venice, 1520-23) on. Cited by folio of the Talmud and opening word(s) of the commentary.

Daniel: a book of the *Bible.

Derech Eretz (דֶּרֶךְ אֶרֶץ, "Manners"): a tractate of the *Talmud.

Derech Eretz Zuta (דֶּרֶךְ אֶרֶץ זוּטָא, "The Smaller 'Manners'"): a tractate of the *Talmud.

Derech Mitzvotecha (דֶּרֶךְ מִצְוֹתֶךָ, "The Way of Your Commandments" [Psalms 119:32]): Rabbi Menachem Mendel of Lubavitch (1789-1866). Chassidic discourses. Paltova, 1911.

Deuteronomy: a book of the *Bible.

Ecclesiastes: a book of the *Bible.

Eichah Rabbah (אֵיכָה רַבָּה): the *Midrash on the book of Lamentations.

Eiruvin (עֵרוּבִין, "Mixing [Domains]"): a tractate of the *Talmud.

Ein Yaakov (עֵין יַעֲקֹב, "The Eye of Jacob" [Genesis 33:28]): Rabbi Yaakov ibn Chaviv (c. 1445-c. 1516). Compendium of the aggadic material of the *Talmud. Salonika, 1516-22; standard edition: Vilna, 1869-74.

Emek HaMelech: see Luria, Rabbi Yitzchak.

Esther: a book of the *Bible.

Etz Chaim: see Luria, Rabbi Yitzchak.

Etz Yosef (עֵץ יוֹסֵף, "The Tree of Joseph" [Ezekiel 37:19]): Rabbi Chanoch Zundel of Byalistok (19th century). Commentary on the aggadic material of the *Talmud, printed in standard editions of **Ein Yaakov*.

Exodus: a book of the *Bible.

Ezekiel: a book of the *Bible.

Ezra: a book of the *Bible.

Genesis: a book of the *Bible.

Gur Aryeh (גּוּר אַרְיֵה, "A Lion Cub" [Genesis 49:9]): Rabbi Yehudah Liva (1512-1609). Super-commentary on *Rashi on the *Torah. Prague, 1578.

Habakkuk: a book of the *Bible.

Haggai: a book of the *Bible.

HaYom Yom (הַיּוֹם יוֹם, "Today is..."): Rabbi Menachem Mendel Schneersohn of Lubavitch (the Lubavitcher Rebbe). Compendium of Chassidic teachings arranged according to the days of the year. Cited according to date of entry. New York: Kehot, 1943.

Hosea: a book of the *Bible.

I am Asleep yet My Heart is Awake [Song of Songs 5:2]: Rabbi Yitzchak Ginsburgh. Jerusalem: Gal Einai, 1984.

Igeret HaKodesh (אִגֶּרֶת הַקֹּדֶשׁ, "The Holy Letter"): Rabbi Shneur Zalman of Liadi (1745-1812). Fourth section of the **Tanya*.

Igeret HaNechamah (אִגֶּרֶת הַנֶּחָמָה, "The Letter of Consolation"): Rabbi Maimon ben Yosef (?-c. 1170, father of the *Rambam). Warsaw, 1912; Jerusalem, 1945.

Igeret HaTeshuvah (אִגֶּרֶת הַתְּשׁוּבָה, "The Letter on *Teshuvah*"): Rabbi Shneur Zalman of Liadi (1745-1812). Third section of the **Tanya*.

Igrot Kodesh Admor HaRayatz (אִגְּרוֹת קֹדֶשׁ אַדְמוֹ"ר הָרַיַּ"ץ) Correspondence of Rabbi Yosef Yitzchak of Lubavitch (1880-1950). 14 vols. New York: Kehot, 1982-98.

Igrot Kodesh of the Rebbe (אִגְּרוֹת קֹדֶשׁ) Correspondence of Rabbi Menachem Mendel Schneersohn of Lubavitch, the Lubavitcher Rebbe. 25 volumes to date. New York: Kehot, 1987 on.

Igrot Moshe (אִגְּרוֹת מֹשֶׁה, "The Letters of Moshe"): Responsa of Rabbi Moshe Feinstein (1895-1986). New York: 1959-63.

Imrei Binah (אִמְרֵי בִינָה, "Words of Understanding" [Proverbs 1:2]): Rabbi Dovber of Lubavitch (1773-1827). Chassidic discourses. Kapust, 1821.

Isaiah: a book of the *Bible.

Jeremiah: a book of the *Bible.

Job: a book of the *Bible.

Joel: a book of the *Bible.

Jonah: a book of the *Bible.

Joshua: a book of the *Bible.

Judges: a book of the *Bible.

Karnei Or (קַרְנֵי אוֹר, "Rays of Light"): Yehudah Leib Krinsky. Part of *Mechokekei Yehudah*, a super-commentary on *Ibn Ezra on the Torah.

K'lalei HaChinuch veHaHadrachah (כְּלָלֵי הַחִנּוּךְ וְהַהַדְרָכָה, "Principles of Education and Guidance"): Rabbi Yosef Yitzchak of Lubavitch (1880-1950). Chassidic discourse, published in **Sefer HaSichot 5703*.

Kehilat Yaakov (קְהִלַּת יַעֲקֹב, "The Congregation of Jacob" [Deuteronomy 33:4]): Rabbi Yaakov Tzvi Yallish (?-1825) Encyclopedia of Kabbalistic terminology. Lemberg, 1870.

Kesef Tzaruf (כֶּסֶף צָרוּף, "Refined Silver" [Psalms 12:7]): Rabbi Yoshiahu Pinto (c. 1565-1648) Commentary on the book of Proverbs. Amsterdam, 1729.

Keter Shem Tov (כֶּתֶר שֵׁם טוֹב, "The Crown of a Good Name" [*Avot* 4:13]): Rabbi Aharon of Opt. Collection of Chassidic teachings of Rabbi Yisrael Ba'al Shem Tov (1698-1760). Zolkova, 1794. Cited according to the Kehot (NY, 1972) edition.

Ketubot (כְּתֻבּוֹת, "Marriage Contracts"): a tractate of the *Talmud.

Kidushin (קִדּוּשִׁין, "Betrothals"): a tractate of the *Talmud.

Kimchi, Rabbi David: see Commentary on the Bible.

Kings: a book of the *Bible.

Kitzurim VeHe'arot leSefer Likutei Amarim (קִצּוּרִים וְהֶעָרוֹת לְסֵפֶר לקוטי אמרים, "Synopses and Notes to the *Tanya*"): Rabbi Menachem Mendel of Lubavitch (1789-1866). Commentary on the **Tanya.* New York: Kehot, 1948.

Klal Gadol BaTorah (כְּלָל גָּדוֹל בַּתּוֹרָה, "A Great Principle of the Torah"): Rabbi Yitzchak Ginsburgh. Rechovot: Gal Einai, 1999.

Kohelet Rabbah (קֹהֶלֶת רַבָּה): the *Midrash to the book of *Ecclesiastes.

Korban HaEidah (קָרְבַּן הָעֵדָה, "The Sacrifice of the Congregation"): Rabbi David Frankel (1707-1762). Commentary on the Jerusalem *Talmud. Dessau, 1743; Berlin, 1757–62.

Kuntres Acharon (קוּנְטְרֵס אַחֲרוֹן, "The Last Pamphlet"): Rabbi Shneur Zalman of Liadi (1745-1812). Fifth section of the **Tanya.*

Lamentations: a book of the *Bible.

Lev LaDa'at (לֵב לָדַעַת, "A Heart to Know" [Deuteronomy 29:3]): Rabbi Yitzchak Ginsburgh. Bat Ayin: Gal Einai, 1990.

Leviticus: a book of the *Bible.

Likutei Amarim **(the** *Maggid)* (לִקּוּטֵי אֲמָרִים - הַמַּגִּיד [מִמעזריטש], "Collected Teachings of the Maggid" of Mezeritch): Rabbi Dovber (the *maggid*) of Mezeritch (?-1772). Chassidic teachings. Koretz, 1781. Cited according to the Kehot (NY, 1980) edition.

Likutei Diburim (לִקּוּטֵי דִּבּוּרִים, "Collected Sayings"): Rabbi Yosef Yitzchak of Lubavitch (1880-1950). Chassidic teachings and lore. Poland, 1933 on.

Likutei Moharan (לִקּוּטֵי מוֹהֲרַ"ן, "Collected [Teachings of] Rabbi Nachman"): Rabbi Nachman of Breslov (1772-1810). Chassidic teachings. Ostraha, 1806; Zolkava, 1809. Cited by volume and discourse (*torah*).

Likutei Sichot (לִקּוּטֵי שִׂיחוֹת, "Collected Addresses"): Rabbi Menachem Mendel Schneersohn of Lubavitch (the Lubavitcher Rebbe). Thirty-seven volumes published to date. New York: Kehot, 1962 on.

Likutei Torah (לִקּוּטֵי תּוֹרָה, "Collected [Teachings on the] Torah"): Rabbi Shneur Zalman of Liadi (1745-1812). Chassidic discourses. Continuation of **Torah Or*, published with glosses of Rabbi Menachem Mendel of Lubavitch (1789-1866). Zhitomer, 1848.

Liturgy: The standard liturgy used today was originally compiled by the Men of the Great Assembly, the Sanhedrin that functioned roughly from the period after the rebuilding of the first Temple (353 BCE) to the beginning of the period of Alexander the Great (313 BCE). Although additions and variations have been added to this basic core throughout the historical dispersion of the Jewish people, resulting in several versions (or *nuscha'ot*) of the liturgy, the basic core remains common to all versions. The text of the liturgy they instituted was fixed according to Divine inspiration (the Great Assembly included a number of prophets) and is thus inviolate and almost as infinite in depth as the Torah itself.

Living in Divine Space: Rabbi Yitzchak Ginsburgh. Rechovot: Gal Einai, 1997.

Luria, Rabbi Yitzchak (1534-1572): Central figure of Kabbalah, whose teachings form the core of Kabbalistic doctrine and the basis for understanding the **Zohar*. Known by the acronym *Arizal* (אֲרִיזַ"ל): הָאֱלֹקִי רַבֵּנוּ יִצְחָק זִכְרוֹנוֹ לִבְרָכָה, "the G-dly Rabbi Yitzchak [Luria Ashkenazi], of blessed memory." His teachings were recorded primarily by Rabbi Chaim Vital (1543-1620), whose writings have reached us in several versions:

1. The "Eight Gates" (שְׁמוֹנָה שְׁעָרִים), edited by Rabbi Shmuel Vital (?-1677), comprising (in alphabetical order):

   a. ***Sha'ar HaGilgulim*** (שַׁעַר הַגִּלְגּוּלִים, "The Gate of Reincarnations"). Jerusalem, 1868.
   b. ***Sha'ar HaKavanot*** (שַׁעַר הַכַּוָּנוֹת, "The Gate of *Kavanot*"). Salonika, 1852.
   c. ***Sha'ar HaHakdamot*** (שַׁעַר הַהַקְדָּמוֹת, "The Gate of Introductions"). Salonika, 1862.
   d. ***Sha'ar HaMitzvot*** (שַׁעַר הַמִּצְוֹת, "The Gate of the Commandments"). Salonika, 1852.

e. ***Sha'ar HaPesukim*** (שַׁעַר הַפְּסוּקִים, "The Gate of Biblical Verses"). Jerusalem, 1868.
f. ***Sha'ar Ma'amarei Rashbi*** (שַׁעַר מַאֲמָרֵי רַשְׁבִּ"י, "The Gate of the Sayings of Rabbi Shimon bar Yochai"). Salonika, 1862.
g. ***Sha'ar Ma'amarei Razal*** (שַׁעַר מַאֲמָרֵי רַזַ"ל, "The Gate of Rabbinic Sayings"). Salonika, 1862.
h. ***Sha'ar Ruach HaKodesh*** (שַׁעַר רוּחַ הַקֹּדֶשׁ, "The Gate of the Holy Spirit"). Jerusalem, 1868.

2. The "Tree of Life" (עֵץ חַיִּים) series, edited by Rabbi Meir Popperos (1624-1662), comprising:

a. *Derech Etz Chaim*. Published as ***Etz Chaim*** (עֵץ חַיִּים, "The Tree of Life" [Genesis 2:9]). Koretz, 1782. This work is divided into "chambers," which are further subdivided into "gates" and chapters, but since the "gates" are numbered independently of the "chambers," citation is by "gate" and chapter only.

b. *Pri Etz Chaim*. Published in three parts:

i. ***Pri Etz Chaim*** (פְּרִי עֵץ חַיִּים, "The Fruit of the Tree of Life"). Exposition of the liturgy). Koretz, 1785.
ii. ***Ta'amei HaMitzvot*** (טַעֲמֵי הַמִּצְוֹת, "Reasons for the Commandments"). Zolkova, 1775.
iii. ***Sha'ar HaYichudim*** (שַׁעַר הַיִּחוּדִים, "The Gate of Unifications"). Koretz, 1783.

c. *Nof Etz Chaim*. Published partially as:

i. ***Zohar HaRakia*** (זֹהַר הָרָקִיעַ, "The Brightness of the Firmament" [Daniel 12:3]). Commentary on the *Zohar. Koretz, 1785.
ii. ***Likutei Torah*** (לִקּוּטֵי תּוֹרָה, "Collected [teachings on the] Torah"). Zalkova, 1775.
iii. The commentary on the Talmud was not published, but extraneous material not written by R. Chaim Vital was published as ***Likutei HaShas*** (לִקּוּטֵי הַשַּׁ"ס). ?, 1783.
iv. ***Sefer HaGilgulim*** (סֵפֶר הַגִּלְגּוּלִים, "The Book of Reincarnations"). On transmigration. Part 1: Frankfort on the Main, 1684. With part 2 (edited by Rabbi Natan Shapiro): Premishla, 1875.

3. Works edited by Rabbi Yaakov Tzemach (1570-1665):

a. ***Mavo Shearim*** (מָבוֹא שְׁעָרִים, "Introduction to the Gates"). Koretz, 1784.
b. ***Olat Tamid*** (עוֹלַת תָּמִיד, "A Perpetual Burnt-Offering" [Numbers 28:6]).

c. ***Kehilat Ya'akov*** (קְהִלַּת יַעֲקֹב, "The Congregation of Jacob" [Deuteronomy 33:4]).
d. ***Otzarot Chaim*** (אוֹצְרוֹת חַיִּים, "Treasures of Life").
e. ***Zohar HaRakia*** (זֹהַר הָרָקִיעַ, "The Brilliance of the Firmament" [Daniel 12:3]). This is not the *Zohar HaRakia* mentioned above.
f. ***Adam Yashar I*** (אָדָם יָשָׁר, "Upright Man" [Ecclesiastes 7:29]). Printed, with errors, as ***Arba Mei'ot Shekel Kesef*** (אַרְבַּע מֵאוֹת שֶׁקֶל כֶּסֶף, "Four Hundred Talents of Silver" [Genesis 23:14]).
g. ***Adam Yashar II***. Second version, combining *Kehilat Ya'akov* and *Adam Yashar I*.
h. ***Eidut B'Ya'akov*** (עֵדוּת בְּיַעֲקֹב, "Testimony in Jacob" [Psalms 78:5]). Third version, combining *Otzarot Chaim* and *Adam Yashar II*.
i. ***Kol B'Rama*** (קוֹל בְּרָמָה, "A Voice in Ramah" [Jeremiah 31:15]). Commentary on the *Idra Rabbah*, a part of the **Zohar*.

4. Miscellaneous works, including:

a. ***Sefer HaLikutim*** (סֵפֶר הַלִּקּוּטִים, "The Book of Collected Teachings"). Jerusalem, 1913.
b. ***Limudei Atzilut*** (לִמּוּדֵי אֲצִילוּת, "Teachings of *Atzilut*"). Levov, 1850; Munkatch, 1897.
c. ***Machberet HaKodesh*** (מַחְבֶּרֶת הַקֹּדֶשׁ, "The Holy Compendium"). Koretz, 1783.

In 1962 (reprint, 1988), Rabbi Yehudah Tzvi Brandwein republished an improved edition of the "Eight Gates" series, *Etz Chaim, Pri Etz Chaim, Mavo Shearim, Likutei Torah, Ta'amei HaMitzvot, Arba Me'ot Shekel Kesef, Olat Tamid*, and *Sefer HaLikutim* with his own notes and cross-references. Unfortunately, this edition does not follow the pagination of the previous editions.

Most of the material in the first edition is paralleled in the second and third editions. The presentation of the material in the "Eight Gates" series is considered more precise, while the editions of Rabbi Meir Popperos and his student Rabbi Yaakov Tzemach are richer, partly due to the inclusion of material recorded by other students of the Arizal other than Rabbi Chaim Vital. These series are therefore traditionally studied together, according to the following scheme, and in the following order:

1	*Mavo Shearim* and *Sha'ar HaHakdamot*	*Etz Chaim*
2	*Sha'ar HaKavanot*	*Pri Etz Chaim*
3	*Sha'ar HaPesukim*	*Likutei Torah* and *Sefer HaLikutim*
4	*Sha'ar HaMitzvot*	*Ta'amei HaMitzvot*
5	*Sha'ar Ma'amarei Razal*	*Likutei HaShas*
6	*Sha'ar Ma'amarei Rashbi*	*Zohar HaRakia and Kol B'Ramah*
7	*Sha'ar HaGilgulim*	*Sefer HaGilgulim*
8	*Sha'ar Ruach HaKodesh*	*Sha'ar HaYichudim*

In addition, other students of the Arizal recorded his teachings. Although these works are considered less reliable than those of Rabbi Chaim Vital, they are also cited in *Chassidut* (see *Igrot Kodesh* of the Rebbe, vol. 11, p. 167, cited in *Sha'arei Halachah Uminhag* vol. 3, p. 175). Amongst these works are:

a. ***Emek HaMelech*** (עֵמֶק הַמֶּלֶךְ, "The Valley of the King" [Genesis 14:17]): Rabbi Naftali Bacharach (1st half of the 17th century). Amsterdam, 1648, based on the teachings of Rabbi Yisrael Seruk (?-before 1604).

b. ***Sefer HaKavanot*** (סֵפֶר הַכַּוָּנוֹת, "The Book of *Kavanot*"): Rabbi Moshe Trinko. Yesnitz, 1723.

c. ***Kanfei Yonah*** (כַּנְפֵי יוֹנָה, "The Wings of a Dove" [Psalms 68:14]): Rabbi Menachem Azariah of Fano (1548-1620). Koretz, 1786.

Ma'amarei Admor HaEmtza'i (מַאֲמָרֵי אַדְמוּ"ר הָאֶמְצָעִי, "Discourses of Rabbi Dovber of Lubavitch," 1773-1827): Series of Chassidic discourses, published according to the books of the *Bible, etc. Nineteen volumes published to date. New York: Kehot, 1985 on.

Ma'amarei Admor HaZaken (מַאֲמָרֵי אַדְמוּ"ר הַזָּקֵן, "Discourses of Rabbi Shneur Zalman of Liadi," 1745-1812): Series of Chassidic discourses, published according to the year of their delivery, topic, book of the *Bible, etc. Twenty-four volumes published to date. New York: Kehot, 1955 on.

Magen Avot (מָגֵן אָבוֹת, "The Shield of the Fathers" [liturgy]): Rabbi Shlomo Zalman of Kapust (1830-1900). Chassidic discourses. Berditchev, 1902.

Magen Avraham (מָגֵן אַבְרָהָם, "The Shield of Abraham" [liturgy]): Rabbi Avraham Gumbiner (c. 1637-1683). Commentary on the **Shulchan Aruch*. Dyhernfurth, 1692.

Makot (מַכּוֹת, "Injuries"): a tractate of the *Talmud.

Malachi: a book of the *Bible.

Malchut Yisrael (מַלְכוּת יִשְׂרָאֵל, "The Kingdom of Israel"): Rabbi Yitzchak Ginsburgh. Rechovot: Gal Einai, 1999 on.

Mavo Shearim: see Luria, Rabbi Yitzchak.

Meor Einaim (מְאוֹר עֵינַיִם, "The Light of the Eyes" [Proverbs 15:30]): Rabbi Menachem Nachum of Chernobyl (1730-1798). Chassidic teachings. Slavota, 1798.

Meor Einaim (מְאוֹר עֵינַיִם, "The Light of the Eyes" [Proverbs 15:30]): Rabbi Yoshiahu Pinto (c. 1565-1648). Commentary on the aggadic passages of the *Talmud. Amsterdam, 1643. Printed in standard editions of **Ein Yaakov*.

Mechilta (מְכִילְתָּא, "The Measure"): Halachic *Midrash to the book of *Exodus. Constantinople, 1515.

Megilah (מְגִלָּה, "The Scroll [of Esther]"): a tractate of the *Talmud.

Mei HaShiloach (מֵי הַשִּׁלוֹחַ, "The Waters of the Shiloach" [Isaiah 8:6]): Rabbi Mordechai Yosef Leiner of Izhbitz (1801-1854). Chassidic teachings. Vienna: 1860; Lublin: 1922.

Menachot (מְנָחוֹת, "Flour Offerings"): a tractate of the *Talmud.

Menorat HaMaor (מְנוֹרַת הַמָּאוֹר, "The Candelabrum of Light" [Exodus 35:14]): Rabbi Yitzchak Abuhav (end of 14th century). Ethics. Constantinople, 1514.

Micah: a book of the *Bible.

Midrash (מִדְרָשׁ, "seeking"; pl. מִדְרָשִׁים, Midrashim): the second major body of the oral Torah (after the *Talmud), consisting of halachic or homiletic material couched as linguistic analyses of the Biblical text. An individual work of midrashic material is also called a Midrash; a specific analysis is called a midrash.

The Midrash is a corpus of many works written over the span of several centuries (roughly the second to the eighth CE), mostly in the Holy Land. The chief collection of homiletic midrashic material is the *Rabbah* ("great") series, covering the five books of Moses and the five scrolls. Other important collections are

Midrash ... *Midrash Tanchuma, *Midrash Tehilim, Pesikta d'Rav Kahana, *Pirkei d'Rabbi Eliezer* and **Tana d'vei Eliahu*. Several later collections contain material that has reached us in its original form. These include **Midrash HaGadol* and **Yalkut Shimoni*. There are many smaller, minor Midrashim, as well; some of these are to be found in the collection **Otzar HaMidrashim*. Halachic Midrashim include the **Mechilta*, the **Sifra* and the **Sifrei*.

Midrash Eleh Ezkerah (מִדְרָשׁ אֵלֶּה אֶזְכְּרָה, "The Midrash on 'I will Remember These' [Psalms 42:5]"): A minor *Midrash.

Midrash HaGadol (מִדְרָשׁ הַגָּדוֹל, "The Great Midrash"): 13th century compendium of midrashic material, including material missing from older midrashic collections.

Midrash Mishlei (מִדְרָשׁ מִשְׁלֵי): the *Midrash on the book of *Proverbs.

Midrash Shmuel (מִדְרָשׁ שְׁמוּאֵל): the *Midrash on the book of *Samuel.

Midrash Tanchuma (מִדְרָשׁ תַּנְחוּמָא): *a Midrash on the Torah from the school of Rabbi Tanchuma.

Midrash Tehilim (מִדְרָשׁ תְּהִלִּים): the *Midrash on the book of *Psalms.

Mishlei Yisrael (מִשְׁלֵי יִשְׂרָאֵל, "The Parables of Israel"): Meir Wachsman. Anthology of Parables from the Bible, the Talmud, the Midrash, and medieval Jewish literature. Jerusalem, 1933.

Mishnah: see Talmud.

Mishnat Chasidim (מִשְׁנַת חֲסִידִים, "The Teachings of the Pious"): Rabbi Emanuel Chai Rikki (1688-1743). Kabbalah. Amsterdam, 1727.

Mishneh Torah (מִשְׁנֵה תוֹרָה, "Repetition of the Torah" [Deuteronomy 17:18]): Rabbi Moshe ben Maimon (Maimonides, 1135-1205). Codification of Jewish law. Rome, before 1480.

Mivchar HaPeninim (מִבְחַר הַפְּנִינִים, "Selected Pearls"): attributed to Rabbi Shlomo ibn Gabirol (c. 1020-c. 1057). Trans. Rabbi Yehudah ibn Tibbon. Cremona, 1558.

Moed Katan (מוֹעֵד קָטָן, "The Lesser Festival"): a tractate of the *Talmud.

Moreh Nevuchim (מוֹרֶה נְבֻכִים, "A Guide for the Perplexed"): Rabbi Moshe ben Maimon (Maimonides, 1135-1205). Philosophy. Rome, before 1480.

Muda'ut Tivit (מוּדָעוּת טִבְעִית, "Natural Consciousness"): Rabbi Yitzchak Ginsburgh. Rechovot: Gal Einai, 1999.

Nahar Shalom (נָהָר שָׁלוֹם, "The Peaceful River" [Isaiah 66:12]): Rabbi Shalom Sharabi (1720-1777). Lurianic Kabbalah. Salonika, 1806.

Nahum: a book of the *Bible.

Nazir (נָזִיר, "The Nazarite"): a tractate of the *Talmud.

Nedarim (נְדָרִים, "Vows"): a tractate of the *Talmud.

Nidah (נִדָּה, "The Menstruate"): a tractate of the *Talmud.

Nitzotzei Orot (נִצוֹצֵי אוֹרוֹת, "Sparks of Light"): Rabbi Chaim Yosef David Azulai (1727-1806). Commentary on the **Zohar*.

Numbers: a book of the *Bible.

Obadiah: a book of the *Bible.

Ohalot: a tractate of the *Talmud.

Or HaChamah (אוֹר הַחַמָּה, "The Light of the Sun" [Isaiah 30:26]): Rabbi Avraham Azulai (1570-1643). Commentary on the **Zohar*. Vols. 1 & 2: Jerusalem, 1876; Vol. 3: Salonika, 1842; Vol. 4: Premishla, 1898.

Or HaSechel (אוֹר הַשֵּׂכֶל, "The Light of the Intellect"): Rabbi Avraham Abulafia (1240-after 1291). Kabbalah. Jerusalem, 1999.

Or HaTorah (אוֹר הַתּוֹרָה, "The Light of the Torah" [*Ketubot* 111b]): Rabbi Menachem Mendel of Lubavitch (1789-1866). Chassidic discourses. Forty volumes. New York: Kehot, 1950 on.

Or Torah (אוֹר תּוֹרָה, "The Light of Torah" [*Ketubot* 111b]): Rabbi Dovber (the *maggid*) of Mezeritch (?-1773). Chassidic teachings. Koretz, 1804. Cited according to the Kehot (NY, 1980) edition.

Otiot d'Rabbi Akiva (אוֹתִיּוֹת דְּרַבִּי עֲקִיבָא, "The Letters [of the Hebrew Alphabet expounded] by Rabbi Akiva"): a minor *midrash. Published, *inter alia*, in **Otzar HaMidrashim*, p. 408.

Otzar HaMidrashim (אוֹצַר הַמִּדְרָשִׁים, "A Treasury of Midrashim"): Yehudah David Eisenstein (1854-1956). Collection of articles on the various Midrashim and texts of many small Midrashim, published in 1915.

Pardes Rimonim (פַּרְדֵּס רִמּוֹנִים, "The Pomegranate Orchard" [Song of Songs 4:13]): Rabbi Moshe Cordevero (1522-1570). Summary of pre-Lurianic Kabbalah. Cracow, 1592.

Peah (פֵּאָה, "The Corner [of the Field]"): a tractate of the *Talmud.

Pelach HaRimon (פֶּלַח הָרִמּוֹן, "The Segment of the Pomegranate" [Song of Songs 4:3, 6:7]): Rabbi Hillel of Partich (1795-1864). Chassidic discourses. Vilna, 1887; New York: Kehot, 1955 on.

Pele Yoetz (פֶּלֶא יוֹעֵץ, "Wondrous Advisor" [Isaiah 9:5]): Rabbi Eliezer Papo (1786-1824). Ethics. Constantinople, 1825.

Pesachim (פְּסָחִים, "Passover Offerings"): a tractate of the *Talmud.

Pesikta Zotarta (פְּסִיקְתָּא זוּטַרְתָּא, "The Lesser *Pesikta*"): *Midrash. Also known as *Midrash Lekach Tov* (מִדְרָשׁ לֶקַח טוֹב).

Pirkei d'Rabbi Eliezer (פִּרְקֵי דְרַבִּי אֱלִיעֶזֶר, "The Chapters of Rabbi Eliezer"): *Midrash.

Pokeiach Ivrim (פֹּקֵחַ עִוְרִים, "He Opens the Eyes of the Blind" [Psalms 146:8]): Rabbi Dovber of Lubavitch (1773-1827). Chassidic discourse. First published in 1817; included in **Ma'amarei Admor HaEmtza'i—Kuntresim* (New York: Kehot, 1991).

Pri Etz Chaim: see Luria, Rabbi Yitzchak.

Proverbs: a book of the *Bible.

Psalms: a book of the *Bible.

Ramataim Tzofim (רָמָתַיִם צוֹפִים, "*Ramataim Tzofim*" [1 Samuel 1:1]): Rabbi Shmuel of Shinove (?-1873). Commentary on **Tana d'vei Eliahu*. Jerusalem, 1954.

Rambam (**R**abbi **M**oshe **b**en **M**aimon): see Commentary on the Mishnah, *Mishneh Torah*.

Ramban (**R**abbi **M**oshe **b**en **N**achman): see Commentary on the Bible.

Rashi (**R**abbi **Sh**lomo **Y**itzchaki): see Commentary on the Bible, Talmud.

Rechovot HaNahar (רְחֹבוֹת הַנָּהָר, "The Widening of the River" [Genesis 36:37]): Rabbi Shalom Sharabi (1720-1777). Lurianic Kabbalah. Salonika, 1806.

Reishit Chochmah (רֵאשִׁית חָכְמָה, "The Beginning of Wisdom" [Psalms 111:10]): Rabbi Eliahu di Vidas (16th century). Ethics, based on Kabbalah. Venice, 1579.

Reshimot (רְשִׁימוֹת, "Notes"): Rabbi Menachem Mendel Schneersohn of Lubavitch (the Lubavitcher Rebbe). New York: Kehot, 1995 on.

Rosh HaShanah (רֹאשׁ הַשָּׁנָה, "The New Year"): a tractate of the *Talmud.

Rut Rabbah (רוּת רַבָּה): the *Midrash on the book of *Ruth.

Rut Zuta (רוּת זוּטָא) ed. Buber: *Midrash on the book of Ruth.

Ruth: a book of the *Bible.

Samuel: a book of the *Bible.

Sanhedrin (סַנְהֶדְרִין, "The Sanhedrin"): a tractate of the *Talmud.

Seder HaYom (סֵדֶר הַיּוֹם, "The Order of the Day"): Rabbi Moshe Machir (16th century). Ethics, rules of conduct. Venice, 1599.

Sefat Emet (שְׂפַת אֱמֶת, "The Lip of Truth" [Proverbs 12:19]): Rabbi Yehudah Leib Alter of Ger (1847-1905). Chassidic teachings. Piotrokov-Cracow, 1905-1952.

Sefer HaGilgulim: see Luria, Rabbi Yitzchak.

Sefer HaHalachot (סֵפֶר הַהֲלָכוֹת, "The Book of Laws"): Rabbi Yitzchak al-Fasi (1013-1103). Summary of the legal material of the Talmud applicable during the exile. Printed in the standard editions of the Talmud.

Sefer HaLikutim: see Luria, Rabbi Yitzchak.

Sefer HaMa'amarim (סֵפֶר הַמַּאֲמָרִים, "The Book of Discourses"): general name for books of Chassidic discourses by Chabad rebbes. If followed by a year from 5643-5680, refers to discourses by Rabbi Shalom Dovber of Lubavitch (1860-1920); if by a year from 5680-5711 [or the word *Kuntresim*], to discourses by Rabbi Yosef Yitzchak of Lubavitch (1880-1950); if by a year from 5711-5752 [or the word *Melukat*], to discourses by Rabbi Menachem Mendel of Lubavitch (the Lubavitcher Rebbe).

Sefer HaSichot (סֵפֶר הַשִּׂיחוֹת, "The Book of Addresses"): general name for books of addresses by Chabad rebbes. If followed by a year from 5680-5711, refers to addresses by Rabbi Yosef Yitzchak of Lubavitch (1880-1950); if by a year from 5711-5752, to discourses by Rabbi Menachem Mendel of Lubavitch (the Lubavitcher Rebbe).

Sefer Yetzirah (סֵפֶר יְצִירָה, "The Book of Formation"): a fundamental text of Kabbalah, containing teachings that date back to Abraham, redacted by Rabbi Akiva (2nd century). Mantua, 1562. English translation by Aryeh Kaplan, York Beach, Maine: Weiser, 1990.

Semachot (שְׂמָחוֹת, "[Non-] Joyous Occasions"): a tractate of the *Talmud.

Sha'ar HaGilgulim: see Luria, Rabbi Yitzchak.

Sha'ar HaKavanot : see Luria, Rabbi Yitzchak.

Sha'ar HaPesukim: see Luria, Rabbi Yitzchak.

Sha'ar HaYichud (שַׁעַר הַיִּחוּד, "The Gate of Unity"): Rabbi Dovber of Lubavitch (1773-1827). Chassidic discourse. Kapust, 1820.

Sha'ar HaYichud VehaEmunah (שַׁעַר הַיִּחוּד וְהָאֱמוּנָה, "The Gate of Unity and Faith"): Rabbi Shneur Zalman of Liadi (1745-1812). Second part of the **Tanya*.

Sha'ar Ma'amarei Razal: see Luria, Rabbi Yitzchak.

Sha'arei Ahavah v'Ratzon (שַׁעֲרֵי אַהֲבָה וְרָצוֹן, "Gates of Love and Will"): Rabbi Yitzchak Ginsburgh. Jerusalem: Gal Einai, 1996

Sha'arei Halachah Uminhag (שַׁעֲרֵי הֲלָכָה וּמִנְהָג, "Gates of Law and Custom"): Compendium of halachic rulings of Rabbi Menachem Mendel Schneersohn of Lubavitch (the Lubavitcher Rebbe), by Rabbi Yosef Yitzchak Havlin. Jerusalem: Kehot-Heichal Menachem, 1993.

Shabbat (שַׁבָּת, "The Sabbath"): a tractate of the *Talmud.

Shechinah Beineihem (שְׁכִינָה בֵּינֵיהֶם, "The Divine Presence Between Them" [*Avot* 3:2]): Rabbi Yitzchak Ginsburgh. Jerusalem: Gal Einai, 1987.

Shemot Rabbah (שְׁמוֹת רַבָּה): the *Midrash on the book of *Exodus.

Shevuot (שְׁבוּעוֹת, "Oaths"): a tractate of the *Talmud.

Shir HaShirim Rabbah (שִׁיר הַשִּׁירִים רַבָּה): the *Midrash on the book of *Song of Songs.

Shirat Yisrael (שִׁירַת יִשְׂרָאֵל, "The Song of Israel"): Rabbi Moshe ibn Ezra (c. 1055-after 1135), trans. Rabbi Ben Tzion Halper. Leipzig, 1924.

Shnei Luchot HaBrit (שְׁנֵי לוּחוֹת הַבְּרִית, "The Two Tablets of the Covenant" [after Deuteronomy 9:11]): Rabbi Yeshayahu Horowitz (1560-1630). Kabbalah, *halachah*, ethics. Amsterdam, 1648-9.

Shulchan Aruch (שֻׁלְחָן עָרוּךְ, "The Set Table" [Ezekiel 23:41]): Rabbi Yosef Karo (1488-1575). The Code of Jewish law. Cited by volume name (*Orach Chaim, Even HaEzer, Yoreh Deah,* and *Choshen Mishpat*), chapter, and paragraph. Venice, 1564.

Shulchan Aruch HaRav (שֻׁלְחָן עָרוּךְ הָרַב, "'The Set Table' of the Rabbi"): Rabbi Shneur Zalman of Liadi (1745-1812). Update of the **Shulchan Aruch*. Cited similarly to the *Shulchan Aruch*. Kapust, 1814.

Siddur Beit Yaakov (סִדּוּר בֵּית יַעֲקֹב, "The Prayerbook of the House of Jacob" [Psalms 114:1, etc.]): Rabbi Yaakov of Emden (1695-1776). Prayerbook with ethical and Kabbalistic commentary. Lemberg, 1904.

Siddur im Dach (סִדּוּר עִם דַּא"ח, "A Prayerbook with Chassidic Commentary"): Rabbi Dovber of Lubavitch (1773-1827). Chassidic discourses on the prayerbook. Kapust, 1816.

Sifra (סִפְרָא, "The Book," also called *Torat Kohanim*, תּוֹרַת כֹּהֲנִים, "The Law of the Priests"): halachic Midrash to the book of *Leviticus.

Sifrei (סִפְרֵי, "The Books"): halachic Midrash to the books of *Numbers and *Deuteronomy.

Sod HaShem Lireiav (סוֹד ה' לִירֵאָיו, "The Secret of G-d is to Those who Fear Him" [Psalms 25:14]): Rabbi Yitzchak Ginsburgh. Jerusalem: Gal Einai, 1985.

Song of Songs: a book of the *Bible.

Sotah (סוֹטָה, "The Suspected Adulteress"): a tractate of the *Talmud.

Sukah (סֻכָּה, "The Booth"): a tractate of the *Talmud.

Ta'amei HaMitzvot: see Luria, Rabbi Yitzchak.

Ta'anit (תַּעֲנִית, "The Fast"): a tractate of the *Talmud.

Taharat Yisrael (טָהֳרַת יִשְׂרָאֵל, "The Purity of Israel"): Rabbi Yisrael Yitzchak Yanovsky of Prague. Laws of Family Purity. Belogrei, Piotrokov, Warsaw, 1910-23.

Talmud (תַּלְמוּד, "learning"): the written version of the greater part of the oral *Torah, comprising mostly legal but also much homiletic and even some explicitly mystical material.

The Talmud comprises the *Mishnah* (מִשְׁנָה, "repetition") and the *Gemara* (גְּמָרָא, "completion"). The *Mishnah* is the basic compendium of the laws (each known as a *mishnah*) comprising the oral Torah, redacted by Rabbi Yehudah the Prince in the second century CE. The *Mishnah* was elaborated upon over the next few centuries in the academies of the Holy Land and Babylonia; this material is the *Gemara*.

There are thus two Talmuds: the one composed in the Holy Land, known as the *Talmud Yerushalmi* ("The Jerusalem Talmud"), completed in the third century, and the one composed in Babylonia, known as the *Talmud Bavli* ("The Babylonian Talmud), completed in the sixth century.

The *Mishnah*—and *ipso facto* the Talmud—is divided into tractates. References to the *Mishnah* are simply the name of the tractate followed by the number of the chapter and individual *mishnah*. The Jerusalem Talmud was first printed in Venice, 1523-24. Although subsequent editions have generally followed the same pagination as this edition, it is nonetheless cited by chapter and *halachah* (i.e., individual *mishnah*) number, as is the *Mishnah*. References to it are therefore prefaced by "*Y.*," to distinguish them from references to the *Mishnah* itself. The Babylonian Talmud was first printed in its entirety in Venice, 1520-23, and subsequent editions have followed the same pagination as this edition, as well. References to the tractates of the *Talmud Bavli* are simply by tractate name followed by page and column ("a" or "b").

Tamid (תָּמִיד, "The Daily Offering"): a tractate of the *Talmud.

Tana d'vei Eliahu Rabbah (תָּנָא דְּבֵי אֵלִיָּהוּ רַבָּה, "The Larger [collection of the] Teachings of the School of Eliahu"): *Midrash.

Tana d'vei Eliahu Zuta (תָּנָא דְּבֵי אֵלִיָּהוּ זוּטָא, "The Smaller [collection of the] Teachings of the School of Eliahu"): *Midrash.

Tanya (תַּנְיָא, "It has been taught"): Rabbi Shneur Zalman of Liadi (1745-1812). Seminal work of Chabad *Chassidut*. Also known as *Likutei Amarim* (לִקּוּטֵי אֲמָרִים, "Collected Teachings") and *Sefer shel Beinonim* (סֵפֶר שֶׁל בֵּינוֹנִים, "The Book of the *Beinonim*"). Slavita, 1796. English translation (Rabbis Nissan Mindel, Nisen Mangel, Zalman Posner, Jacob Immanuel Schochet): New York: Kehot, 1962-69.

Tanya b'Tzeiruf Ma'arei Mekomot (תַּנְיָא בְּצֵרוּף מַאַרֵי מְקוֹמוֹת, "*Tanya* with Sources"): Rabbi Aharon Chitrik (contemporary). Collection of source material and commentary on the **Tanya*. Cited by chapter (and for precision, sometimes by page number as well). New York: Kehot, 1992 on.

Targum (תַּרְגּוּם, "Translation"): the Aramaic translation of the Bible. The translation of the Five Books of Moses is that of Onkelos (2nd century); that of the Prophets is that of Yonatan ben Uziel (1st century). See *Megilah* 3a.

Terumot (תְּרוּמוֹת, "Donations"): a tractate of the *Talmud.

Teshuvat HaShanah (תְּשׁוּבַת הַשָּׁנָה, "The Repentance of the Year" [1 Chronicles 20:1]): Rabbi Yitzchak Ginsburgh. Rechovot: Gal Einai, 1997.

The Alef-Beit: see *The Hebrew Letters*.

The Dynamic Corporation: Rabbi Yitzchak Ginsburgh. Rechovot: Gal Einai, 1996.

The Hebrew Letters: Rabbi Yitzchak Ginsburgh. Published also as *The Alef-Beit*. Jerusalem: Gal Einai, 1991.

Tikunei Zohar (תִּקּוּנֵי זֹהַר, "Rectifications of the *Zohar*"): Additions to the **Zohar*. Mantua, 1558; Constantinople, 1719, 1740. Cited according to section and page number (according to the second Constantinople edition, which is followed by most subsequent editions).

Toldot Yaakov Yosef (תּוֹלְדוֹת יַעֲקֹב יוֹסֵף, "The Generations of Jacob are Joseph" [Genesis 37:2]): Rabbi Yaakov Yosef of Polnoye (1704-1794). Sermons on the *Torah, containing the earliest recordings of the teachings of Rabbi Yisrael Ba'al Shem Tov (1698-1760). Koretz, 1780.

Torah (תּוֹרָה, "teaching"): G-d's will and wisdom as communicated to man. It pre-existed creation, and G-d used the Torah as His blueprint in creating the world.

G-d certainly communicated the teachings of the Torah in some form to Adam, who then transmitted them orally from generation to generation. However, G-d "officially" gave the Torah to mankind c. 1313 BCE (and during the ensuing 40 years) at Mt. Sinai through Moses. The Ten Commandments were pronounced in the presence of the entire Jewish people.

G-d gave the Torah in two parts: the written Torah and the oral Torah. The written Torah originally consisted of the Five Books of Moses (the "Pentateuch"), the other books being added later (see Bible). The oral Torah was communicated together with the Five Books of Moses as an explanation of the laws and lore included in it. This material was later written down by the sages of the oral Torah in the form of the *Talmud, the *Midrash, and the **Zohar*. (All references to "our sages" in this book refer to the sages who transmitted the oral Torah as recorded in these works.)

Torah Or (תּוֹרָה אוֹר, "Torah Light" [Proverbs 6:23]): Rabbi Shneur Zalman of Liadi (1745-1812). Chassidic discourses. Kapust, 1837. Cf. *Likutei Torah*.

Torat Shalom (תּוֹרַת שָׁלוֹם, "The Teaching of Shalom"): Rabbi Shalom Dovber of Lubavitch (1860-1920). Addresses. New York: Kehot, 1946.

Torat Shmuel (תּוֹרַת שְׁמוּאֵל, "The Teaching of Shmuel"): General name for books of Chassidic discourses by Rabbi Shmuel of Lubavitch (1834-1882), subtitled by the year of their delivery or the opening words of the first discourse in the series.

Tosefot (תּוֹסָפוֹת, "Additions"): Medieval commentary on the *Talmud, printed on the same page as the Talmudic text from the latter's first printing (Venice, 1520-23) on. Cited by folio of the Talmud and opening word(s) of the commentary.

Tzeva'at HaRibash (צַוָּאַת הָרִיבָ"שׁ, "The Will of Rabbi Yisrael Ba'al Shem"): Collection of teachings of Rabbi Yisrael Ba'al Shem Tov (1698-1760) and Rabbi Dovber (the *maggid*) of Mezeritch (?-1773). New York: Kehot, 1975,1982. English translation (Rabbi J. Immanuel Schochet): New York: Kehot, 1999.

Uktzin (עֻקְצִין, "Stalks"): a tractate of the *Talmud.

Vayikra Rabbah (וַיִּקְרָא רַבָּה): the *Midrash on the book of *Leviticus.

Yadaim (יָדַיִם, "Hands"): a tractate of the *Talmud.

Yahel Or (יָהֵל אוֹר, "Light will Glow" [see Job 31:26]): Yehudah Leib Krinsky. Part of *Mechokekei Yehudah*, a super-commentary on *Ibn Ezra on the Torah.

Yalkut Shimoni (יַלְקוּט שִׁמְעוֹנִי, "The Shimon Collection"): Rabbi Shimon Ashkenazi (14th century). Compendium of midrashic material, including material missing from older midrashic collections. Salonika, 1521-26.

Yevamot (יְבָמוֹת, "Levirite Marriage"): a tractate of the *Talmud.

Yom Malkeinu (יוֹם מַלְכֵּנוּ, "The Day of our King" [Hosea 7:5]): Collection of Chassidic teachings of Rabbi Menachem Mendel Schneersohn (the Lubavitcher Rebbe) on birthdays. Kefar Chabad: Kehot, 1984.

Yoma (יוֹמָא, "The Day [of Atonement]"): a tractate of the *Talmud.

Zechariah: a book of the *Bible.

Zephaniah: a book of the *Bible.

Zohar (זֹהַר, "Brilliance"): Rabbi Shimon bar Yochai (2nd century). One of the basic texts of the oral *Torah and Kabbalah. The Zoharic literature includes the *Zohar* proper, the **Tikunei Zohar*, and the **Zohar Chadash*. The *Zohar* was printed in 1558 in both Mantua and Cremona, but standard pagination follows the Mantua edition.

Zohar Chadash (זֹהַר חָדָשׁ, "The New *Zohar*"): Rabbi Shimon bar Yochai (2nd century). Additions to the **Zohar*. Salonika, 1597.

Index

A

B

E

F

G

I

J

K

M

N

O

P

R

S

T

U

V

Y

Z